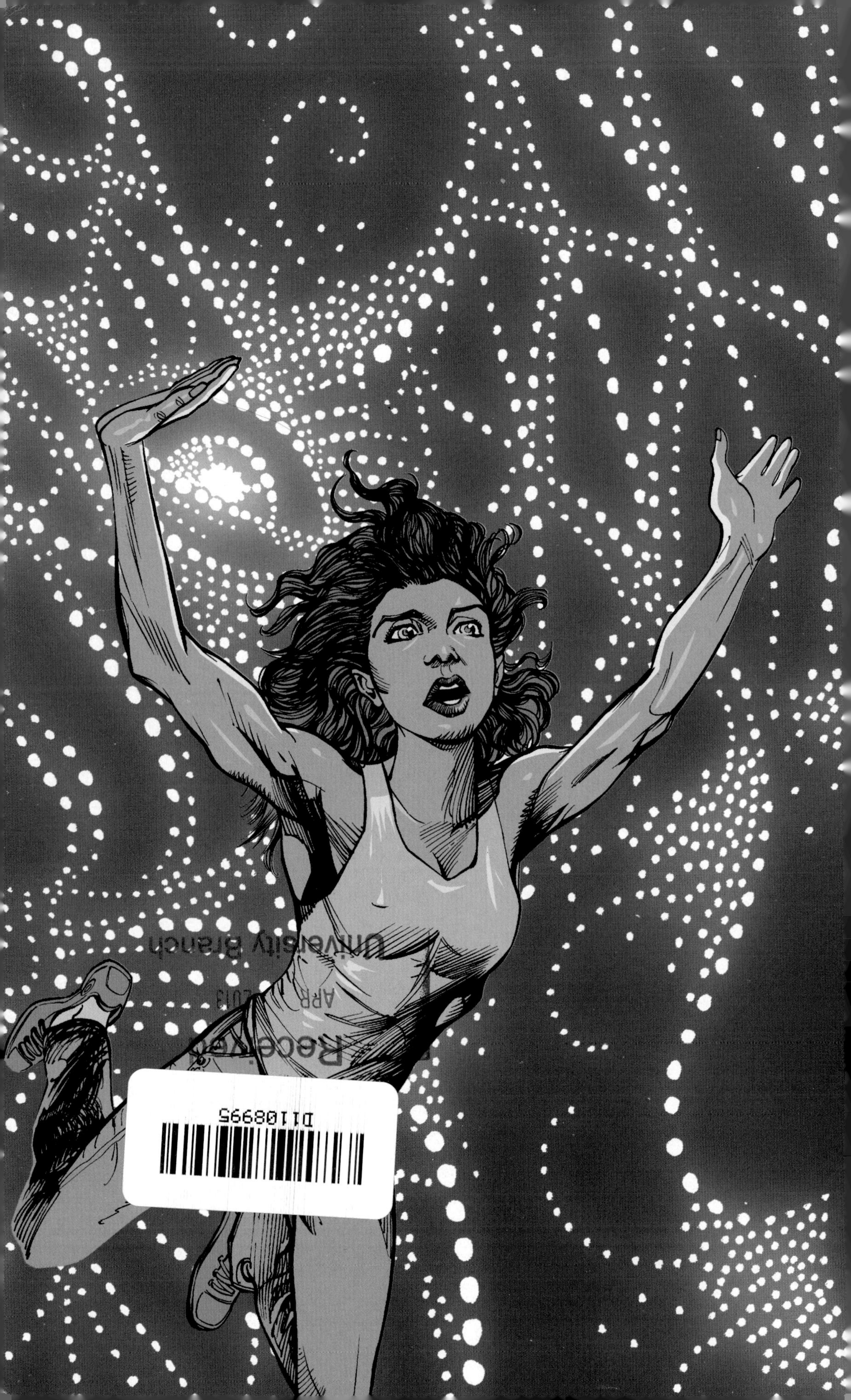

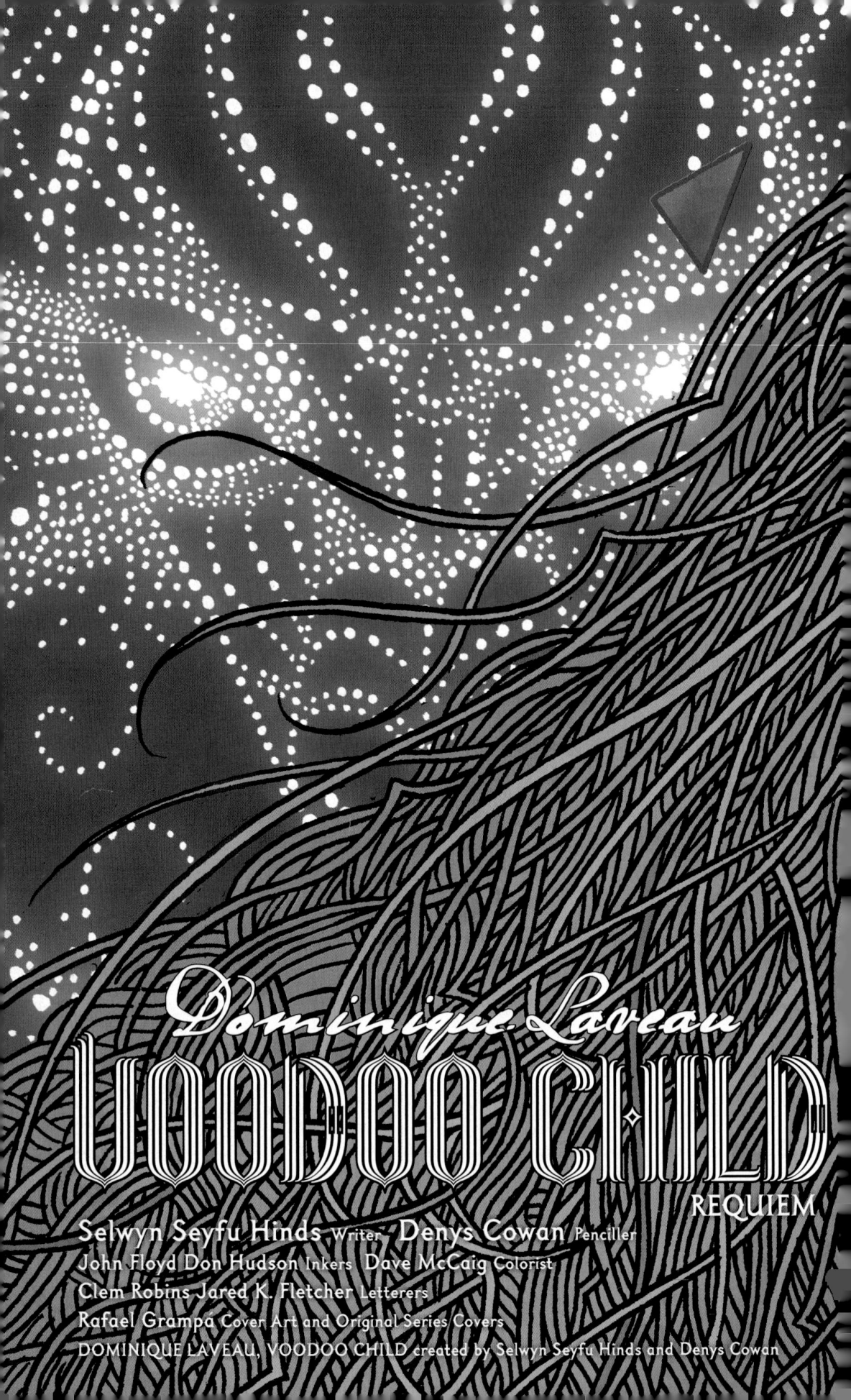

Dominique Laveau
VOODOO CHILD
REQUIEM

Selwyn Seyfu Hinds Writer **Denys Cowan** Penciller
John Floyd Don Hudson Inkers Dave McCaig Colorist
Clem Robins Jared K. Fletcher Letterers
Rafael Grampa Cover Art and Original Series Covers
DOMINIQUE LAVEAU, VOODOO CHILD created by Selwyn Seyfu Hinds and Denys Cowan

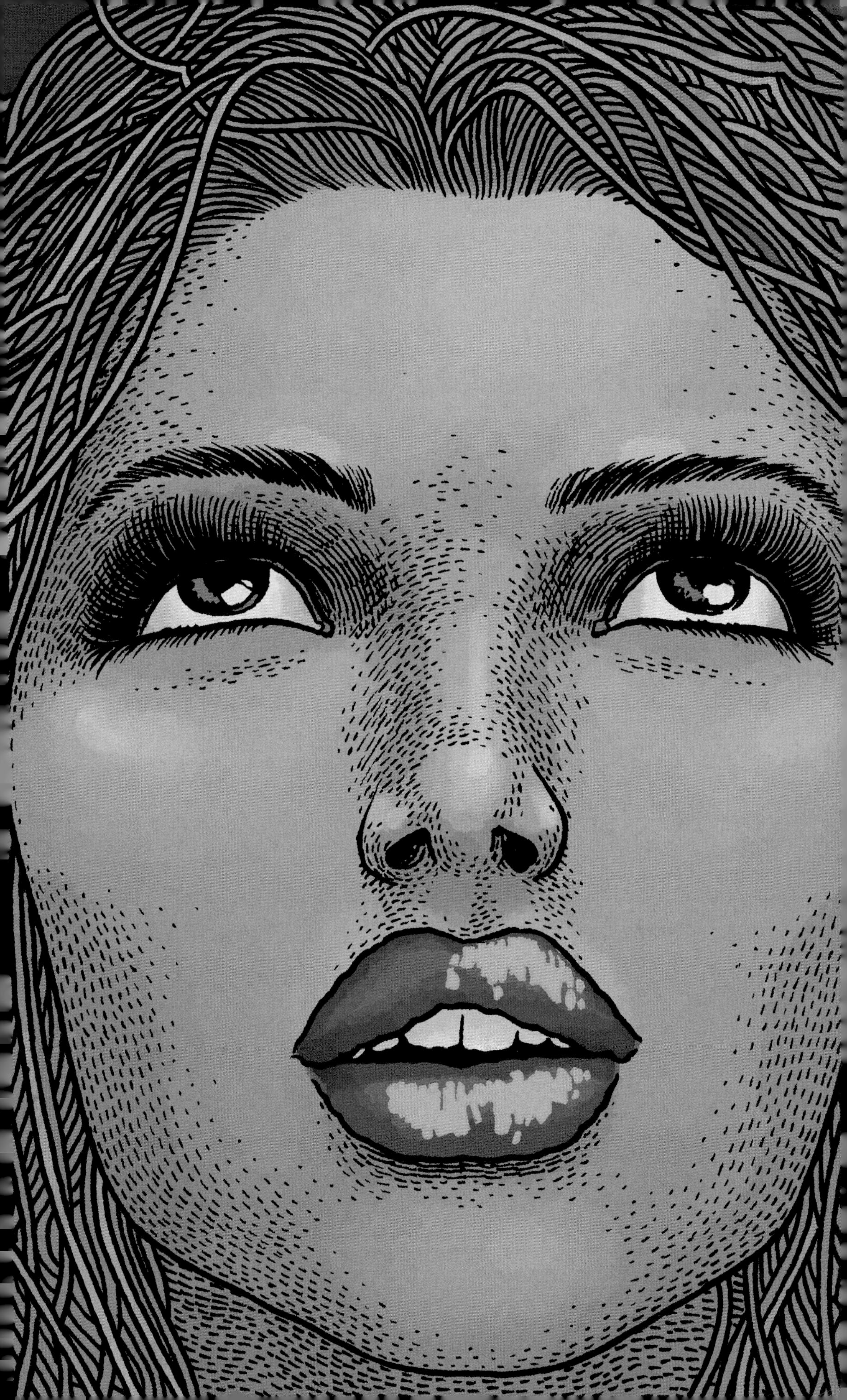

DOMINIQUE LAVEAU, VOODOO CHILD: REQUIEM

Published by DC Comics. Cover and compilation Copyright © 2012 Loco Jumby Inc. and
Denys Cowan. All Rights Reserved.

Originally published in single magazine form in THE UNEXPECTED 1 and DOMINIQUE
LAVEAU, VOODOO CHILD 1-7. Copyright © 2011, 2012 Loco Jumby Inc. and Denys Cowan.
All Rights Reserved. All characters, their distinctive likenesses and related elements featured
in this publication are trademarks of Loco Jumby Inc. and Denys Cowan. VERTIGO is a
trademark of DC Comics. The stories, characters and incidents featured in this publication are
entirely fictional. DC Comics does not read or accept unsolicited submissions of ideas, stories
or artwork.

DC Comics, 1700 Broadway, New York, NY 10019
A Warner Bros. Entertainment Company.
Printed in the USA. First Printing.
ISBN: 978-1-4012-3742-4

Library of Congress Cataloging-in-Publication Data

Hinds, Selwyn Seyfu.
  Dominique Laveau, voodoo child. Volume 1, Requiem / Selwyn Seyfu Hinds, Denys Cowan,
John Floyd.
    p. cm.
  "Originally published in single magazine form in Dominique Laveau: Voodoo Child 1-7, The
Unexpected 1."
  ISBN 978-1-4012-3742-4 (alk. paper)
  1. New Orleans (La.)--Comic books, strips, etc. 2. Graphic novels. I. Cowan, Denys. II. Floyd,
John. III. Title. IV. Title: Requiem.
  PN6727.H533D66 2012
  741.5'973—dc23
                              2012033192

SUSTAINABLE Certified Chain of Custody
FORESTRY At Least 20% Certified Forest Content
INITIATIVE www.sfiprogram.org
SFI-01042
APPLIES TO TEXT STOCK ONLY

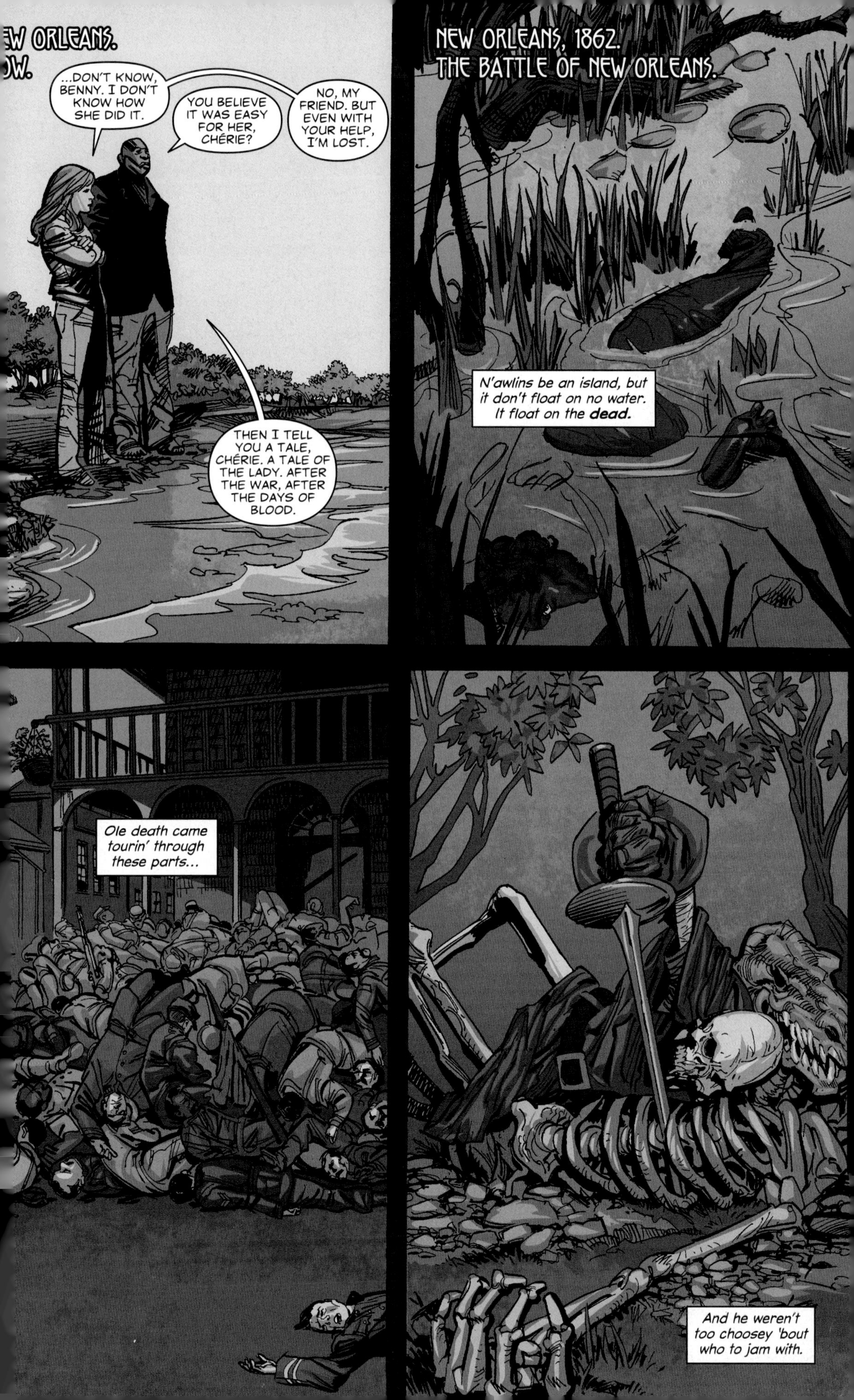
EW ORLEANS.
OW.
...DON'T KNOW, BENNY. I DON'T KNOW HOW SHE DID IT.
YOU BELIEVE IT WAS EASY FOR HER, CHÉRIE?
NO, MY FRIEND. BUT EVEN WITH YOUR HELP, I'M LOST.
THEN I TELL YOU A TALE, CHÉRIE. A TALE OF THE LADY. AFTER THE WAR, AFTER THE DAYS OF BLOOD.
NEW ORLEANS, 1862.
THE BATTLE OF NEW ORLEANS.
N'awlins be an island, but it don't float on no water. It float on the dead.
Ole death came tourin' through these parts...
And he weren't too choosey 'bout who to jam with.

BLiNK

Le prélude à la mort
Une histoire de la...

VOODOO CHIL

SELWYN SEYFU HINDS writer • DENYS COWAN penc
DON HUDSON inks • JARED K. FLETCHER letterer • DAVE McCAIG color
JOE HUGHES assistant editor • KAREN BERGER edi

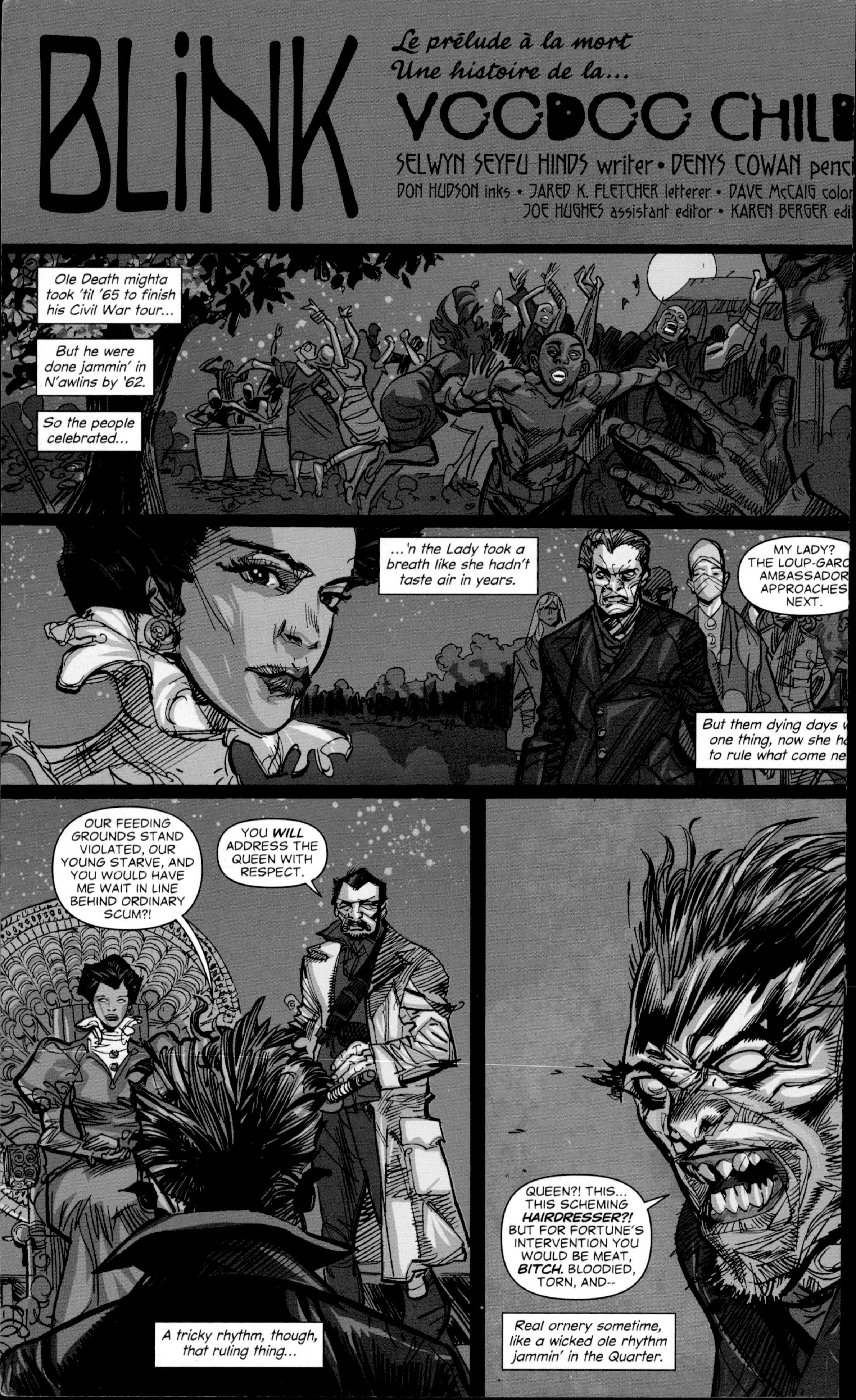
Ole Death mighta took 'til '65 to finish his Civil War tour...
But he were done jammin' in N'awlins by '62.
So the people celebrated...
...'n the Lady took a breath like she hadn't taste air in years.
MY LADY? THE LOUP-GARO AMBASSADOR APPROACHES NEXT.
But them dying days one thing, now she h to rule what come ne
OUR FEEDING GROUNDS STAND VIOLATED, OUR YOUNG STARVE, AND YOU WOULD HAVE ME WAIT IN LINE BEHIND ORDINARY SCUM?!
YOU **WILL** ADDRESS THE QUEEN WITH RESPECT.
A tricky rhythm, though, that ruling thing...
QUEEN?! THIS... THIS SCHEMING ***HAIRDRESSER?!*** BUT FOR FORTUNE'S INTERVENTION YOU WOULD BE MEAT, ***BITCH.*** BLOODIED, TORN, AND--
Real ornery sometime, like a wicked ole rhythm jammin' in the Quarter.

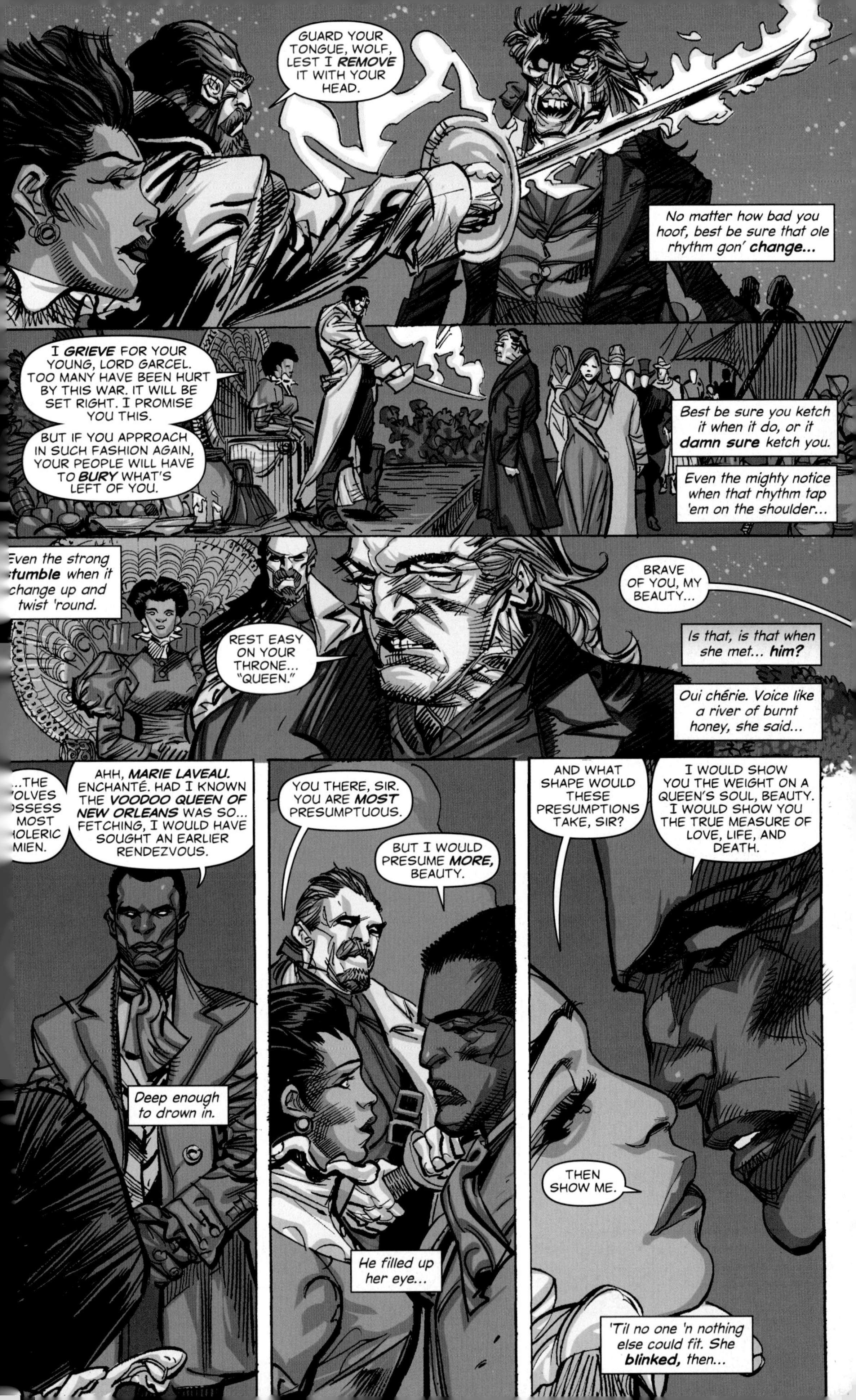
GUARD YOUR TONGUE, WOLF, LEST I REMOVE IT WITH YOUR HEAD.
No matter how bad you hoof, best be sure that ole rhythm gon' change...
I GRIEVE FOR YOUR YOUNG, LORD GARCEL. TOO MANY HAVE BEEN HURT BY THIS WAR. IT WILL BE SET RIGHT. I PROMISE YOU THIS.
BUT IF YOU APPROACH IN SUCH FASHION AGAIN, YOUR PEOPLE WILL HAVE TO BURY WHAT'S LEFT OF YOU.
Best be sure you ketch it when it do, or it damn sure ketch you.
Even the mighty notice when that rhythm tap 'em on the shoulder...
Even the strong stumble when it change up and twist 'round.
REST EASY ON YOUR THRONE... "QUEEN."
BRAVE OF YOU, MY BEAUTY...
Is that, is that when she met... him?
Oui chérie. Voice like a river of burnt honey, she said...
...THE WOLVES POSSESS MOST CHOLERIC MIEN.
AHH, MARIE LAVEAU. ENCHANTÉ. HAD I KNOWN THE VOODOO QUEEN OF NEW ORLEANS WAS SO... FETCHING, I WOULD HAVE SOUGHT AN EARLIER RENDEZVOUS.
Deep enough to drown in.
YOU THERE, SIR. YOU ARE MOST PRESUMPTUOUS.
BUT I WOULD PRESUME MORE, BEAUTY.
He filled up her eye...
AND WHAT SHAPE WOULD THESE PRESUMPTIONS TAKE, SIR?
I WOULD SHOW YOU THE WEIGHT ON A QUEEN'S SOUL, BEAUTY. I WOULD SHOW YOU THE TRUE MEASURE OF LOVE, LIFE, AND DEATH.
THEN SHOW ME.
'Til no one 'n nothing else could fit. She blinked, then...

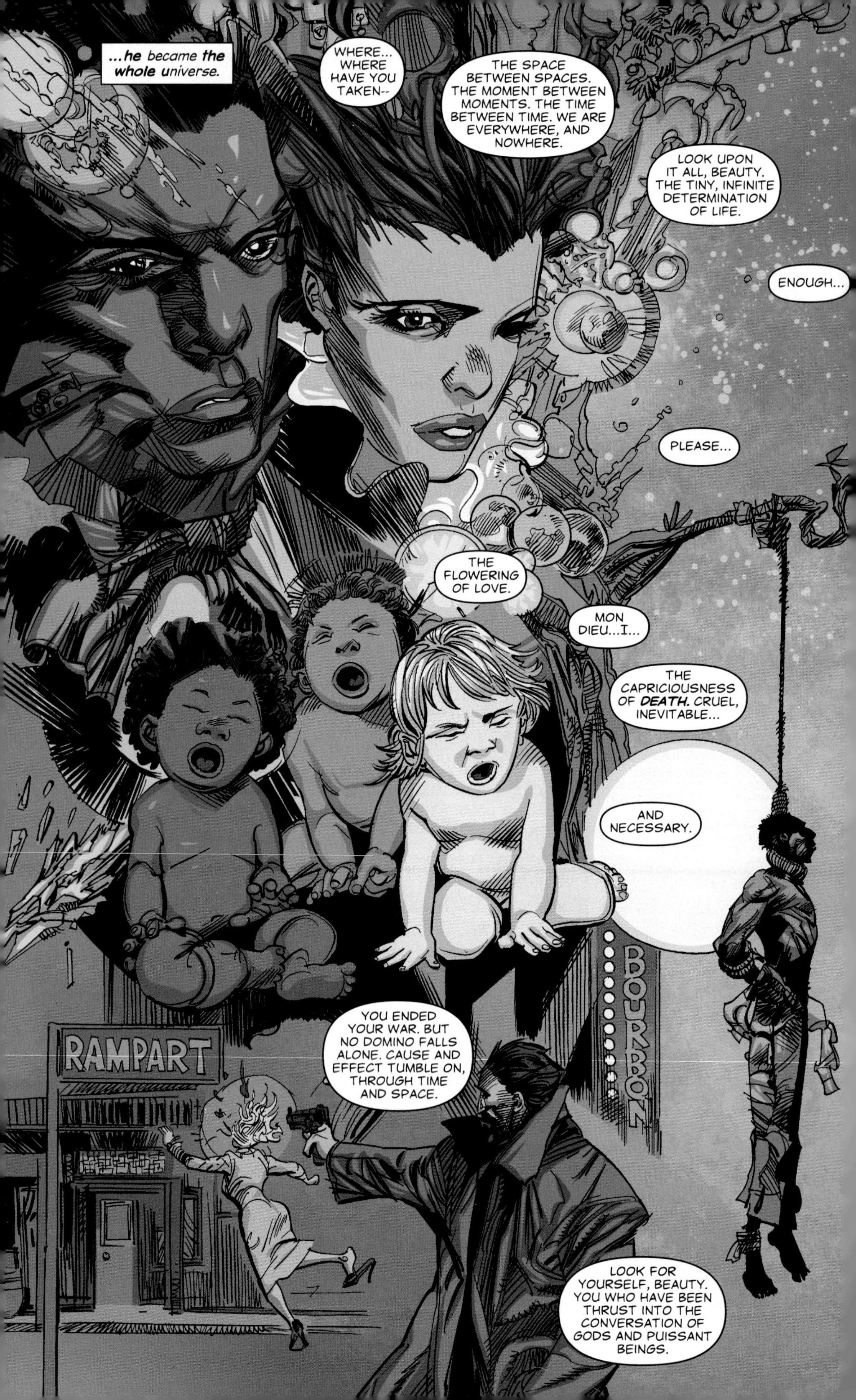
...he became the whole universe.
WHERE... WHERE HAVE YOU TAKEN--
THE SPACE BETWEEN SPACES. THE MOMENT BETWEEN MOMENTS. THE TIME BETWEEN TIME. WE ARE EVERYWHERE, AND NOWHERE.
LOOK UPON IT ALL, BEAUTY. THE TINY, INFINITE DETERMINATION OF LIFE.
ENOUGH...
PLEASE...
THE FLOWERING OF LOVE.
MON DIEU...I...
THE CAPRICIOUSNESS OF DEATH. CRUEL, INEVITABLE...
AND NECESSARY.
BOURBON
RAMPART
YOU ENDED YOUR WAR. BUT NO DOMINO FALLS ALONE. CAUSE AND EFFECT TUMBLE ON, THROUGH TIME AND SPACE.
LOOK FOR YOURSELF, BEAUTY. YOU WHO HAVE BEEN THRUST INTO THE CONVERSATION OF GODS AND PUISSANT BEINGS.

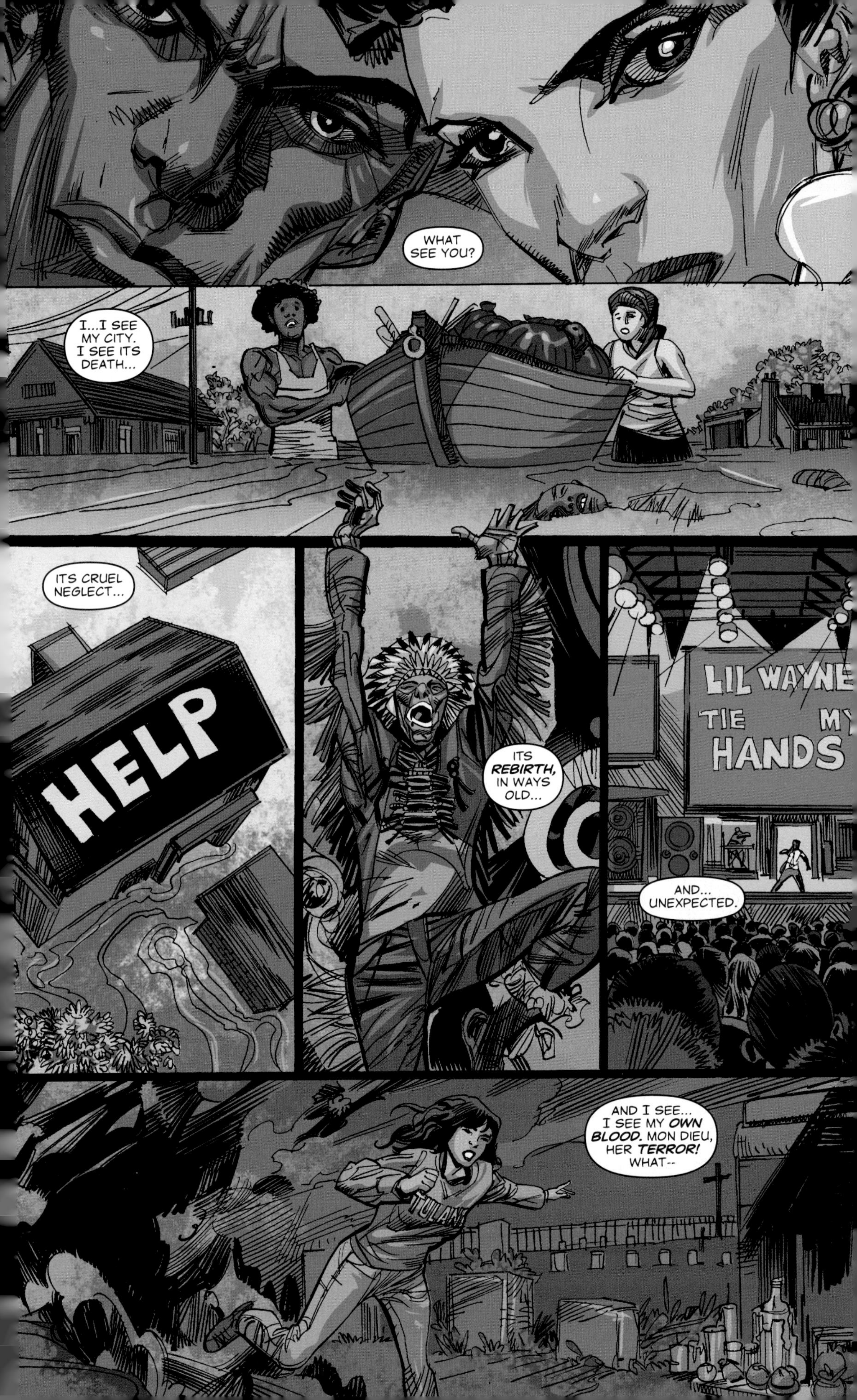
WHAT SEE YOU?
I...I SEE MY CITY. I SEE ITS DEATH...
ITS CRUEL NEGLECT...
HELP
ITS REBIRTH, IN WAYS OLD...
LIL WAYNE
TIE MY HANDS
AND... UNEXPECTED.
AND I SEE... I SEE MY OWN BLOOD. MON DIEU, HER TERROR! WHAT--
TULANE

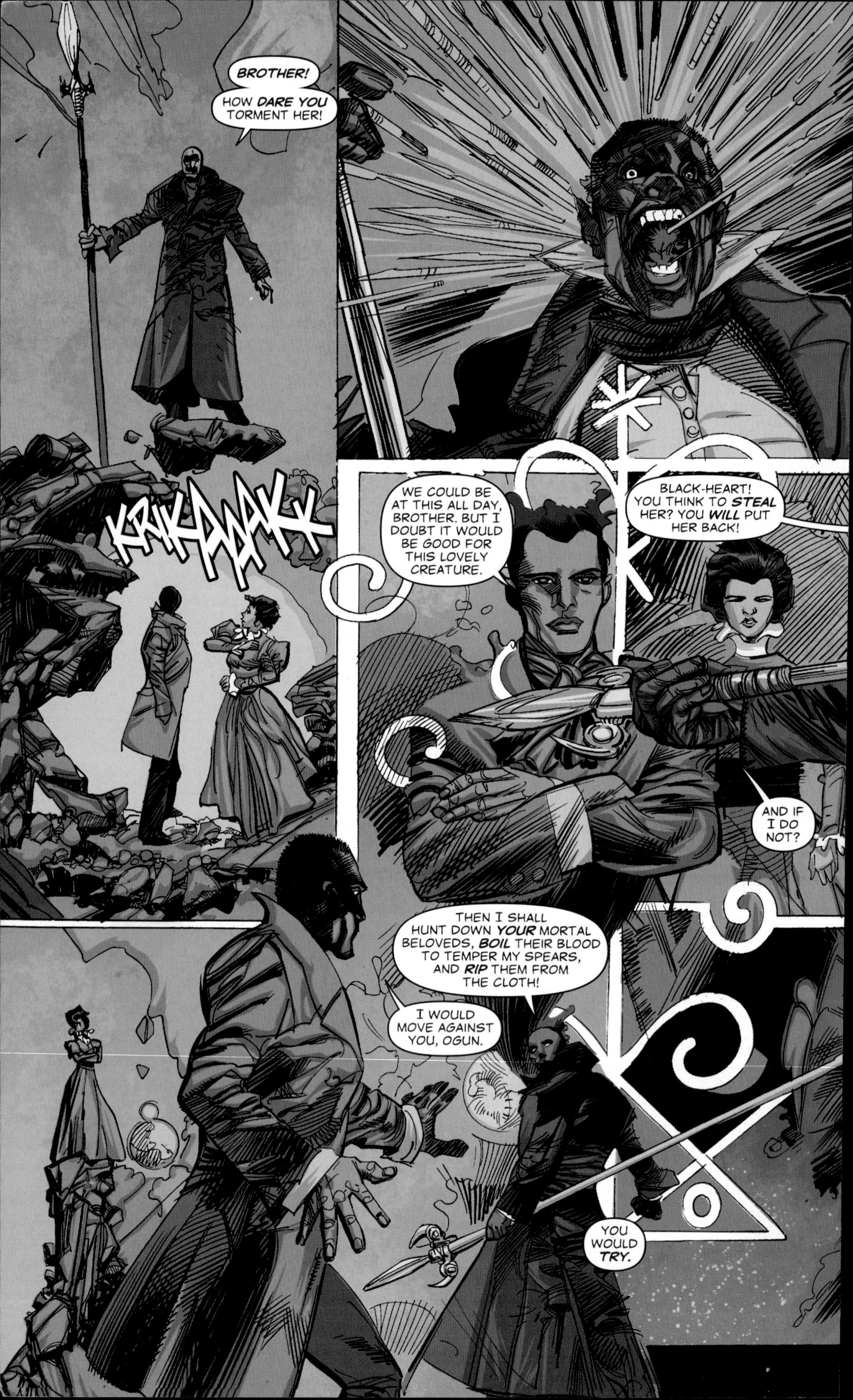
BROTHER!
HOW DARE YOU TORMENT HER!
KRIKRAKK
WE COULD BE AT THIS ALL DAY, BROTHER. BUT I DOUBT IT WOULD BE GOOD FOR THIS LOVELY CREATURE.
BLACK-HEART! YOU THINK TO STEAL HER? YOU WILL PUT HER BACK!
AND IF I DO NOT?
THEN I SHALL HUNT DOWN YOUR MORTAL BELOVEDS, BOIL THEIR BLOOD TO TEMPER MY SPEARS, AND RIP THEM FROM THE CLOTH!
I WOULD MOVE AGAINST YOU, OGUN.
YOU WOULD TRY.

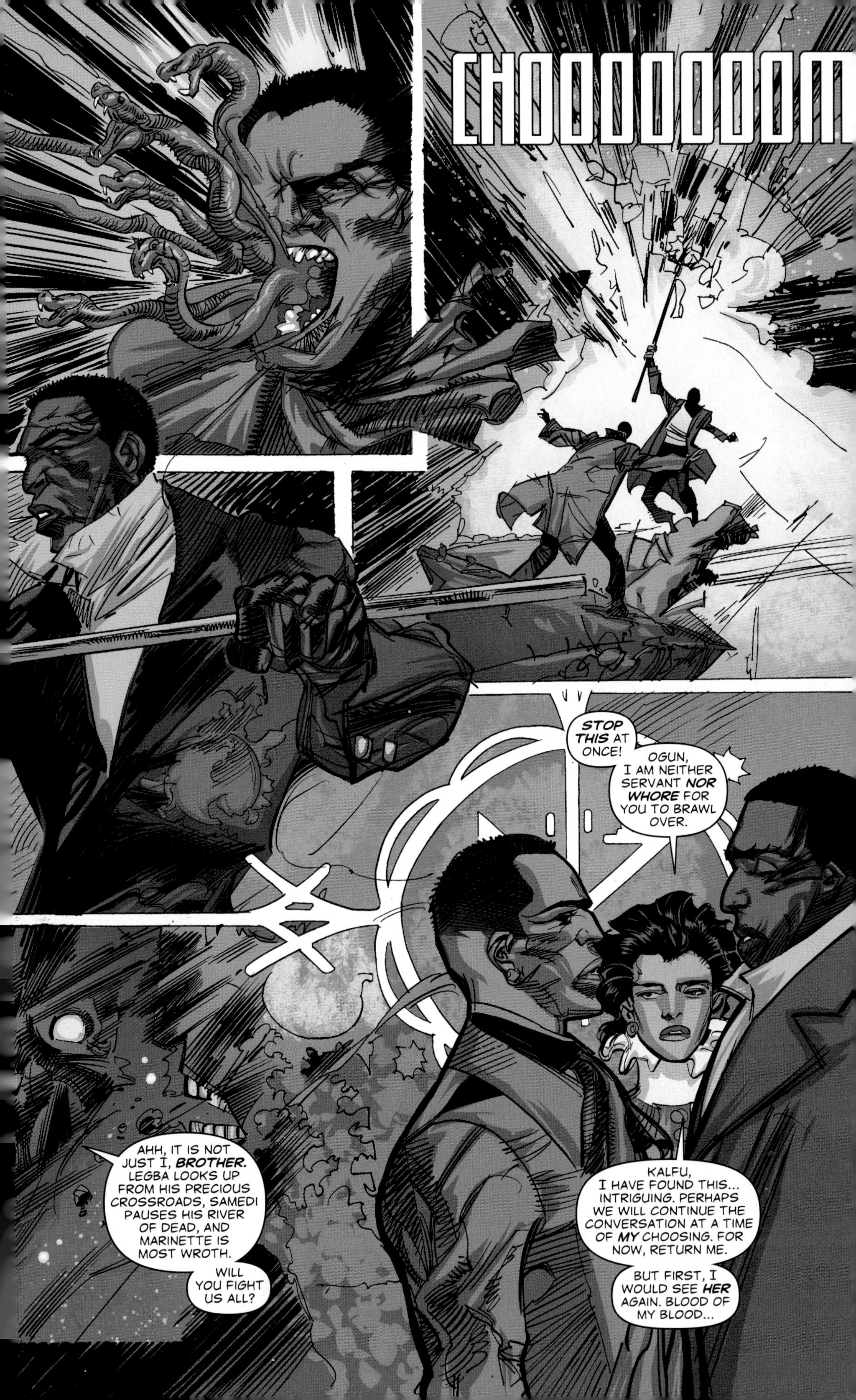
CHOOOOOOOM
STOP THIS AT ONCE!
OGUN, I AM NEITHER SERVANT NOR WHORE FOR YOU TO BRAWL OVER.
AHH, IT IS NOT JUST I, BROTHER. LEGBA LOOKS UP FROM HIS PRECIOUS CROSSROADS, SAMEDI PAUSES HIS RIVER OF DEAD, AND MARINETTE IS MOST WROTH.
WILL YOU FIGHT US ALL?
KALFU, I HAVE FOUND THIS... INTRIGUING. PERHAPS WE WILL CONTINUE THE CONVERSATION AT A TIME OF MY CHOOSING. FOR NOW, RETURN ME.
BUT FIRST, I WOULD SEE HER AGAIN. BLOOD OF MY BLOOD...

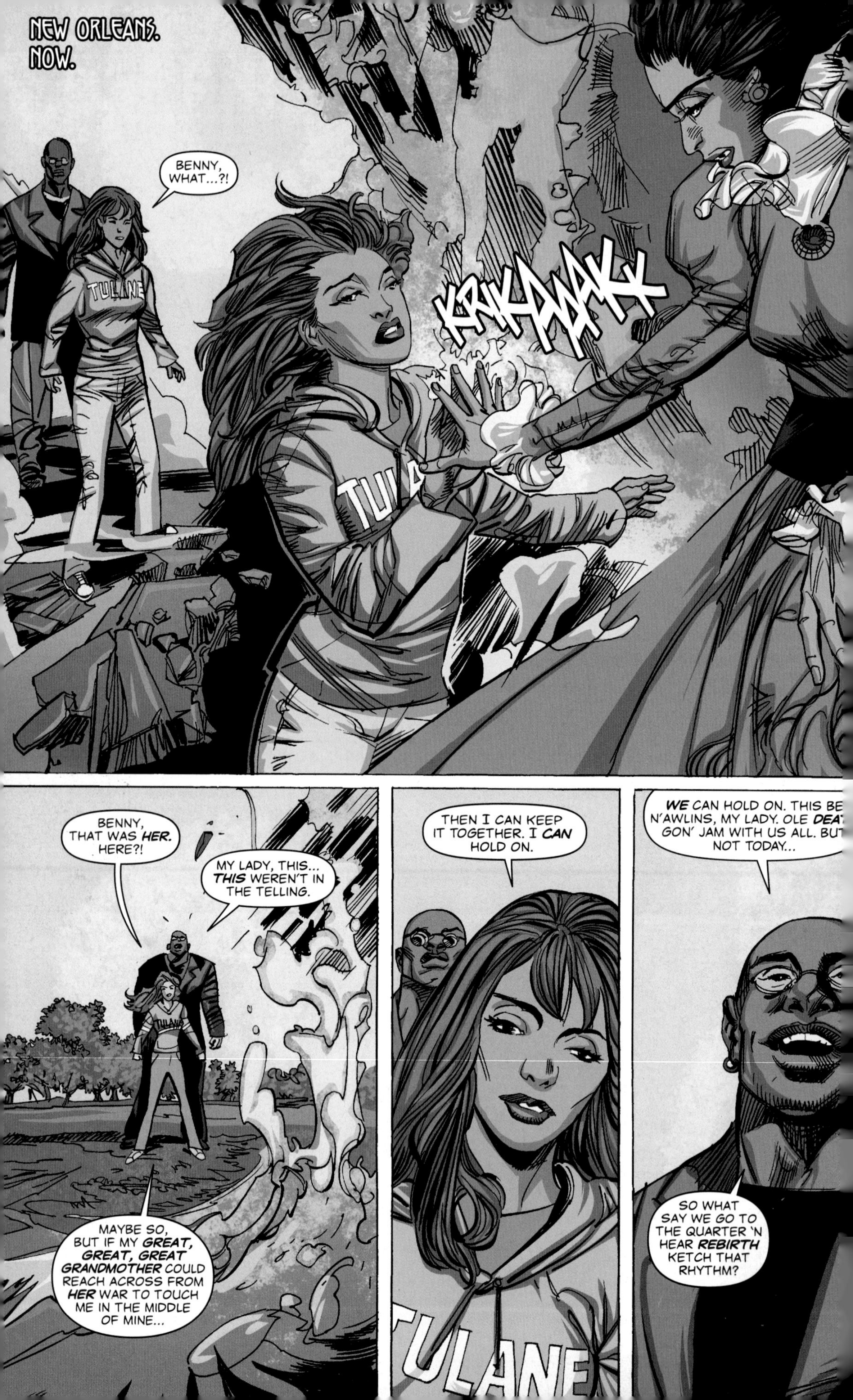
NEW ORLEANS.
NOW.
BENNY, WHAT...?!
KRKAKAKK
BENNY, THAT WAS HER. HERE?!
MY LADY, THIS... THIS WEREN'T IN THE TELLING.
MAYBE SO, BUT IF MY GREAT, GREAT, GREAT GRANDMOTHER COULD REACH ACROSS FROM HER WAR TO TOUCH ME IN THE MIDDLE OF MINE...
THEN I CAN KEEP IT TOGETHER. I CAN HOLD ON.
WE CAN HOLD ON. THIS BE N'AWLINS, MY LADY. OLE DEAT GON' JAM WITH US ALL. BU NOT TODAY...
SO WHAT SAY WE GO TO THE QUARTER 'N HEAR REBIRTH KETCH THAT RHYTHM?
TULANE

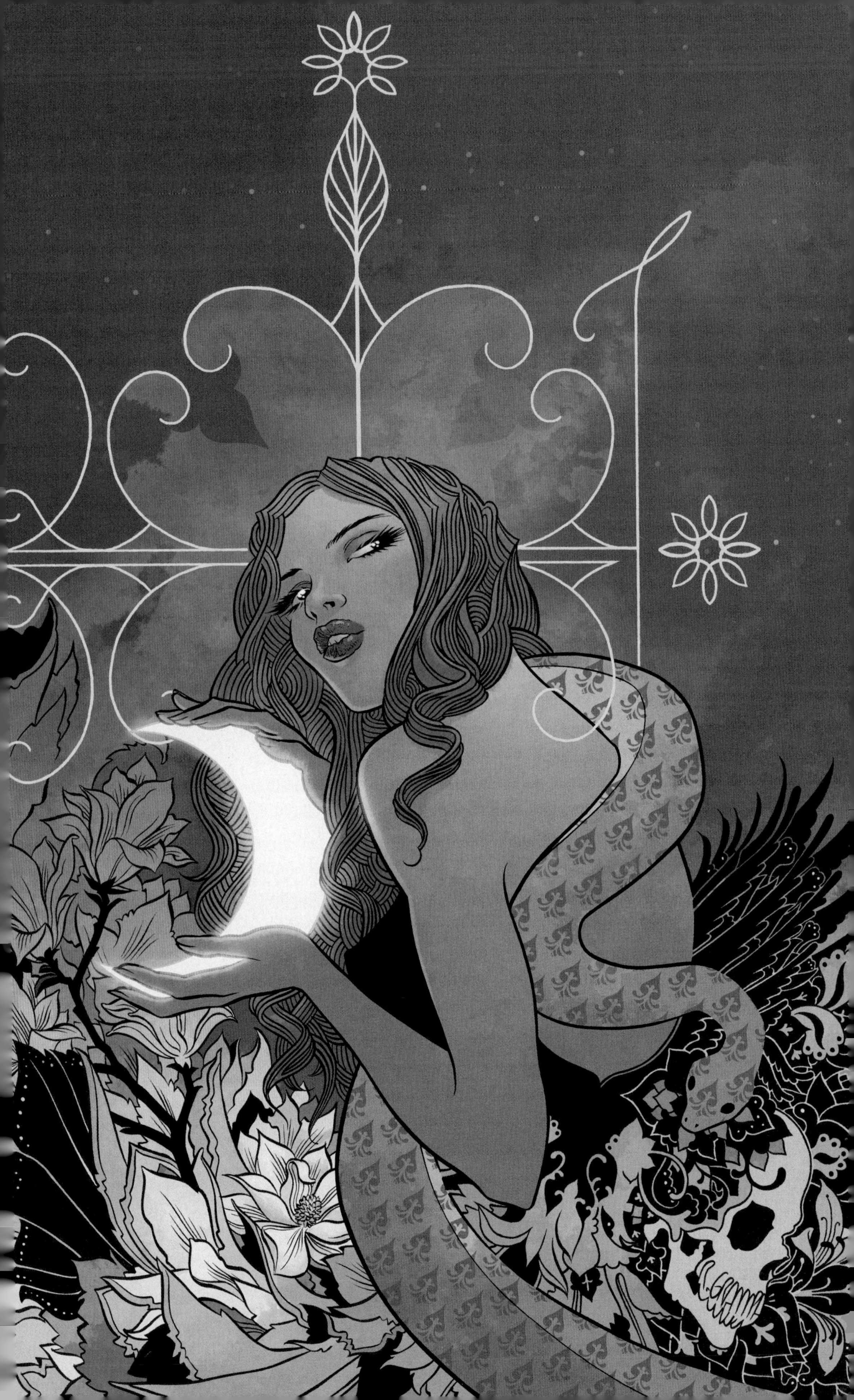

"The bonds have torn. The balance is upset. Order must be restored."

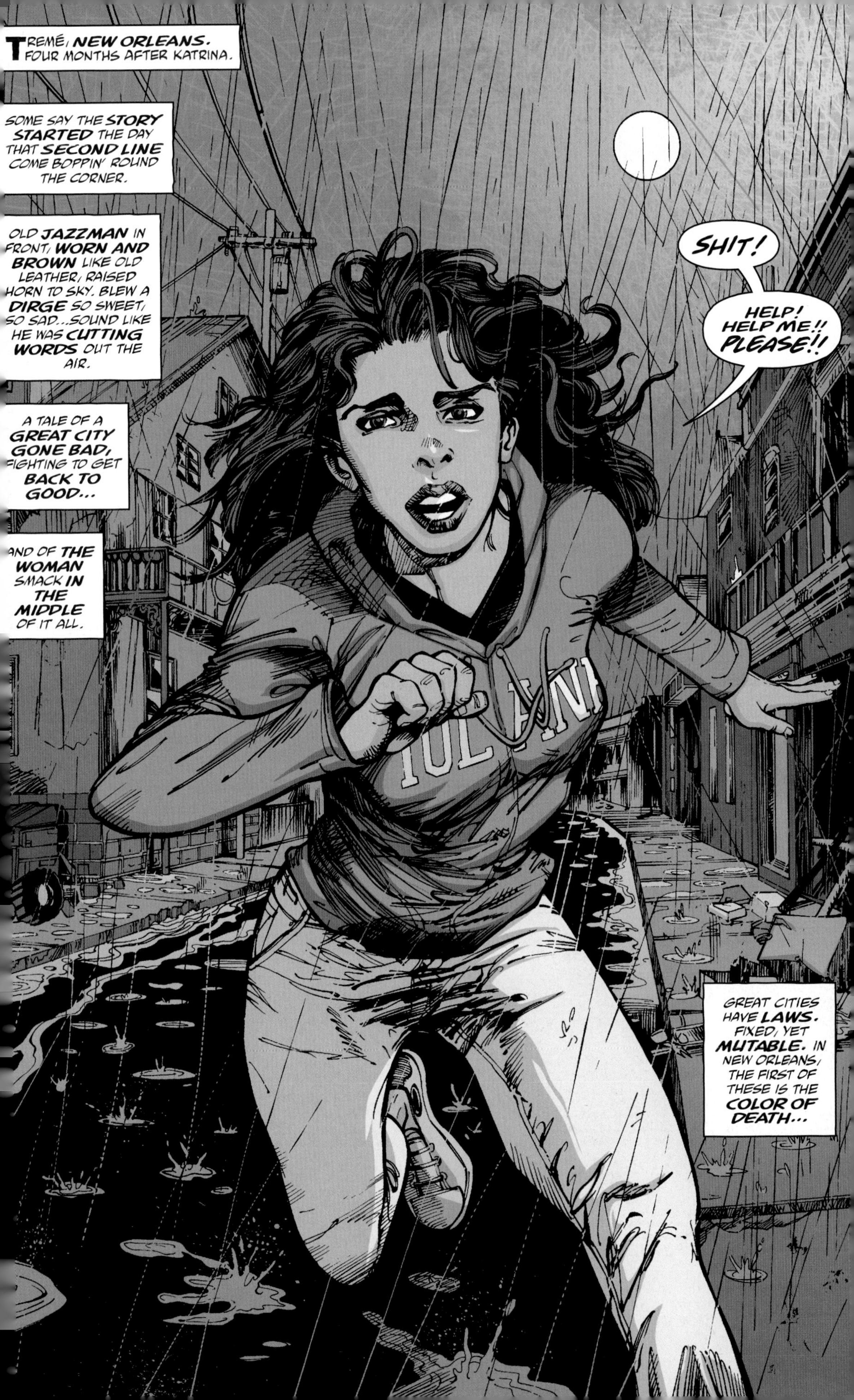
TREMÉ, NEW ORLEANS. FOUR MONTHS AFTER KATRINA.
SOME SAY THE STORY STARTED THE DAY THAT SECOND LINE COME BOPPIN' ROUND THE CORNER.
OLD JAZZMAN IN FRONT, WORN AND BROWN LIKE OLD LEATHER, RAISED HORN TO SKY. BLEW A DIRGE SO SWEET, SO SAD...SOUND LIKE HE WAS CUTTING WORDS OUT THE AIR.
A TALE OF A GREAT CITY GONE BAD, FIGHTING TO GET BACK TO GOOD...
AND OF THE WOMAN SMACK IN THE MIDDLE OF IT ALL.
SHIT!
HELP! HELP ME!! PLEASE!!
GREAT CITIES HAVE LAWS. FIXED, YET MUTABLE. IN NEW ORLEANS, THE FIRST OF THESE IS THE COLOR OF DEATH...

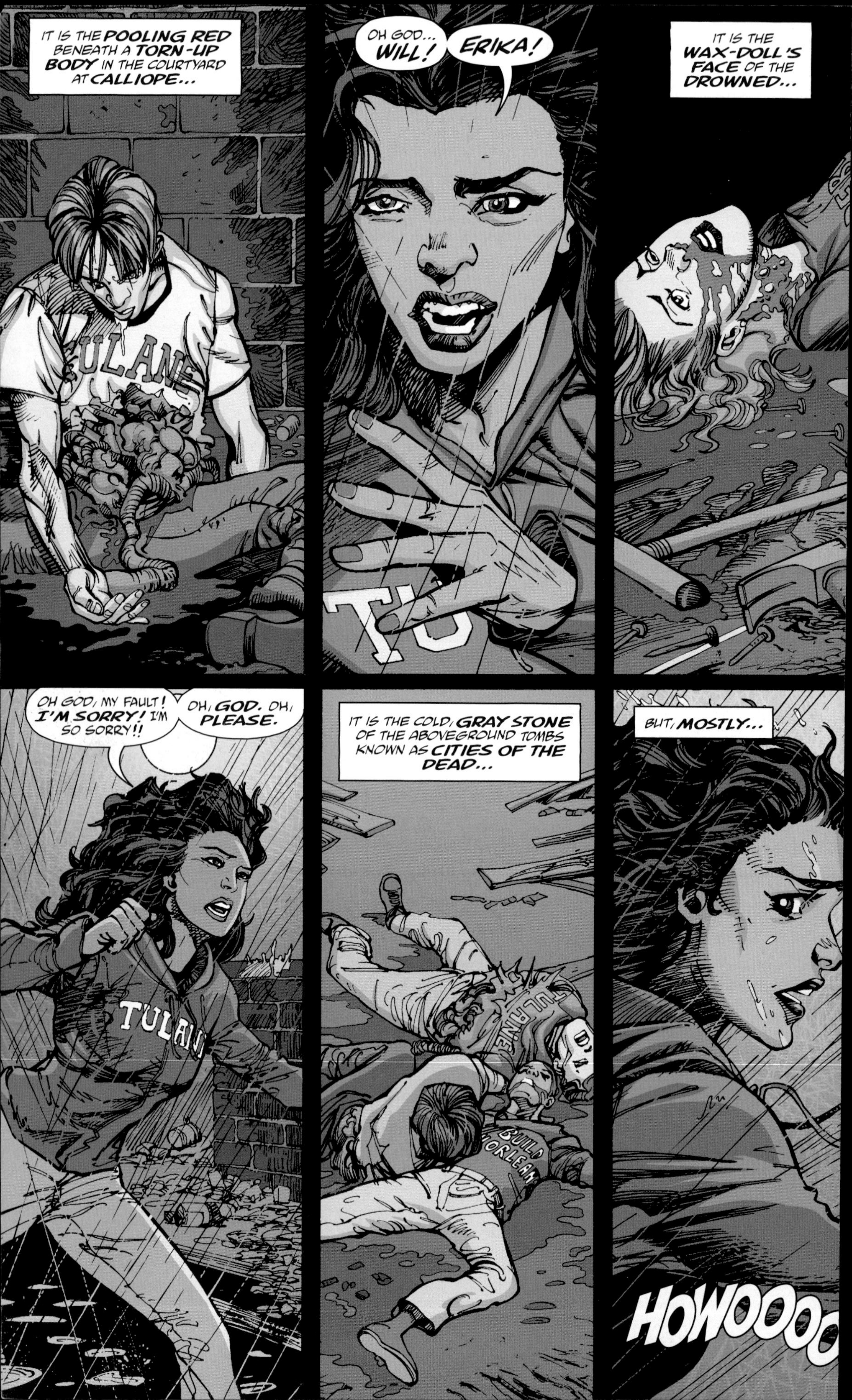
IT IS THE POOLING RED BENEATH A TORN-UP BODY IN THE COURTYARD AT CALLIOPE...
OH GOD... WILL!
ERIKA!
IT IS THE WAX-DOLL'S FACE OF THE DROWNED...
OH GOD, MY FAULT! I'M SORRY! I'M SO SORRY!!
OH, GOD. OH, PLEASE.
IT IS THE COLD, GRAY STONE OF THE ABOVEGROUND TOMBS KNOWN AS CITIES OF THE DEAD...
BUT, MOSTLY...
HOWOOOO

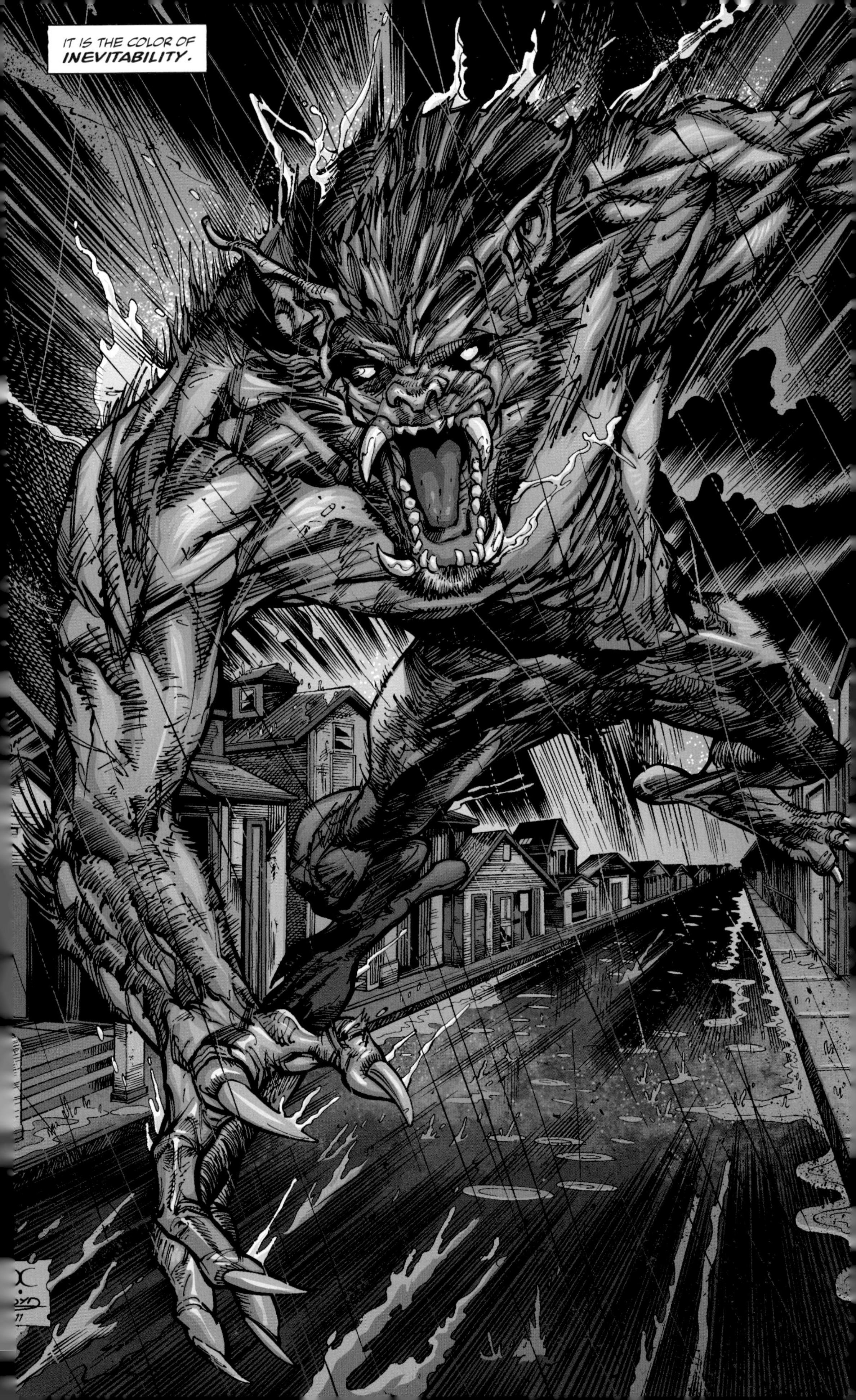
IT IS THE COLOR OF
INEVITABILITY.

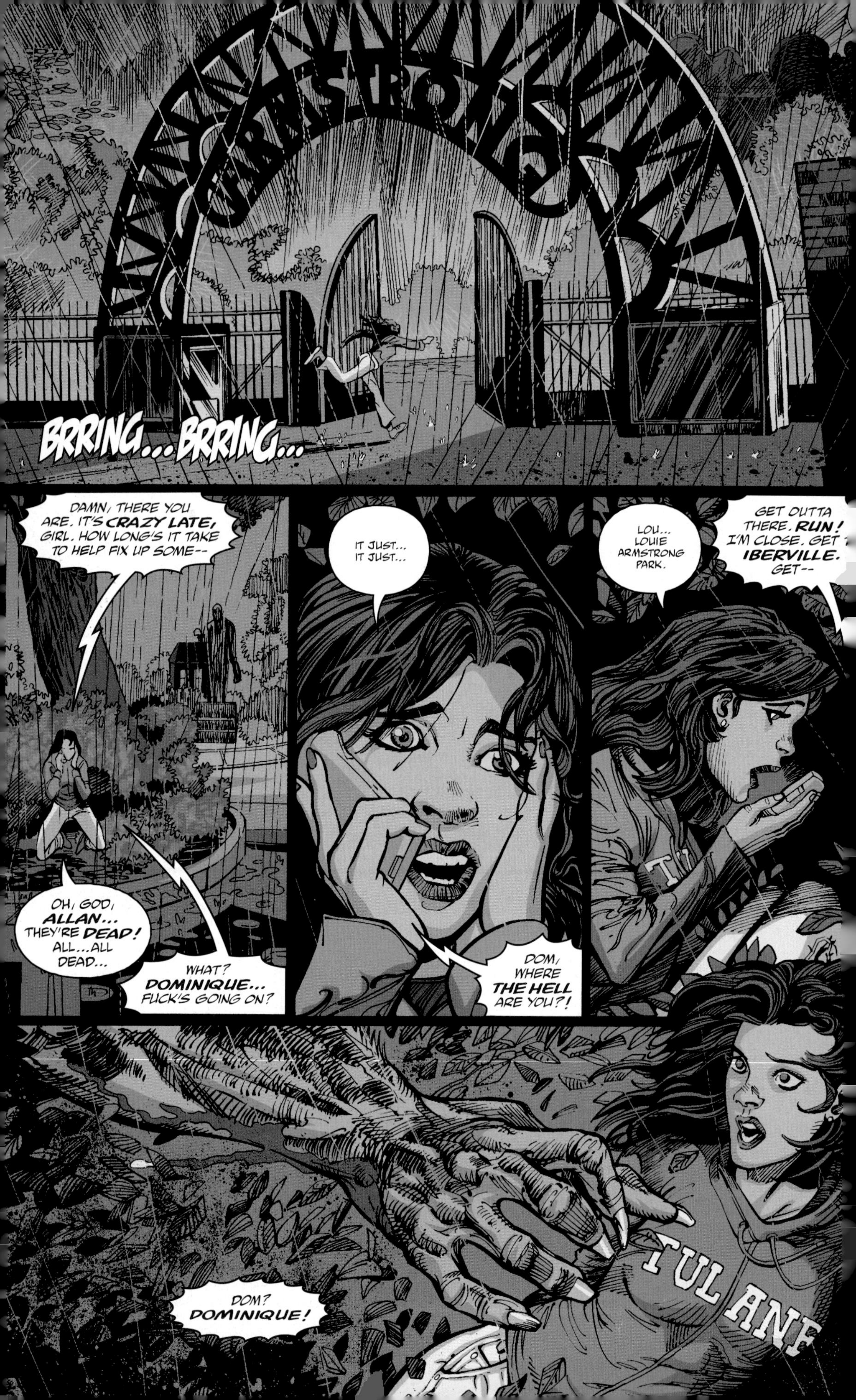
BRRING...BRRING...
DAMN, THERE YOU ARE. IT'S CRAZY LATE, GIRL. HOW LONG'S IT TAKE TO HELP FIX UP SOME--
OH, GOD, ALLAN... THEY'RE DEAD! ALL...ALL DEAD...
WHAT? DOMINIQUE... FUCK'S GOING ON?
IT JUST... IT JUST...
DOM, WHERE THE HELL ARE YOU?!
LOU... LOUIE ARMSTRONG PARK.
GET OUTTA THERE. RUN! I'M CLOSE. GET IBERVILLE. GET--
DOM? DOMINIQUE!

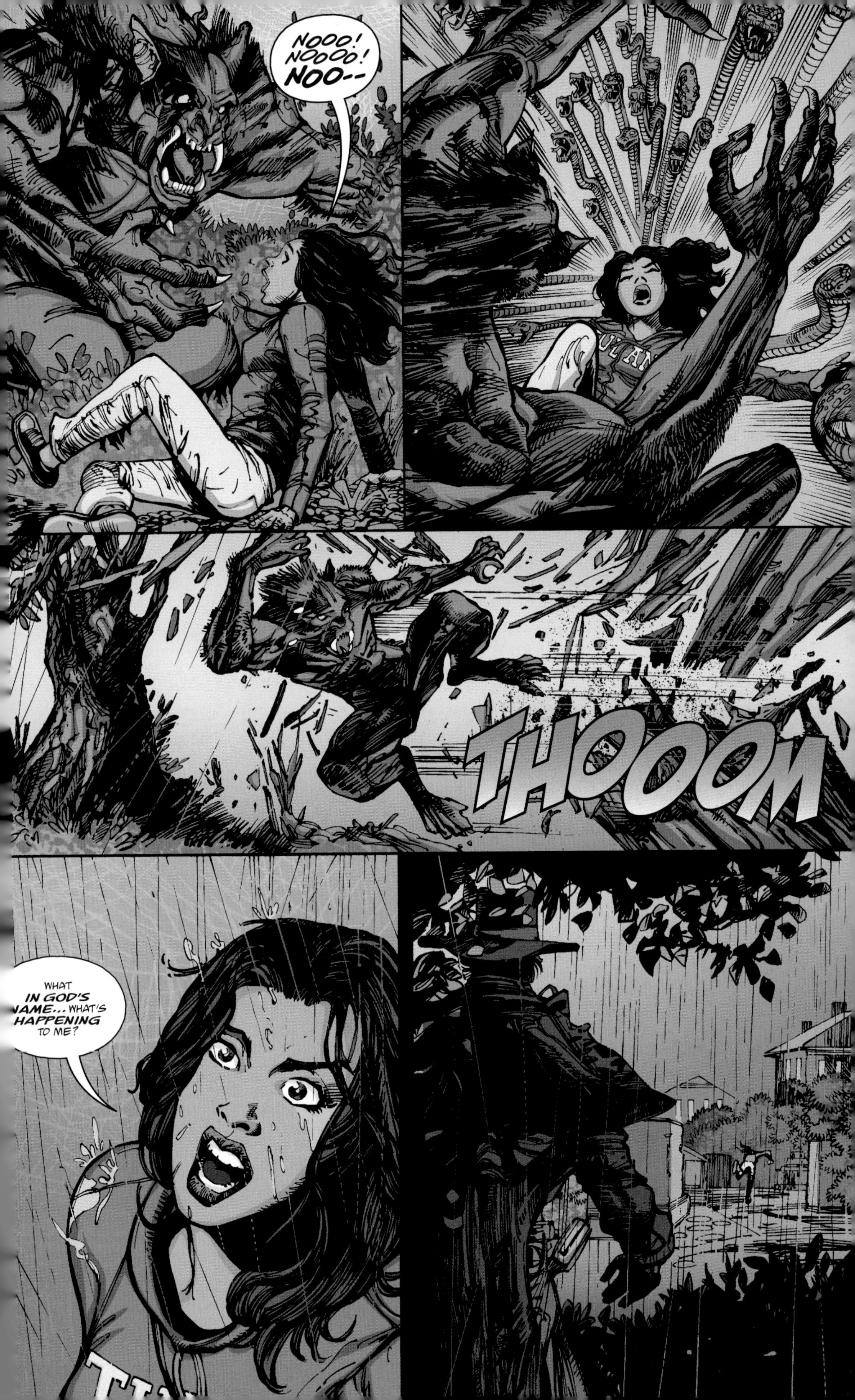
NOOO! NOOOO! NOO--
THOOOM
WHAT IN GOD'S NAME... WHAT'S HAPPENING TO ME?

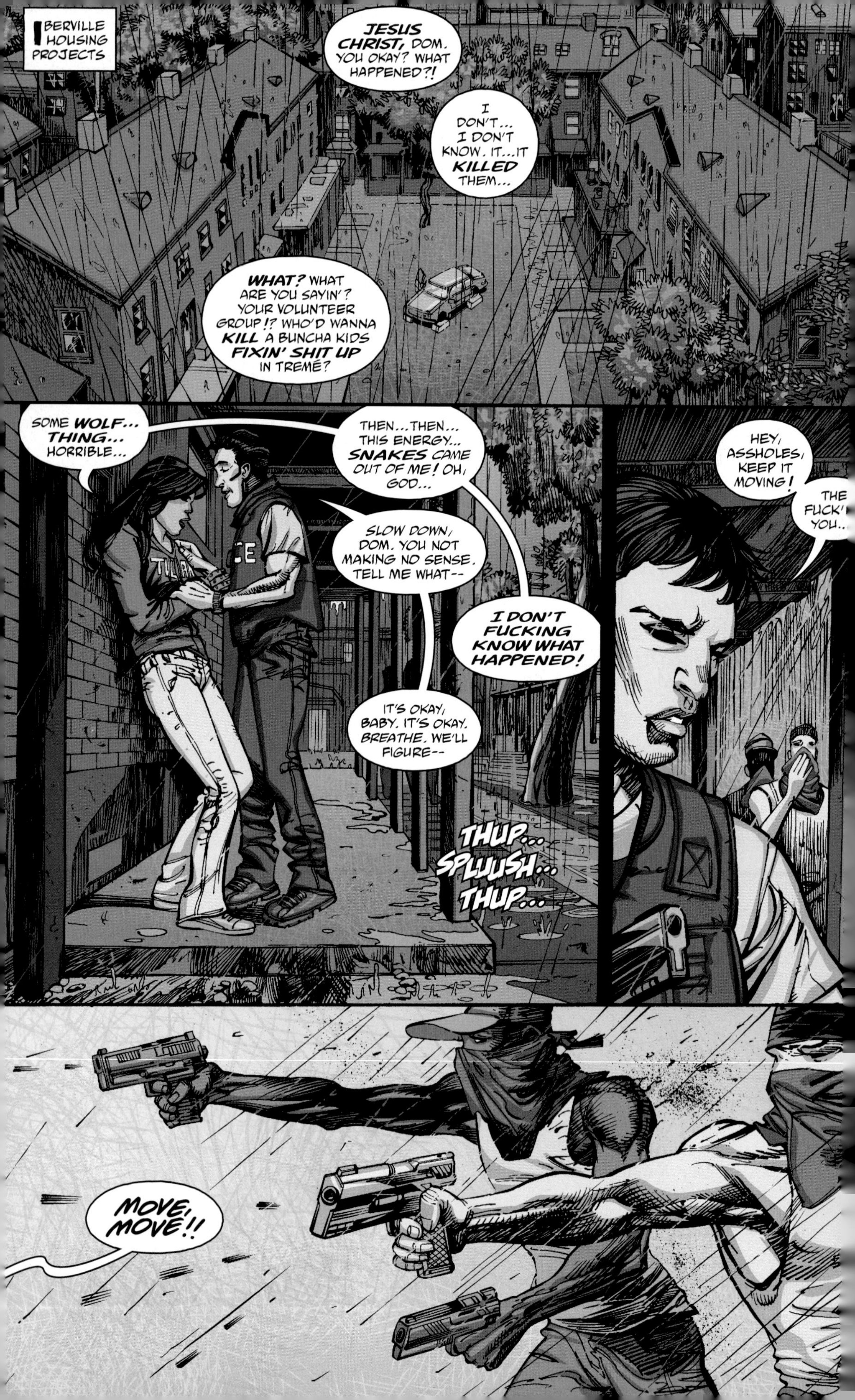
IBERVILLE HOUSING PROJECTS
JESUS CHRIST, DOM. YOU OKAY? WHAT HAPPENED?!
I DON'T... I DON'T KNOW. IT...IT KILLED THEM...
WHAT? WHAT ARE YOU SAYIN'? YOUR VOLUNTEER GROUP!? WHO'D WANNA KILL A BUNCHA KIDS FIXIN' SHIT UP IN TREMÉ?
SOME WOLF... THING... HORRIBLE...
THEN...THEN... THIS ENERGY... SNAKES CAME OUT OF ME! OH, GOD...
SLOW DOWN, DOM. YOU NOT MAKING NO SENSE. TELL ME WHAT--
I DON'T FUCKING KNOW WHAT HAPPENED!
IT'S OKAY, BABY. IT'S OKAY. BREATHE. WE'LL FIGURE--
THUP... SPLUUSH... THUP...
HEY, ASSHOLES, KEEP IT MOVING!
THE FUCK' YOU...
MOVE, MOVE!!

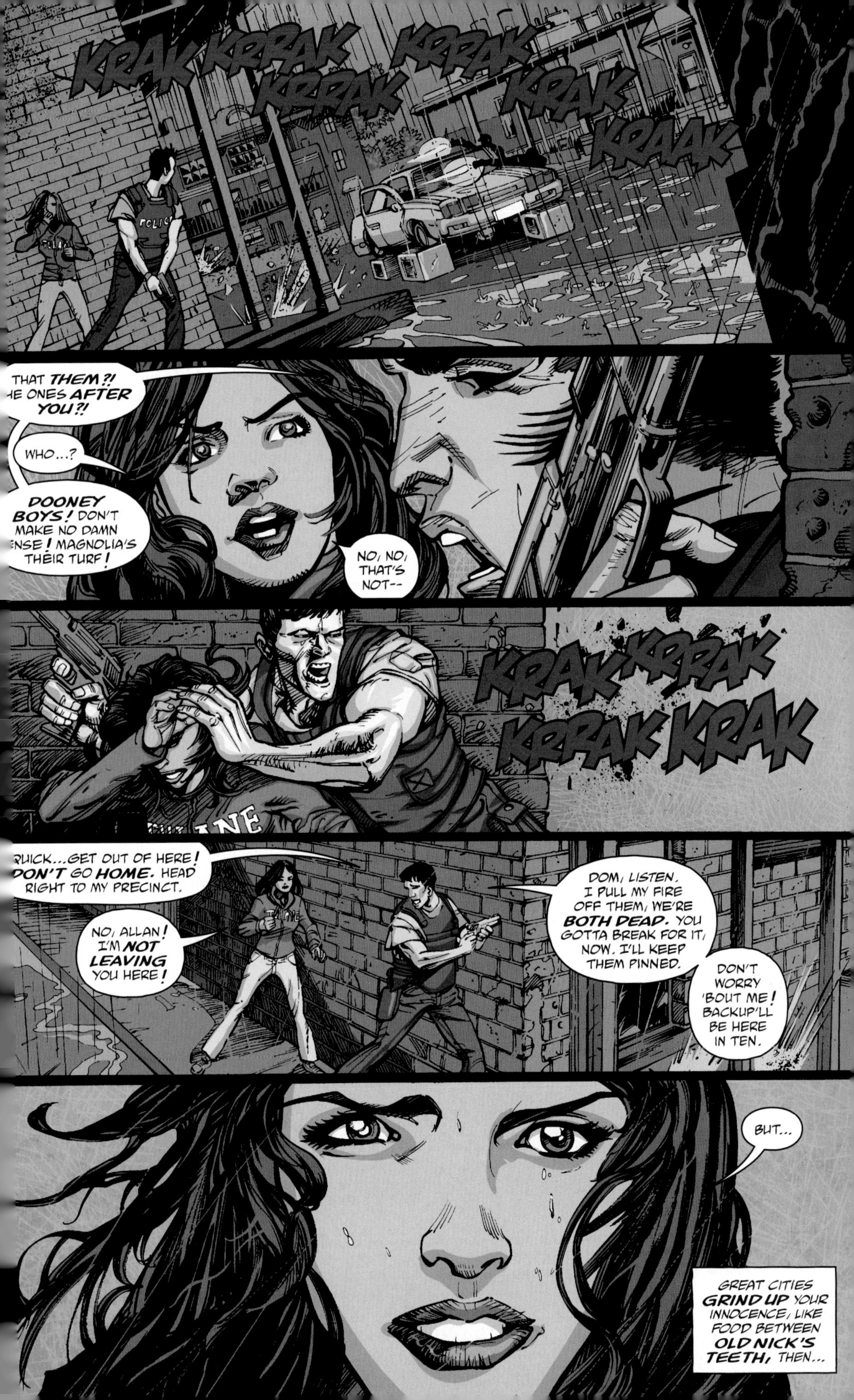
KRAK KRRAK KRRAK KRRAK KRAK KRAAK
THAT THEM?! HE ONES AFTER YOU?!
WHO...?
DOONEY BOYS! DON'T MAKE NO DAMN ENSE! MAGNOLIA'S THEIR TURF!
NO, NO, THAT'S NOT--
KRAK KRRAK KRRAK KRAK
QUICK...GET OUT OF HERE! DON'T GO HOME. HEAD RIGHT TO MY PRECINCT.
NO, ALLAN! I'M NOT LEAVING YOU HERE!
DOM, LISTEN. I PULL MY FIRE OFF THEM, WE'RE BOTH DEAD. YOU GOTTA BREAK FOR IT, NOW. I'LL KEEP THEM PINNED.
DON'T WORRY 'BOUT ME! BACKUP'LL BE HERE IN TEN.
BUT...
GREAT CITIES GRIND UP YOUR INNOCENCE, LIKE FOOD BETWEEN OLD NICK'S TEETH, THEN...

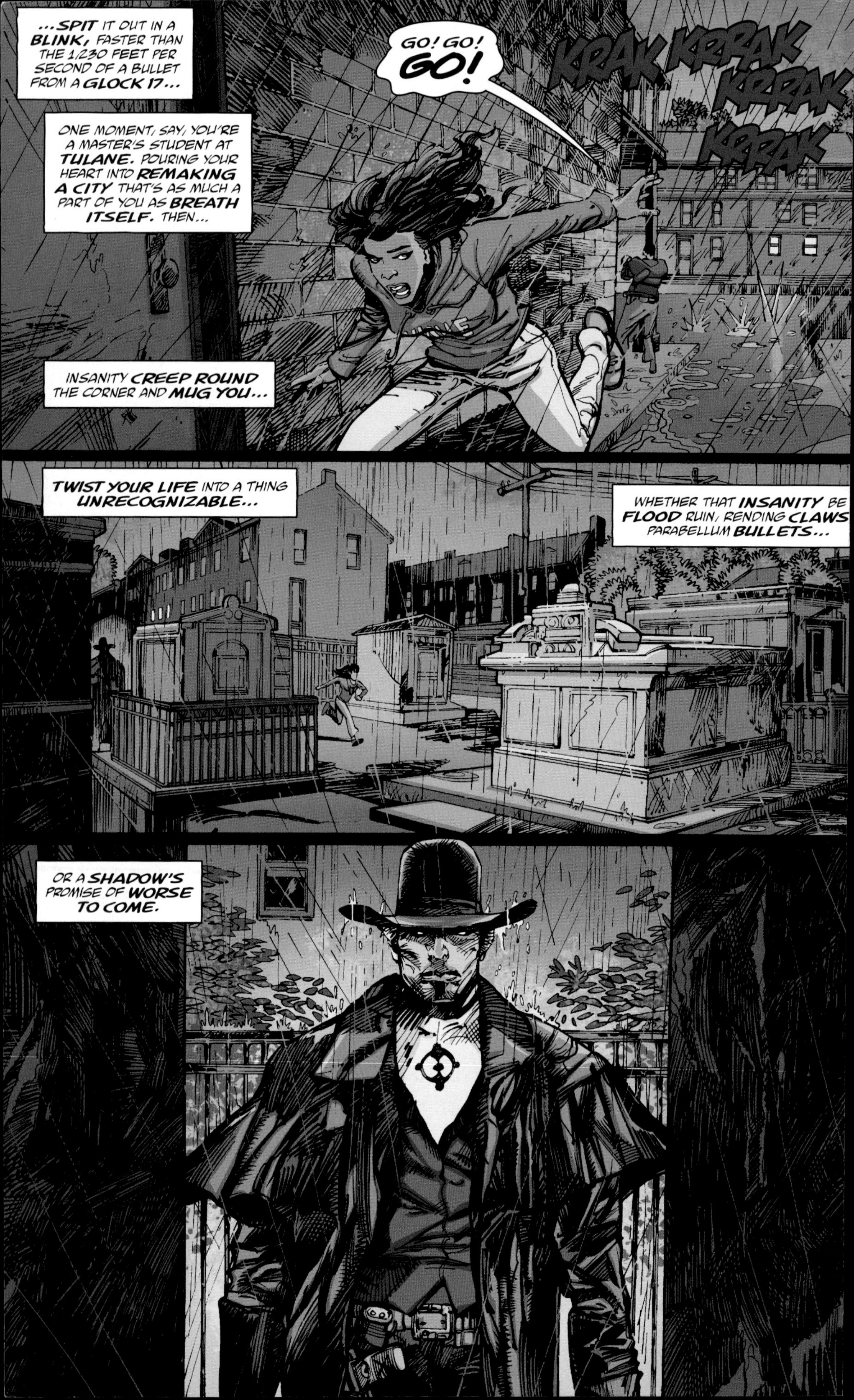

...SPIT IT OUT IN A BLINK, FASTER THAN THE 1,230 FEET PER SECOND OF A BULLET FROM A GLOCK 17...
GO! GO! GO!
KRAK KRRAK KRRAK KRRAK
ONE MOMENT, SAY, YOU'RE A MASTER'S STUDENT AT TULANE. POURING YOUR HEART INTO REMAKING A CITY THAT'S AS MUCH A PART OF YOU AS BREATH ITSELF. THEN...
INSANITY CREEP ROUND THE CORNER AND MUG YOU...
TWIST YOUR LIFE INTO A THING UNRECOGNIZABLE...
WHETHER THAT INSANITY BE FLOOD RUIN, RENDING CLAWS, PARABELLUM BULLETS...
OR A SHADOW'S PROMISE OF WORSE TO COME.

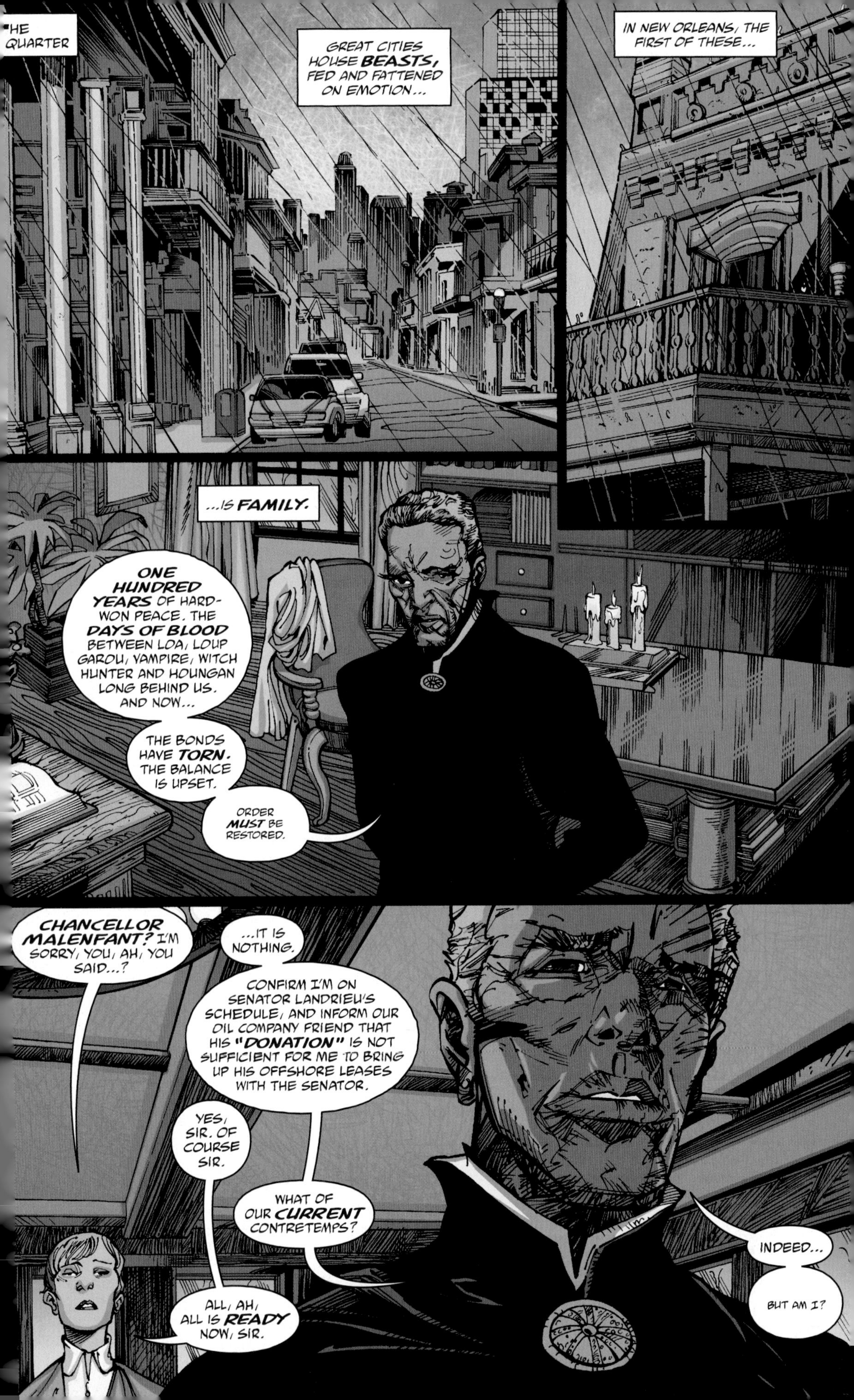
HE QUARTER
GREAT CITIES HOUSE BEASTS, FED AND FATTENED ON EMOTION...
IN NEW ORLEANS, THE FIRST OF THESE...
...IS FAMILY.
ONE HUNDRED YEARS OF HARD-WON PEACE. THE DAYS OF BLOOD BETWEEN LOA, LOUP GAROU, VAMPIRE, WITCH HUNTER AND HOUNGAN LONG BEHIND US. AND NOW...
THE BONDS HAVE TORN. THE BALANCE IS UPSET.
ORDER MUST BE RESTORED.
CHANCELLOR MALENFANT? I'M SORRY, YOU, AH, YOU SAID...?
...IT IS NOTHING.
CONFIRM I'M ON SENATOR LANDRIEU'S SCHEDULE, AND INFORM OUR OIL COMPANY FRIEND THAT HIS "DONATION" IS NOT SUFFICIENT FOR ME TO BRING UP HIS OFFSHORE LEASES WITH THE SENATOR.
YES, SIR. OF COURSE SIR.
WHAT OF OUR CURRENT CONTRETEMPS?
ALL, AH, ALL IS READY NOW, SIR.
INDEED...
BUT AM I?

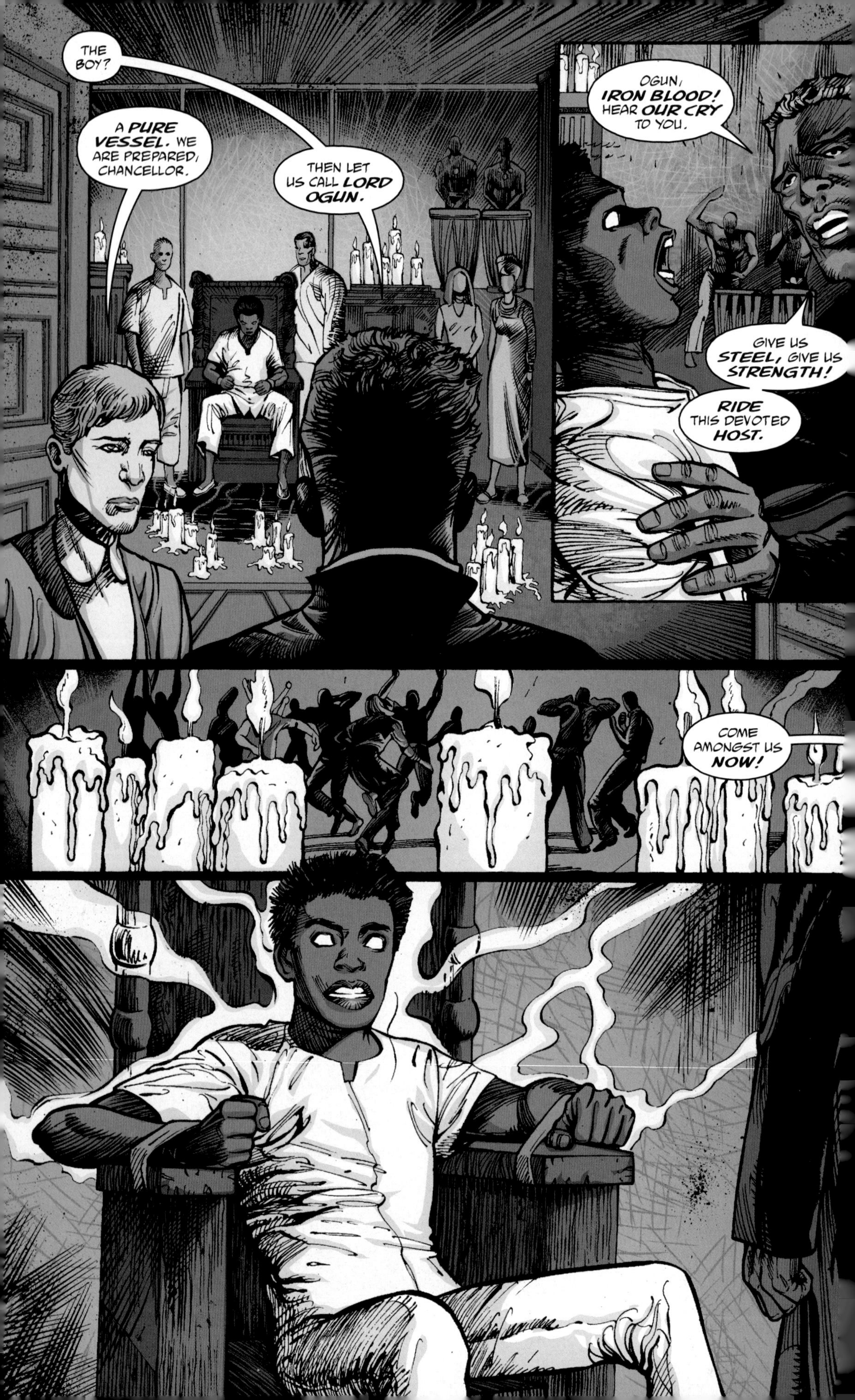
THE BOY?
A PURE VESSEL. WE ARE PREPARED, CHANCELLOR.
THEN LET US CALL LORD OGUN.
OGUN, IRON BLOOD! HEAR OUR CRY TO YOU.
GIVE US STEEL, GIVE US STRENGTH!
RIDE THIS DEVOTED HOST.
COME AMONGST US NOW!

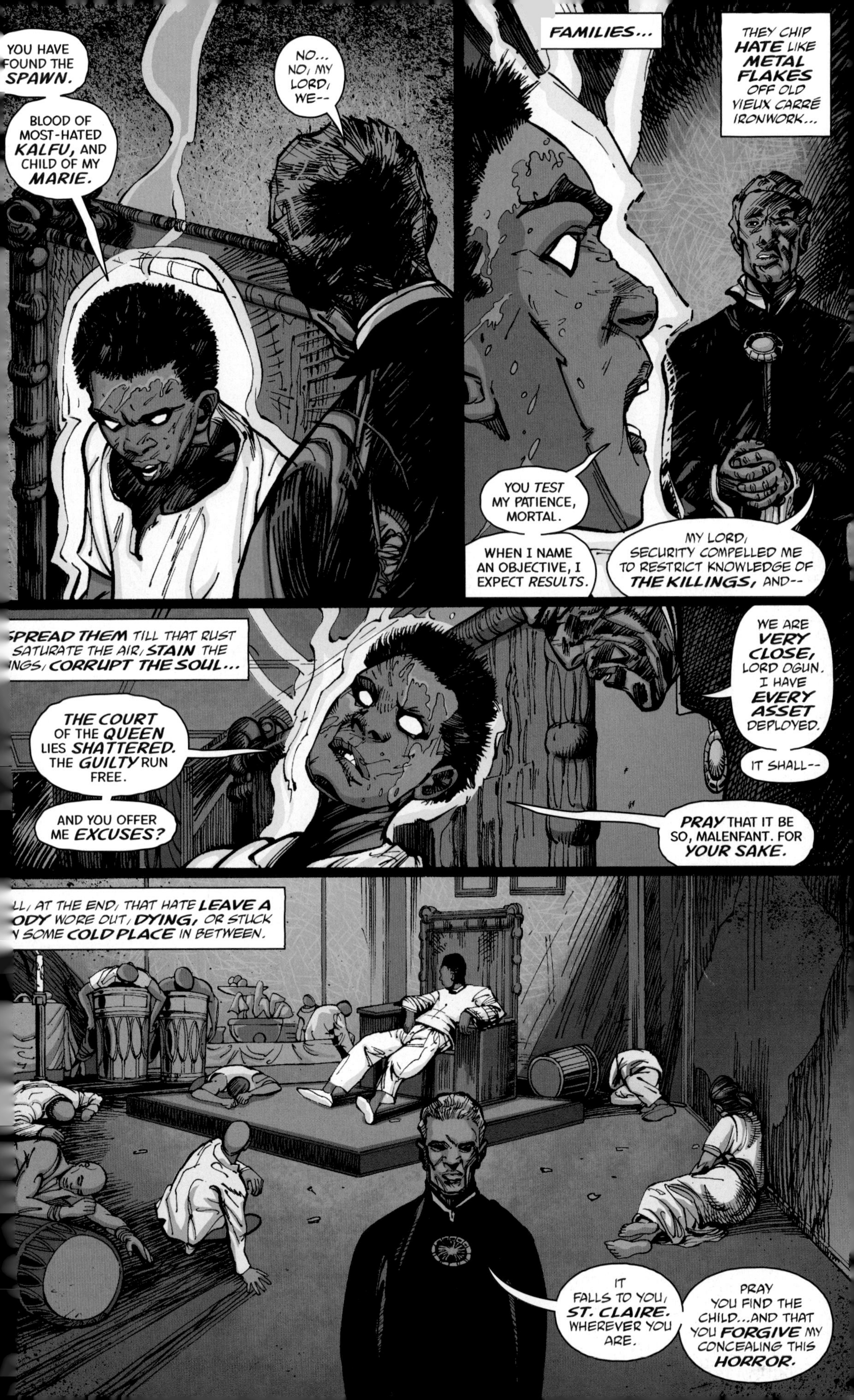
YOU HAVE FOUND THE SPAWN.
BLOOD OF MOST-HATED KALFU, AND CHILD OF MY MARIE.
NO... NO, MY LORD, WE--
FAMILIES...
THEY CHIP HATE LIKE METAL FLAKES OFF OLD VIEUX CARRÉ IRONWORK...
YOU TEST MY PATIENCE, MORTAL.
WHEN I NAME AN OBJECTIVE, I EXPECT RESULTS.
MY LORD, SECURITY COMPELLED ME TO RESTRICT KNOWLEDGE OF THE KILLINGS, AND--
SPREAD THEM TILL THAT RUST SATURATE THE AIR, STAIN THE NGS, CORRUPT THE SOUL...
THE COURT OF THE QUEEN LIES SHATTERED. THE GUILTY RUN FREE.
AND YOU OFFER ME EXCUSES?
WE ARE VERY CLOSE, LORD OGUN. I HAVE EVERY ASSET DEPLOYED.
IT SHALL--
PRAY THAT IT BE SO, MALENFANT. FOR YOUR SAKE.
LL, AT THE END, THAT HATE LEAVE A ODY WORE OUT, DYING, OR STUCK N SOME COLD PLACE IN BETWEEN.
IT FALLS TO YOU, ST. CLAIRE. WHEREVER YOU ARE.
PRAY YOU FIND THE CHILD...AND THAT YOU FORGIVE MY CONCEALING THIS HORROR.

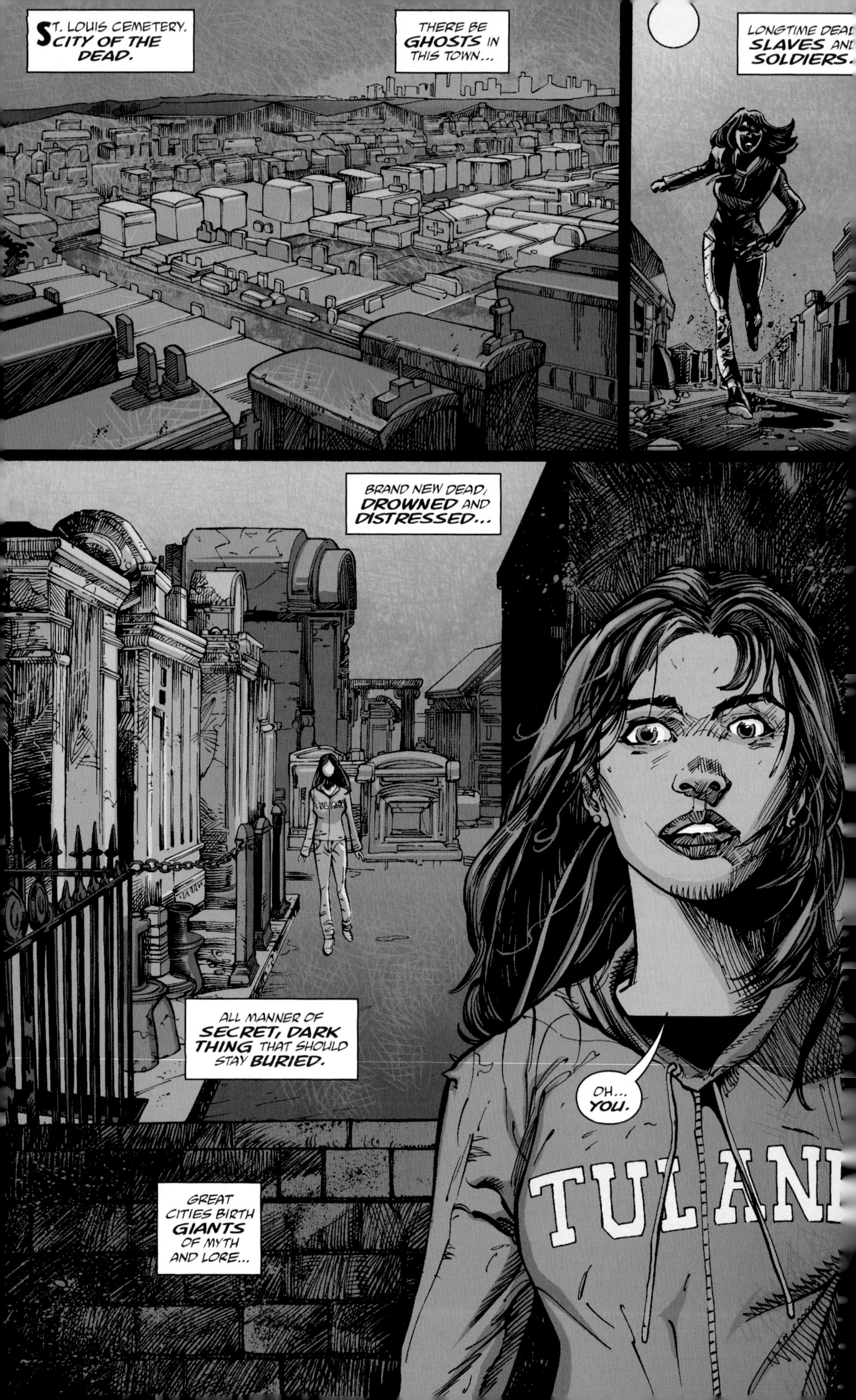
ST. LOUIS CEMETERY. CITY OF THE DEAD.
THERE BE GHOSTS IN THIS TOWN...
LONGTIME DEAD SLAVES AND SOLDIERS.
BRAND NEW DEAD, DROWNED AND DISTRESSED...
ALL MANNER OF SECRET, DARK THING THAT SHOULD STAY BURIED.
GREAT CITIES BIRTH GIANTS OF MYTH AND LORE...
OH... YOU.
TULANE

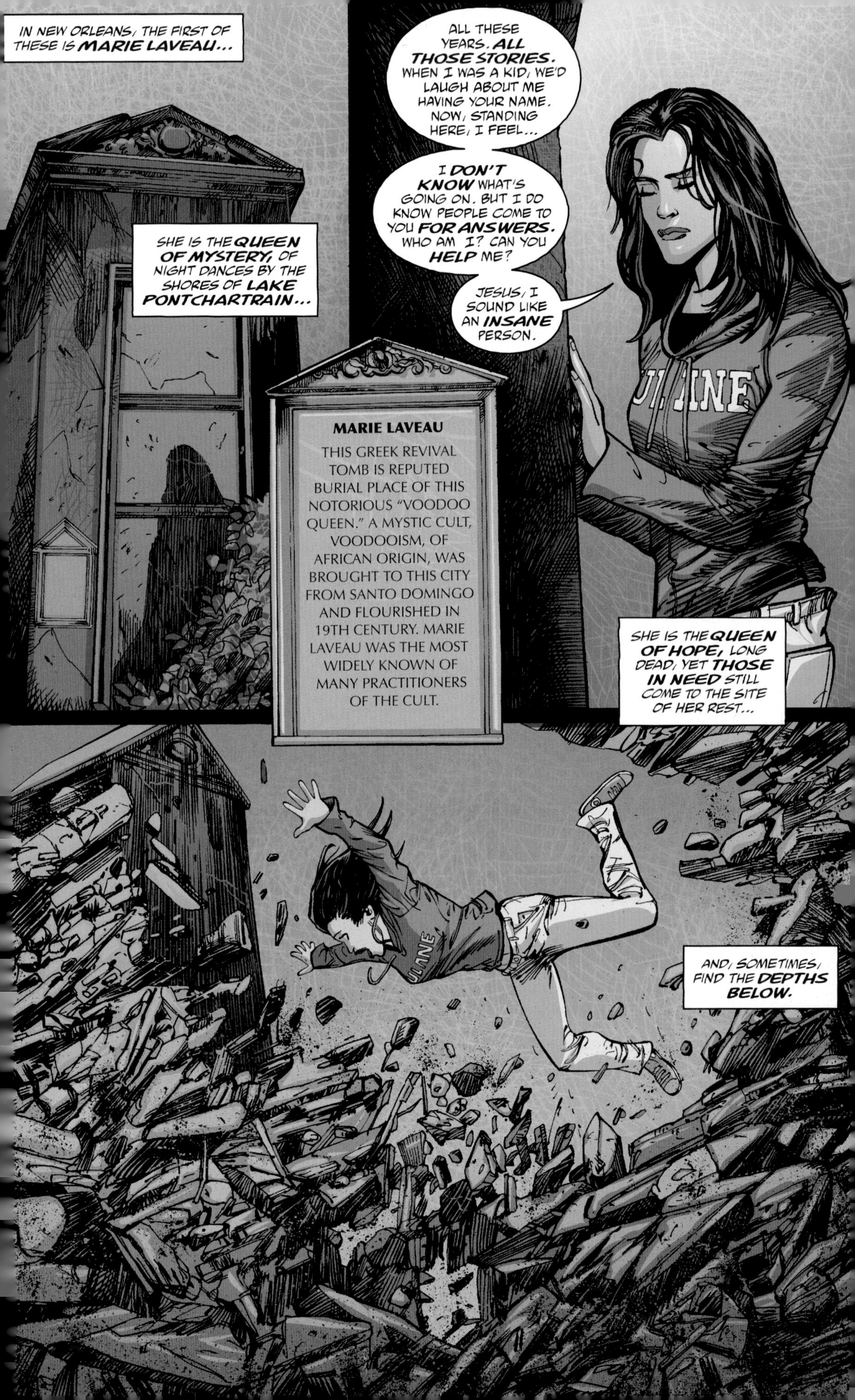
IN NEW ORLEANS, THE FIRST OF THESE IS MARIE LAVEAU...
ALL THESE YEARS. ALL THOSE STORIES. WHEN I WAS A KID, WE'D LAUGH ABOUT ME HAVING YOUR NAME. NOW, STANDING HERE, I FEEL...
I DON'T KNOW WHAT'S GOING ON. BUT I DO KNOW PEOPLE COME TO YOU FOR ANSWERS. WHO AM I? CAN YOU HELP ME?
JESUS, I SOUND LIKE AN INSANE PERSON.
SHE IS THE QUEEN OF MYSTERY, OF NIGHT DANCES BY THE SHORES OF LAKE PONTCHARTRAIN...
MARIE LAVEAU
THIS GREEK REVIVAL TOMB IS REPUTED BURIAL PLACE OF THIS NOTORIOUS "VOODOO QUEEN." A MYSTIC CULT, VOODOOISM, OF AFRICAN ORIGIN, WAS BROUGHT TO THIS CITY FROM SANTO DOMINGO AND FLOURISHED IN 19TH CENTURY. MARIE LAVEAU WAS THE MOST WIDELY KNOWN OF MANY PRACTITIONERS OF THE CULT.
SHE IS THE QUEEN OF HOPE, LONG DEAD, YET THOSE IN NEED STILL COME TO THE SITE OF HER REST...
AND, SOMETIMES, FIND THE DEPTHS BELOW.

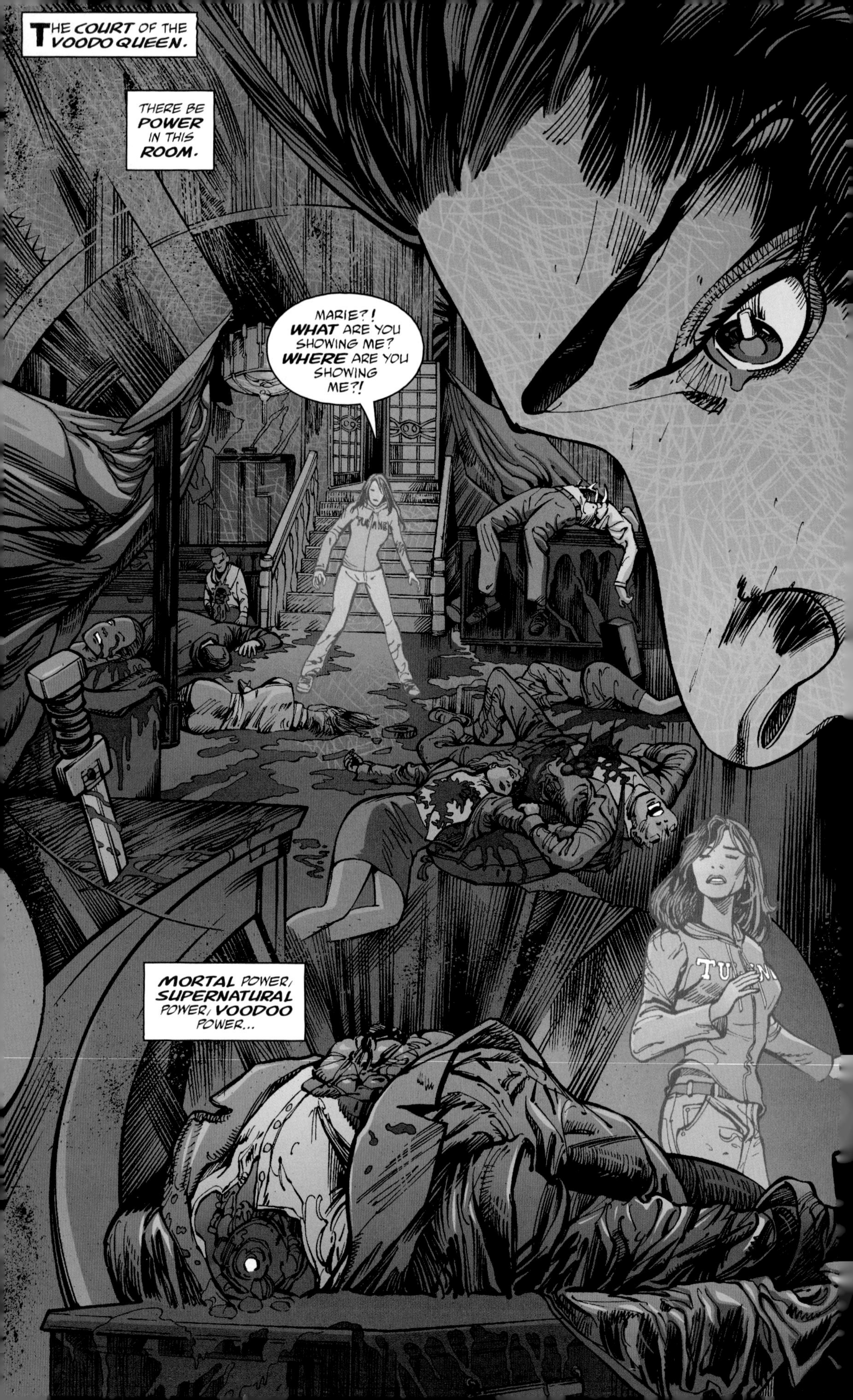
THE COURT OF THE VOODO QUEEN.
THERE BE POWER IN THIS ROOM.
MARIE?! WHAT ARE YOU SHOWING ME? WHERE ARE YOU SHOWING ME?!
MORTAL POWER, SUPERNATURAL POWER, VOODOO POWER...

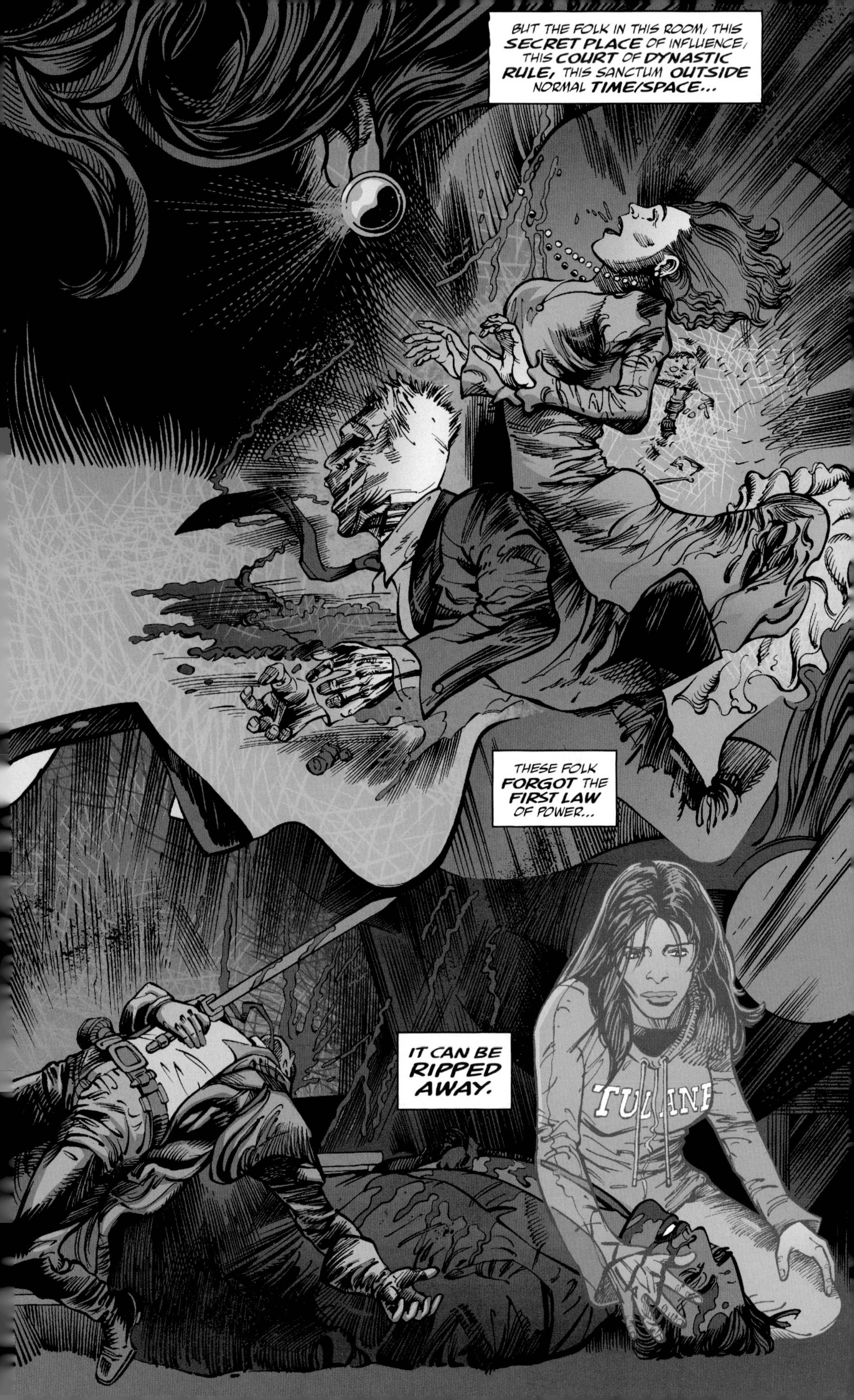
BUT THE FOLK IN THIS ROOM, THIS SECRET PLACE OF INFLUENCE, THIS COURT OF DYNASTIC RULE, THIS SANCTUM OUTSIDE NORMAL TIME/SPACE...
THESE FOLK FORGOT THE FIRST LAW OF POWER...
IT CAN BE RIPPED AWAY.
TULANE

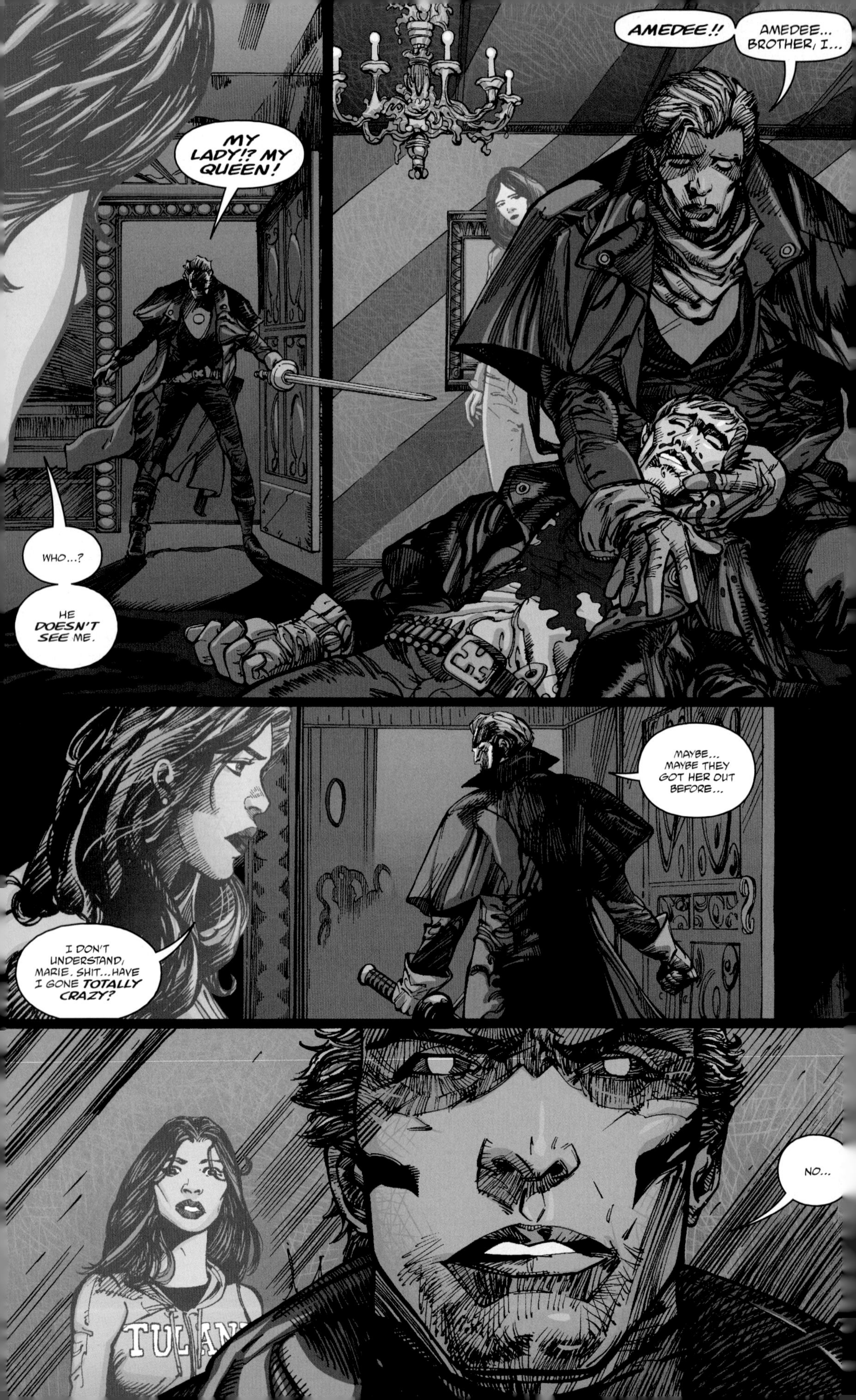
MY LADY!? MY QUEEN!
AMEDEE!!
AMEDEE... BROTHER, I...
WHO...?
HE DOESN'T SEE ME.
MAYBE... MAYBE THEY GOT HER OUT BEFORE...
I DON'T UNDERSTAND, MARIE. SHIT...HAVE I GONE TOTALLY CRAZY?
NO...
TULAN

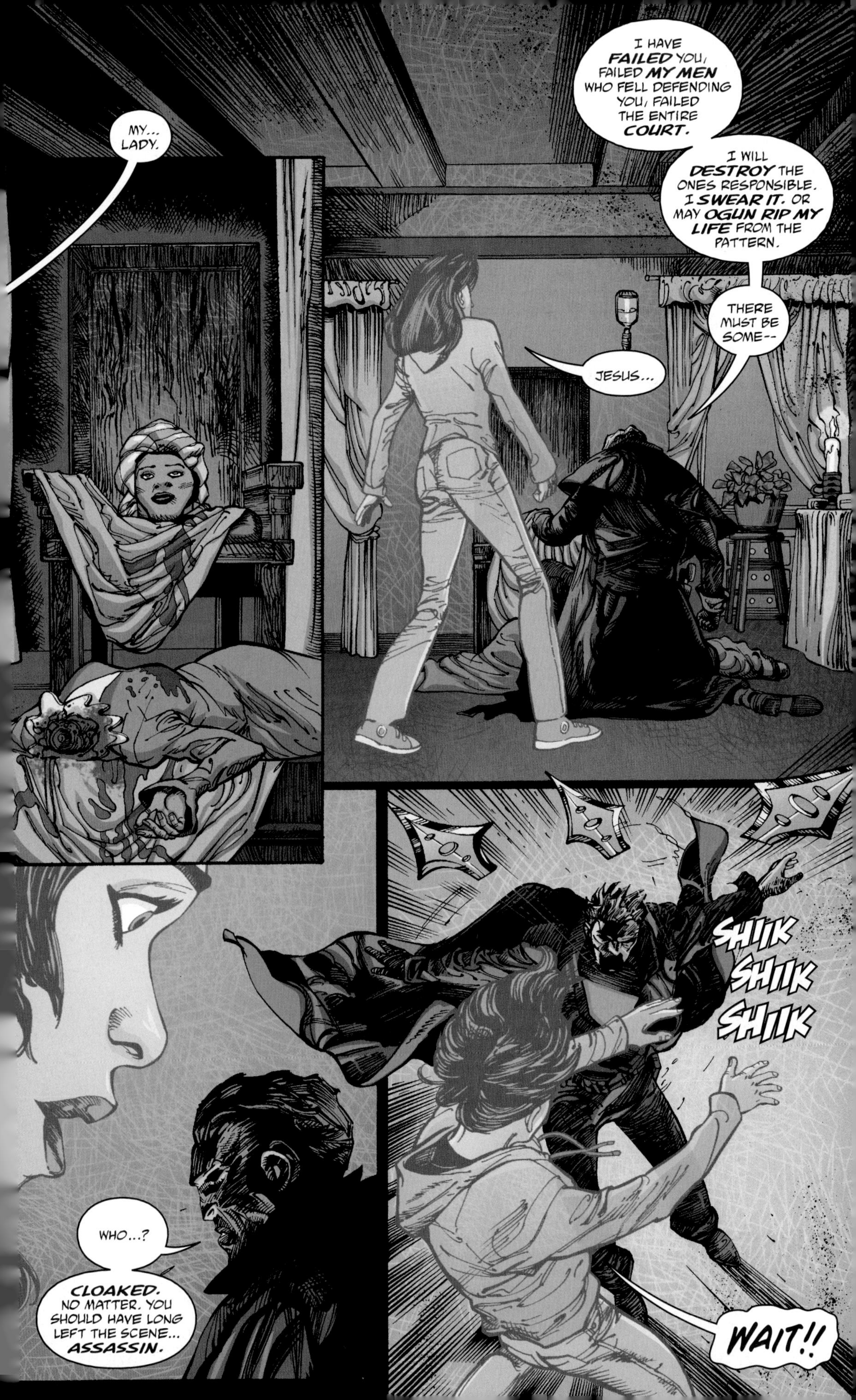

MY... LADY.
I HAVE FAILED YOU, FAILED MY MEN WHO FELL DEFENDING YOU, FAILED THE ENTIRE COURT.
I WILL DESTROY THE ONES RESPONSIBLE. I SWEAR IT. OR MAY OGUN RIP MY LIFE FROM THE PATTERN.
THERE MUST BE SOME--
JESUS...
WHO...?
CLOAKED. NO MATTER. YOU SHOULD HAVE LONG LEFT THE SCENE... ASSASSIN.
SHIIK SHIIK SHIIK
WAIT!!

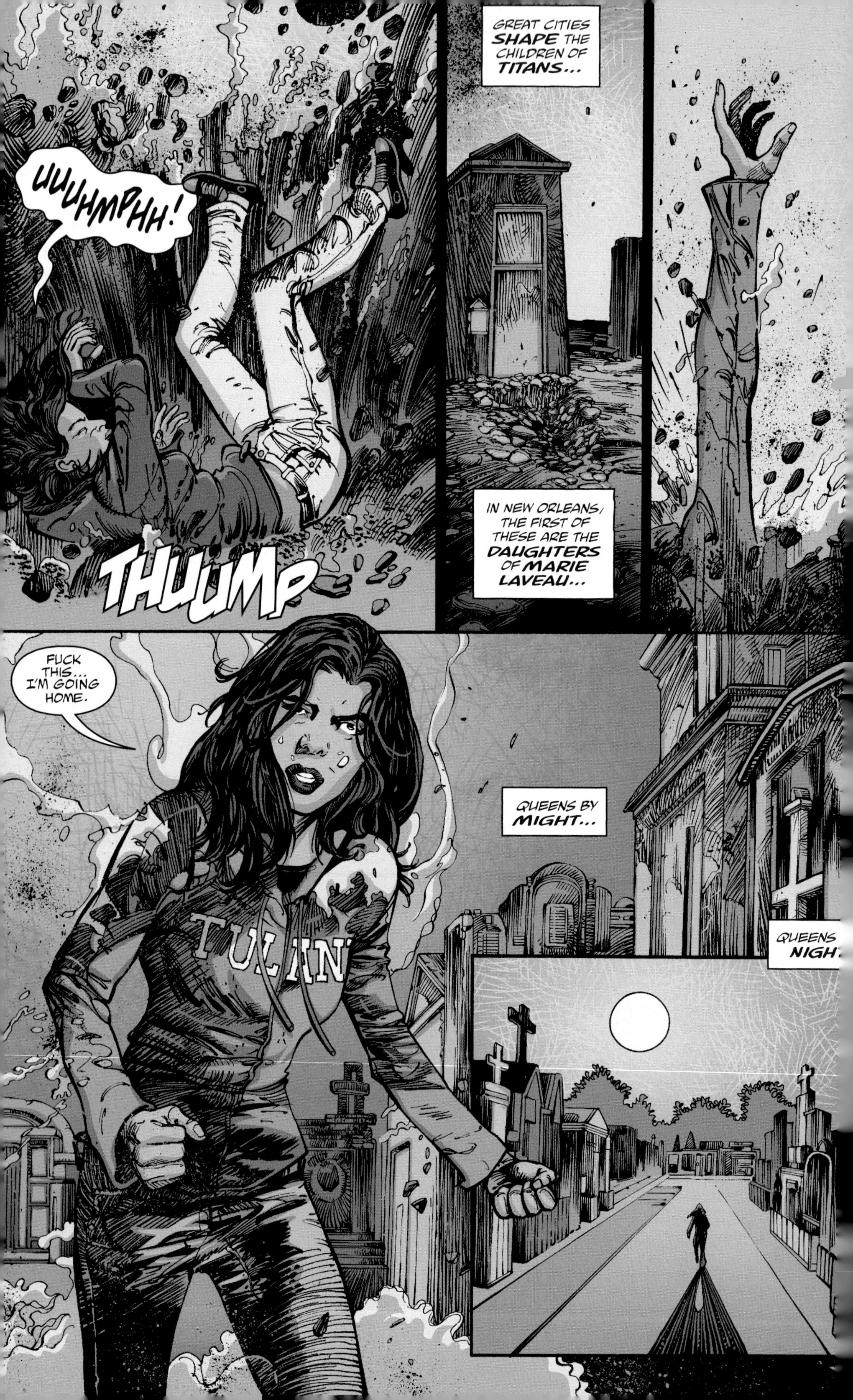
UUUHMPHH!
THUUMP
GREAT CITIES SHAPE THE CHILDREN OF TITANS...
IN NEW ORLEANS, THE FIRST OF THESE ARE THE DAUGHTERS OF MARIE LAVEAU...
FUCK THIS... I'M GOING HOME.
TULANE
QUEENS BY MIGHT...
QUEENS OF NIGHT.

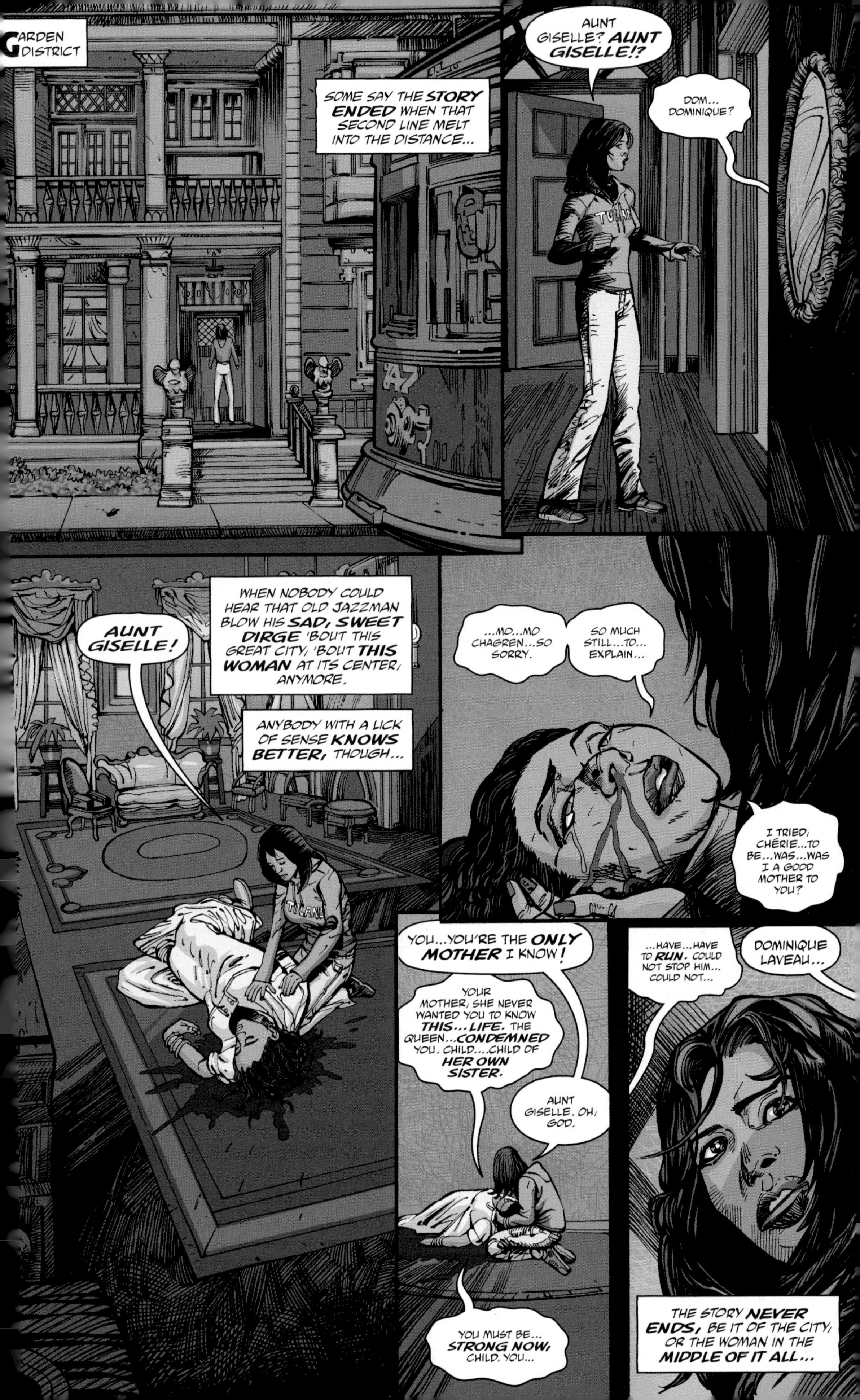
GARDEN DISTRICT
SOME SAY THE STORY ENDED WHEN THAT SECOND LINE MELT INTO THE DISTANCE...
AUNT GISELLE? AUNT GISELLE!?
DOM... DOMINIQUE?
WHEN NOBODY COULD HEAR THAT OLD JAZZMAN BLOW HIS SAD, SWEET DIRGE 'BOUT THIS GREAT CITY, 'BOUT THIS WOMAN AT ITS CENTER, ANYMORE.
AUNT GISELLE!
ANYBODY WITH A LICK OF SENSE KNOWS BETTER, THOUGH...
...MO...MO CHAGREN...SO SORRY.
SO MUCH STILL...TO... EXPLAIN...
I TRIED, CHÉRIE...TO BE...WAS...WAS I A GOOD MOTHER TO YOU?
YOU...YOU'RE THE ONLY MOTHER I KNOW!
YOUR MOTHER, SHE NEVER WANTED YOU TO KNOW THIS...LIFE. THE QUEEN...CONDEMNED YOU, CHILD....CHILD OF HER OWN SISTER.
AUNT GISELLE. OH, GOD.
YOU MUST BE... STRONG NOW, CHILD. YOU...
...HAVE...HAVE TO RUN. COULD NOT STOP HIM... COULD NOT...
DOMINIQUE LAVEAU...
THE STORY NEVER ENDS, BE IT OF THE CITY, OR THE WOMAN IN THE MIDDLE OF IT ALL...

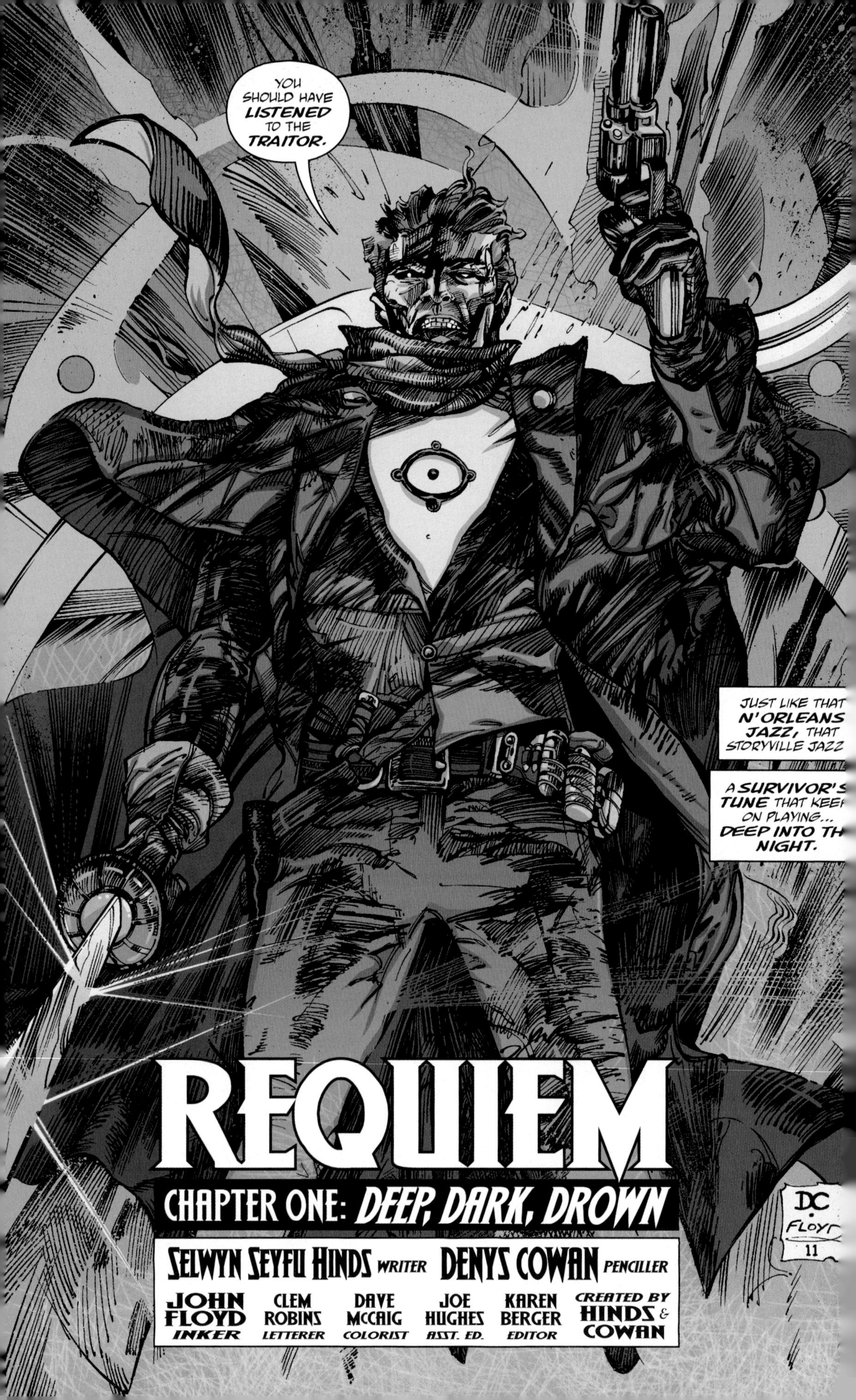
YOU SHOULD HAVE LISTENED TO THE TRAITOR.
JUST LIKE THAT N'ORLEANS JAZZ, THAT STORYVILLE JAZZ
A SURVIVOR'S TUNE THAT KEE ON PLAYING... DEEP INTO TH NIGHT.
REQUIEM
CHAPTER ONE: DEEP, DARK, DROWN
SELWYN SEYFU HINDS WRITER DENYS COWAN PENCILLER
JOHN FLOYD INKER
CLEM ROBINS LETTERER
DAVE McCAIG COLORIST
JOE HUGHES ASST. ED.
KAREN BERGER EDITOR
CREATED BY HINDS & COWAN
DC
11

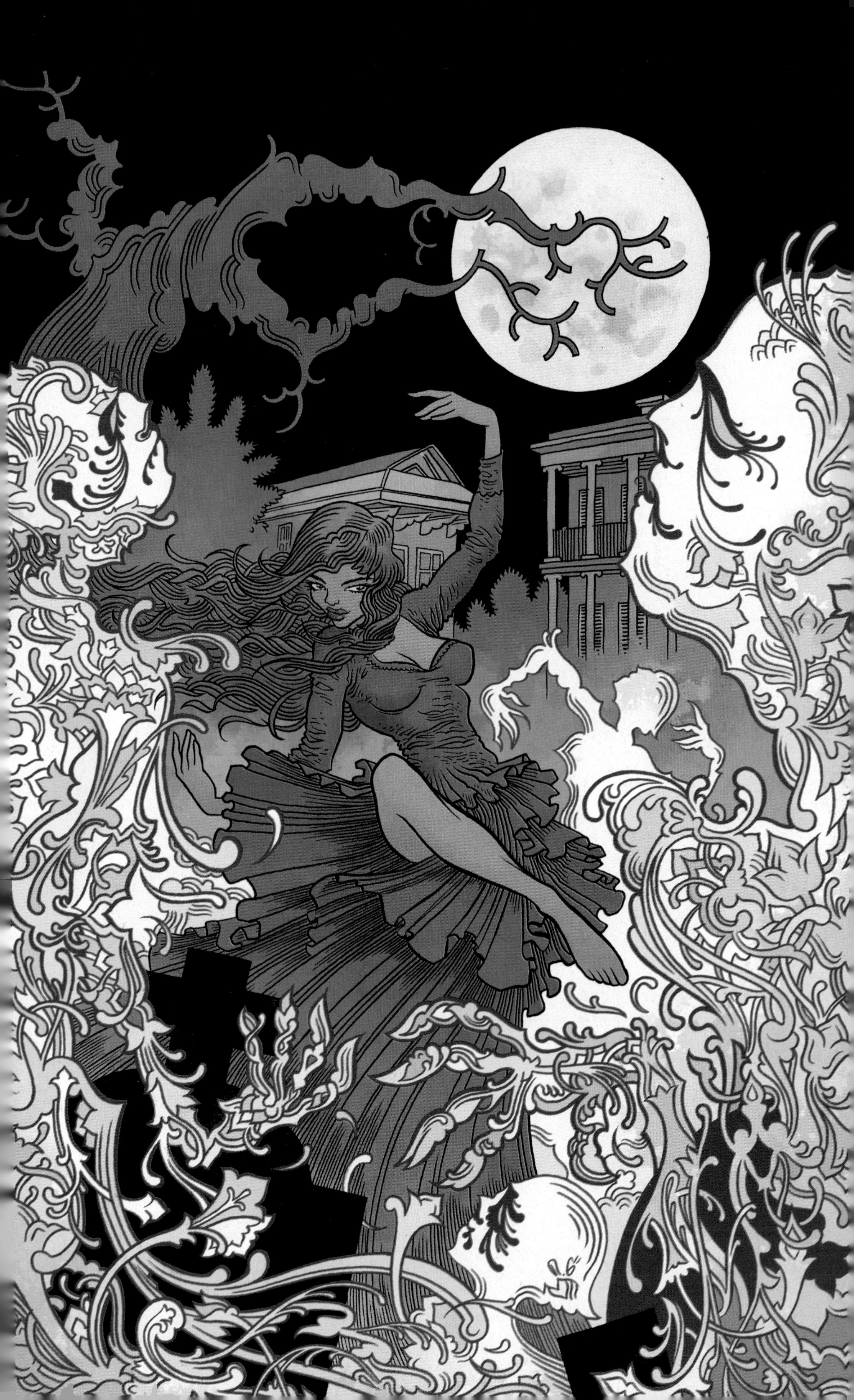

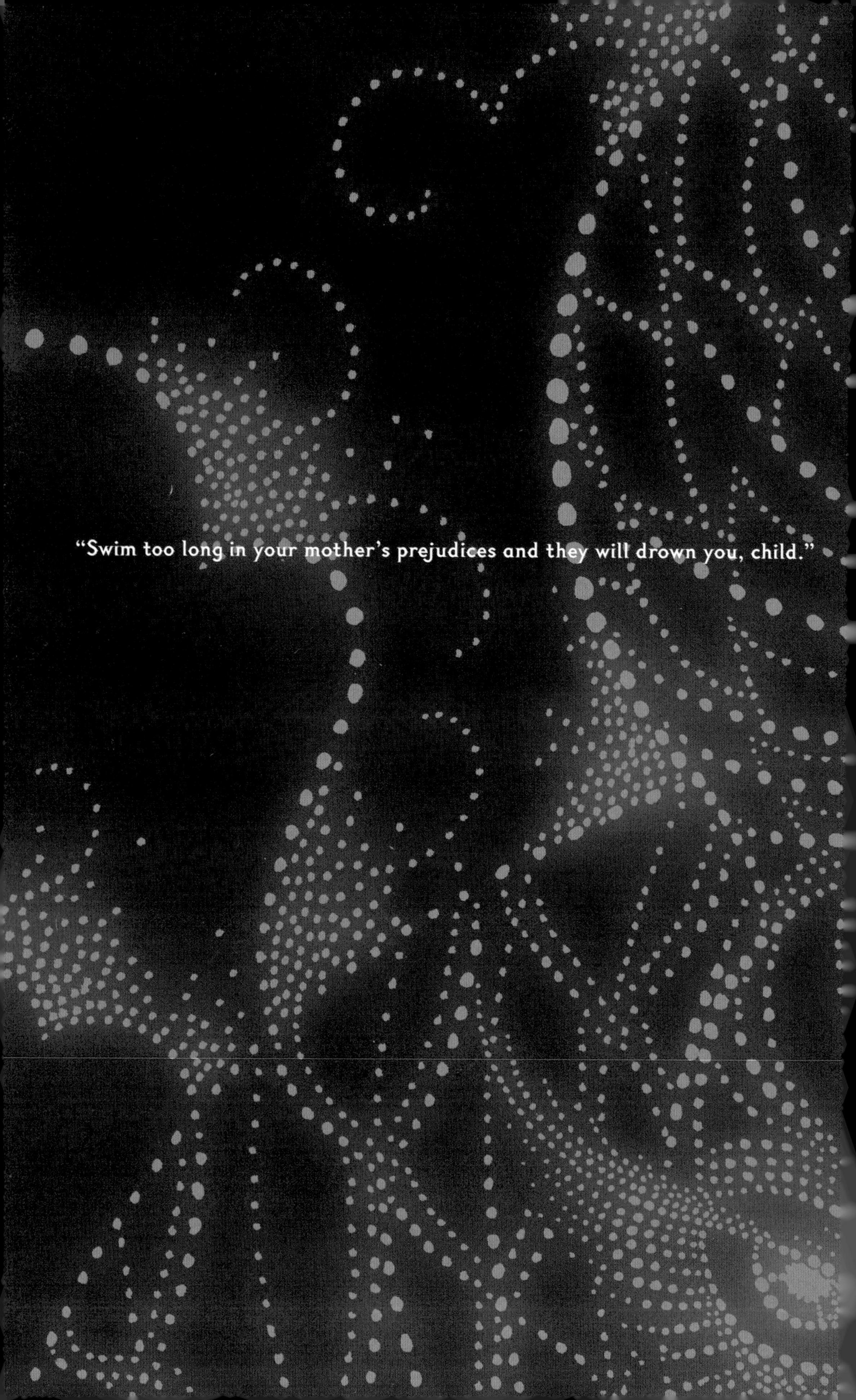
"Swim too long in your mother's prejudices and they will drown you, child."

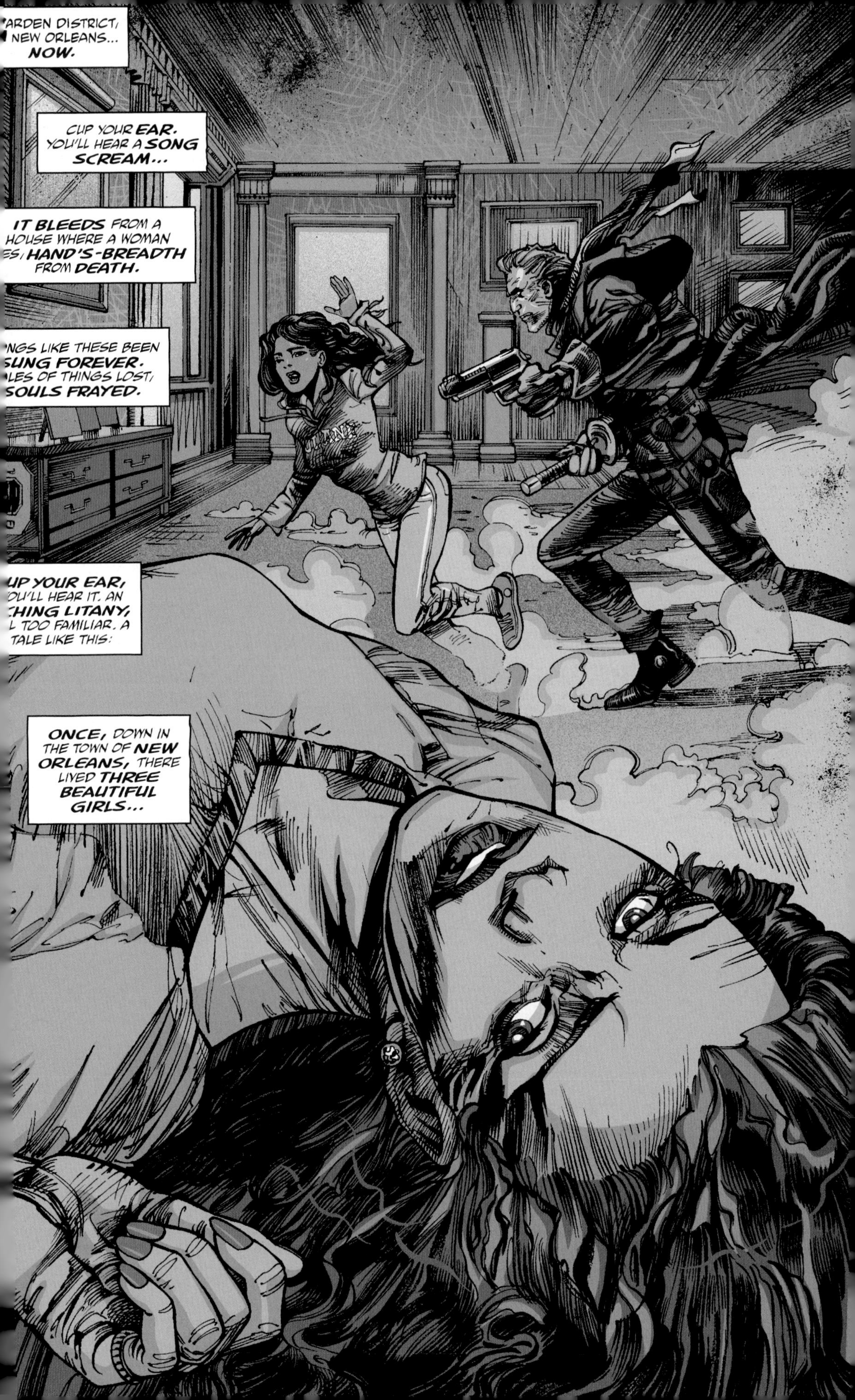
ARDEN DISTRICT, NEW ORLEANS... NOW.
CUP YOUR EAR. YOU'LL HEAR A SONG SCREAM...
IT BLEEDS FROM A HOUSE WHERE A WOMAN ES, HAND'S-BREADTH FROM DEATH.
NGS LIKE THESE BEEN SUNG FOREVER. LES OF THINGS LOST, SOULS FRAYED.
UP YOUR EAR, OU'LL HEAR IT. AN CHING LITANY, L TOO FAMILIAR. A TALE LIKE THIS:
ONCE, DOWN IN THE TOWN OF NEW ORLEANS, THERE LIVED THREE BEAUTIFUL GIRLS...

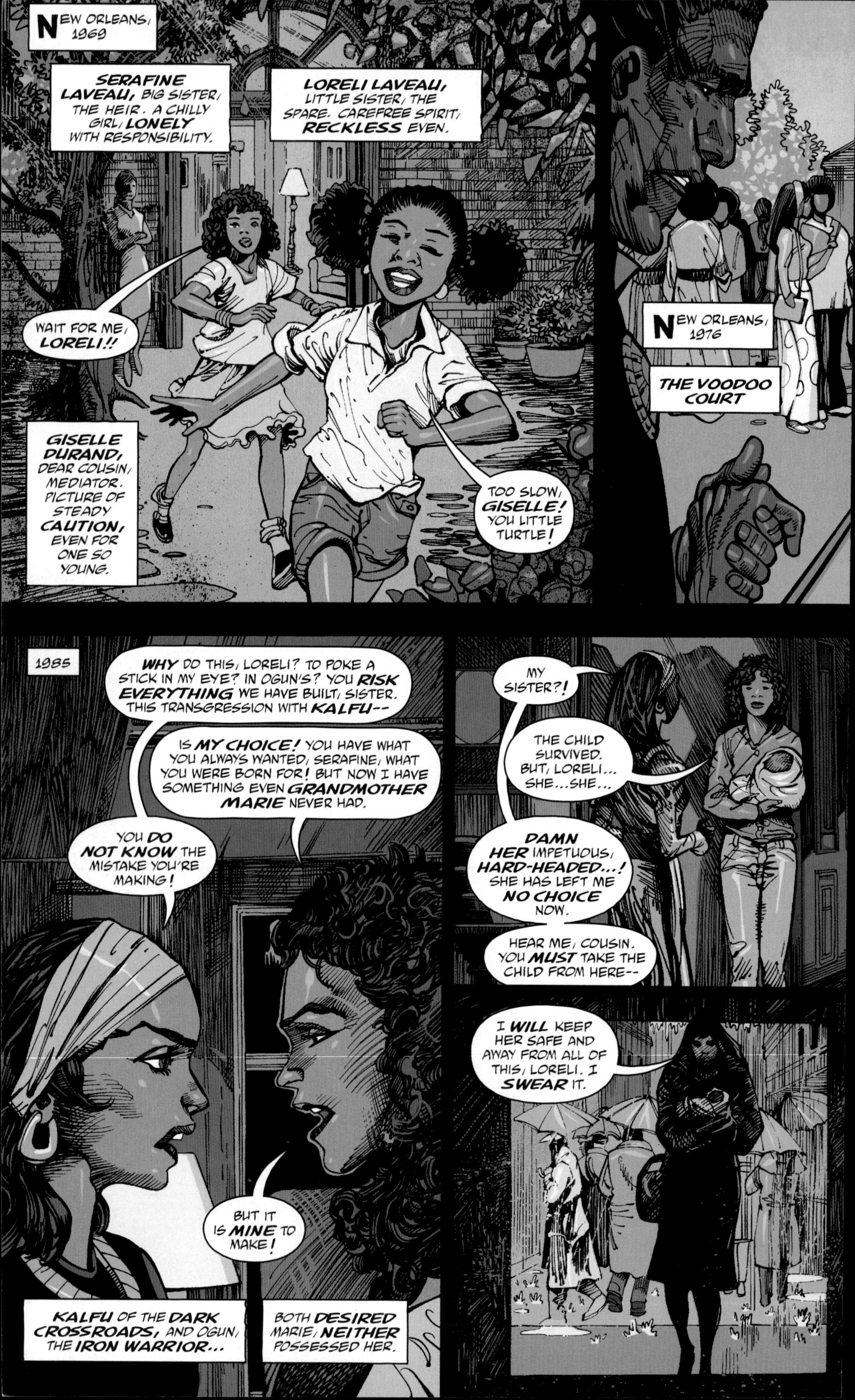
NEW ORLEANS, 1969
SERAFINE LAVEAU, BIG SISTER, THE HEIR. A CHILLY GIRL, LONELY WITH RESPONSIBILITY.
LORELI LAVEAU, LITTLE SISTER, THE SPARE. CAREFREE SPIRIT, RECKLESS EVEN.
WAIT FOR ME, LORELI!!
GISELLE DURAND, DEAR COUSIN, MEDIATOR. PICTURE OF STEADY CAUTION, EVEN FOR ONE SO YOUNG.
TOO SLOW, GISELLE! YOU LITTLE TURTLE!
NEW ORLEANS, 1976
THE VOODOO COURT
1985
WHY DO THIS, LORELI? TO POKE A STICK IN MY EYE? IN OGUN'S? YOU RISK EVERYTHING WE HAVE BUILT, SISTER. THIS TRANSGRESSION WITH KALFU--
IS MY CHOICE! YOU HAVE WHAT YOU ALWAYS WANTED, SERAFINE, WHAT YOU WERE BORN FOR! BUT NOW I HAVE SOMETHING EVEN GRANDMOTHER MARIE NEVER HAD.
YOU DO NOT KNOW THE MISTAKE YOU'RE MAKING!
BUT IT IS MINE TO MAKE!
KALFU OF THE DARK CROSSROADS, AND OGUN, THE IRON WARRIOR...
BOTH DESIRED MARIE, NEITHER POSSESSED HER.
MY SISTER?!
THE CHILD SURVIVED. BUT, LORELI... SHE...SHE...
DAMN HER IMPETUOUS, HARD-HEADED...! SHE HAS LEFT ME NO CHOICE NOW.
HEAR ME, COUSIN. YOU MUST TAKE THE CHILD FROM HERE--
I WILL KEEP HER SAFE AND AWAY FROM ALL OF THIS, LORELI. I SWEAR IT.

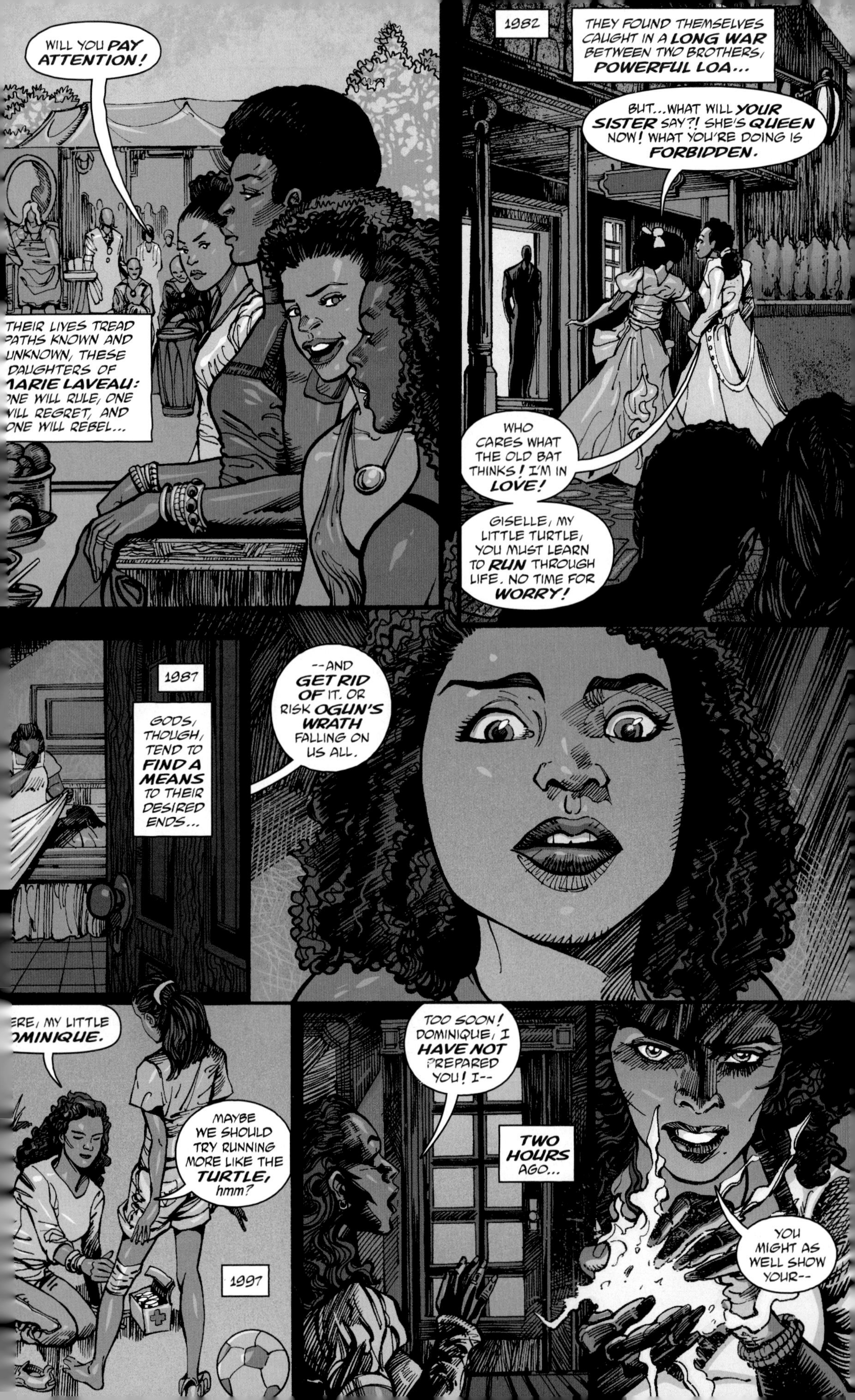
WILL YOU PAY ATTENTION!
THEIR LIVES TREAD PATHS KNOWN AND UNKNOWN, THESE DAUGHTERS OF MARIE LAVEAU: ONE WILL RULE, ONE WILL REGRET, AND ONE WILL REBEL...
1982
THEY FOUND THEMSELVES CAUGHT IN A LONG WAR BETWEEN TWO BROTHERS, POWERFUL LOA...
BUT...WHAT WILL YOUR SISTER SAY?! SHE'S QUEEN NOW! WHAT YOU'RE DOING IS FORBIDDEN.
WHO CARES WHAT THE OLD BAT THINKS! I'M IN LOVE!
GISELLE, MY LITTLE TURTLE, YOU MUST LEARN TO RUN THROUGH LIFE. NO TIME FOR WORRY!
1987
GODS, THOUGH, TEND TO FIND A MEANS TO THEIR DESIRED ENDS...
--AND GET RID OF IT. OR RISK OGUN'S WRATH FALLING ON US ALL.
ERE, MY LITTLE OMINIQUE.
MAYBE WE SHOULD TRY RUNNING MORE LIKE THE TURTLE, hmm?
1997
TOO SOON! DOMINIQUE, I HAVE NOT PREPARED YOU! I--
TWO HOURS AGO...
YOU MIGHT AS WELL SHOW YOUR--

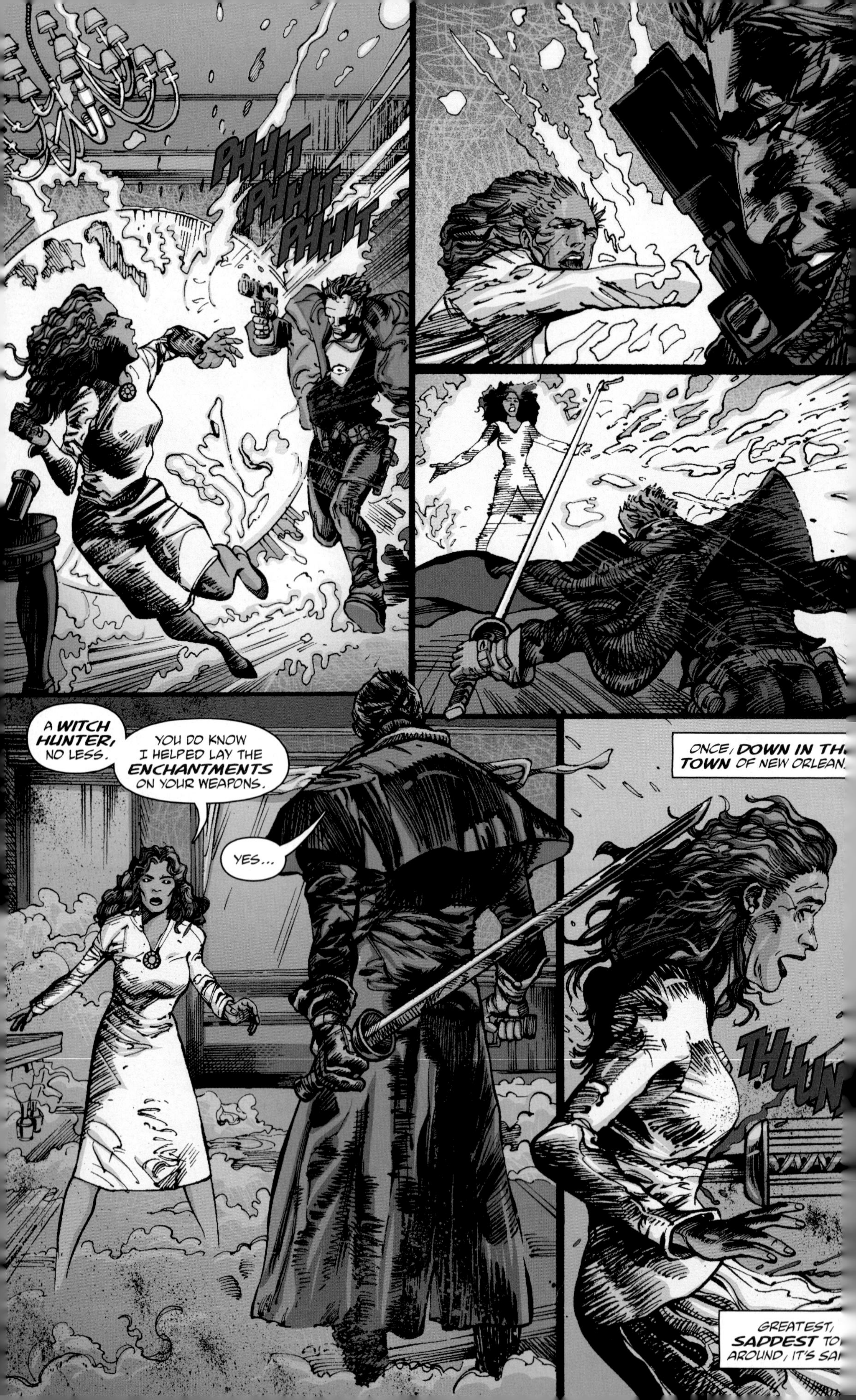

PHHIT
PHHIT
PHHIT
A WITCH HUNTER, NO LESS.
YOU DO KNOW I HELPED LAY THE ENCHANTMENTS ON YOUR WEAPONS.
YES...
ONCE, DOWN IN TH
TOWN OF NEW ORLEAN
THUUN
GREATEST,
SADDEST TO
AROUND, IT'S SA

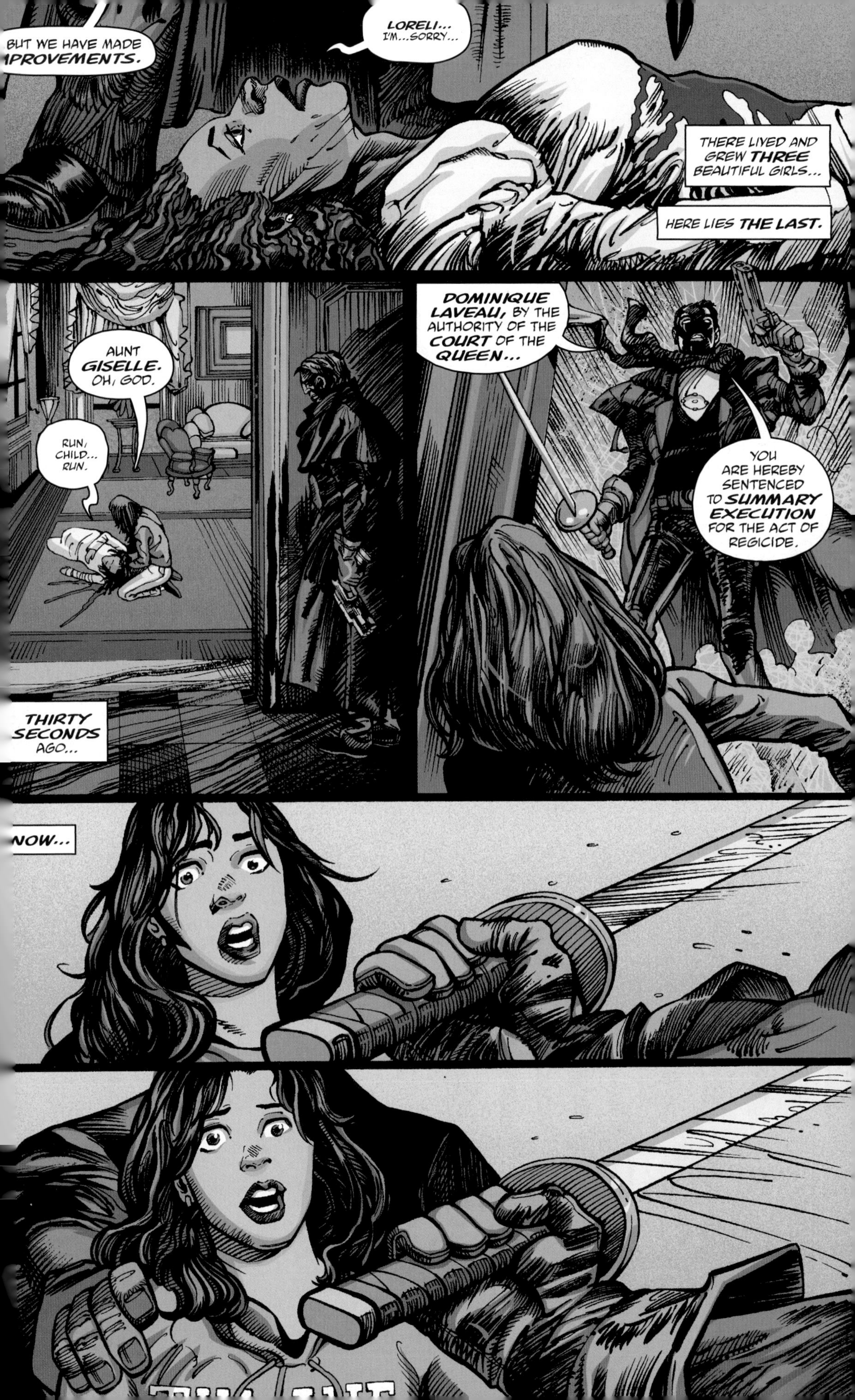

BUT WE HAVE MADE
IPROVEMENTS.
LORELI...
I'M...SORRY...
THERE LIVED AND GREW THREE BEAUTIFUL GIRLS...
HERE LIES THE LAST.
AUNT GISELLE. OH, GOD.
RUN, CHILD... RUN.
THIRTY SECONDS AGO...
DOMINIQUE LAVEAU, BY THE AUTHORITY OF THE COURT OF THE QUEEN...
YOU ARE HEREBY SENTENCED TO SUMMARY EXECUTION FOR THE ACT OF REGICIDE.
NOW...

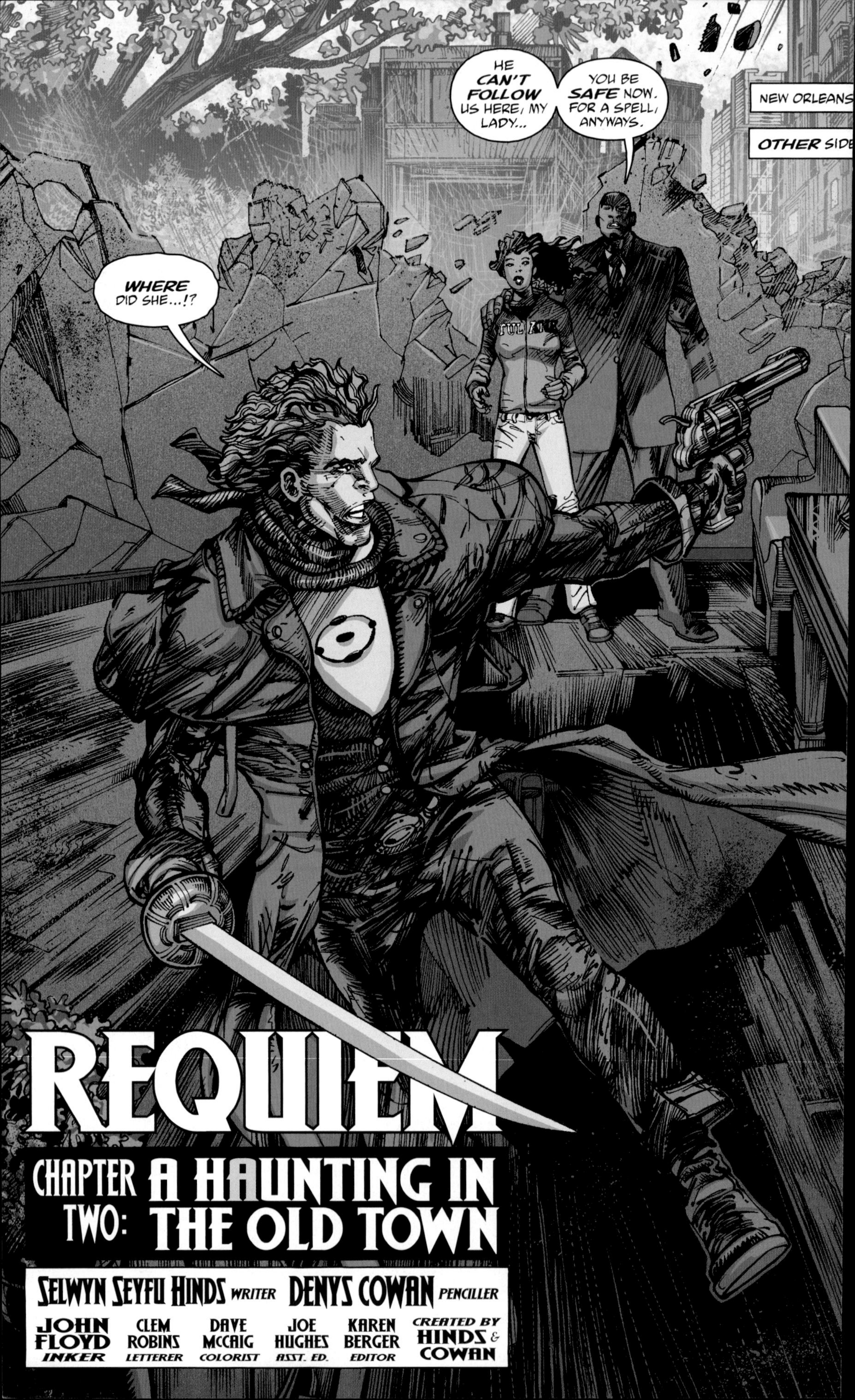
NEW ORLEANS
OTHER SIDE
HE CAN'T FOLLOW US HERE, MY LADY...
YOU BE SAFE NOW. FOR A SPELL, ANYWAYS.
WHERE DID SHE...!?
REQUIEM
CHAPTER TWO: A HAUNTING IN THE OLD TOWN
SELWYN SEYFU HINDS WRITER DENYS COWAN PENCILLER
JOHN FLOYD INKER
CLEM ROBINS LETTERER
DAVE McCAIG COLORIST
JOE HUGHES ASST. ED.
KAREN BERGER EDITOR
CREATED BY HINDS & COWAN

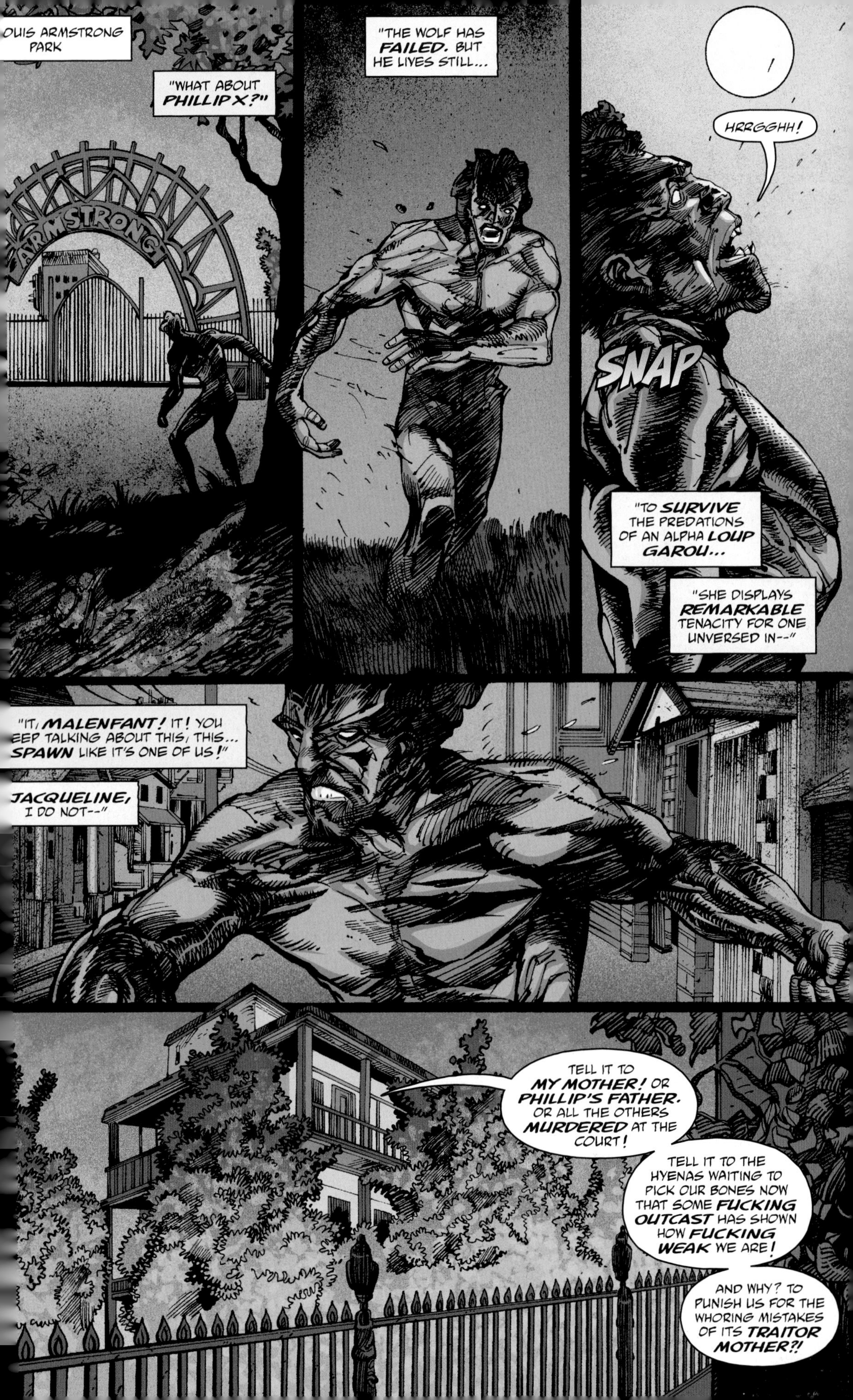

OUIS ARMSTRONG PARK
"WHAT ABOUT PHILLIP X?"
ARMSTRONG
"THE WOLF HAS FAILED. BUT HE LIVES STILL...
HRRGGHH!
SNAP
"TO SURVIVE THE PREDATIONS OF AN ALPHA LOUP GAROU...
"SHE DISPLAYS REMARKABLE TENACITY FOR ONE UNVERSED IN--"
"IT, MALENFANT! IT! YOU EEP TALKING ABOUT THIS, THIS... SPAWN LIKE IT'S ONE OF US!"
JACQUELINE, I DO NOT--"
TELL IT TO MY MOTHER! OR PHILLIP'S FATHER. OR ALL THE OTHERS MURDERED AT THE COURT!
TELL IT TO THE HYENAS WAITING TO PICK OUR BONES NOW THAT SOME FUCKING OUTCAST HAS SHOWN HOW FUCKING WEAK WE ARE!
AND WHY? TO PUNISH US FOR THE WHORING MISTAKES OF ITS TRAITOR MOTHER?!

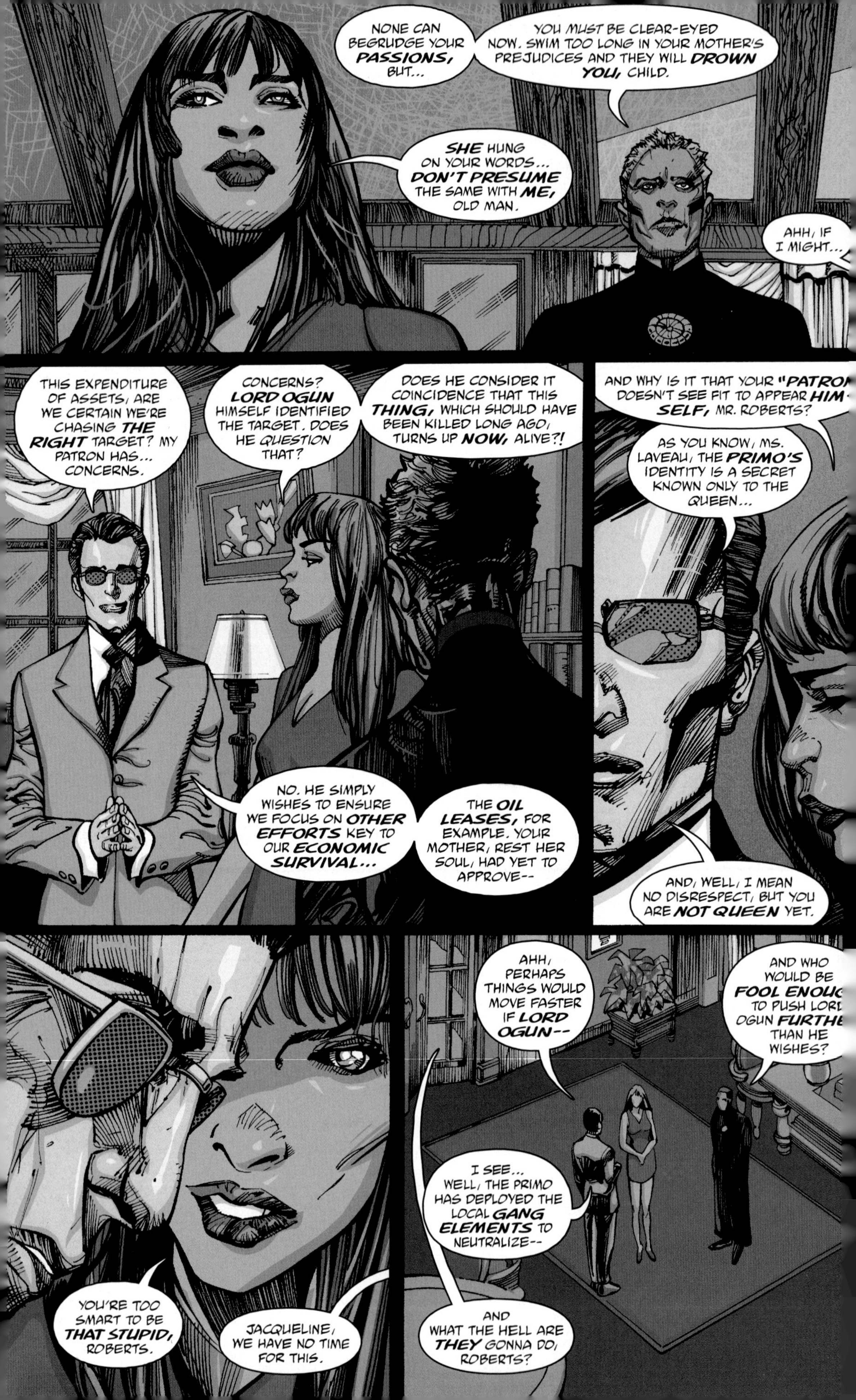
NONE CAN BEGRUDGE YOUR PASSIONS, BUT...
YOU MUST BE CLEAR-EYED NOW. SWIM TOO LONG IN YOUR MOTHER'S PREJUDICES AND THEY WILL DROWN YOU, CHILD.
SHE HUNG ON YOUR WORDS... DON'T PRESUME THE SAME WITH ME, OLD MAN.
AHH, IF I MIGHT...
THIS EXPENDITURE OF ASSETS, ARE WE CERTAIN WE'RE CHASING THE RIGHT TARGET? MY PATRON HAS... CONCERNS.
CONCERNS? LORD OGUN HIMSELF IDENTIFIED THE TARGET. DOES HE QUESTION THAT?
DOES HE CONSIDER IT COINCIDENCE THAT THIS THING, WHICH SHOULD HAVE BEEN KILLED LONG AGO, TURNS UP NOW, ALIVE?!
NO. HE SIMPLY WISHES TO ENSURE WE FOCUS ON OTHER EFFORTS KEY TO OUR ECONOMIC SURVIVAL...
THE OIL LEASES, FOR EXAMPLE. YOUR MOTHER, REST HER SOUL, HAD YET TO APPROVE--
AND WHY IS IT THAT YOUR "PATRON" DOESN'T SEE FIT TO APPEAR HIMSELF, MR. ROBERTS?
AS YOU KNOW, MS. LAVEAU, THE PRIMO'S IDENTITY IS A SECRET KNOWN ONLY TO THE QUEEN...
AND, WELL, I MEAN NO DISRESPECT, BUT YOU ARE NOT QUEEN YET.
YOU'RE TOO SMART TO BE THAT STUPID, ROBERTS.
JACQUELINE, WE HAVE NO TIME FOR THIS.
AHH, PERHAPS THINGS WOULD MOVE FASTER IF LORD OGUN--
AND WHO WOULD BE FOOL ENOUGH TO PUSH LORD OGUN FURTHER THAN HE WISHES?
I SEE... WELL, THE PRIMO HAS DEPLOYED THE LOCAL GANG ELEMENTS TO NEUTRALIZE--
AND WHAT THE HELL ARE THEY GONNA DO, ROBERTS?

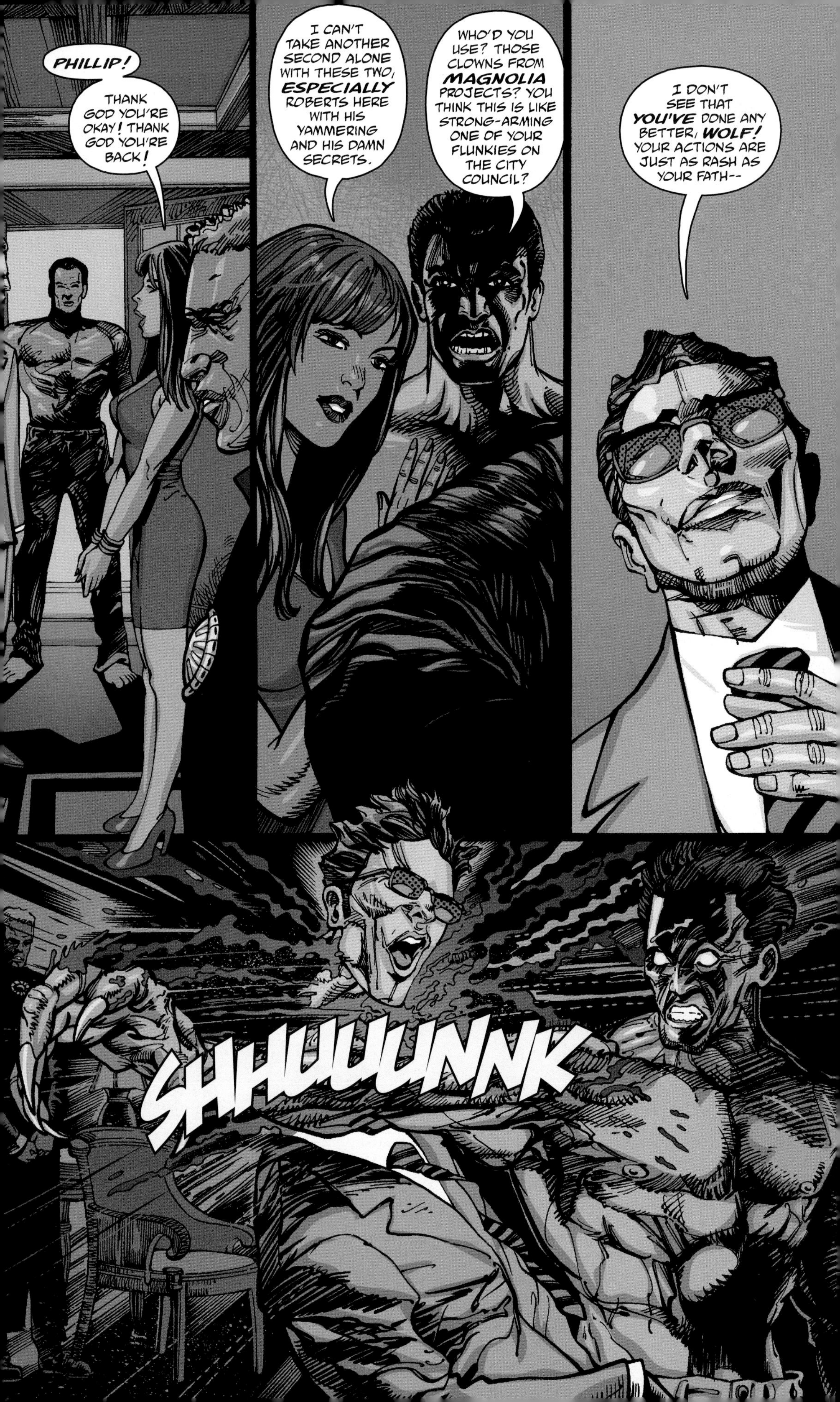
PHILLIP!
THANK GOD YOU'RE OKAY! THANK GOD YOU'RE BACK!
I CAN'T TAKE ANOTHER SECOND ALONE WITH THESE TWO, ESPECIALLY ROBERTS HERE WITH HIS YAMMERING AND HIS DAMN SECRETS.
WHO'D YOU USE? THOSE CLOWNS FROM MAGNOLIA PROJECTS? YOU THINK THIS IS LIKE STRONG-ARMING ONE OF YOUR FLUNKIES ON THE CITY COUNCIL?
I DON'T SEE THAT YOU'VE DONE ANY BETTER, WOLF! YOUR ACTIONS ARE JUST AS RASH AS YOUR FATH--
SHHUUUUNNK

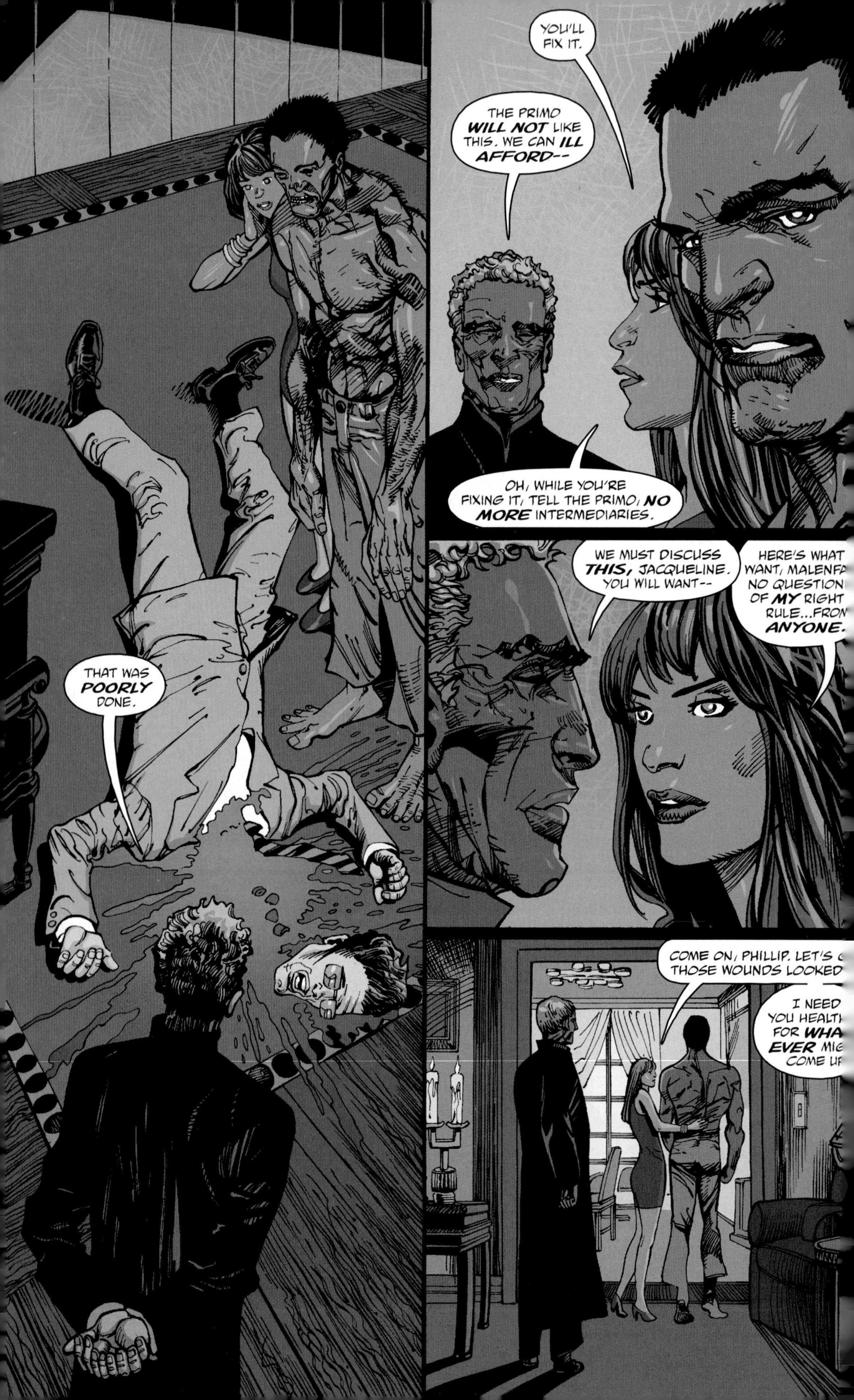
THAT WAS POORLY DONE.
THE PRIMO WILL NOT LIKE THIS. WE CAN ILL AFFORD--
YOU'LL FIX IT.
OH, WHILE YOU'RE FIXING IT, TELL THE PRIMO, NO MORE INTERMEDIARIES.
WE MUST DISCUSS THIS, JACQUELINE. YOU WILL WANT--
HERE'S WHAT WANT, MALENFA NO QUESTION OF MY RIGHT RULE...FROM ANYONE.
COME ON, PHILLIP. LET'S THOSE WOUNDS LOOKED
I NEED YOU HEALTH FOR WHA EVER MIG COME UP

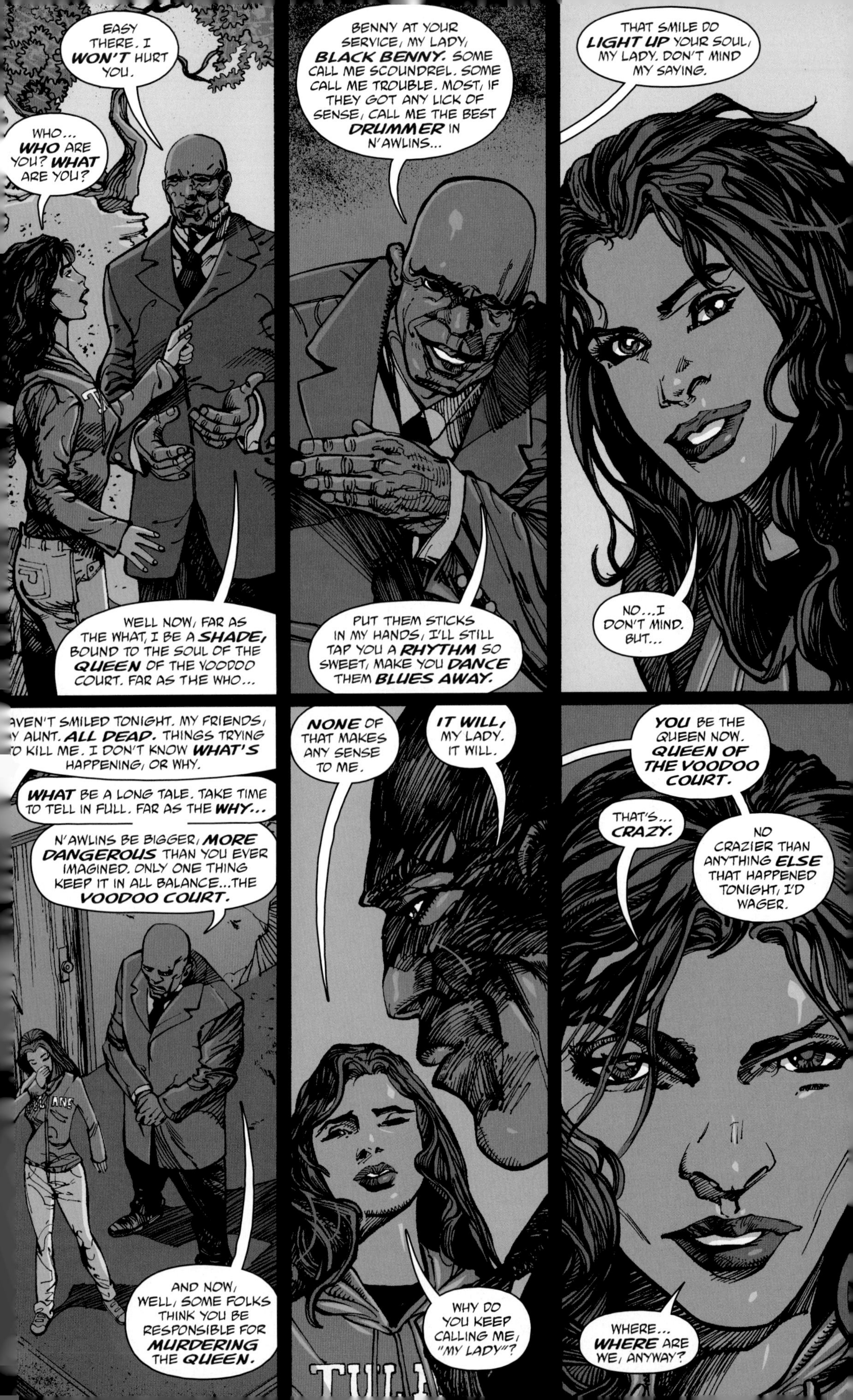
EASY THERE. I WON'T HURT YOU.
WHO... WHO ARE YOU? WHAT ARE YOU?
WELL NOW, FAR AS THE WHAT, I BE A SHADE, BOUND TO THE SOUL OF THE QUEEN OF THE VOODOO COURT. FAR AS THE WHO...
BENNY AT YOUR SERVICE, MY LADY, BLACK BENNY. SOME CALL ME SCOUNDREL. SOME CALL ME TROUBLE. MOST, IF THEY GOT ANY LICK OF SENSE, CALL ME THE BEST DRUMMER IN N'AWLINS...
PUT THEM STICKS IN MY HANDS, I'LL STILL TAP YOU A RHYTHM SO SWEET, MAKE YOU DANCE THEM BLUES AWAY.
THAT SMILE DO LIGHT UP YOUR SOUL, MY LADY. DON'T MIND MY SAYING.
NO...I DON'T MIND. BUT...
AVEN'T SMILED TONIGHT. MY FRIENDS, Y AUNT. ALL DEAD. THINGS TRYING O KILL ME. I DON'T KNOW WHAT'S HAPPENING, OR WHY.
WHAT BE A LONG TALE. TAKE TIME TO TELL IN FULL. FAR AS THE WHY...
N'AWLINS BE BIGGER, MORE DANGEROUS THAN YOU EVER IMAGINED. ONLY ONE THING KEEP IT IN ALL BALANCE...THE VOODOO COURT.
AND NOW, WELL, SOME FOLKS THINK YOU BE RESPONSIBLE FOR MURDERING THE QUEEN.
NONE OF THAT MAKES ANY SENSE TO ME.
IT WILL, MY LADY. IT WILL.
WHY DO YOU KEEP CALLING ME, "MY LADY"?
YOU BE THE QUEEN NOW. QUEEN OF THE VOODOO COURT.
THAT'S... CRAZY.
NO CRAZIER THAN ANYTHING ELSE THAT HAPPENED TONIGHT, I'D WAGER.
WHERE... WHERE ARE WE, ANYWAY?

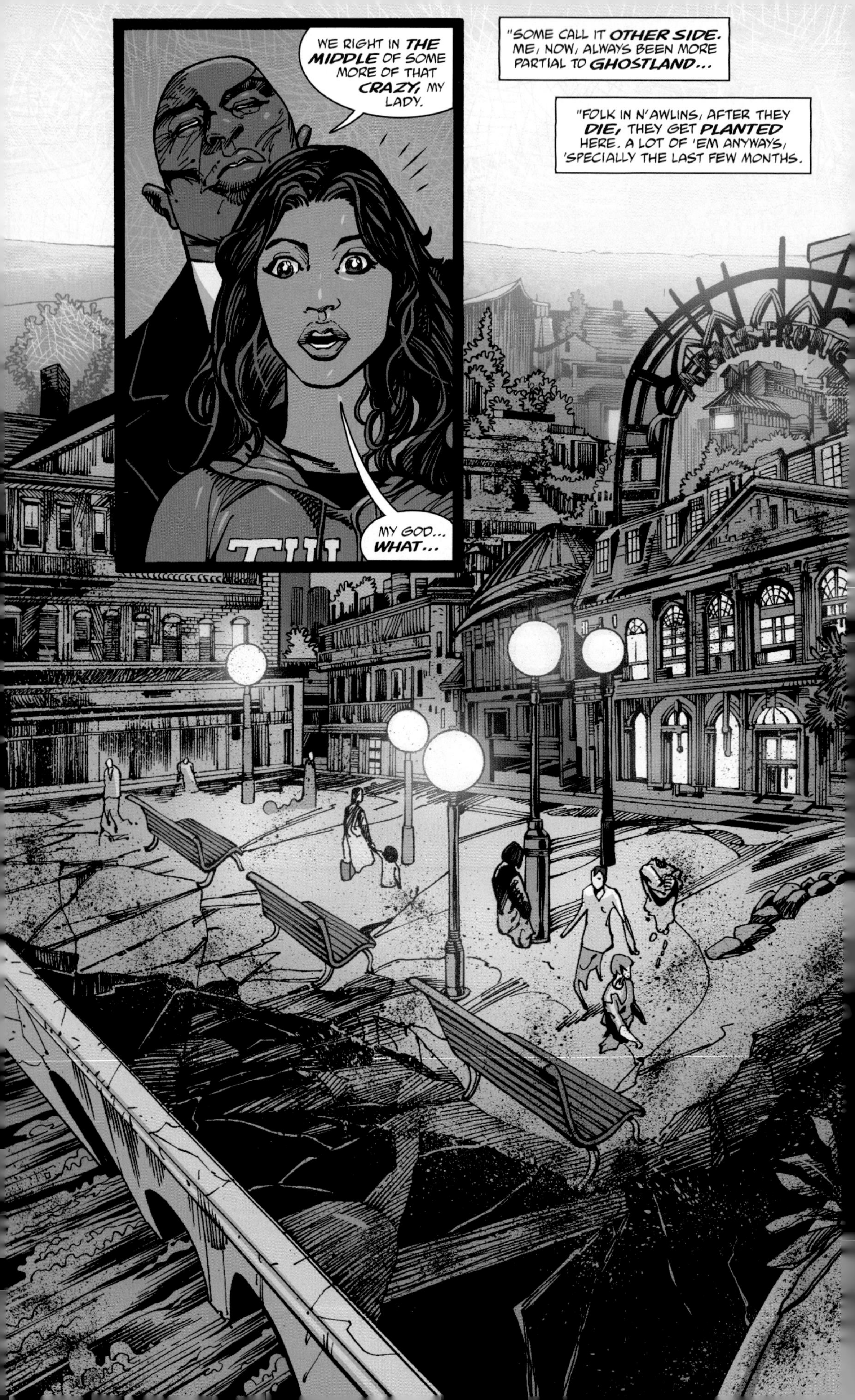
WE RIGHT IN THE MIDDLE OF SOME MORE OF THAT CRAZY, MY LADY.
MY GOD... WHAT...
"SOME CALL IT OTHER SIDE. ME, NOW, ALWAYS BEEN MORE PARTIAL TO GHOSTLAND...
"FOLK IN N'AWLINS, AFTER THEY DIE, THEY GET PLANTED HERE. A LOT OF 'EM ANYWAYS, 'SPECIALLY THE LAST FEW MONTHS.

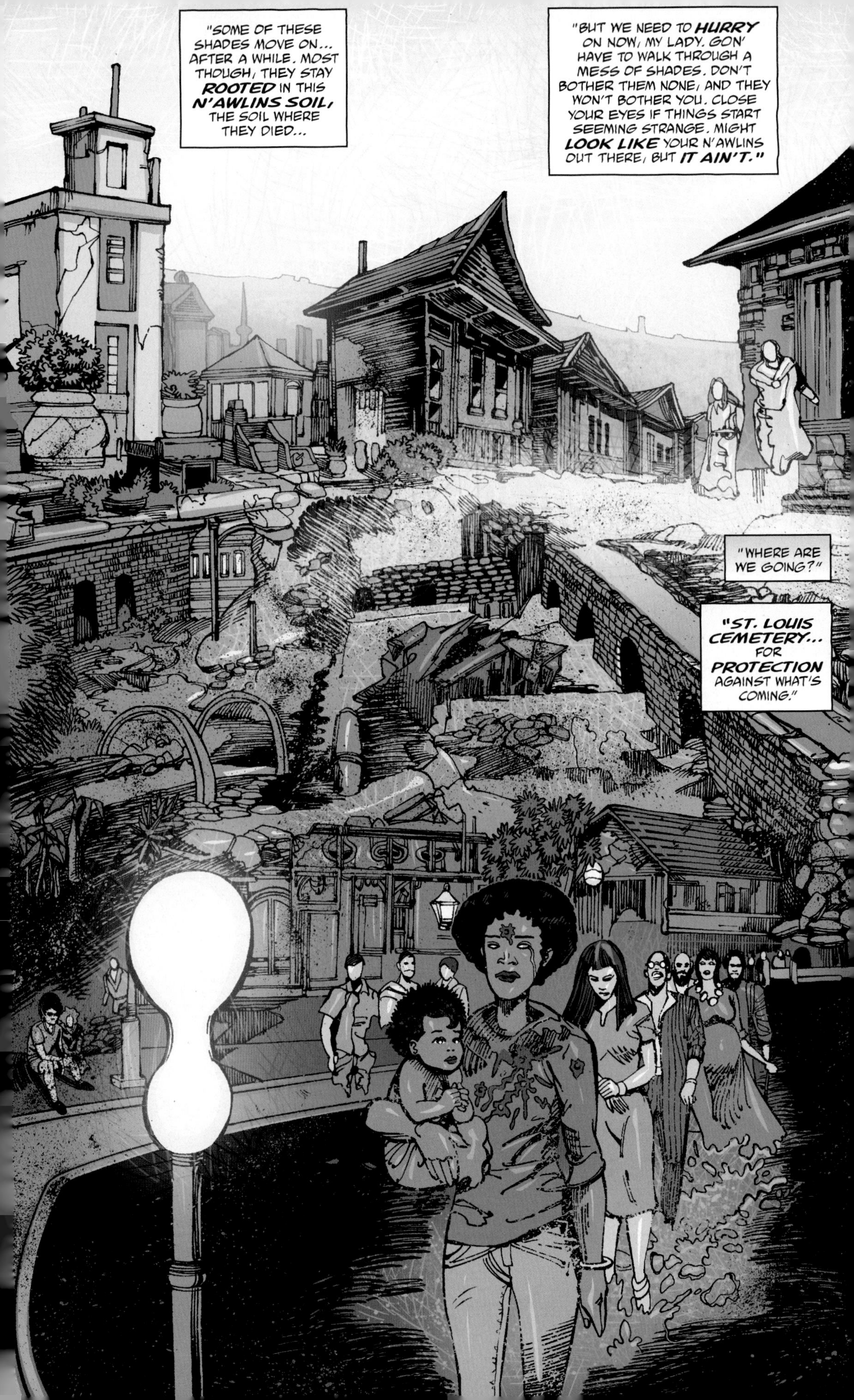
"SOME OF THESE SHADES MOVE ON... AFTER A WHILE. MOST THOUGH, THEY STAY ROOTED IN THIS N'AWLINS SOIL, THE SOIL WHERE THEY DIED...
"BUT WE NEED TO HURRY ON NOW, MY LADY. GON' HAVE TO WALK THROUGH A MESS OF SHADES. DON'T BOTHER THEM NONE, AND THEY WON'T BOTHER YOU. CLOSE YOUR EYES IF THINGS START SEEMING STRANGE. MIGHT LOOK LIKE YOUR N'AWLINS OUT THERE, BUT IT AIN'T."
"WHERE ARE WE GOING?"
"ST. LOUIS CEMETERY... FOR PROTECTION AGAINST WHAT'S COMING."

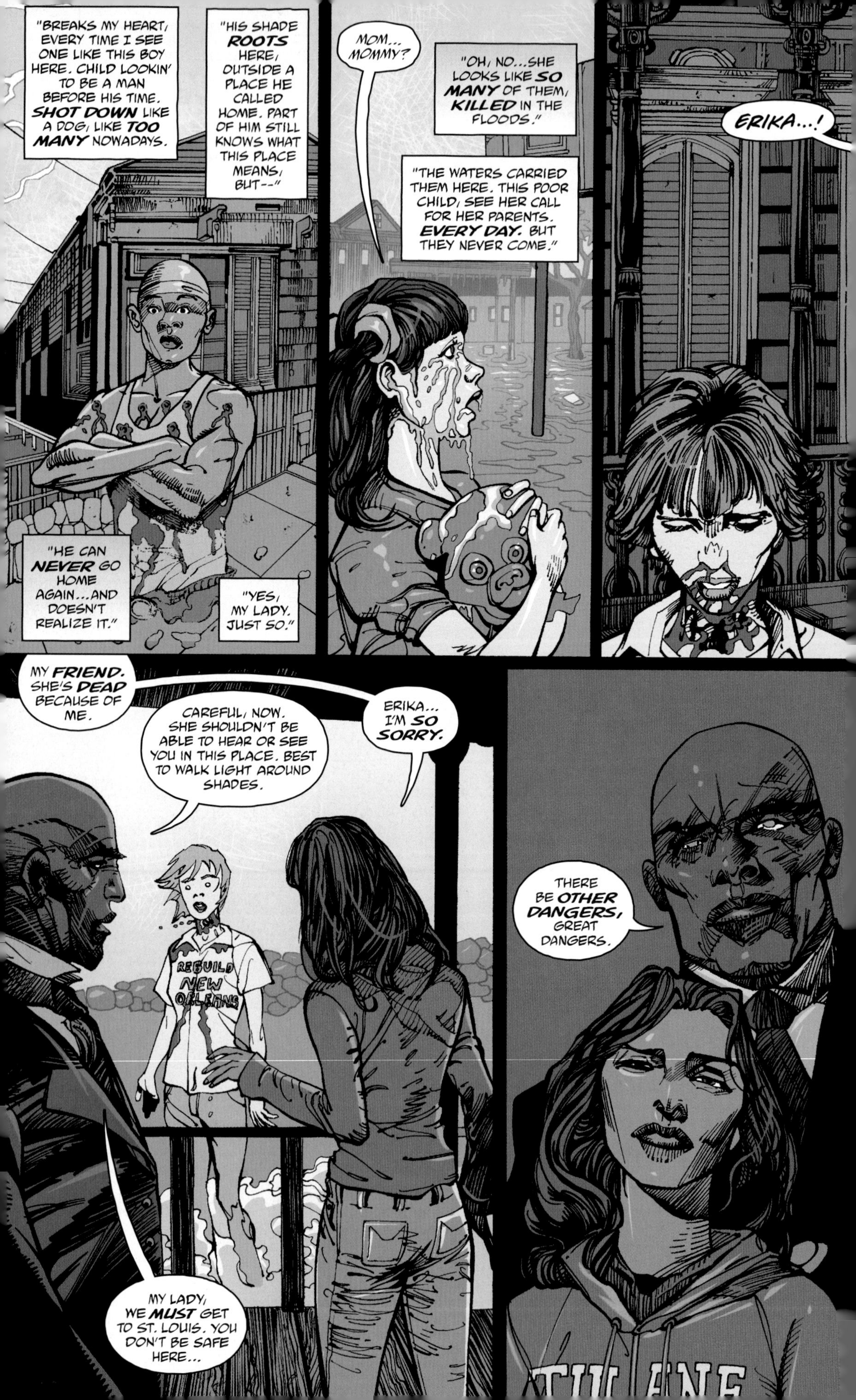
"BREAKS MY HEART, EVERY TIME I SEE ONE LIKE THIS BOY HERE. CHILD LOOKIN' TO BE A MAN BEFORE HIS TIME. SHOT DOWN LIKE A DOG, LIKE TOO MANY NOWADAYS.
"HIS SHADE ROOTS HERE, OUTSIDE A PLACE HE CALLED HOME. PART OF HIM STILL KNOWS WHAT THIS PLACE MEANS, BUT--"
"HE CAN NEVER GO HOME AGAIN...AND DOESN'T REALIZE IT."
"YES, MY LADY. JUST SO."
MOM... MOMMY?
"OH, NO...SHE LOOKS LIKE SO MANY OF THEM, KILLED IN THE FLOODS."
"THE WATERS CARRIED THEM HERE. THIS POOR CHILD, SEE HER CALL FOR HER PARENTS. EVERY DAY. BUT THEY NEVER COME."
ERIKA...!
MY FRIEND. SHE'S DEAD BECAUSE OF ME.
CAREFUL, NOW. SHE SHOULDN'T BE ABLE TO HEAR OR SEE YOU IN THIS PLACE. BEST TO WALK LIGHT AROUND SHADES.
ERIKA... I'M SO SORRY.
REBUILD NEW ORLEANS
MY LADY, WE MUST GET TO ST. LOUIS. YOU DON'T BE SAFE HERE...
THERE BE OTHER DANGERS, GREAT DANGERS.
TULANE

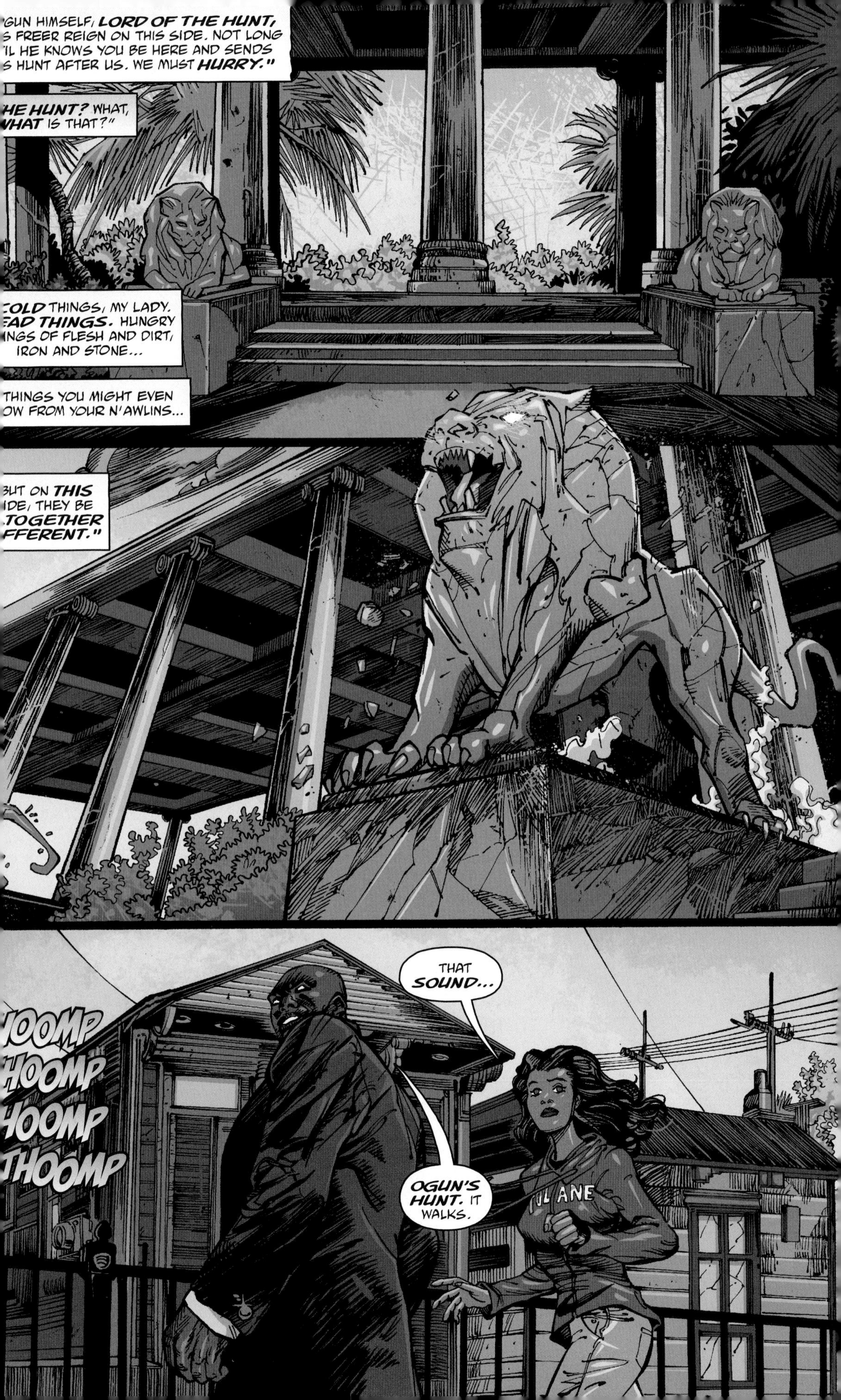
"GUN HIMSELF, LORD OF THE HUNT, S FREER REIGN ON THIS SIDE. NOT LONG 'IL HE KNOWS YOU BE HERE AND SENDS S HUNT AFTER US. WE MUST HURRY."
HE HUNT? WHAT, WHAT IS THAT?"
COLD THINGS, MY LADY. EAD THINGS. HUNGRY NGS OF FLESH AND DIRT, IRON AND STONE...
THINGS YOU MIGHT EVEN OW FROM YOUR N'AWLINS...
BUT ON THIS IDE, THEY BE TOGETHER FFERENT."
HOOMP HOOMP HOOMP THOOMP
THAT SOUND...
OGUN'S HUNT. IT WALKS.

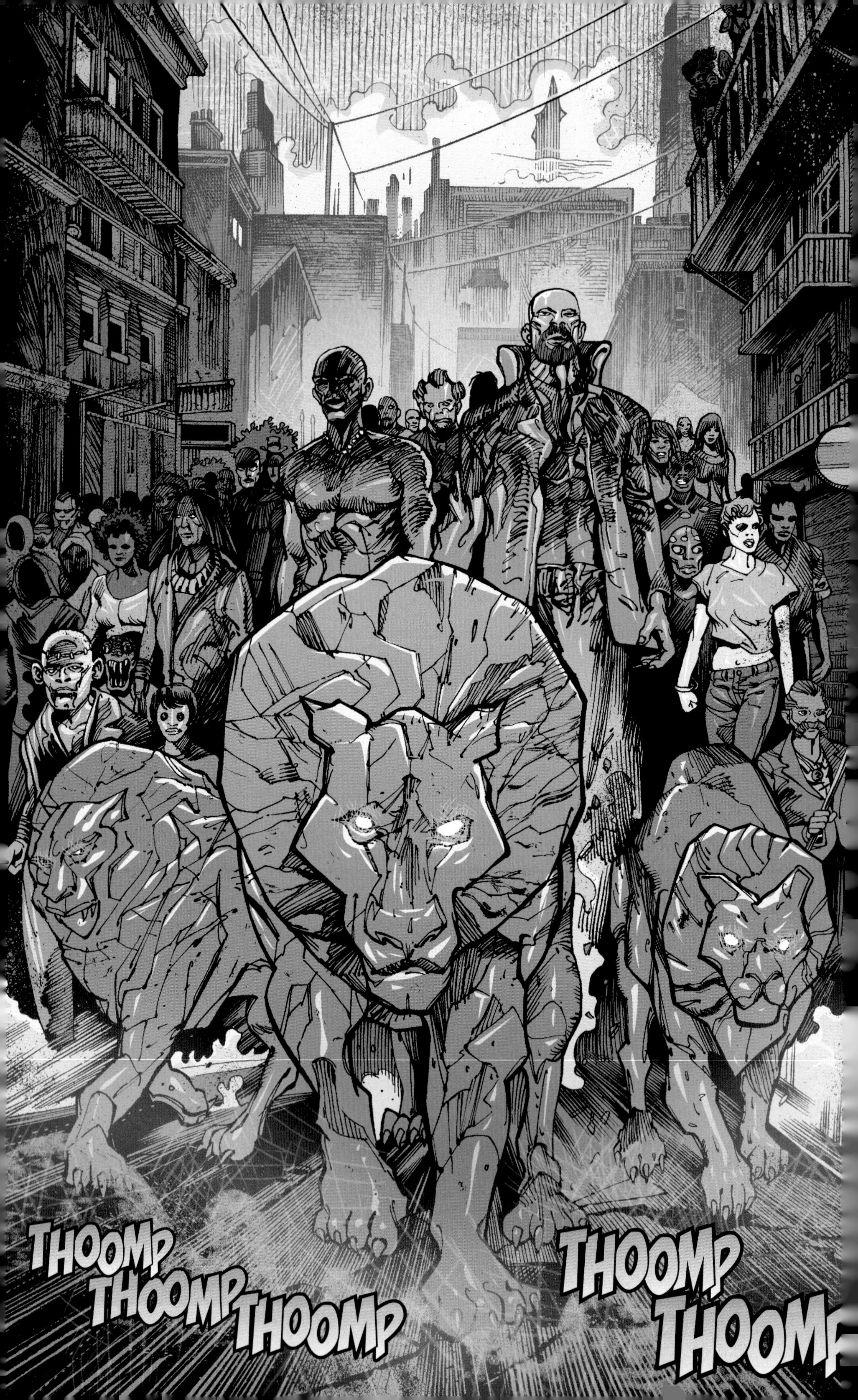
THOOMP
THOOMP
THOOMP
THOOMP
THOOMP

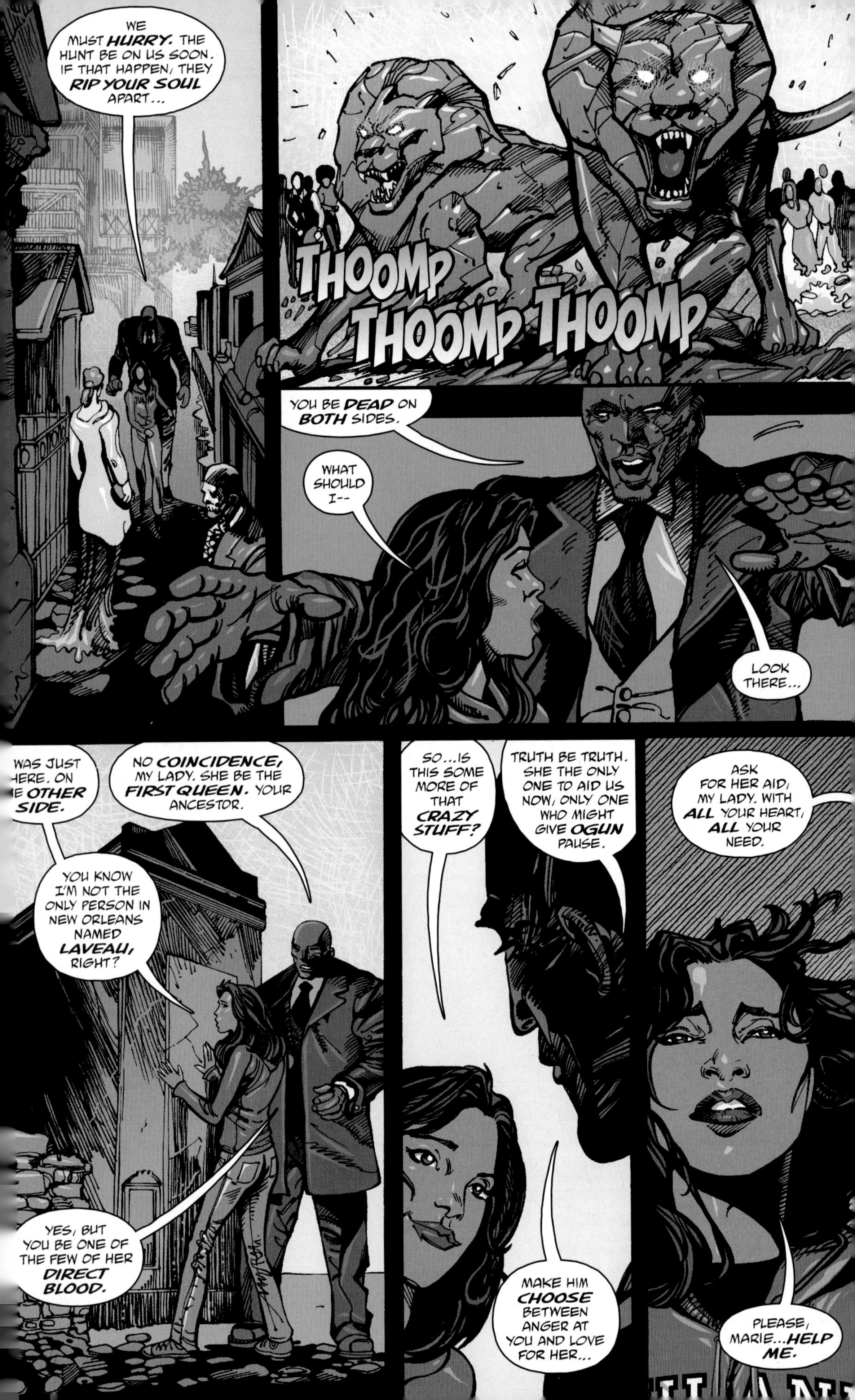

WE MUST HURRY. THE HUNT BE ON US SOON. IF THAT HAPPEN, THEY RIP YOUR SOUL APART...
THOOMP
THOOMP THOOMP
YOU BE DEAD ON BOTH SIDES.
WHAT SHOULD I--
LOOK THERE...
WAS JUST HERE. ON E OTHER SIDE.
NO COINCIDENCE, MY LADY. SHE BE THE FIRST QUEEN. YOUR ANCESTOR.
YOU KNOW I'M NOT THE ONLY PERSON IN NEW ORLEANS NAMED LAVEAU, RIGHT?
YES, BUT YOU BE ONE OF THE FEW OF HER DIRECT BLOOD.
SO...IS THIS SOME MORE OF THAT CRAZY STUFF?
TRUTH BE TRUTH. SHE THE ONLY ONE TO AID US NOW, ONLY ONE WHO MIGHT GIVE OGUN PAUSE.
MAKE HIM CHOOSE BETWEEN ANGER AT YOU AND LOVE FOR HER...
ASK FOR HER AID, MY LADY. WITH ALL YOUR HEART, ALL YOUR NEED.
PLEASE, MARIE...HELP ME.

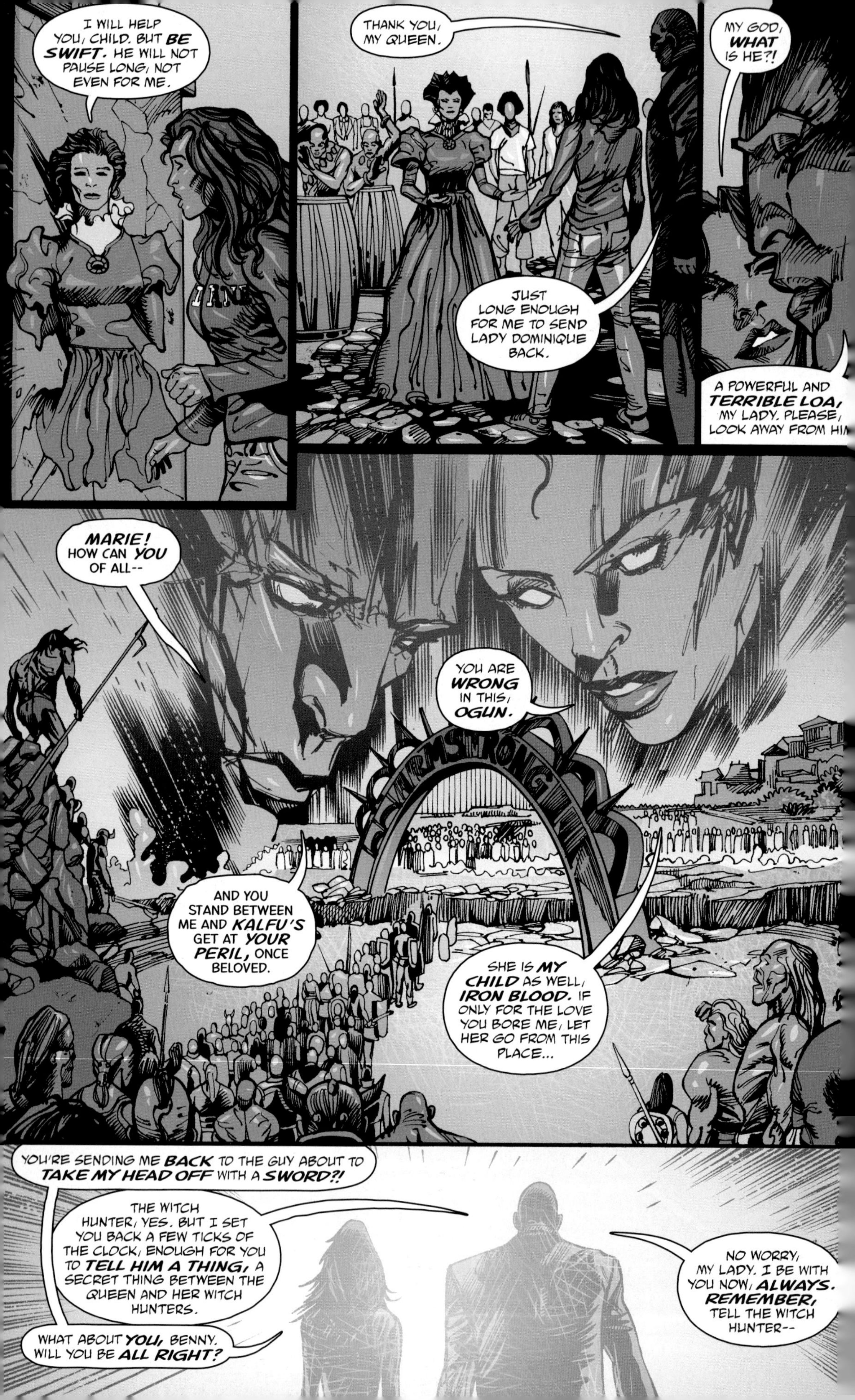

I WILL HELP YOU, CHILD. BUT BE SWIFT. HE WILL NOT PAUSE LONG, NOT EVEN FOR ME.
THANK YOU, MY QUEEN.
JUST LONG ENOUGH FOR ME TO SEND LADY DOMINIQUE BACK.
MY GOD, WHAT IS HE?!
A POWERFUL AND TERRIBLE LOA, MY LADY. PLEASE, LOOK AWAY FROM HI
MARIE! HOW CAN YOU OF ALL--
YOU ARE WRONG IN THIS, OGUN.
AND YOU STAND BETWEEN ME AND KALFU'S GET AT YOUR PERIL, ONCE BELOVED.
SHE IS MY CHILD AS WELL, IRON BLOOD. IF ONLY FOR THE LOVE YOU BORE ME, LET HER GO FROM THIS PLACE...
YOU'RE SENDING ME BACK TO THE GUY ABOUT TO TAKE MY HEAD OFF WITH A SWORD?!
THE WITCH HUNTER, YES. BUT I SET YOU BACK A FEW TICKS OF THE CLOCK, ENOUGH FOR YOU TO TELL HIM A THING, A SECRET THING BETWEEN THE QUEEN AND HER WITCH HUNTERS.
WHAT ABOUT YOU, BENNY. WILL YOU BE ALL RIGHT?
NO WORRY, MY LADY. I BE WITH YOU NOW, ALWAYS. REMEMBER, TELL THE WITCH HUNTER--

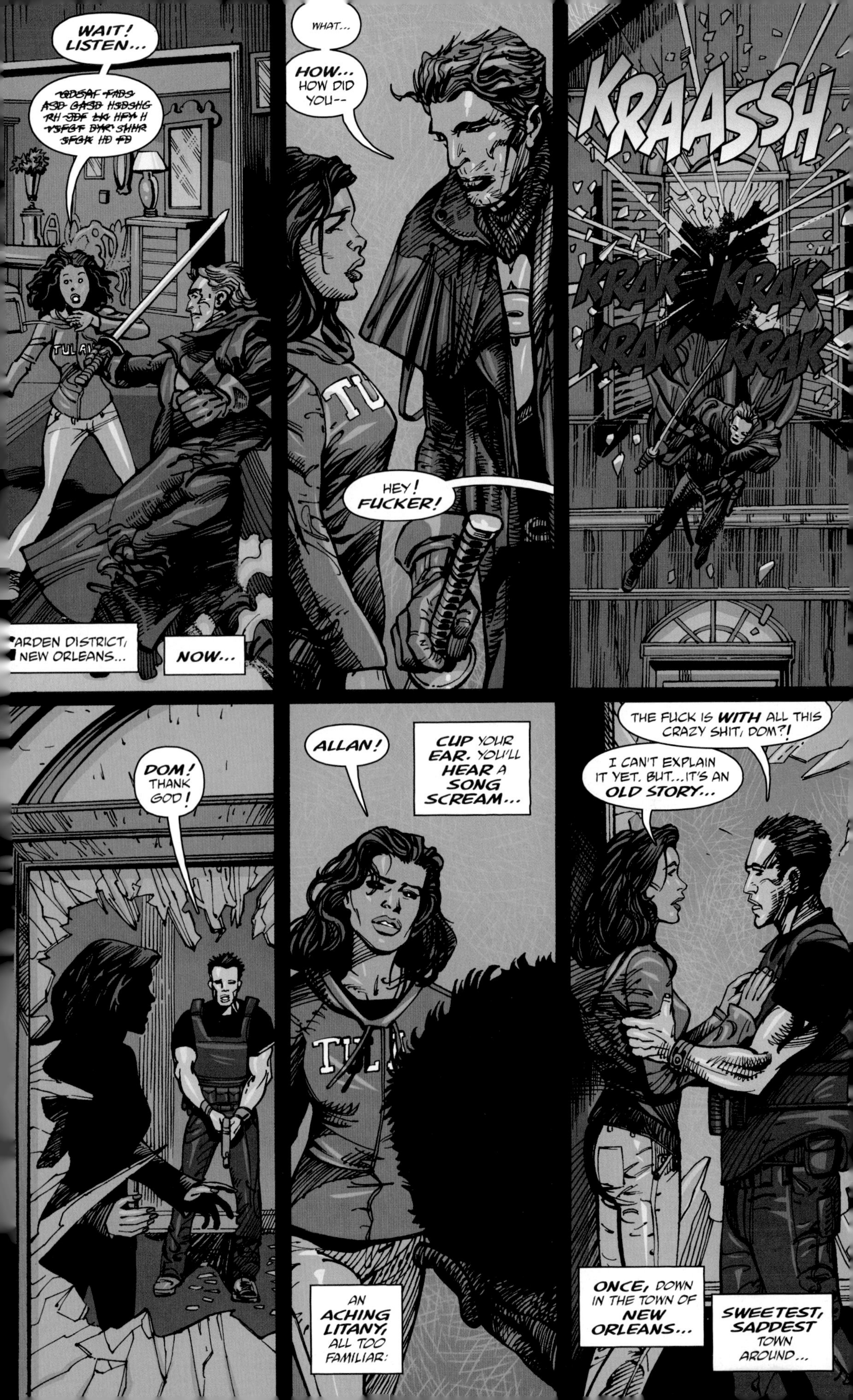
WAIT! LISTEN...
ARDEN DISTRICT, NEW ORLEANS...
NOW...
WHAT...
HOW... HOW DID YOU--
HEY! FUCKER!
KRAASSH
KRAK KRAK
KRAK KRAK
DOM! THANK GOD!
ALLAN!
CUP YOUR EAR. YOU'LL HEAR A SONG SCREAM...
AN ACHING LITANY, ALL TOO FAMILIAR:
THE FUCK IS WITH ALL THIS CRAZY SHIT, DOM?!
I CAN'T EXPLAIN IT YET. BUT...IT'S AN OLD STORY...
ONCE, DOWN IN THE TOWN OF NEW ORLEANS...
SWEETEST, SADDEST TOWN AROUND...

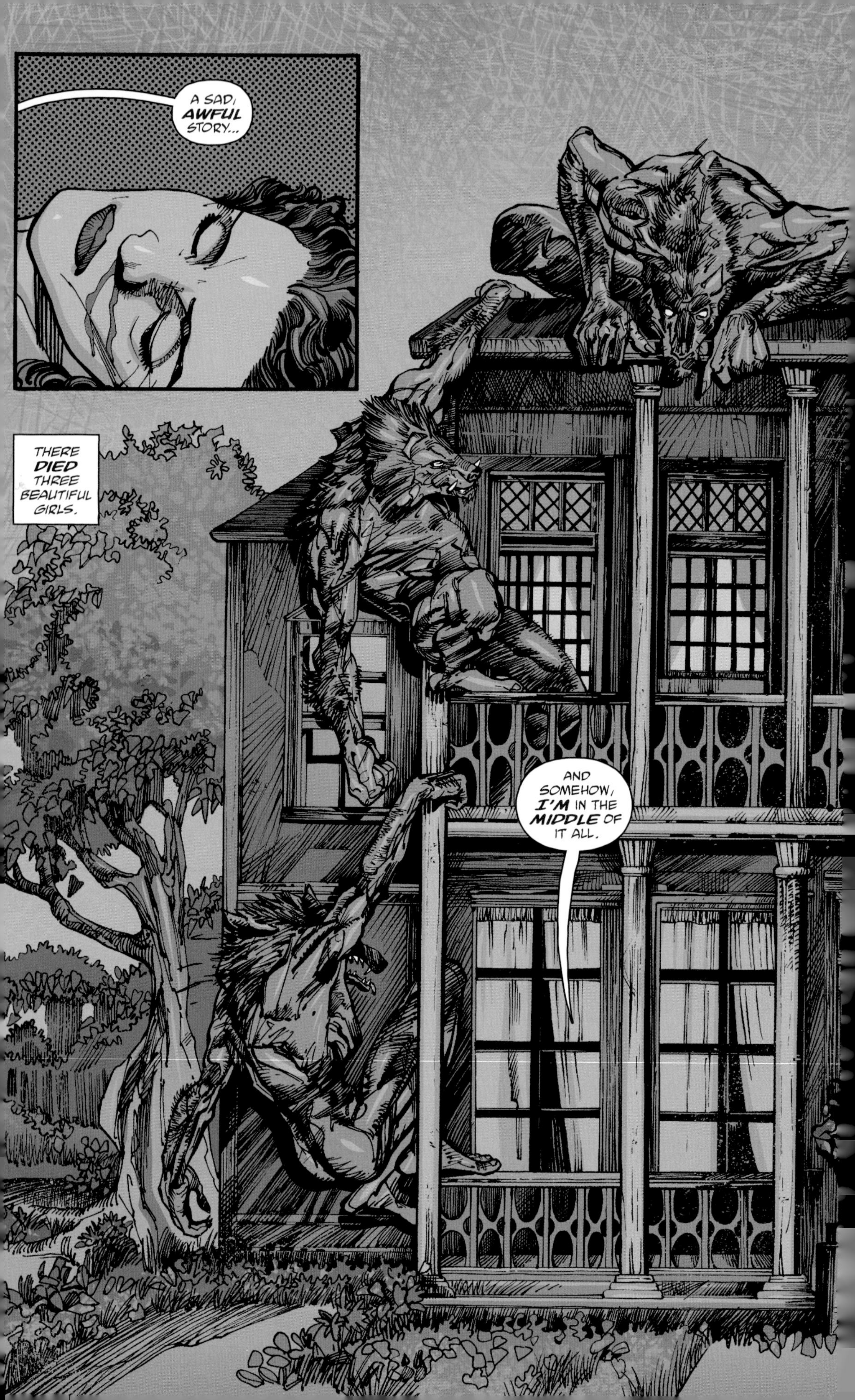
A SAD, AWFUL STORY...
THERE DIED THREE BEAUTIFUL GIRLS.
AND SOMEHOW, I'M IN THE MIDDLE OF IT ALL.

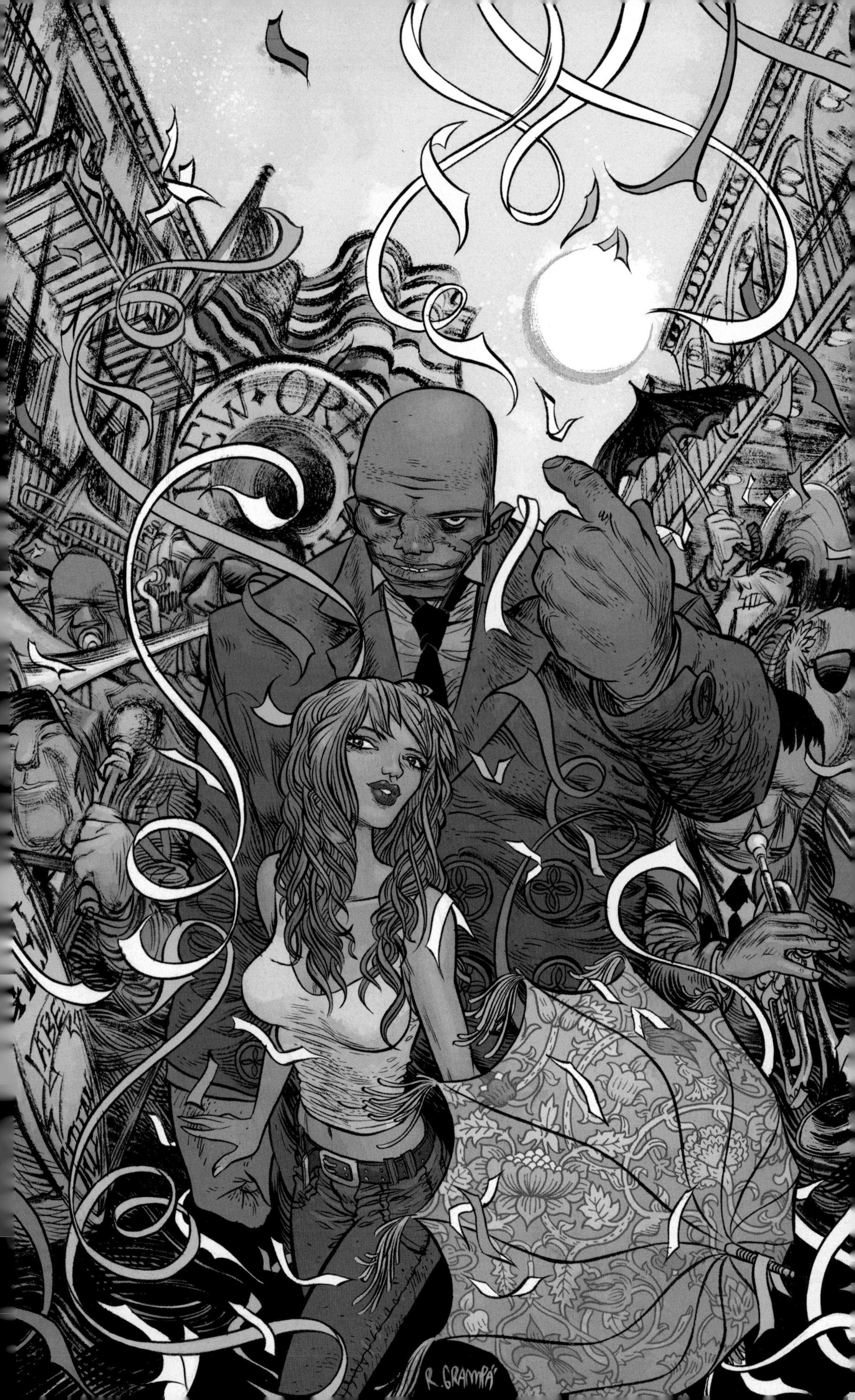
R. GRAMPÁ

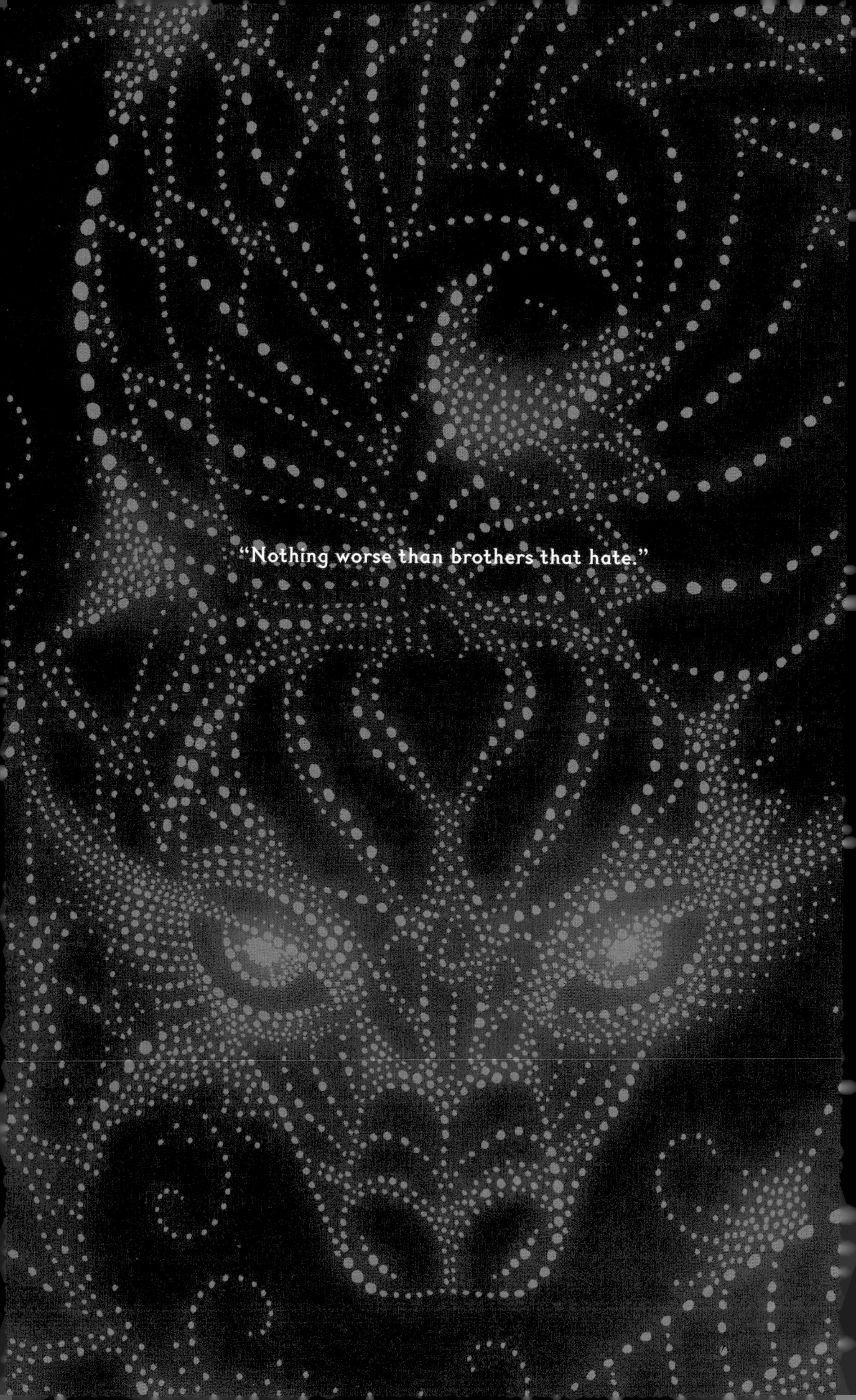
"Nothing worse than brothers that hate."

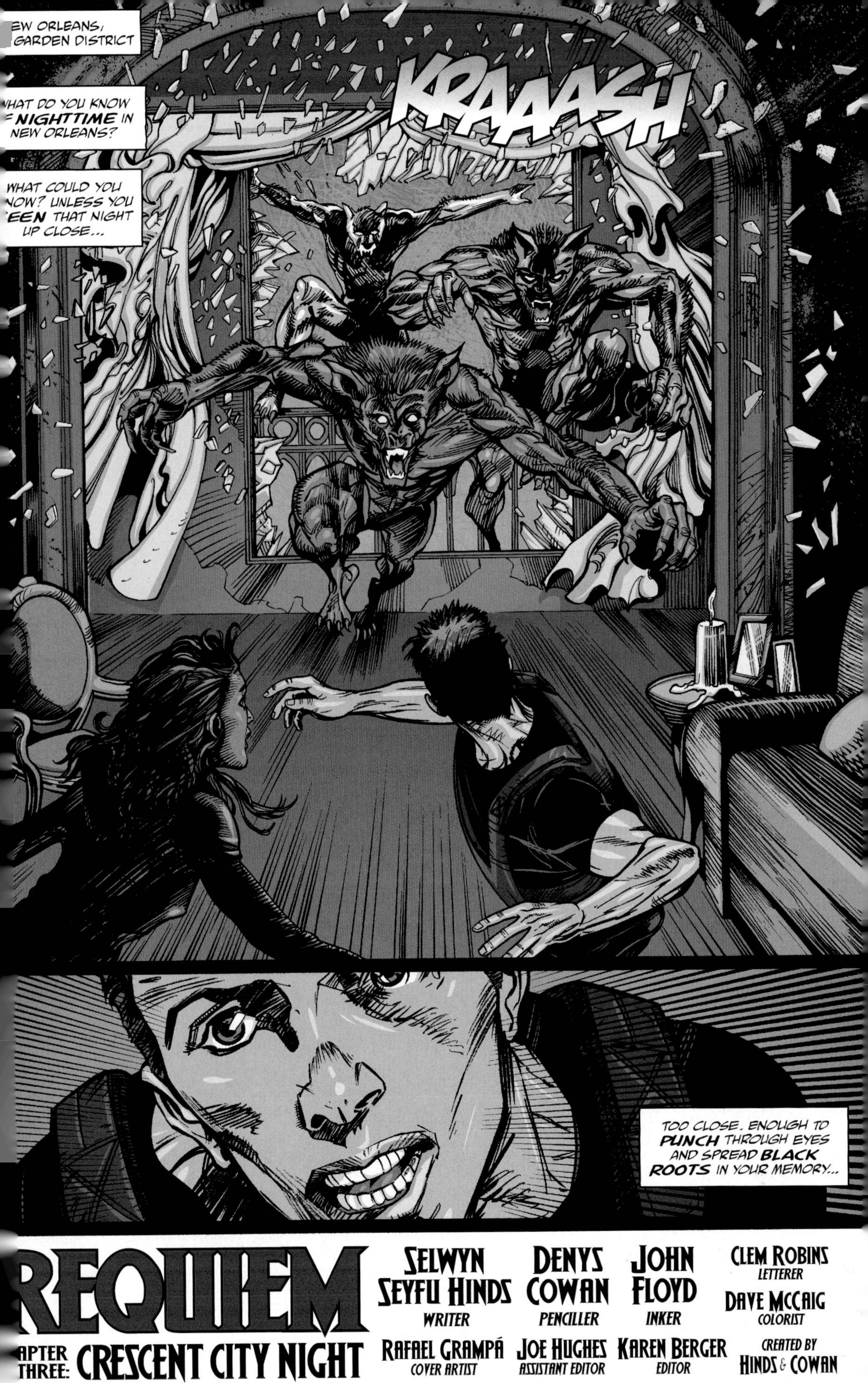
EW ORLEANS, GARDEN DISTRICT
HAT DO YOU KNOW F NIGHTTIME IN NEW ORLEANS?
WHAT COULD YOU NOW? UNLESS YOU EEN THAT NIGHT UP CLOSE...
KRAAASH
TOO CLOSE. ENOUGH TO PUNCH THROUGH EYES AND SPREAD BLACK ROOTS IN YOUR MEMORY...

REQUIEM

APTER THREE: CRESCENT CITY NIGHT

SELWYN SEYFU HINDS WRITER
DENYS COWAN PENCILLER
JOHN FLOYD INKER
CLEM ROBINS LETTERER
DAVE MCCAIG COLORIST
RAFAEL GRAMPÁ COVER ARTIST
JOE HUGHES ASSISTANT EDITOR
KAREN BERGER EDITOR
CREATED BY **HINDS & COWAN**

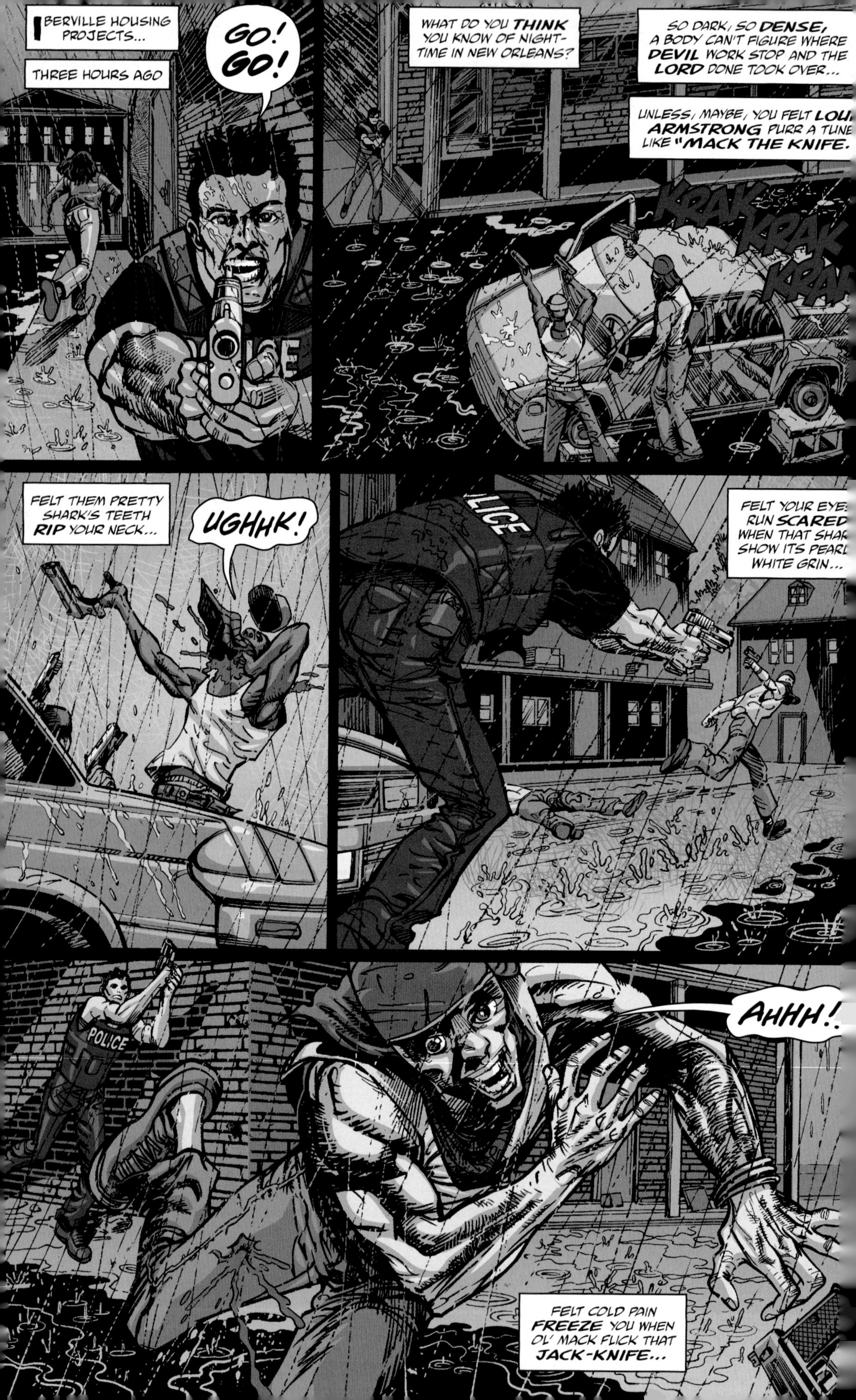
IBERVILLE HOUSING PROJECTS...
THREE HOURS AGO
GO! GO!
WHAT DO YOU THINK YOU KNOW OF NIGHT-TIME IN NEW ORLEANS?
SO DARK, SO DENSE, A BODY CAN'T FIGURE WHERE DEVIL WORK STOP AND THE LORD DONE TOOK OVER...
UNLESS, MAYBE, YOU FELT LOUI ARMSTRONG PURR A TUNE LIKE "MACK THE KNIFE."
KRAK KRAK KRAK
FELT THEM PRETTY SHARK'S TEETH RIP YOUR NECK...
UGHHK!
FELT YOUR EYE RUN SCARED WHEN THAT SHAR SHOW ITS PEARL WHITE GRIN...
POLICE
AHHH!
FELT COLD PAIN FREEZE YOU WHEN OL' MACK FLICK THAT JACK-KNIFE...

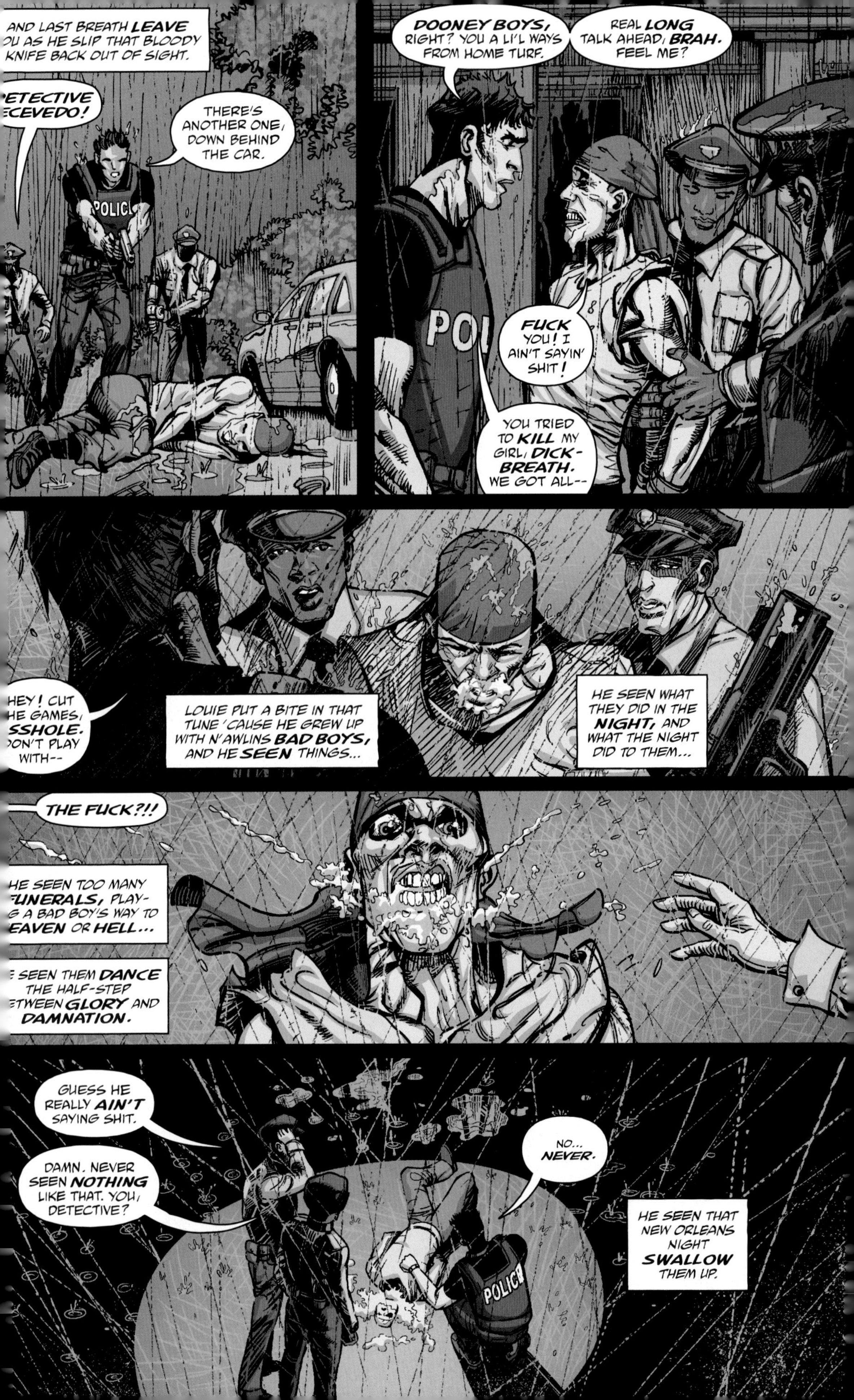

AND LAST BREATH LEAVE
OU AS HE SLIP THAT BLOODY KNIFE BACK OUT OF SIGHT.
ETECTIVE
ECEVEDO!
THERE'S ANOTHER ONE, DOWN BEHIND THE CAR.
POLIC
DOONEY BOYS, RIGHT? YOU A LI'L WAYS FROM HOME TURF.
REAL LONG TALK AHEAD, BRAH. FEEL ME?
POL
FUCK YOU! I AIN'T SAYIN' SHIT!
YOU TRIED TO KILL MY GIRL, DICK-BREATH. WE GOT ALL--
HEY! CUT HE GAMES, SSHOLE. ON'T PLAY WITH--
LOUIE PUT A BITE IN THAT TUNE 'CAUSE HE GREW UP WITH N'AWLINS BAD BOYS, AND HE SEEN THINGS...
HE SEEN WHAT THEY DID IN THE NIGHT, AND WHAT THE NIGHT DID TO THEM...
THE FUCK?!!
HE SEEN TOO MANY FUNERALS, PLAY-G A BAD BOY'S WAY TO EAVEN OR HELL...
E SEEN THEM DANCE THE HALF-STEP ETWEEN GLORY AND DAMNATION.
GUESS HE REALLY AIN'T SAYING SHIT.
DAMN. NEVER SEEN NOTHING LIKE THAT. YOU, DETECTIVE?
NO... NEVER.
HE SEEN THAT NEW ORLEANS NIGHT SWALLOW THEM UP.
POLICE

DOM, **WHERE** ARE YOU?

BABY, IF YOU GET THIS MESSAGE, JUST KNOW YOU'VE **OFFICIALLY** SCARED THE SHIT OUTTA ME...

NOPD, 2ND PRECINCT...

ONE HOUR AGO

LOOK, I'M GONNA PARK OUT BY YOUR AUNT'S, 'CASE YOU GO BY THERE.

AND DOM... THERE'S SOME **WEIRD** SHIT GOING ON HERE, **DANGEROUS** SHIT. BE CARE--

CRIP, CHIK

WHO THE **FUCK'S** THERE?!

YOU GOT **SOME-THING** OVER THERE?!

NAH, IT'S **COOL.** IT'S NOTHING!

JESUS **CHRIST,** ECEVEDO. GET A FUCKING GRIP.

GARDEN DISTRICT

SHFJ BSTRKYF JF DFHG TBF3H YFDASFG FH ~EH!FUOP~

DOM?!

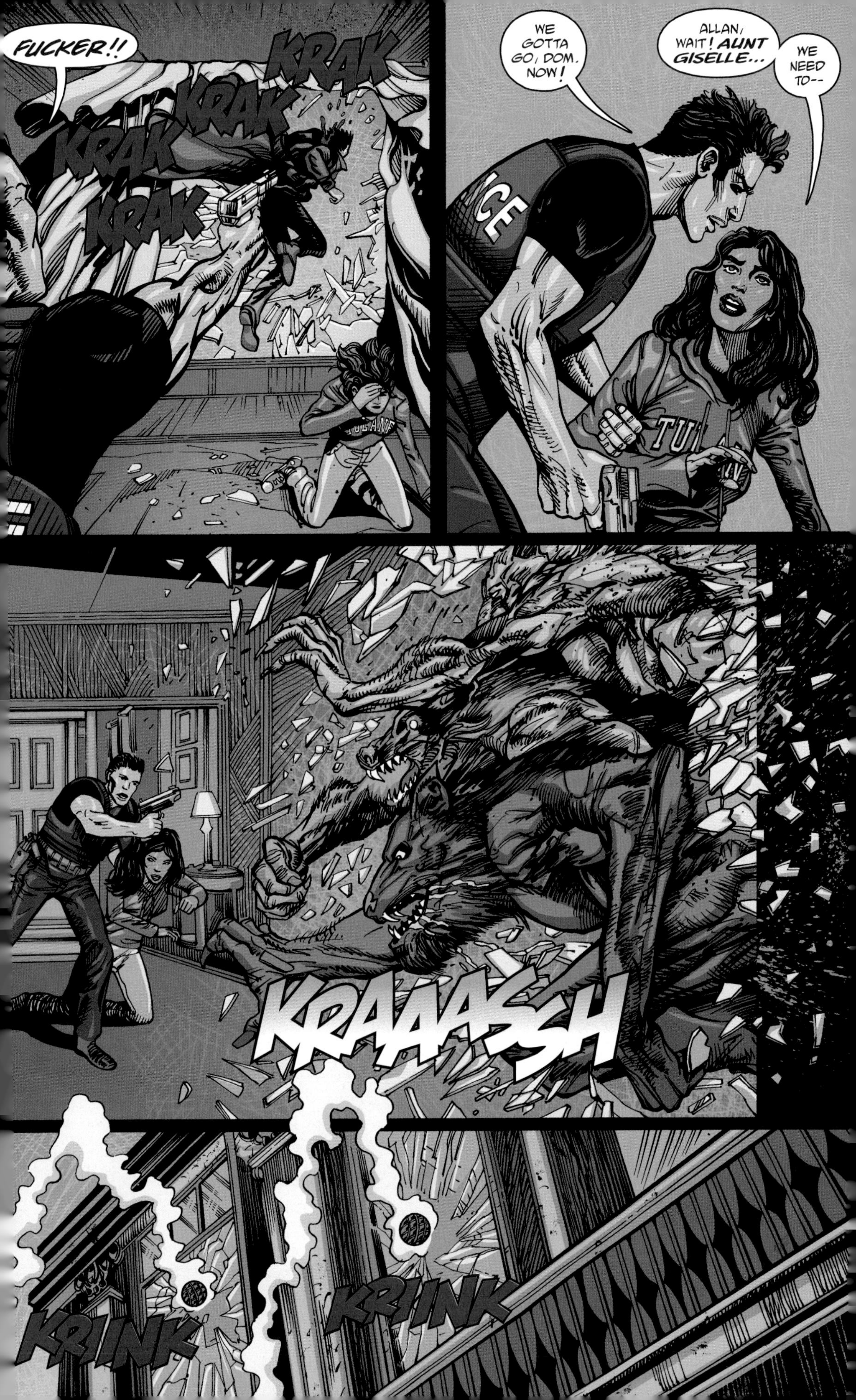
FUCKER!!
KRAK
KRAK
KRAK
KRAK
WE GOTTA GO, DOM. NOW!
ALLAN, WAIT! AUNT GISELLE...
WE NEED TO--
KRAAASH
KRINK
KRINK

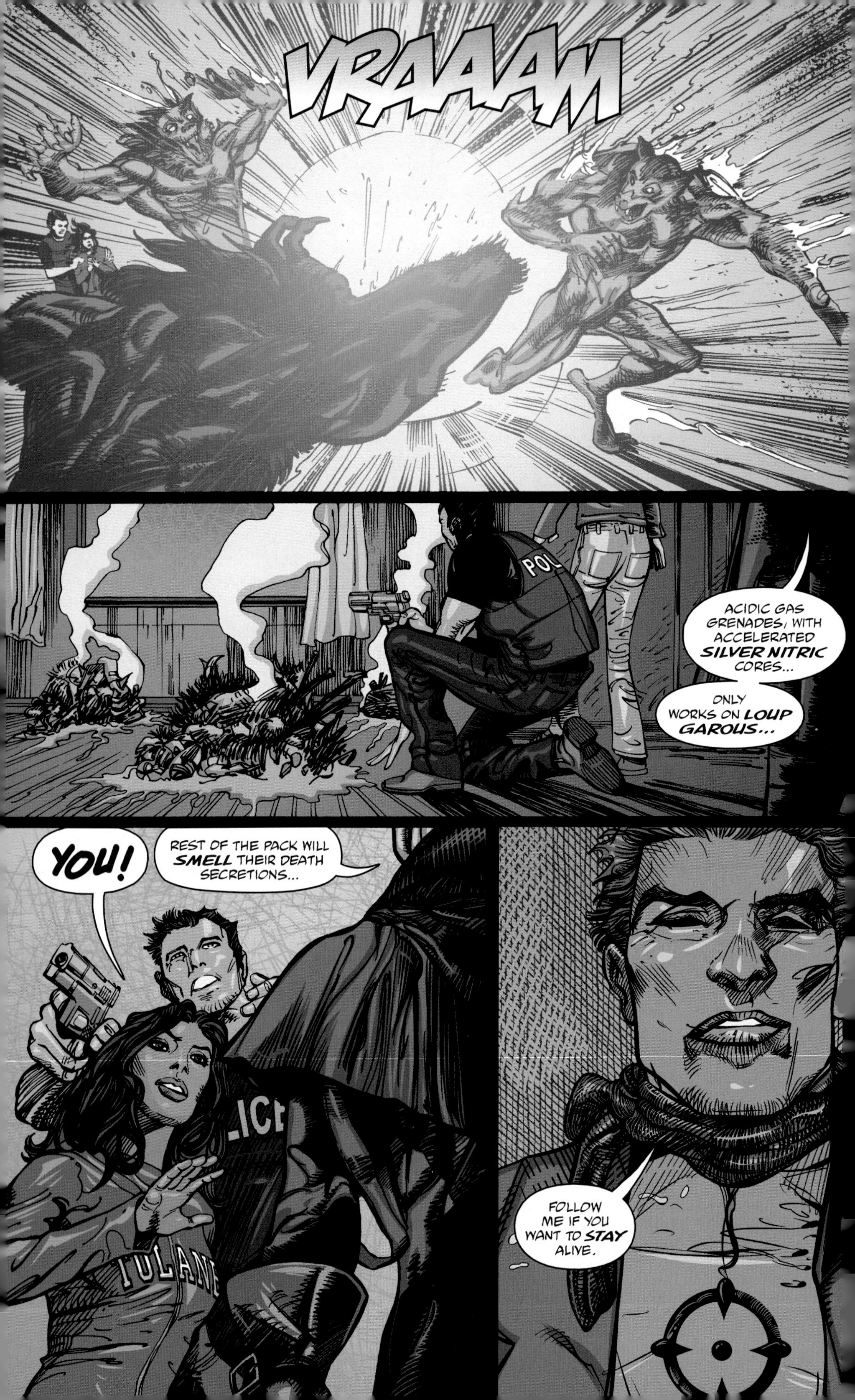
VRAAAM
ACIDIC GAS GRENADES, WITH ACCELERATED SILVER NITRIC CORES...
ONLY WORKS ON LOUP GAROUS...
YOU!
REST OF THE PACK WILL SMELL THEIR DEATH SECRETIONS...
FOLLOW ME IF YOU WANT TO STAY ALIVE.

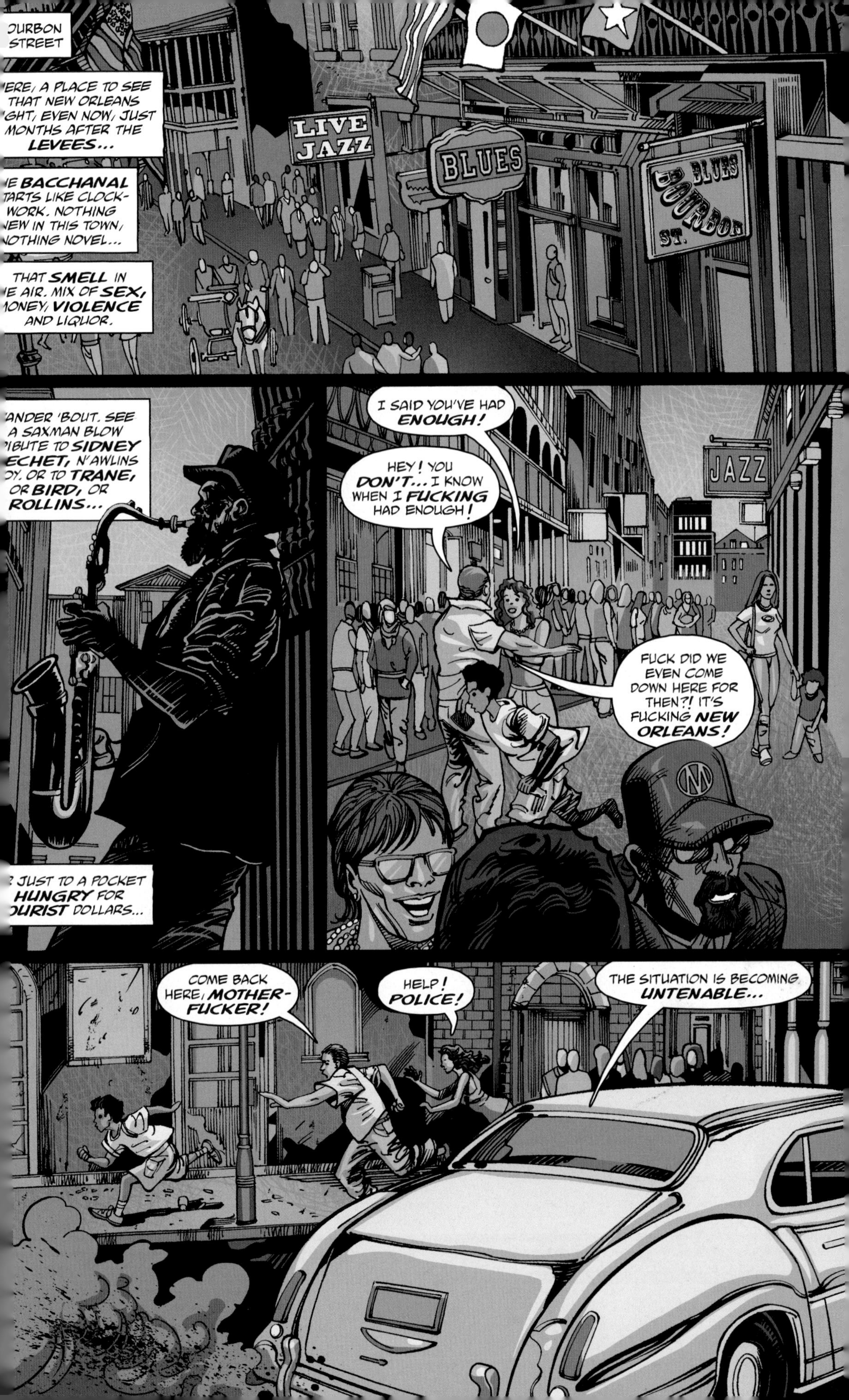

OURBON STREET
ERE, A PLACE TO SEE THAT NEW ORLEANS IGHT, EVEN NOW, JUST MONTHS AFTER THE LEVEES...
E BACCHANAL TARTS LIKE CLOCK-WORK. NOTHING NEW IN THIS TOWN, NOTHING NOVEL...
THAT SMELL IN E AIR. MIX OF SEX, MONEY, VIOLENCE AND LIQUOR.
LIVE JAZZ
BLUES
BLUES BOURBON ST.
ANDER 'BOUT. SEE A SAXMAN BLOW IBUTE TO SIDNEY ECHET, N'AWLINS OY. OR TO TRANE, OR BIRD, OR ROLLINS...
JUST TO A POCKET HUNGRY FOR OURIST DOLLARS...
I SAID YOU'VE HAD ENOUGH!
HEY! YOU DON'T... I KNOW WHEN I FUCKING HAD ENOUGH!
JAZZ
FUCK DID WE EVEN COME DOWN HERE FOR THEN?! IT'S FUCKING NEW ORLEANS!
COME BACK HERE, MOTHER-FUCKER!
HELP! POLICE!
THE SITUATION IS BECOMING UNTENABLE...

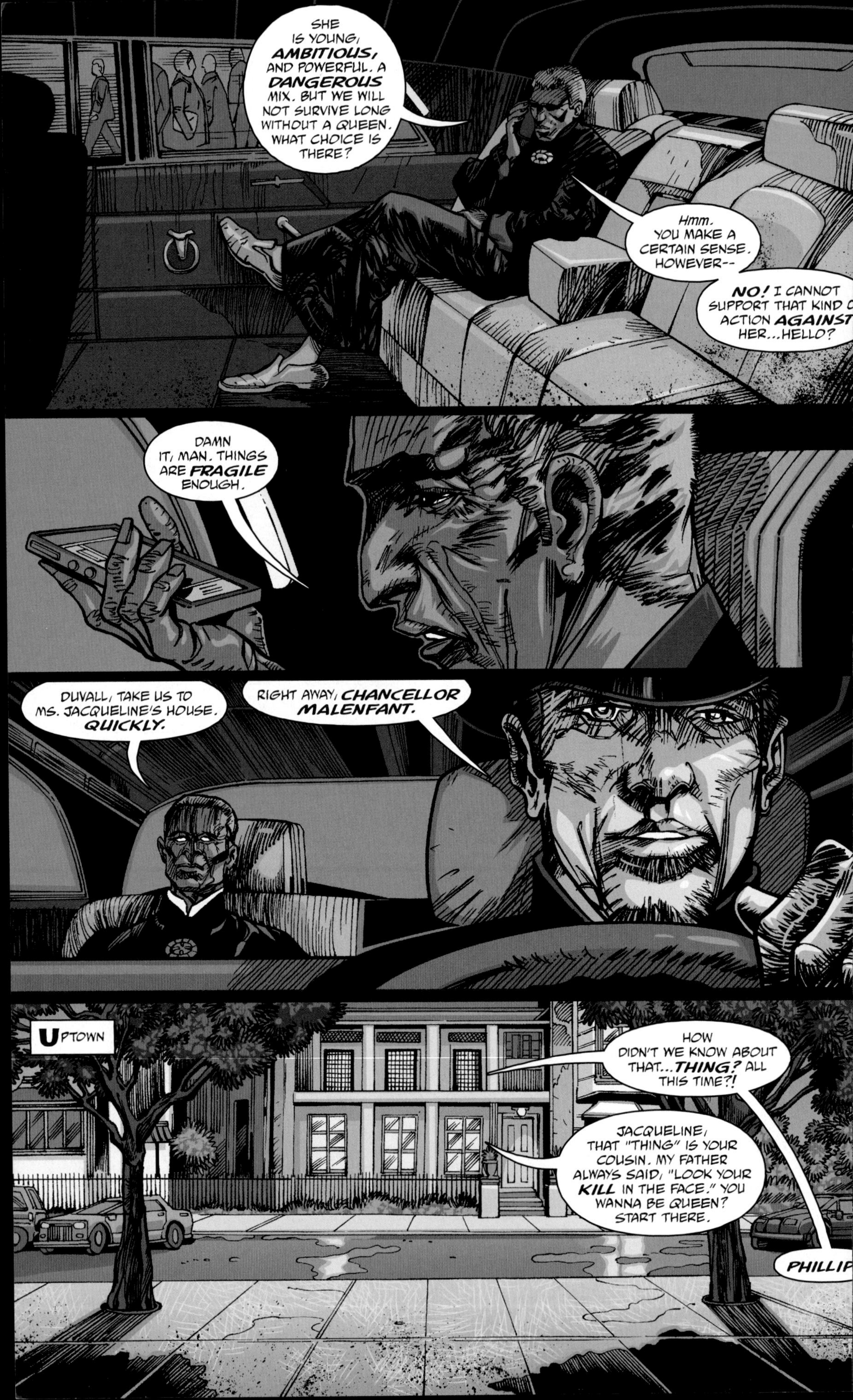
SHE IS YOUNG, AMBITIOUS, AND POWERFUL. A DANGEROUS MIX. BUT WE WILL NOT SURVIVE LONG WITHOUT A QUEEN. WHAT CHOICE IS THERE?
Hmm. YOU MAKE A CERTAIN SENSE. HOWEVER--
NO! I CANNOT SUPPORT THAT KIND O ACTION AGAINST HER...HELLO?
DAMN IT, MAN. THINGS ARE FRAGILE ENOUGH.
DUVALL, TAKE US TO MS. JACQUELINE'S HOUSE. QUICKLY.
RIGHT AWAY, CHANCELLOR MALENFANT.
UPTOWN
HOW DIDN'T WE KNOW ABOUT THAT...THING? ALL THIS TIME?!
JACQUELINE, THAT "THING" IS YOUR COUSIN. MY FATHER ALWAYS SAID, "LOOK YOUR KILL IN THE FACE." YOU WANNA BE QUEEN? START THERE.
PHILLIP

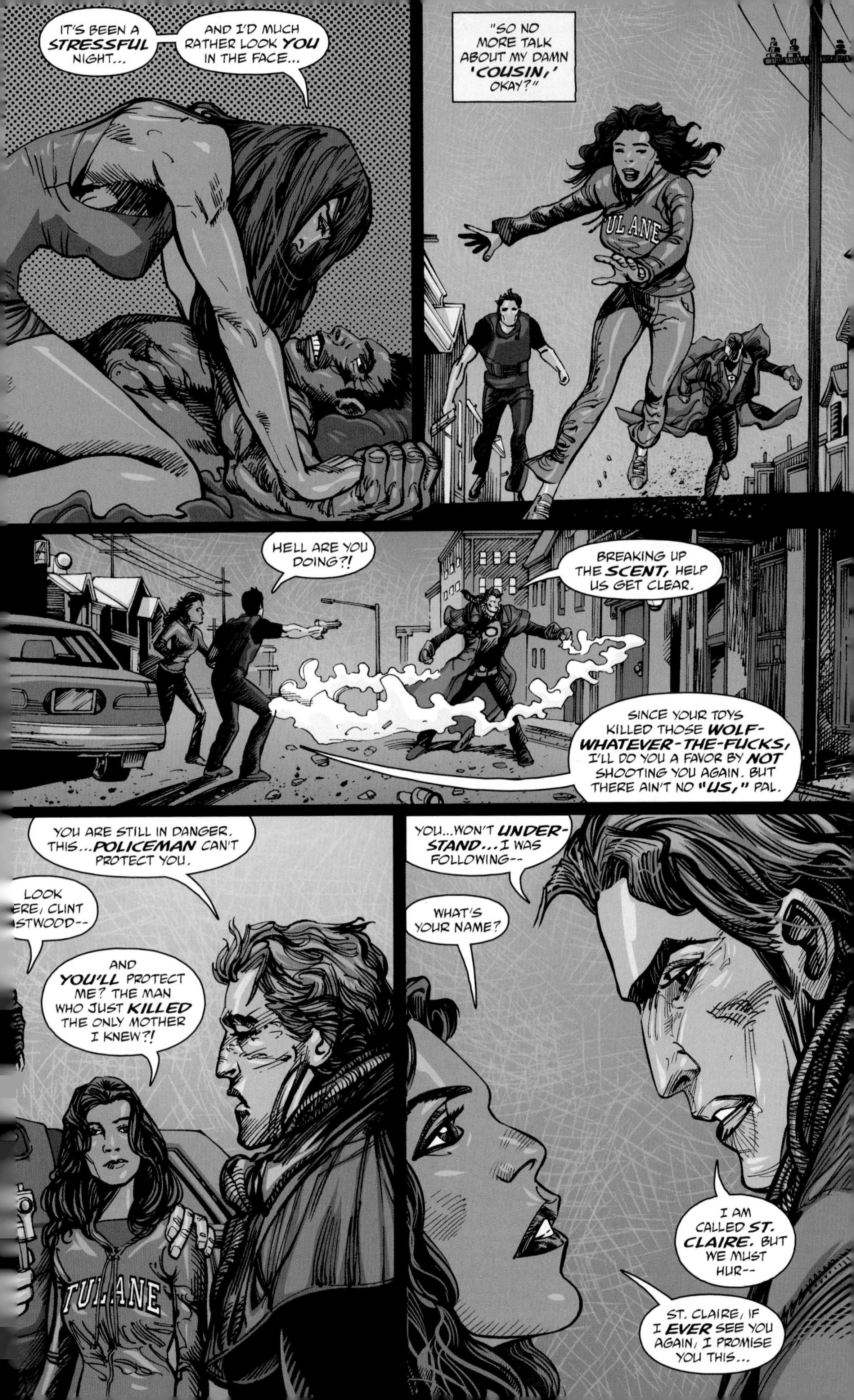
IT'S BEEN A STRESSFUL NIGHT...
AND I'D MUCH RATHER LOOK YOU IN THE FACE...
"SO NO MORE TALK ABOUT MY DAMN 'COUSIN,' OKAY?"
TULANE
HELL ARE YOU DOING?!
BREAKING UP THE SCENT, HELP US GET CLEAR.
SINCE YOUR TOYS KILLED THOSE WOLF-WHATEVER-THE-FUCKS, I'LL DO YOU A FAVOR BY NOT SHOOTING YOU AGAIN. BUT THERE AIN'T NO "US," PAL.
YOU ARE STILL IN DANGER. THIS...POLICEMAN CAN'T PROTECT YOU.
LOOK ERE, CLINT ASTWOOD--
AND YOU'LL PROTECT ME? THE MAN WHO JUST KILLED THE ONLY MOTHER I KNEW?!
TULANE
YOU...WON'T UNDERSTAND...I WAS FOLLOWING--
WHAT'S YOUR NAME?
I AM CALLED ST. CLAIRE. BUT WE MUST HUR--
ST. CLAIRE, IF I EVER SEE YOU AGAIN, I PROMISE YOU THIS...

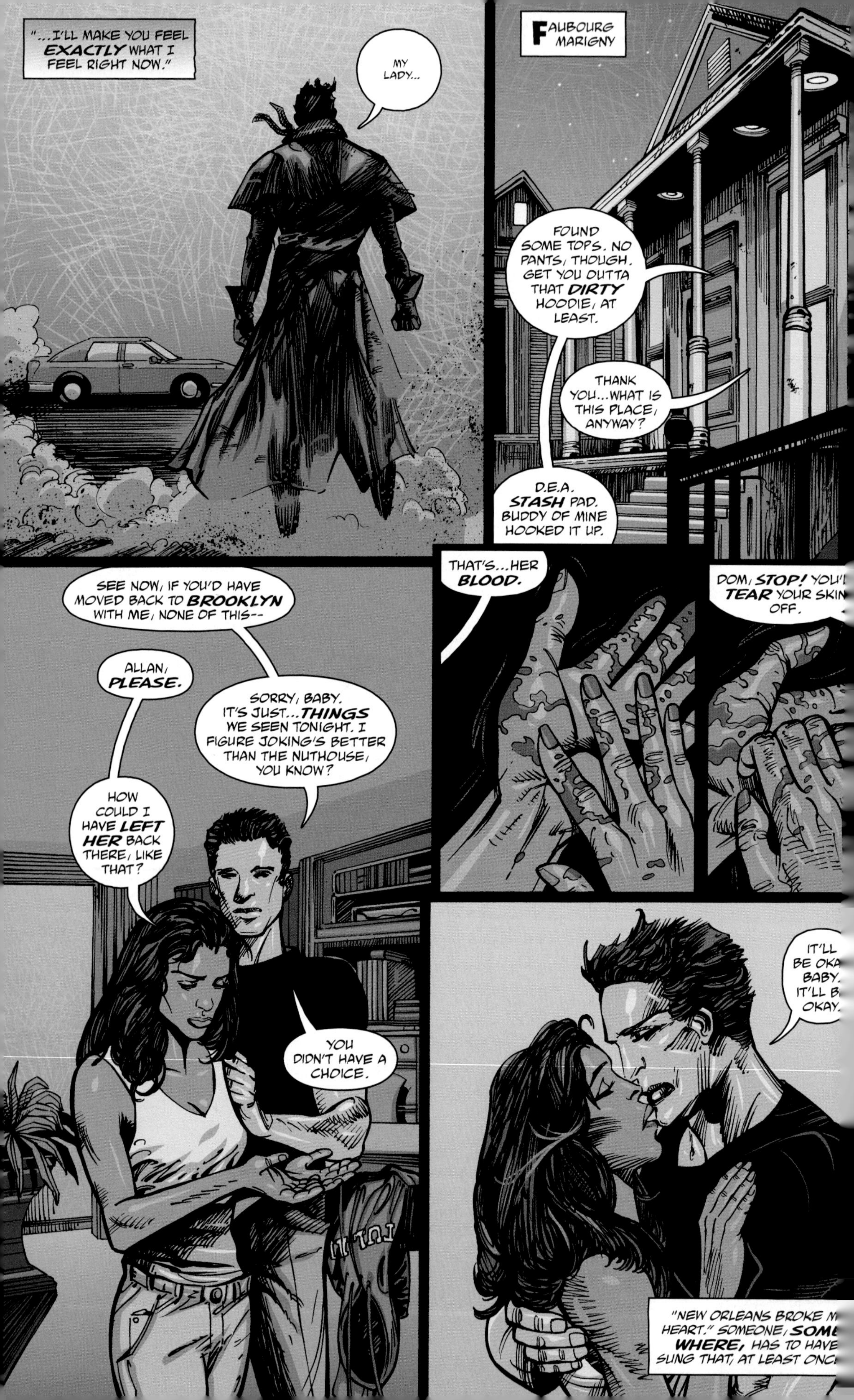
"...I'LL MAKE YOU FEEL EXACTLY WHAT I FEEL RIGHT NOW."
MY LADY...
FAUBOURG MARIGNY
FOUND SOME TOPS. NO PANTS, THOUGH. GET YOU OUTTA THAT DIRTY HOODIE, AT LEAST.
THANK YOU...WHAT IS THIS PLACE, ANYWAY?
D.E.A. STASH PAD. BUDDY OF MINE HOOKED IT UP.
SEE NOW, IF YOU'D HAVE MOVED BACK TO BROOKLYN WITH ME, NONE OF THIS--
ALLAN, PLEASE.
SORRY, BABY. IT'S JUST...THINGS WE SEEN TONIGHT. I FIGURE JOKING'S BETTER THAN THE NUTHOUSE, YOU KNOW?
HOW COULD I HAVE LEFT HER BACK THERE, LIKE THAT?
YOU DIDN'T HAVE A CHOICE.
THAT'S...HER BLOOD.
DOM, STOP! YOU'L TEAR YOUR SKIN OFF.
IT'LL BE OKA BABY. IT'LL B OKAY.
"NEW ORLEANS BROKE M HEART." SOMEONE, SOME WHERE, HAS TO HAVE SUNG THAT, AT LEAST ONC

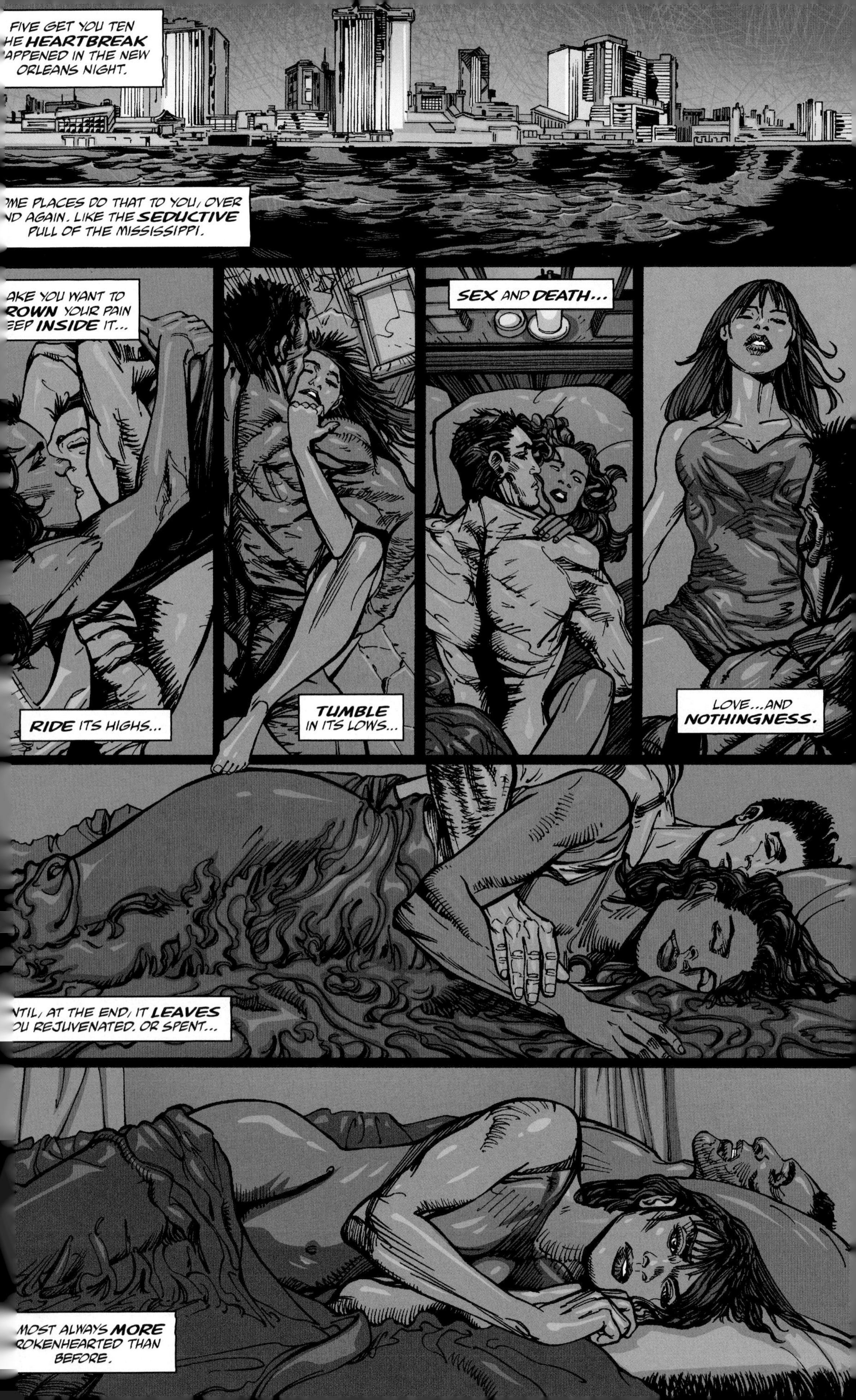
FIVE GET YOU TEN HE HEARTBREAK APPENED IN THE NEW ORLEANS NIGHT.
OME PLACES DO THAT TO YOU, OVER ND AGAIN. LIKE THE SEDUCTIVE PULL OF THE MISSISSIPPI.
AKE YOU WANT TO ROWN YOUR PAIN EEP INSIDE IT...
RIDE ITS HIGHS...
TUMBLE IN ITS LOWS...
SEX AND DEATH...
LOVE...AND NOTHINGNESS.
NTIL, AT THE END, IT LEAVES OU REJUVENATED. OR SPENT...
MOST ALWAYS MORE ROKENHEARTED THAN BEFORE.

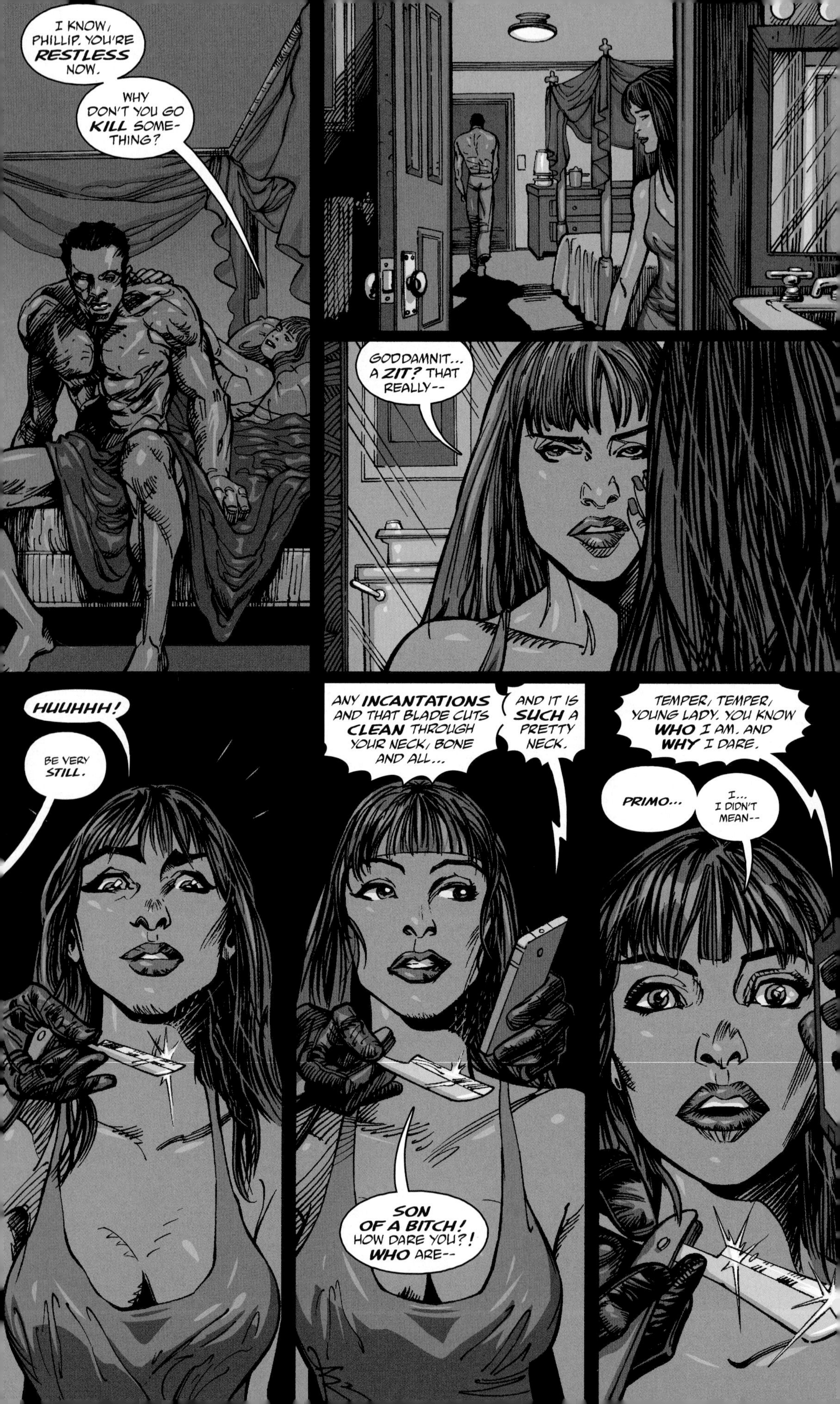
I KNOW, PHILLIP. YOU'RE RESTLESS NOW.
WHY DON'T YOU GO KILL SOME-THING?
GODDAMNIT... A ZIT? THAT REALLY--
HUUHHH!
BE VERY STILL.
ANY INCANTATIONS AND THAT BLADE CUTS CLEAN THROUGH YOUR NECK, BONE AND ALL...
AND IT IS SUCH A PRETTY NECK.
SON OF A BITCH! HOW DARE YOU?! WHO ARE--
TEMPER, TEMPER, YOUNG LADY. YOU KNOW WHO I AM. AND WHY I DARE.
PRIMO...
I... I DIDN'T MEAN--

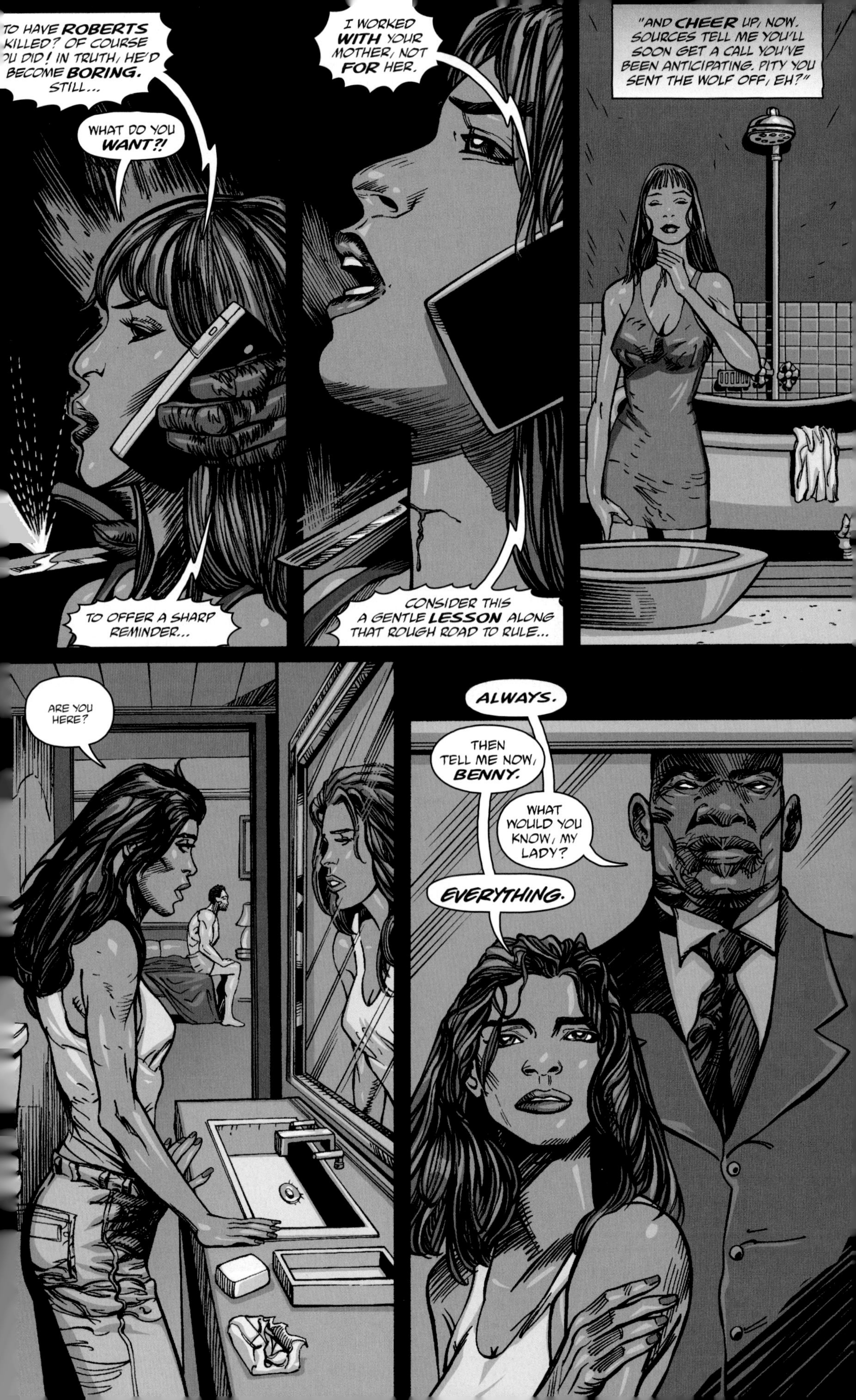
TO HAVE ROBERTS KILLED? OF COURSE OU DID! IN TRUTH, HE'D BECOME BORING. STILL...
WHAT DO YOU WANT?!
TO OFFER A SHARP REMINDER...
I WORKED WITH YOUR MOTHER, NOT FOR HER.
CONSIDER THIS A GENTLE LESSON ALONG THAT ROUGH ROAD TO RULE...
"AND CHEER UP, NOW. SOURCES TELL ME YOU'LL SOON GET A CALL YOU'VE BEEN ANTICIPATING. PITY YOU SENT THE WOLF OFF, EH?"
ARE YOU HERE?
ALWAYS.
THEN TELL ME NOW, BENNY.
WHAT WOULD YOU KNOW, MY LADY?
EVERYTHING.

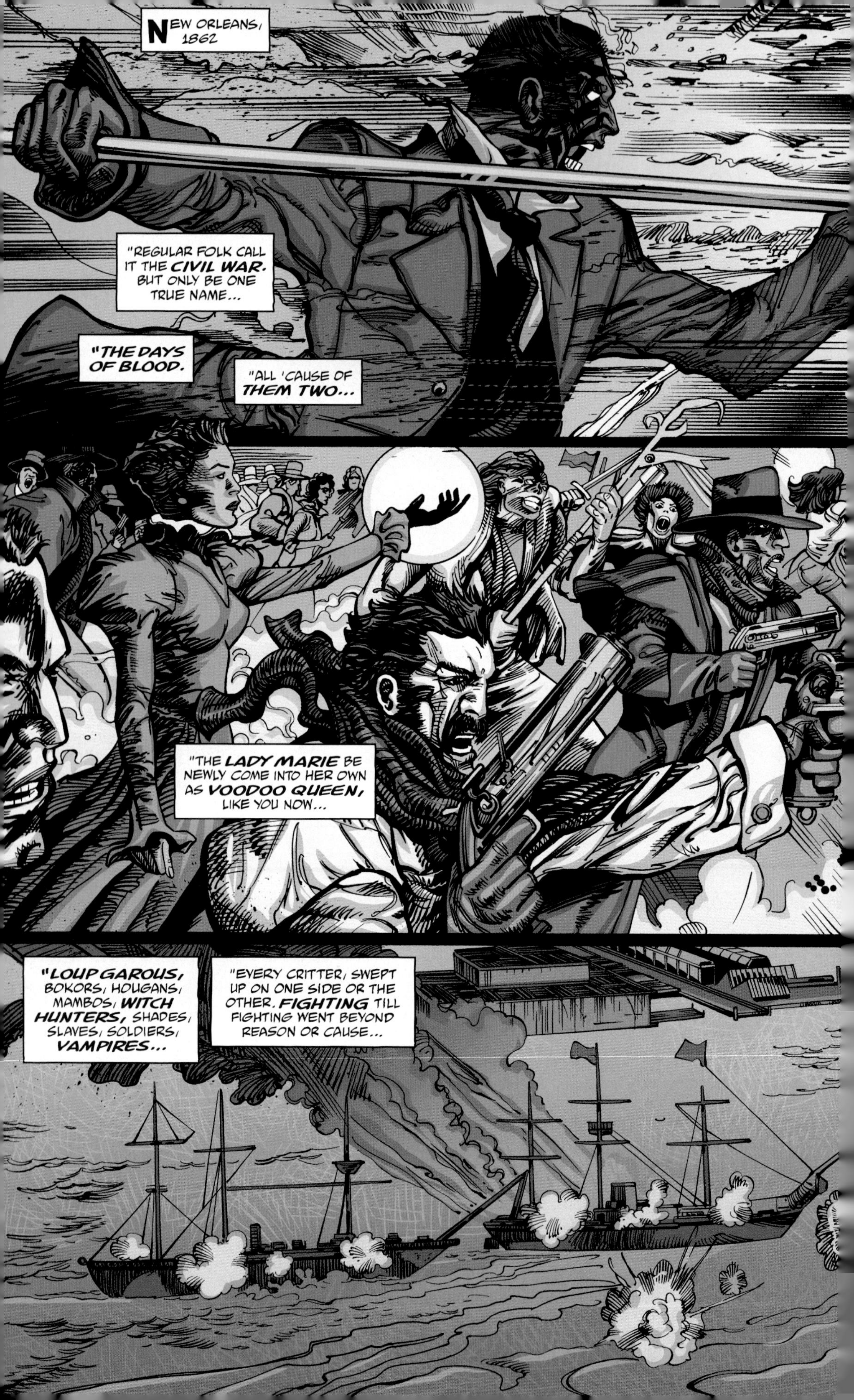
NEW ORLEANS, 1862
"REGULAR FOLK CALL IT THE CIVIL WAR. BUT ONLY BE ONE TRUE NAME...
"THE DAYS OF BLOOD.
"ALL 'CAUSE OF THEM TWO...
"THE LADY MARIE BE NEWLY COME INTO HER OWN AS VOODOO QUEEN, LIKE YOU NOW...
"LOUP GAROUS, BOKORS, HOUGANS, MAMBOS, WITCH HUNTERS, SHADES, SLAVES, SOLDIERS, VAMPIRES...
"EVERY CRITTER, SWEPT UP ON ONE SIDE OR THE OTHER. FIGHTING TILL FIGHTING WENT BEYOND REASON OR CAUSE...

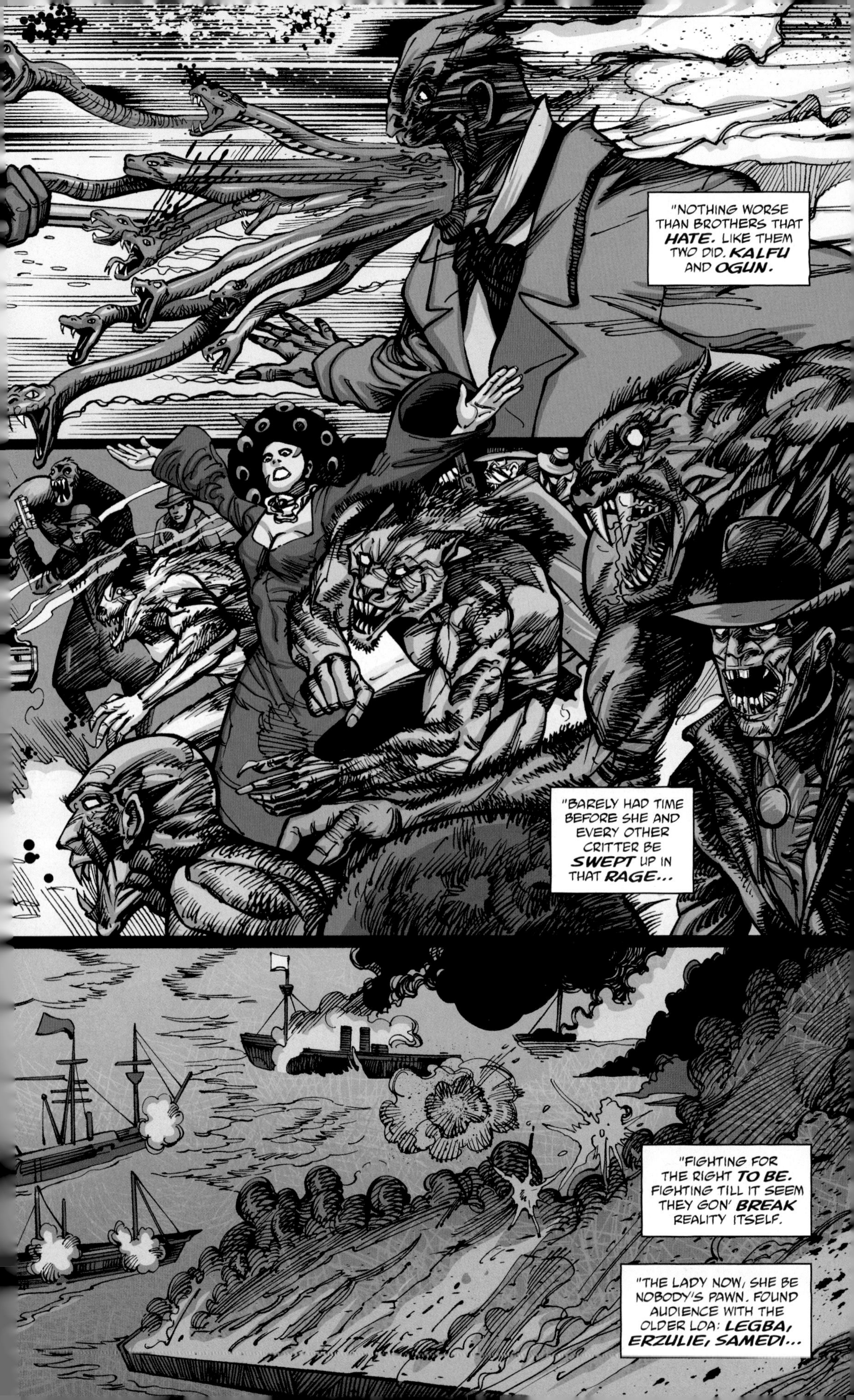
"NOTHING WORSE THAN BROTHERS THAT HATE. LIKE THEM TWO DID. KALFU AND OGUN.
"BARELY HAD TIME BEFORE SHE AND EVERY OTHER CRITTER BE SWEPT UP IN THAT RAGE...
"FIGHTING FOR THE RIGHT TO BE. FIGHTING TILL IT SEEM THEY GON' BREAK REALITY ITSELF.
"THE LADY NOW, SHE BE NOBODY'S PAWN. FOUND AUDIENCE WITH THE OLDER LOA: LEGBA, ERZULIE, SAMEDI...

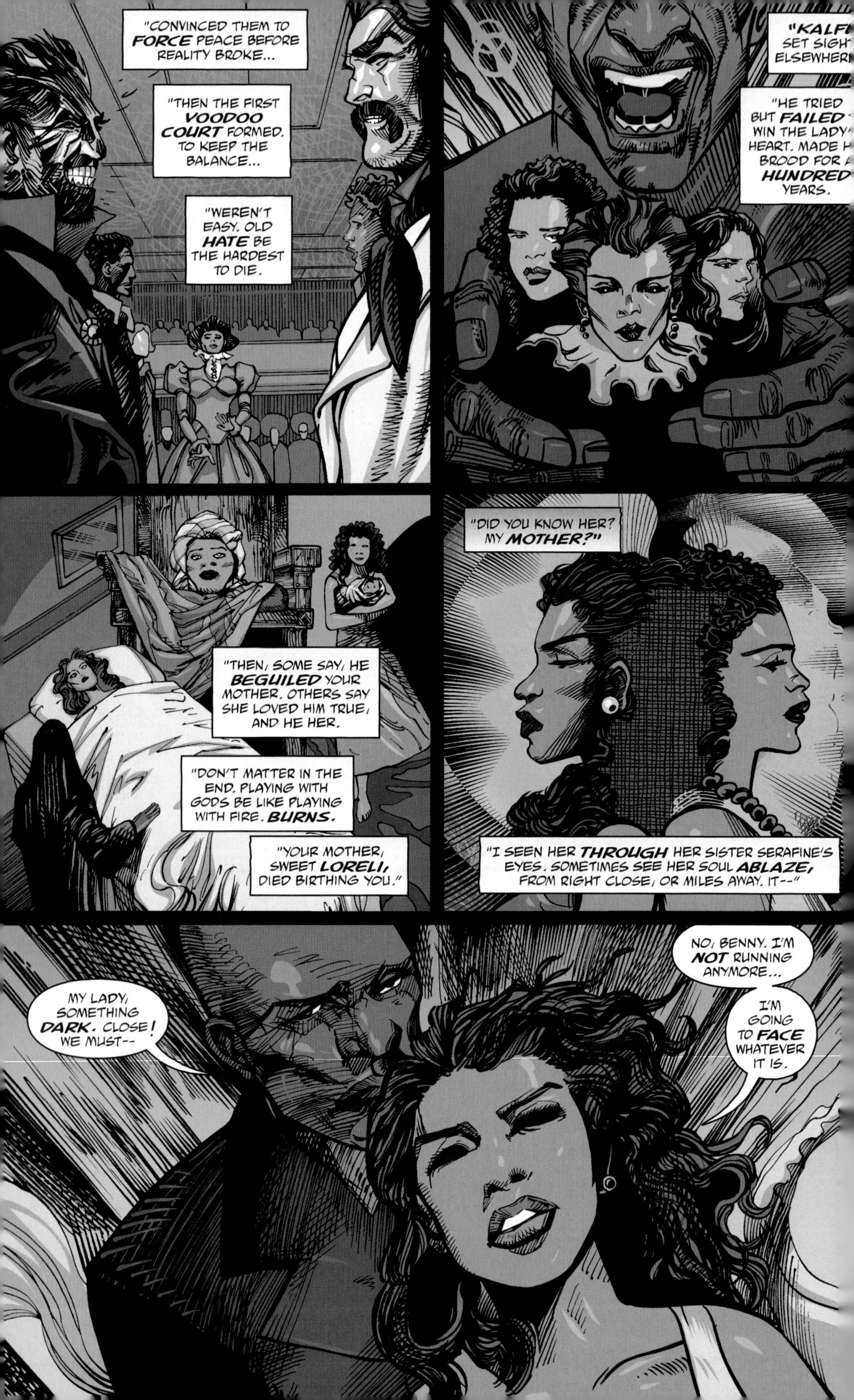
"CONVINCED THEM TO **FORCE** PEACE BEFORE REALITY BROKE...
"THEN THE FIRST **VOODOO COURT** FORMED. TO KEEP THE BALANCE...
"WEREN'T EASY. OLD **HATE** BE THE HARDEST TO DIE.
"HE TRIED BUT **FAILED** WIN THE LADY HEART. MADE H BROOD FOR A **HUNDRED** YEARS.
"THEN, SOME SAY, HE **BEGUILED** YOUR MOTHER. OTHERS SAY SHE LOVED HIM TRUE, AND HE HER.
"DON'T MATTER IN THE END. PLAYING WITH GODS BE LIKE PLAYING WITH FIRE. **BURNS.**
"YOUR MOTHER, SWEET **LORELI,** DIED BIRTHING YOU."
"DID YOU KNOW HER? MY **MOTHER?**"
"I SEEN HER **THROUGH** HER SISTER SERAFINE'S EYES. SOMETIMES SEE HER SOUL **ABLAZE,** FROM RIGHT CLOSE, OR MILES AWAY. IT--"
MY LADY, SOMETHING **DARK.** CLOSE! WE MUST--
NO, BENNY. I'M **NOT** RUNNING ANYMORE...
I'M GOING TO **FACE** WHATEVER IT IS.

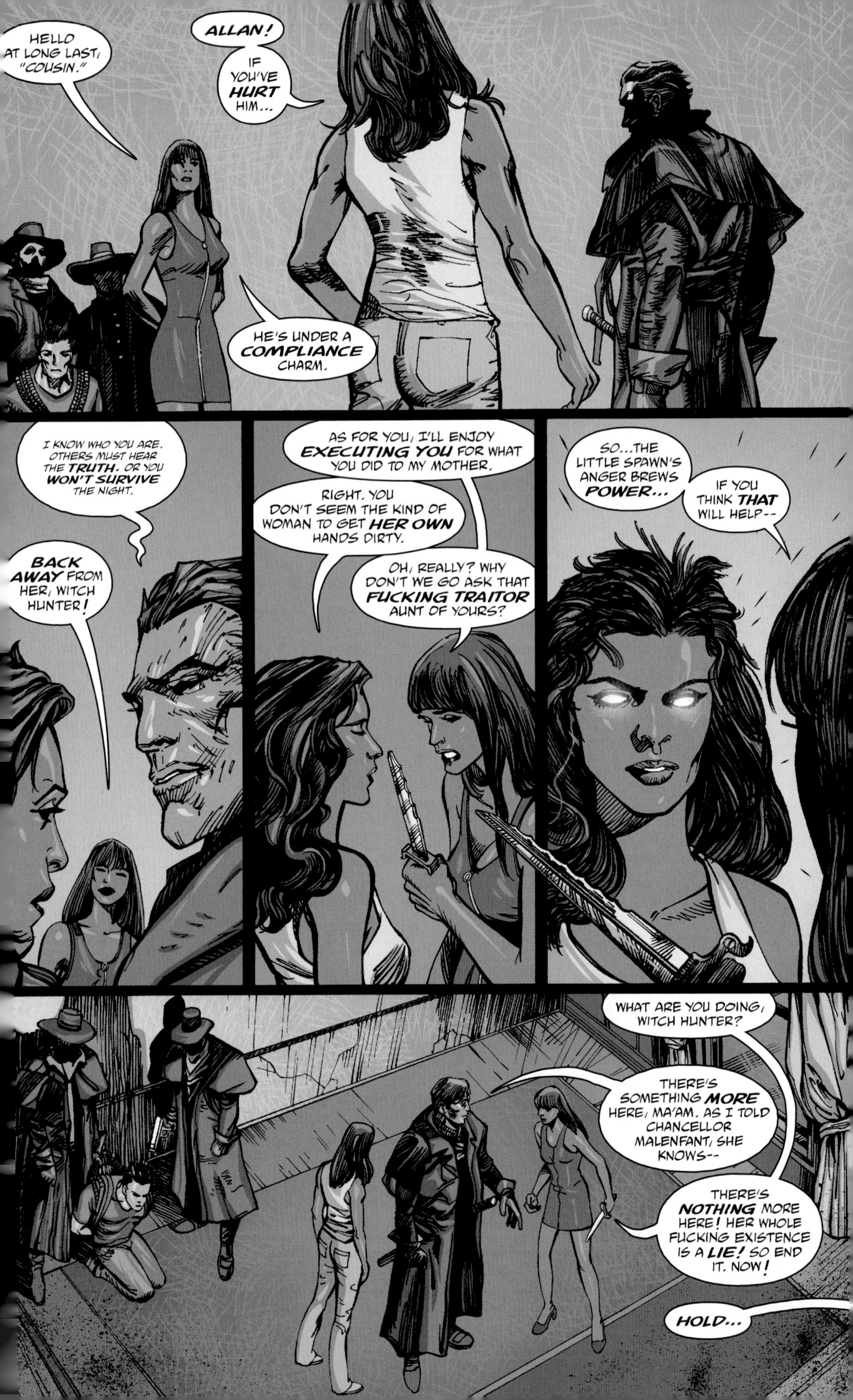
HELLO AT LONG LAST, "COUSIN."
ALLAN!
IF YOU'VE HURT HIM...
HE'S UNDER A COMPLIANCE CHARM.
I KNOW WHO YOU ARE. OTHERS MUST HEAR THE TRUTH. OR YOU WON'T SURVIVE THE NIGHT.
BACK AWAY FROM HER, WITCH HUNTER!
AS FOR YOU, I'LL ENJOY EXECUTING YOU FOR WHAT YOU DID TO MY MOTHER.
RIGHT. YOU DON'T SEEM THE KIND OF WOMAN TO GET HER OWN HANDS DIRTY.
OH, REALLY? WHY DON'T WE GO ASK THAT FUCKING TRAITOR AUNT OF YOURS?
SO...THE LITTLE SPAWN'S ANGER BREWS POWER...
IF YOU THINK THAT WILL HELP--
WHAT ARE YOU DOING, WITCH HUNTER?
THERE'S SOMETHING MORE HERE, MA'AM. AS I TOLD CHANCELLOR MALENFANT, SHE KNOWS--
THERE'S NOTHING MORE HERE! HER WHOLE FUCKING EXISTENCE IS A LIE! SO END IT. NOW!
HOLD...

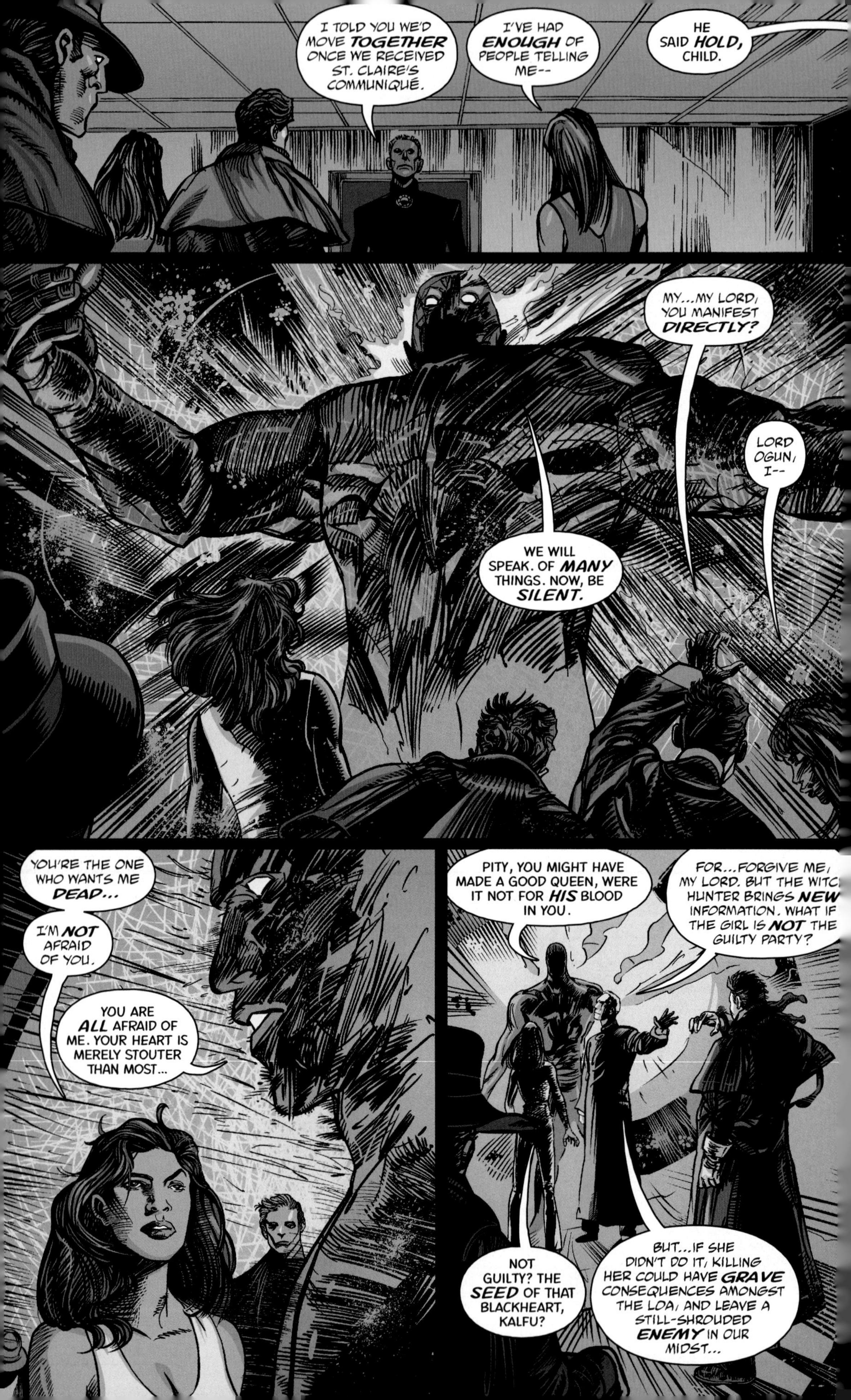
I TOLD YOU WE'D MOVE TOGETHER ONCE WE RECEIVED ST. CLAIRE'S COMMUNIQUÉ.
I'VE HAD ENOUGH OF PEOPLE TELLING ME--
HE SAID HOLD, CHILD.
MY...MY LORD, YOU MANIFEST DIRECTLY?
LORD OGUN, I--
WE WILL SPEAK. OF MANY THINGS. NOW, BE SILENT.
YOU'RE THE ONE WHO WANTS ME DEAD...
I'M NOT AFRAID OF YOU.
YOU ARE ALL AFRAID OF ME. YOUR HEART IS MERELY STOUTER THAN MOST...
PITY, YOU MIGHT HAVE MADE A GOOD QUEEN, WERE IT NOT FOR HIS BLOOD IN YOU.
FOR...FORGIVE ME, MY LORD. BUT THE WITCH HUNTER BRINGS NEW INFORMATION. WHAT IF THE GIRL IS NOT THE GUILTY PARTY?
NOT GUILTY? THE SEED OF THAT BLACKHEART, KALFU?
BUT...IF SHE DIDN'T DO IT, KILLING HER COULD HAVE GRAVE CONSEQUENCES AMONGST THE LOA, AND LEAVE A STILL-SHROUDED ENEMY IN OUR MIDST...

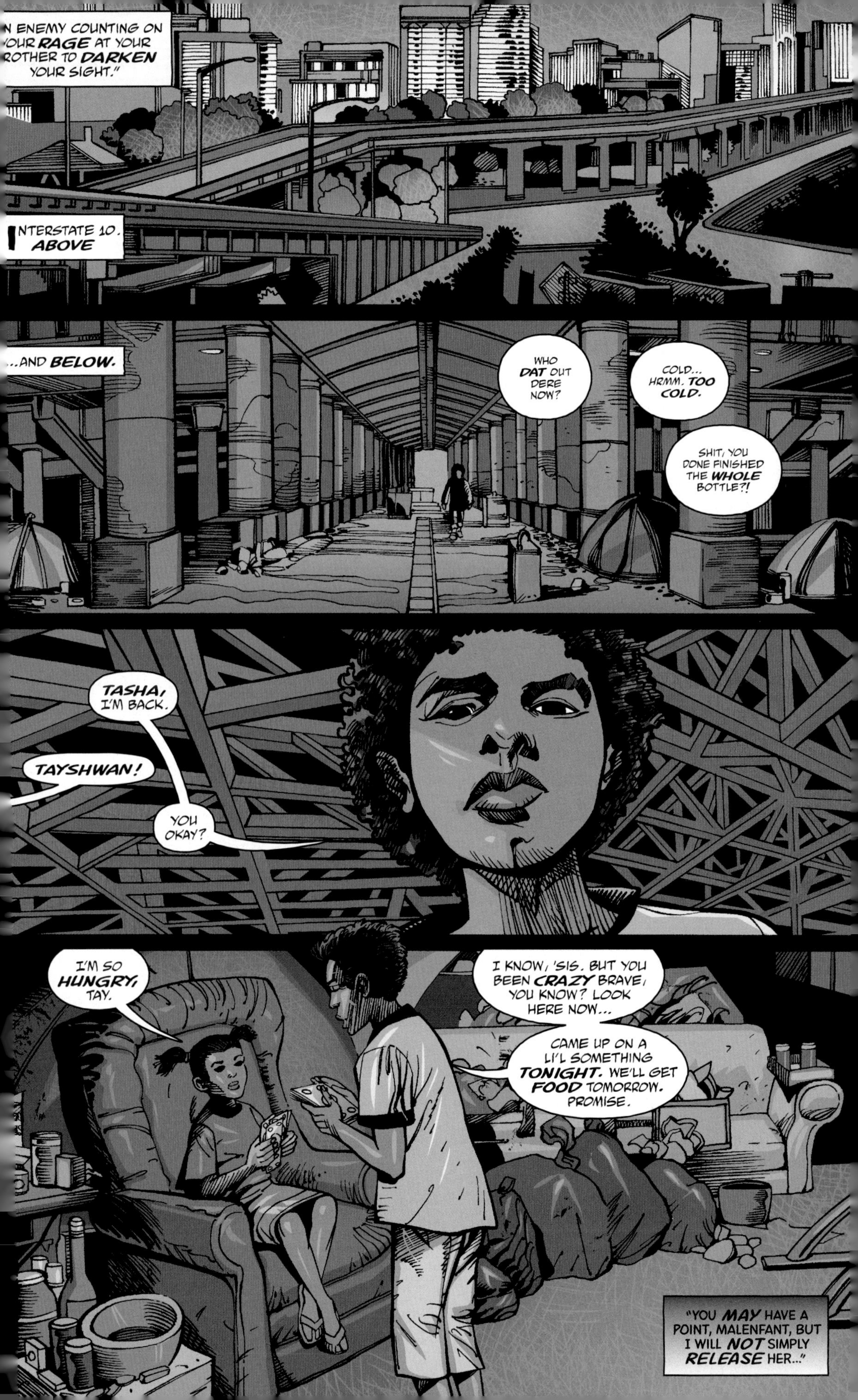

N ENEMY COUNTING ON YOUR RAGE AT YOUR ROTHER TO DARKEN YOUR SIGHT."
NTERSTATE 10. ABOVE
...AND BELOW.
WHO DAT OUT DERE NOW?
COLD... HRMM. TOO COLD.
SHIT, YOU DONE FINISHED THE WHOLE BOTTLE?!
TASHA, I'M BACK.
TAYSHWAN!
YOU OKAY?
I'M SO HUNGRY, TAY.
I KNOW, 'SIS. BUT YOU BEEN CRAZY BRAVE, YOU KNOW? LOOK HERE NOW...
CAME UP ON A LI'L SOMETHING TONIGHT. WE'LL GET FOOD TOMORROW. PROMISE.
"YOU MAY HAVE A POINT, MALENFANT, BUT I WILL NOT SIMPLY RELEASE HER..."

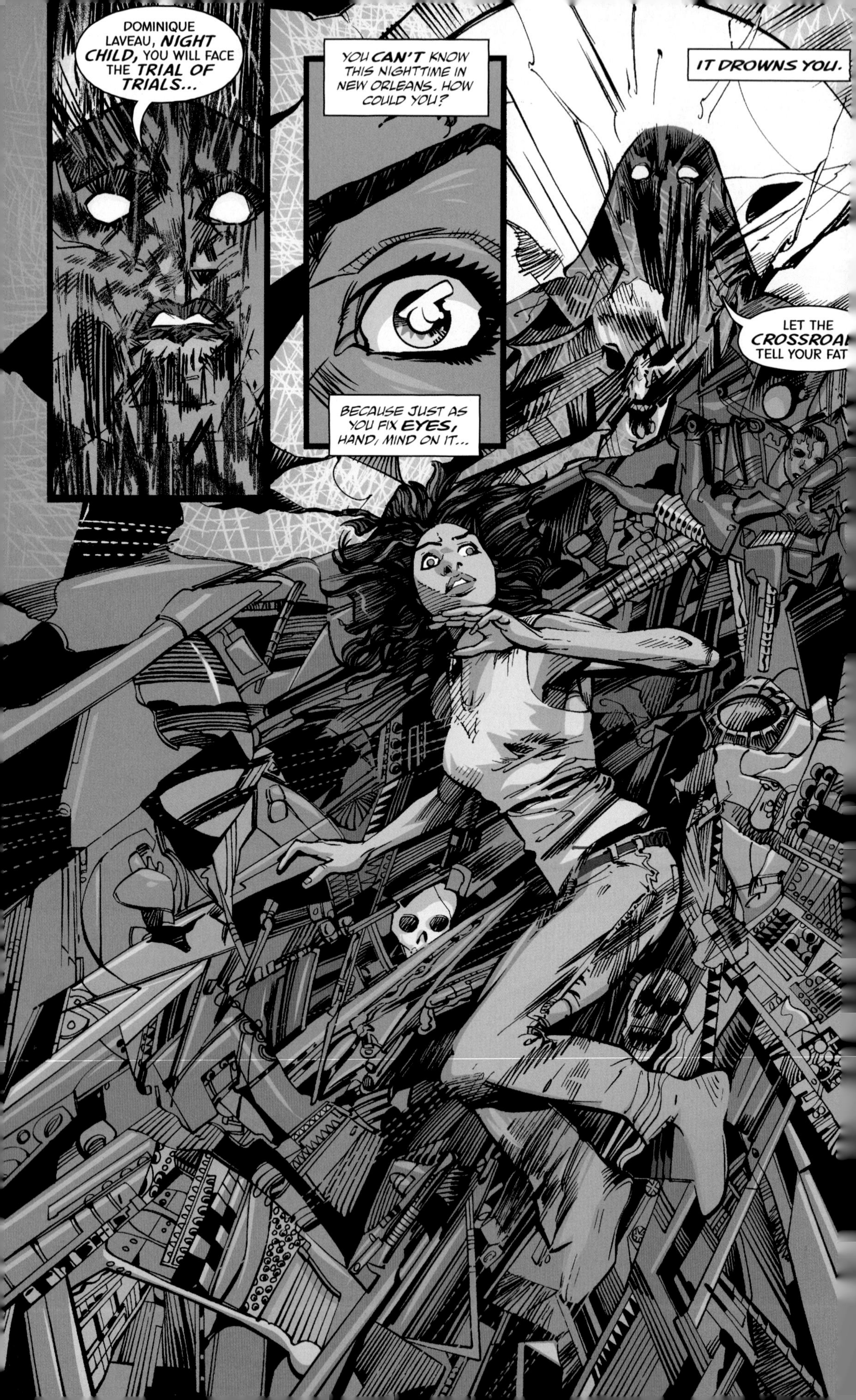
DOMINIQUE LAVEAU, NIGHT CHILD, YOU WILL FACE THE TRIAL OF TRIALS...
YOU CAN'T KNOW THIS NIGHTTIME IN NEW ORLEANS. HOW COULD YOU?
BECAUSE JUST AS YOU FIX EYES, HAND, MIND ON IT...
IT DROWNS YOU.
LET THE CROSSROA
TELL YOUR FAT

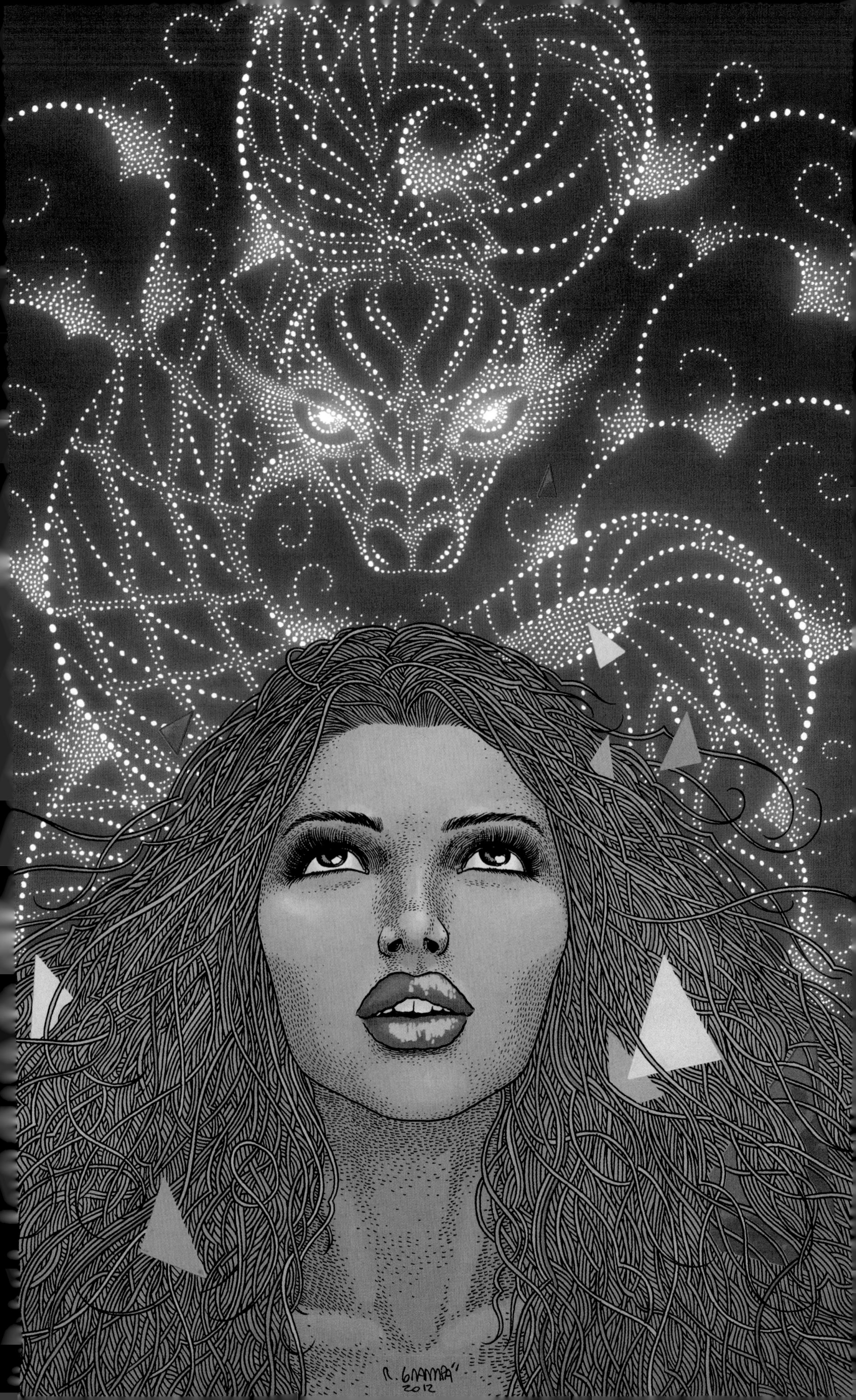
R. GRAMPÁ
2012

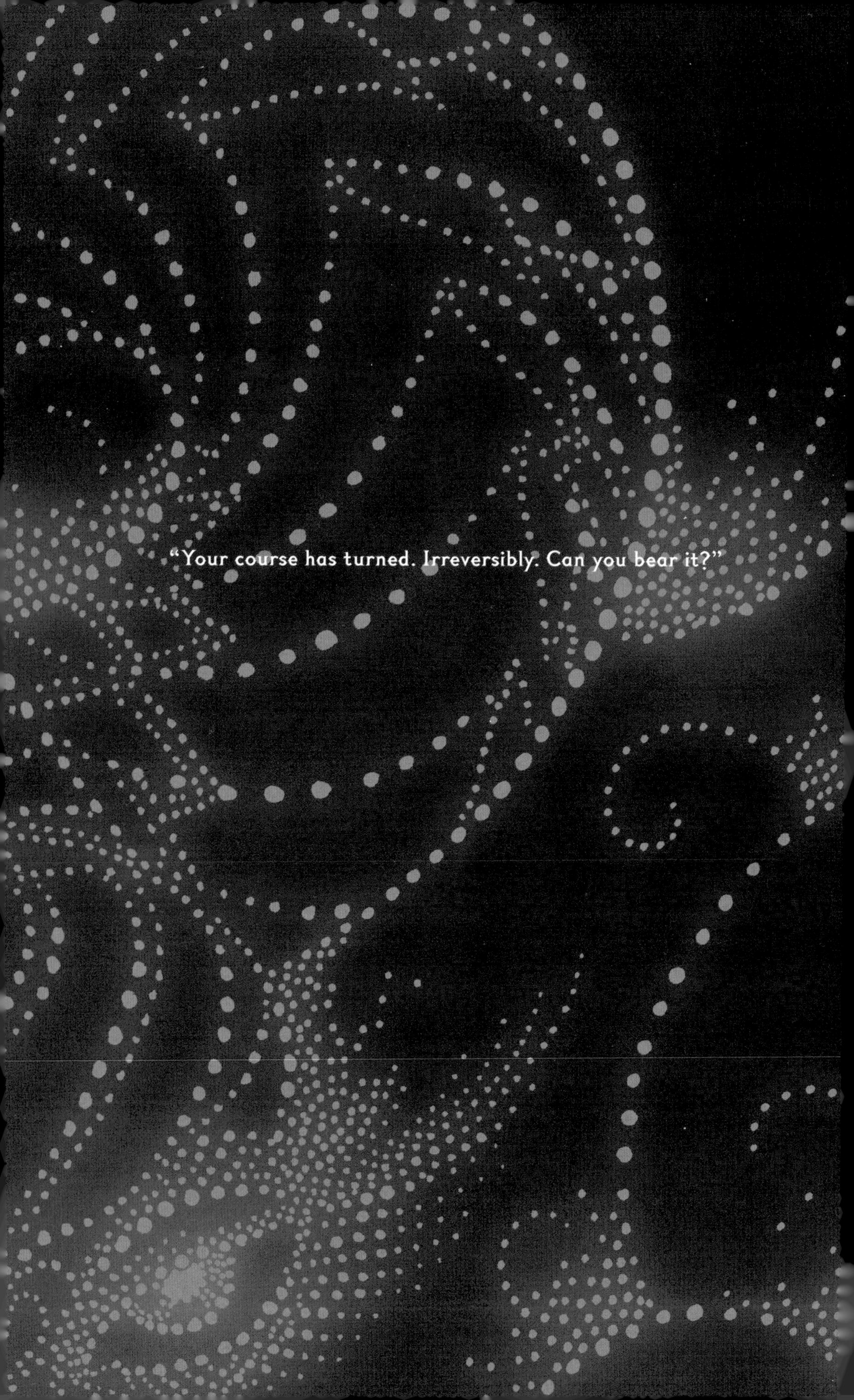
"Your course has turned. Irreversibly. Can you bear it?"

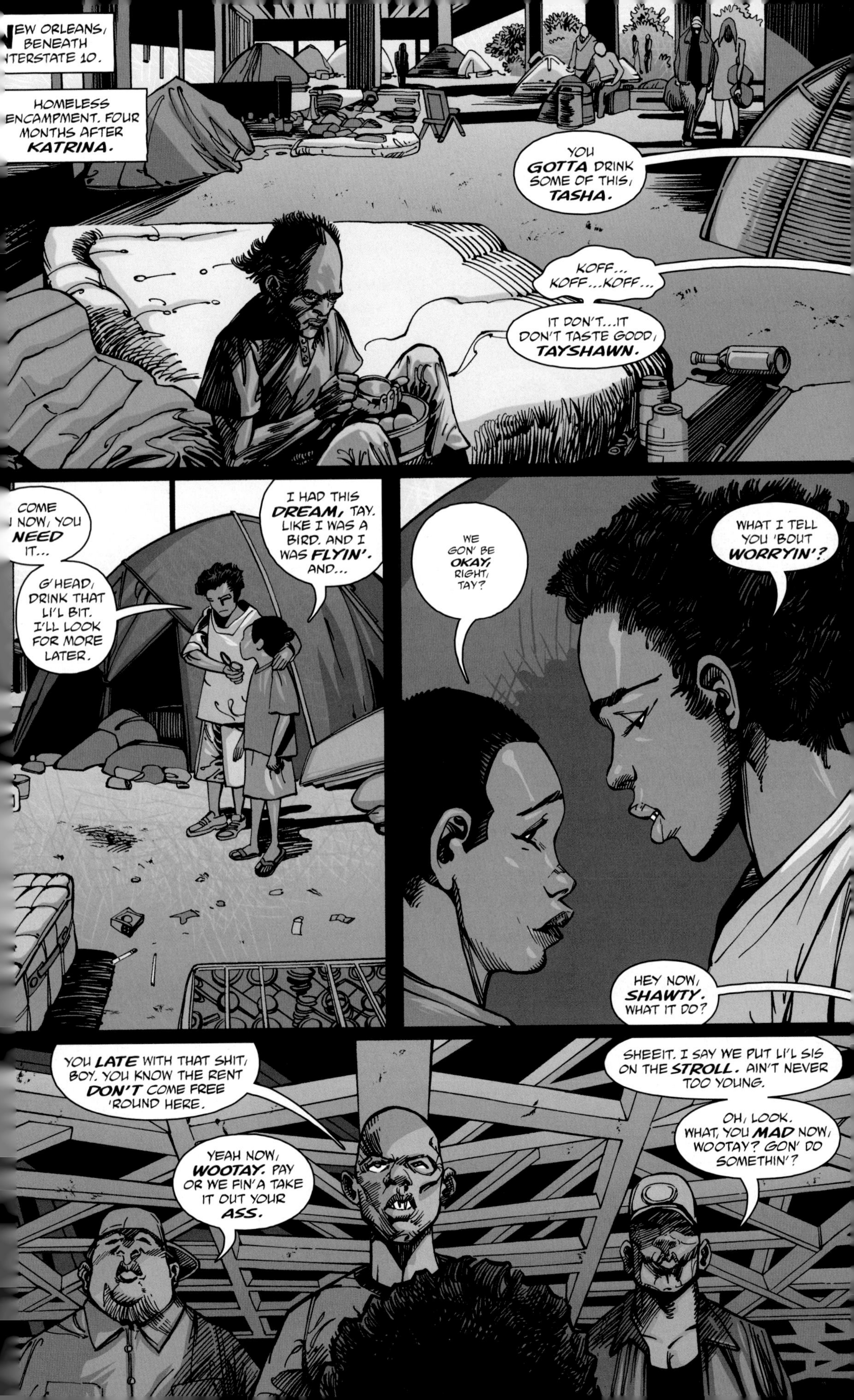

NEW ORLEANS, BENEATH INTERSTATE 10.
HOMELESS ENCAMPMENT. FOUR MONTHS AFTER KATRINA.
YOU GOTTA DRINK SOME OF THIS, TASHA.
KOFF... KOFF...KOFF...
IT DON'T...IT DON'T TASTE GOOD, TAYSHAWN.
COME ON NOW, YOU NEED IT...
G'HEAD, DRINK THAT LI'L BIT. I'LL LOOK FOR MORE LATER.
I HAD THIS DREAM, TAY. LIKE I WAS A BIRD. AND I WAS FLYIN'. AND...
WE GON' BE OKAY, RIGHT, TAY?
WHAT I TELL YOU 'BOUT WORRYIN'?
HEY NOW, SHAWTY. WHAT IT DO?
YOU LATE WITH THAT SHIT, BOY. YOU KNOW THE RENT DON'T COME FREE 'ROUND HERE.
YEAH NOW, WOOTAY. PAY OR WE FIN'A TAKE IT OUT YOUR ASS.
SHEEIT. I SAY WE PUT LI'L SIS ON THE STROLL. AIN'T NEVER TOO YOUNG.
OH, LOOK. WHAT, YOU MAD NOW, WOOTAY? GON' DO SOMETHIN'?

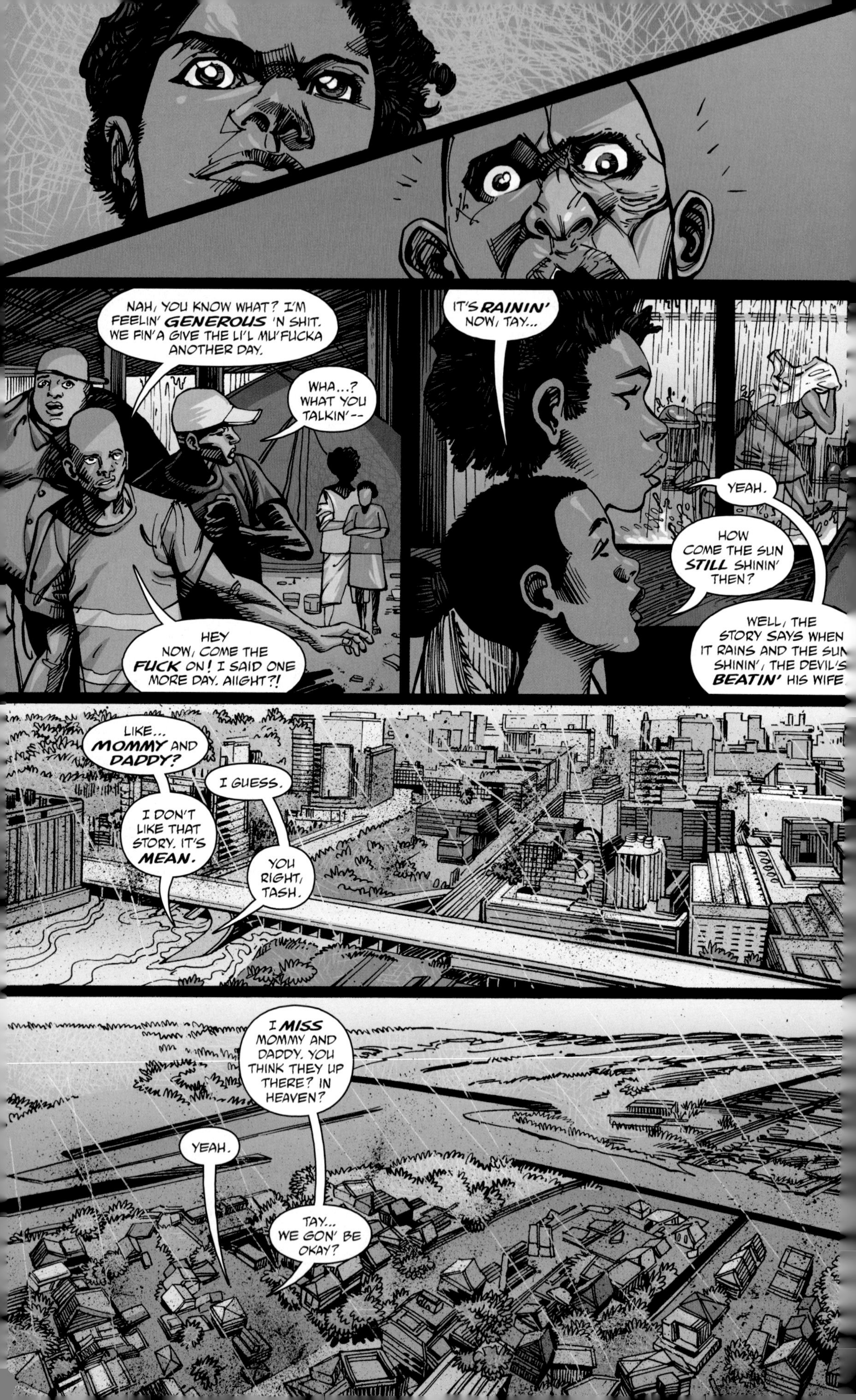
NAH, YOU KNOW WHAT? I'M FEELIN' GENEROUS 'N SHIT. WE FIN'A GIVE THE LI'L MU'FUCKA ANOTHER DAY.
WHA...? WHAT YOU TALKIN'--
HEY NOW, COME THE FUCK ON! I SAID ONE MORE DAY. AIIGHT?!
IT'S RAININ' NOW, TAY...
YEAH.
HOW COME THE SUN STILL SHININ' THEN?
WELL, THE STORY SAYS WHEN IT RAINS AND THE SUN SHININ', THE DEVIL'S BEATIN' HIS WIFE.
LIKE... MOMMY AND DADDY?
I GUESS.
I DON'T LIKE THAT STORY. IT'S MEAN.
YOU RIGHT, TASH.
I MISS MOMMY AND DADDY. YOU THINK THEY UP THERE? IN HEAVEN?
YEAH.
TAY... WE GON' BE OKAY?

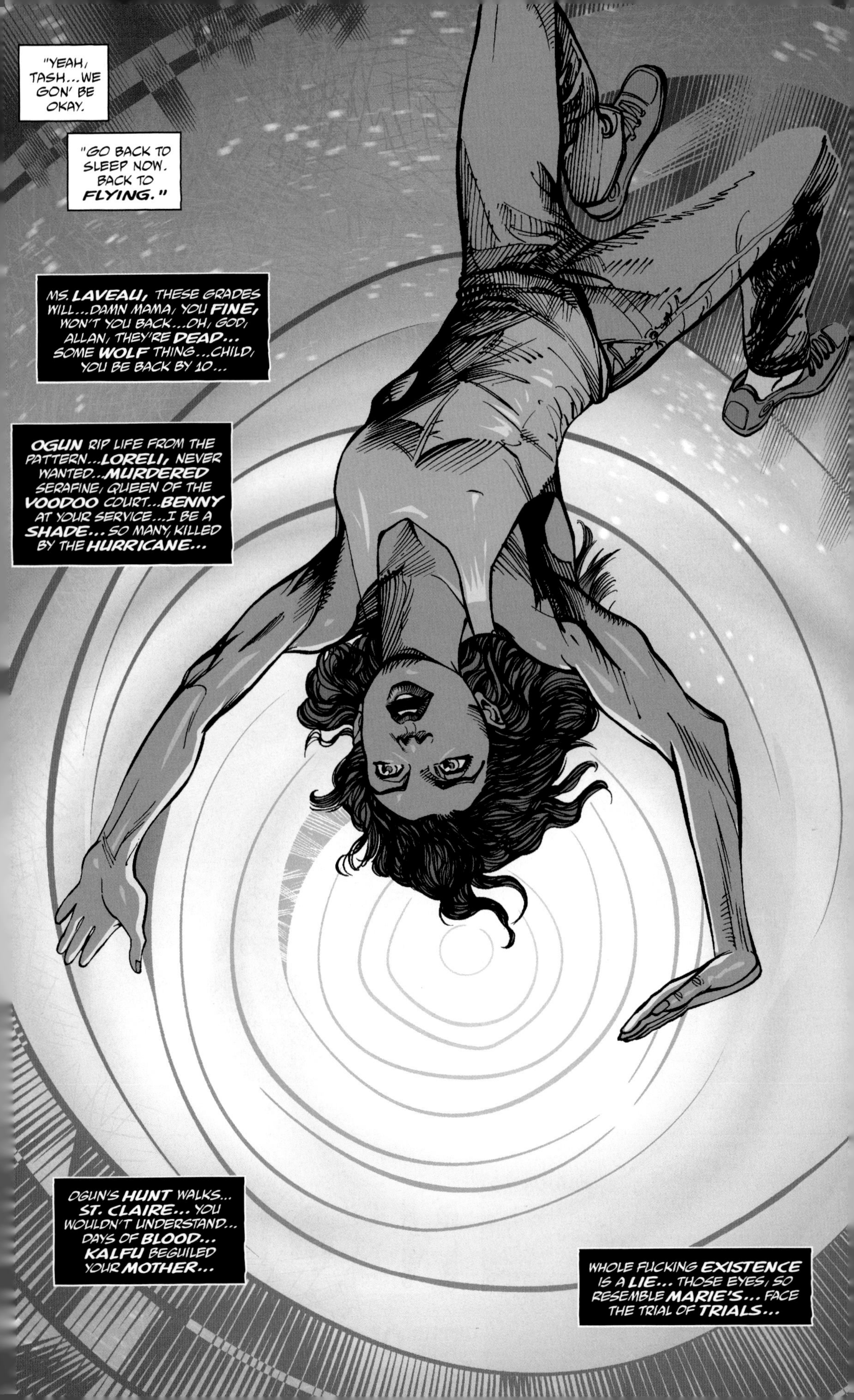
"YEAH, TASH...WE GON' BE OKAY.
"GO BACK TO SLEEP NOW. BACK TO FLYING."
MS. LAVEAU, THESE GRADES WILL...DAMN MAMA, YOU FINE, WON'T YOU BACK...OH, GOD, ALLAN, THEY'RE DEAD... SOME WOLF THING...CHILD, YOU BE BACK BY 10...
OGUN RIP LIFE FROM THE PATTERN...LORELI, NEVER WANTED...MURDERED SERAFINE, QUEEN OF THE VOODOO COURT...BENNY AT YOUR SERVICE...I BE A SHADE...SO MANY, KILLED BY THE HURRICANE...
OGUN'S HUNT WALKS... ST. CLAIRE... YOU WOULDN'T UNDERSTAND... DAYS OF BLOOD... KALFU BEGUILED YOUR MOTHER...
WHOLE FUCKING EXISTENCE IS A LIE... THOSE EYES, SO RESEMBLE MARIE'S... FACE THE TRIAL OF TRIALS...

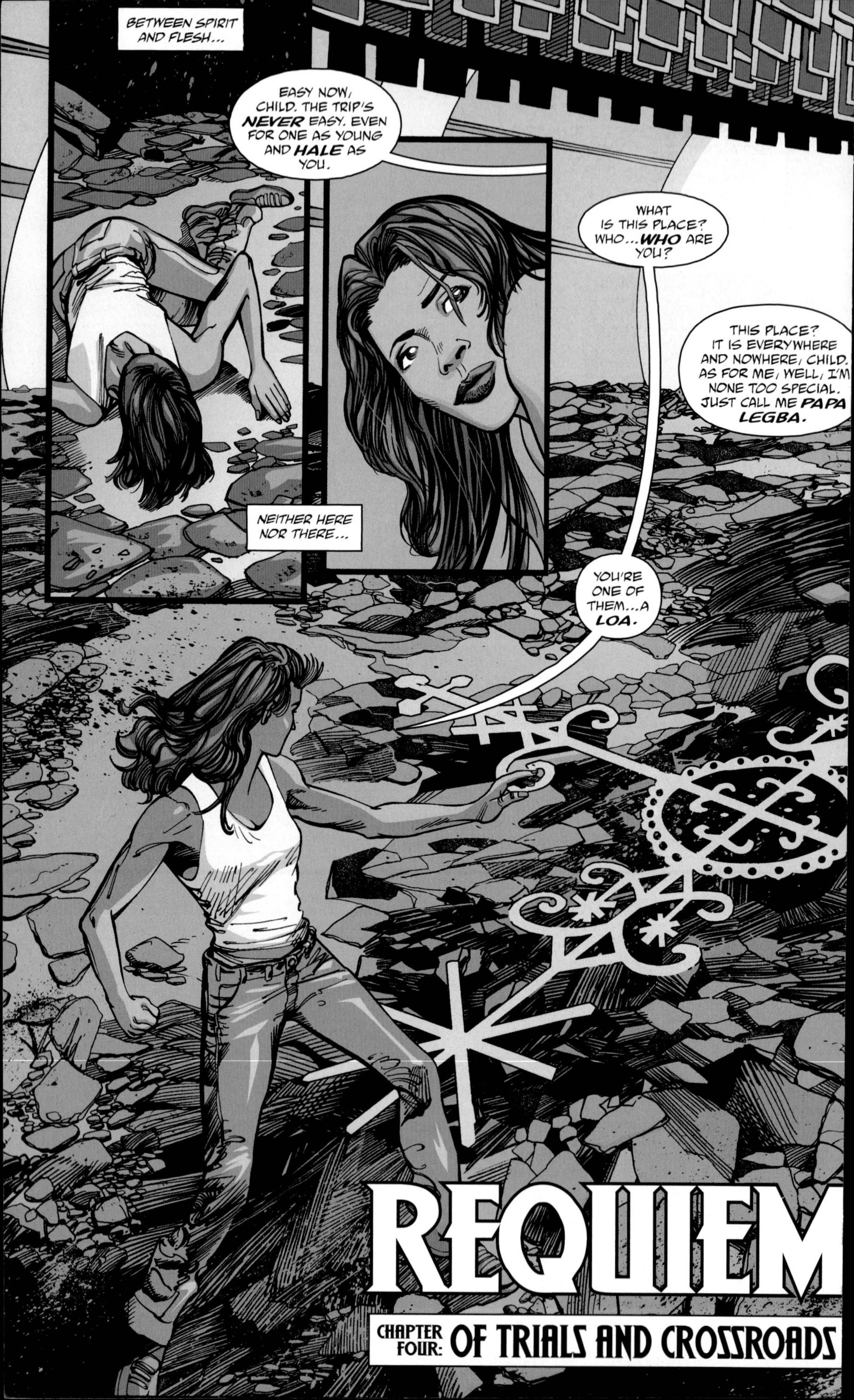
BETWEEN SPIRIT AND FLESH...
EASY NOW, CHILD. THE TRIP'S NEVER EASY. EVEN FOR ONE AS YOUNG AND HALE AS YOU.
NEITHER HERE NOR THERE...
WHAT IS THIS PLACE? WHO...WHO ARE YOU?
THIS PLACE? IT IS EVERYWHERE AND NOWHERE, CHILD. AS FOR ME, WELL, I'M NONE TOO SPECIAL. JUST CALL ME PAPA LEGBA.
YOU'RE ONE OF THEM...A LOA.
REQUIEM
CHAPTER FOUR: OF TRIALS AND CROSSROADS

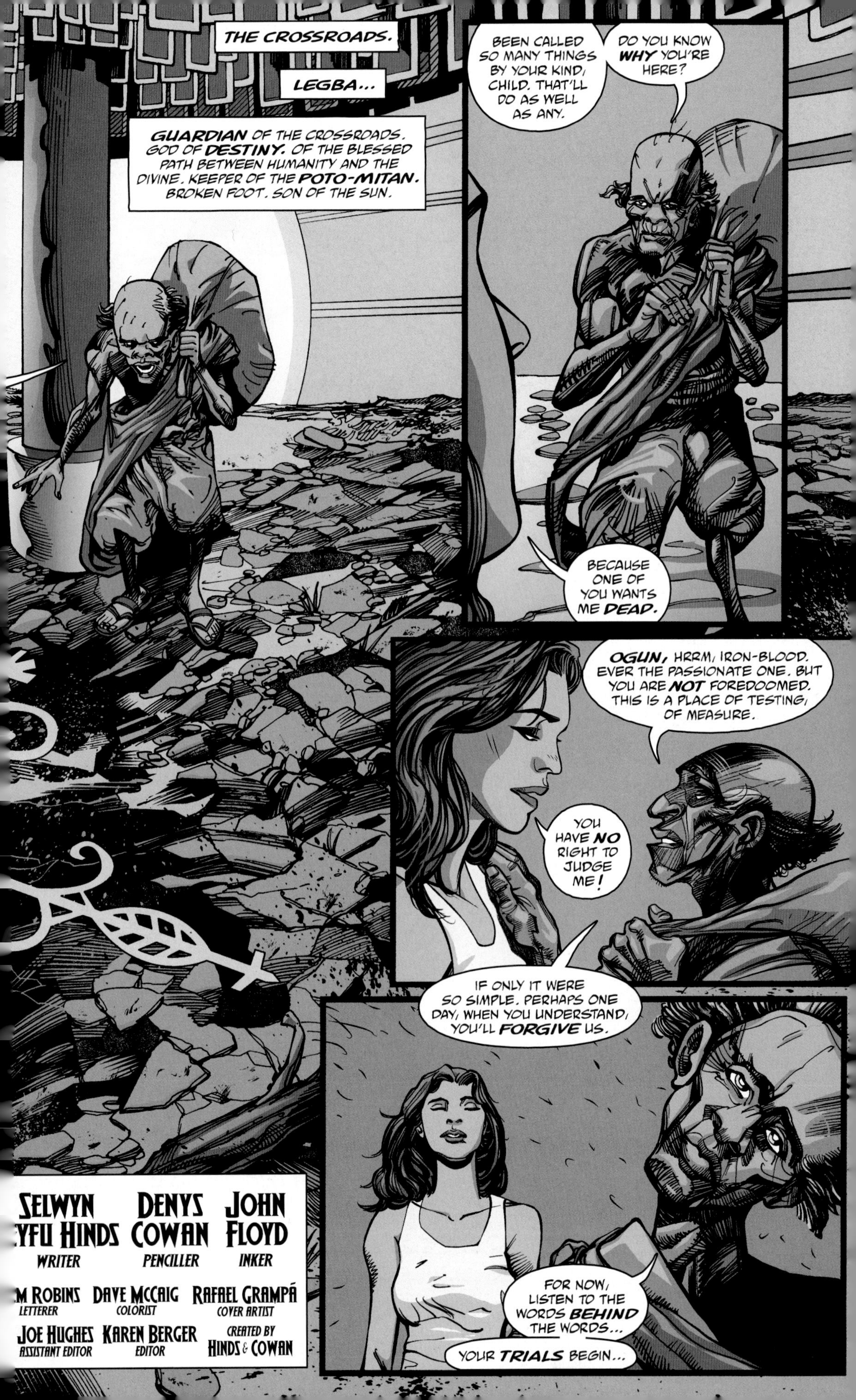
THE CROSSROADS.
LEGBA...
GUARDIAN OF THE CROSSROADS. GOD OF DESTINY. OF THE BLESSED PATH BETWEEN HUMANITY AND THE DIVINE. KEEPER OF THE POTO-MITAN. BROKEN FOOT. SON OF THE SUN.
BEEN CALLED SO MANY THINGS BY YOUR KIND, CHILD. THAT'LL DO AS WELL AS ANY.
DO YOU KNOW WHY YOU'RE HERE?
BECAUSE ONE OF YOU WANTS ME DEAD.
OGUN, HRRM, IRON-BLOOD. EVER THE PASSIONATE ONE. BUT YOU ARE NOT FOREDOOMED. THIS IS A PLACE OF TESTING, OF MEASURE.
YOU HAVE NO RIGHT TO JUDGE ME!
IF ONLY IT WERE SO SIMPLE. PERHAPS ONE DAY, WHEN YOU UNDERSTAND, YOU'LL FORGIVE US.
FOR NOW, LISTEN TO THE WORDS BEHIND THE WORDS...
YOUR TRIALS BEGIN...
SELWYN
YFU HINDS
WRITER
DENYS COWAN
PENCILLER
JOHN FLOYD
INKER
M ROBINS
LETTERER
DAVE McCAIG
COLORIST
RAFAEL GRAMPÁ
COVER ARTIST
JOE HUGHES
ASSISTANT EDITOR
KAREN BERGER
EDITOR
CREATED BY
HINDS & COWAN

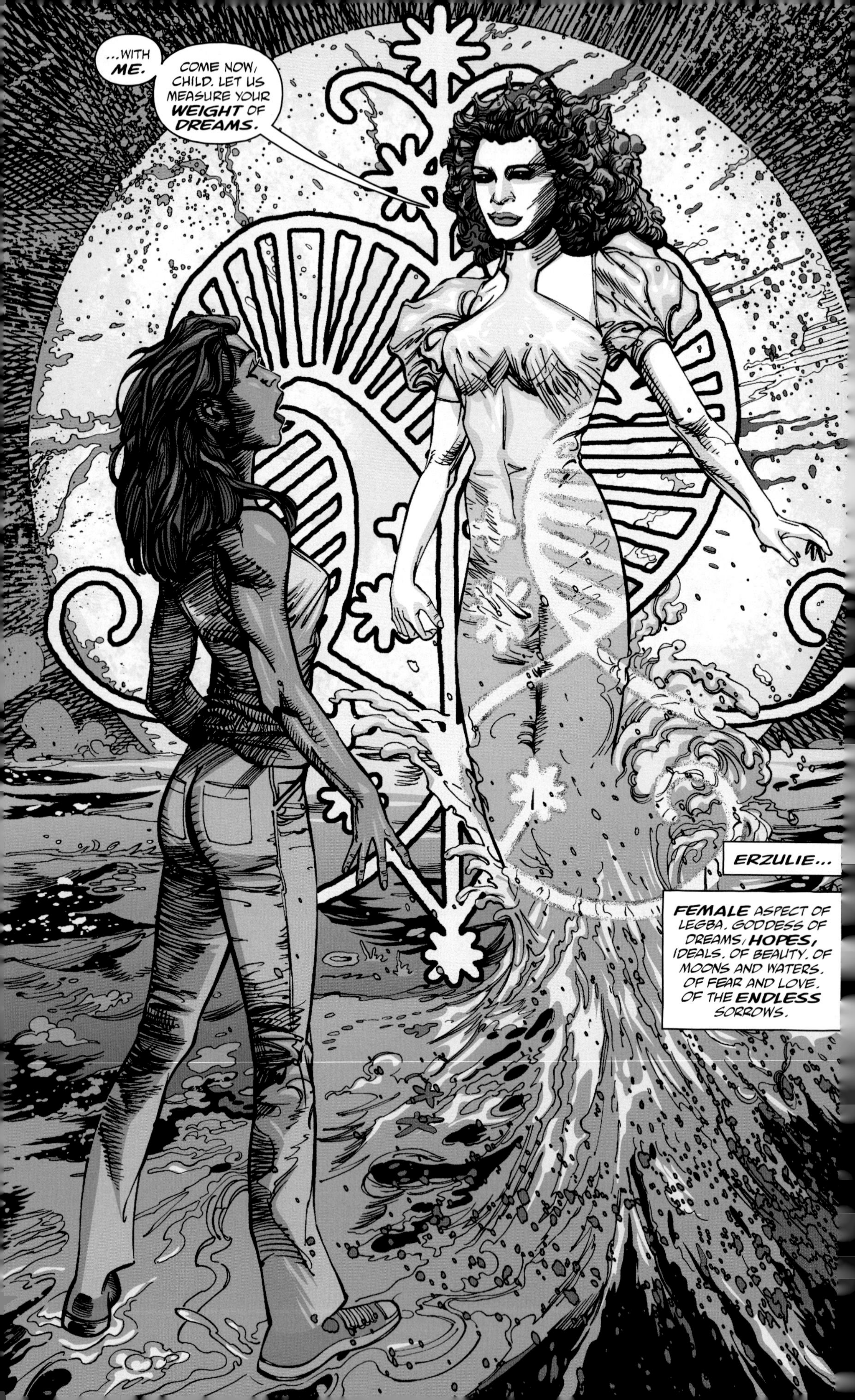
...WITH ME.
COME NOW, CHILD. LET US MEASURE YOUR WEIGHT OF DREAMS.
ERZULIE...
FEMALE ASPECT OF LEGBA. GODDESS OF DREAMS, HOPES, IDEALS. OF BEAUTY. OF MOONS AND WATERS. OF FEAR AND LOVE. OF THE ENDLESS SORROWS.

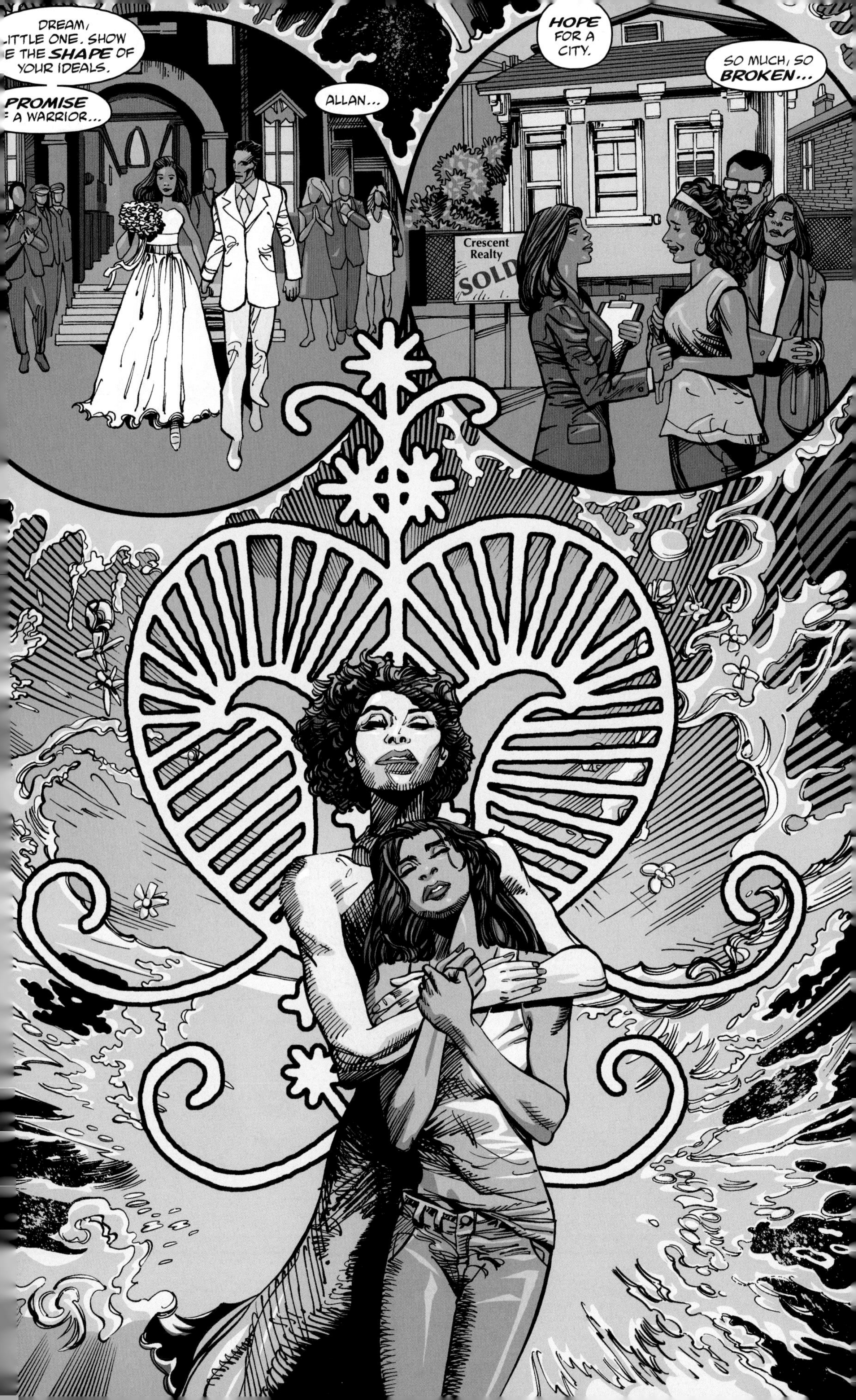
DREAM, LITTLE ONE. SHOW E THE SHAPE OF YOUR IDEALS.
PROMISE F A WARRIOR...
ALLAN...
HOPE FOR A CITY.
SO MUCH, SO BROKEN...
Crescent Realty
SOLD

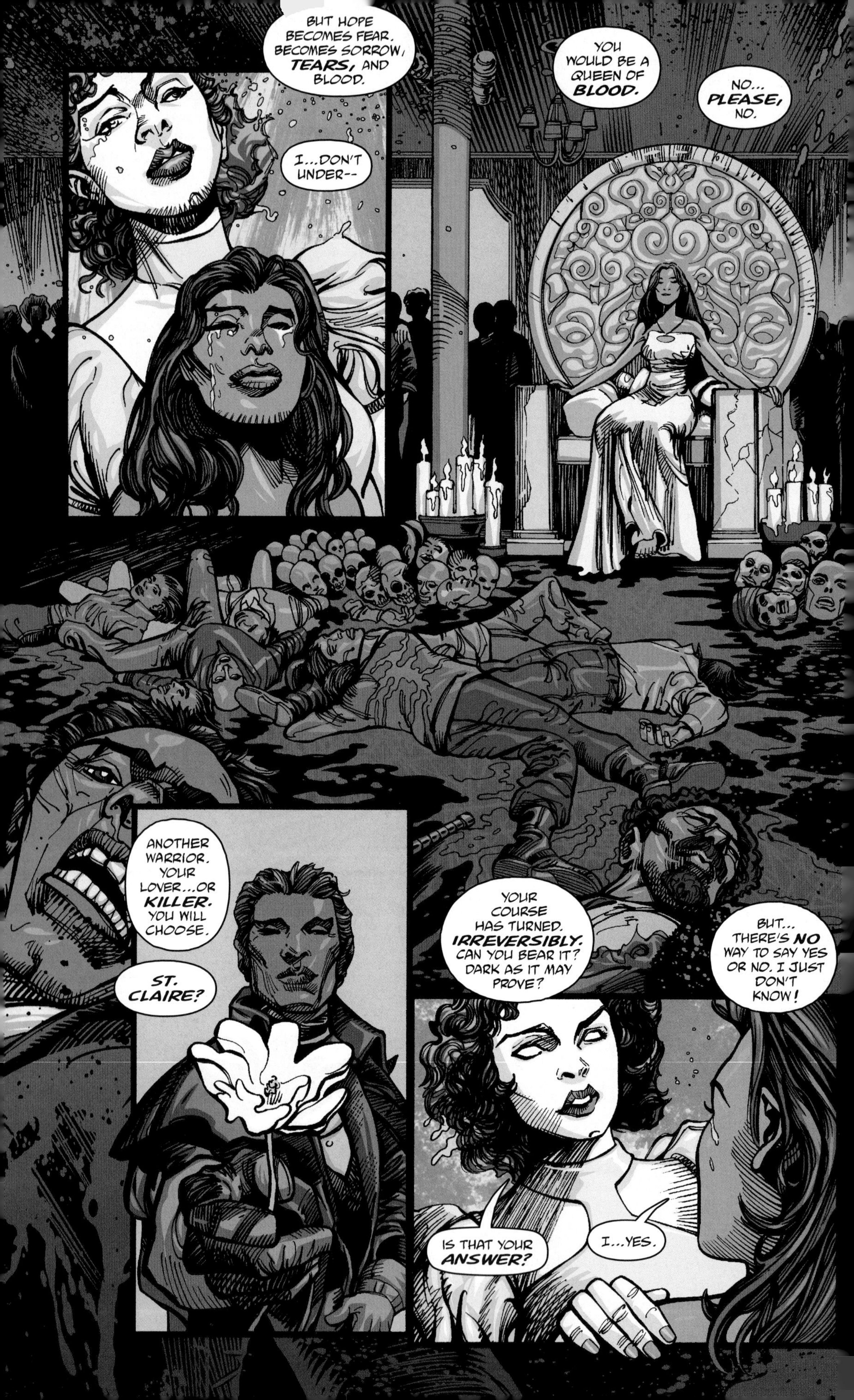
BUT HOPE BECOMES FEAR, BECOMES SORROW, **TEARS,** AND BLOOD.
I...DON'T UNDER--
YOU WOULD BE A QUEEN OF **BLOOD.**
NO... **PLEASE,** NO.
ANOTHER WARRIOR. YOUR LOVER...OR **KILLER.** YOU WILL CHOOSE.
ST. CLAIRE?
YOUR COURSE HAS TURNED. **IRREVERSIBLY.** CAN YOU BEAR IT? DARK AS IT MAY PROVE?
BUT... THERE'S **NO** WAY TO SAY YES OR NO. I JUST DON'T KNOW!
IS THAT YOUR **ANSWER?**
I...YES.

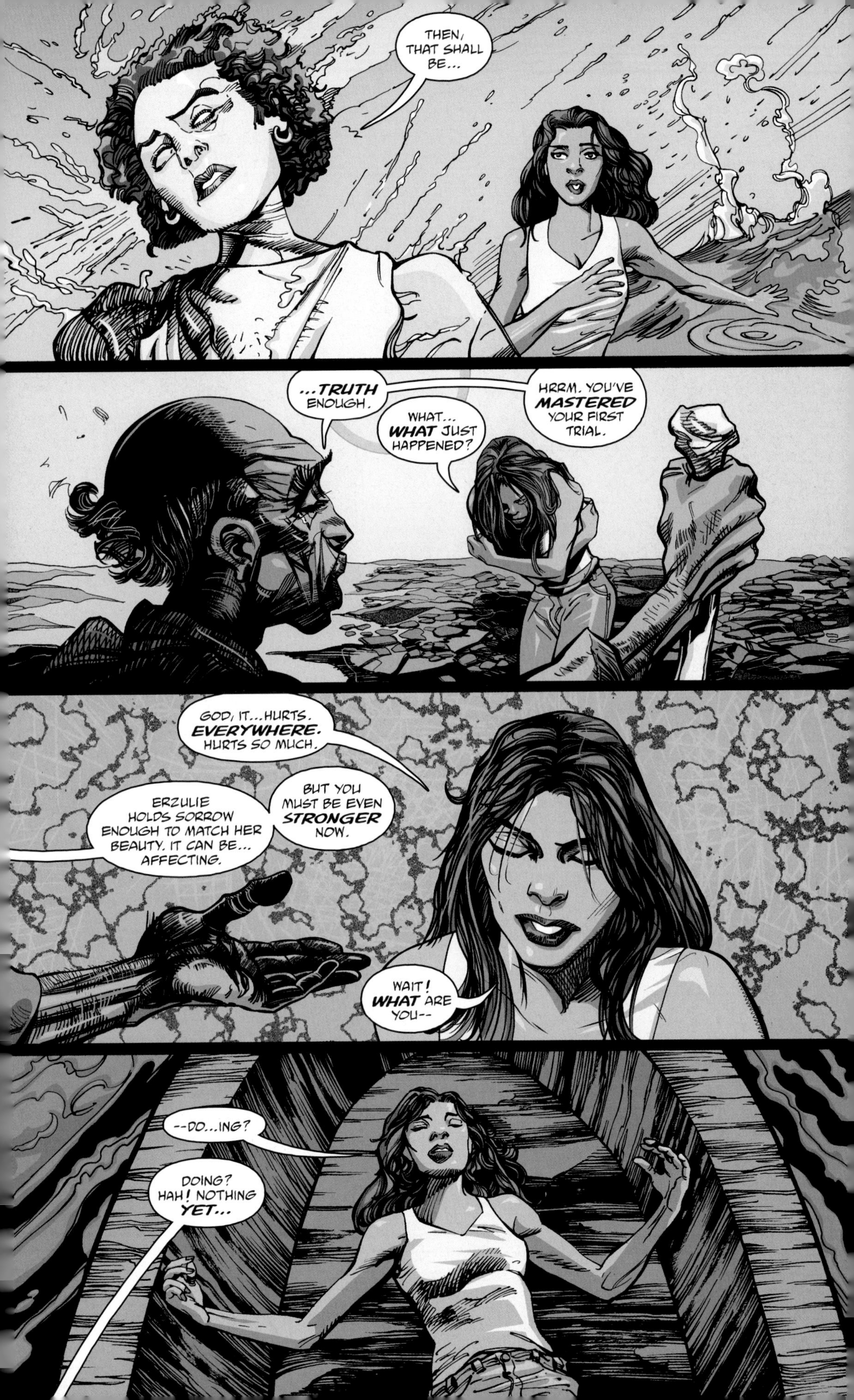
THEN, THAT SHALL BE...
...TRUTH ENOUGH.
HRRM. YOU'VE MASTERED YOUR FIRST TRIAL.
WHAT... WHAT JUST HAPPENED?
GOD, IT...HURTS. EVERYWHERE. HURTS SO MUCH.
ERZULIE HOLDS SORROW ENOUGH TO MATCH HER BEAUTY. IT CAN BE... AFFECTING.
BUT YOU MUST BE EVEN STRONGER NOW.
WAIT! WHAT ARE YOU--
--DO...ING?
DOING? HAH! NOTHING YET...

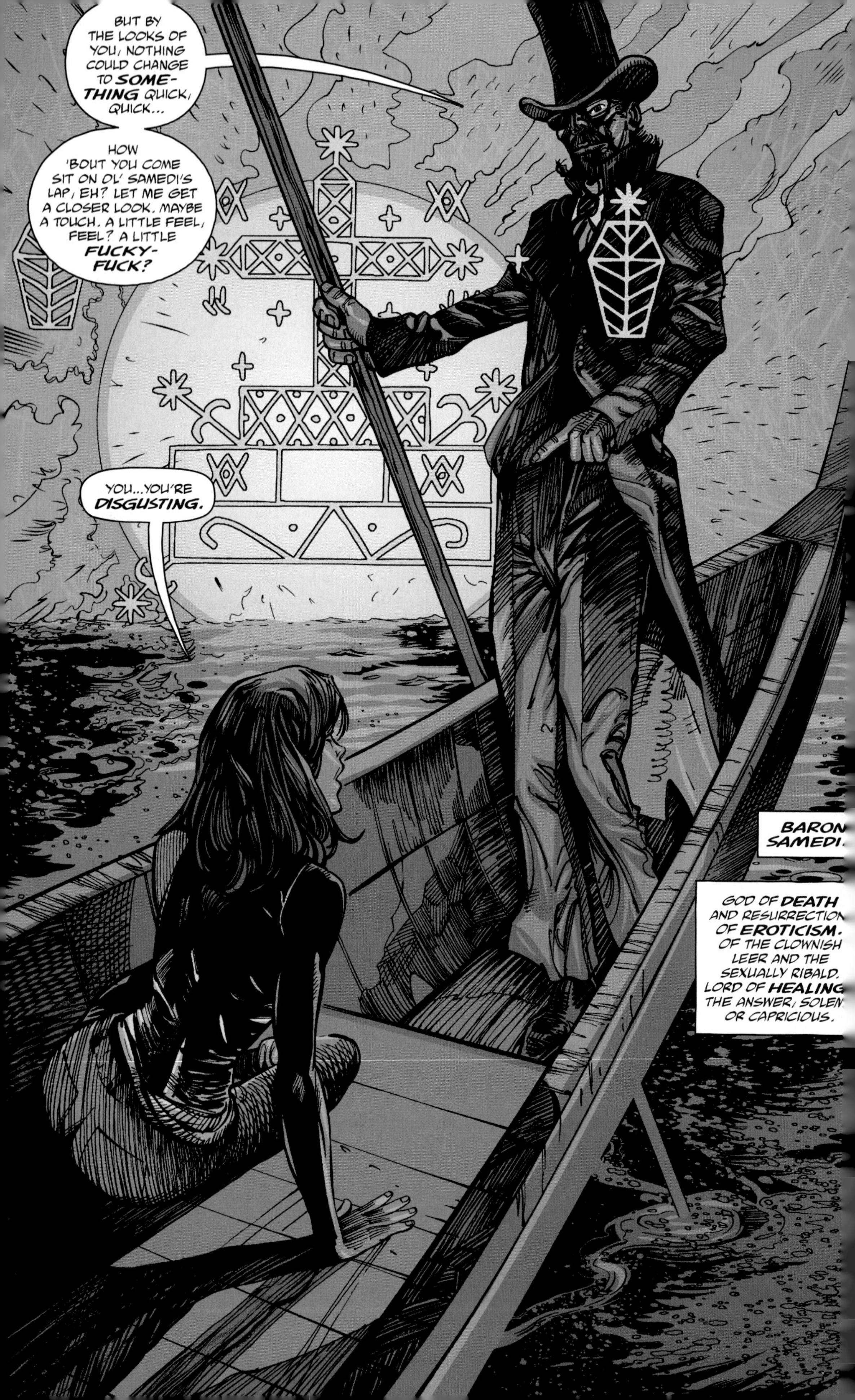

BUT BY THE LOOKS OF YOU, NOTHING COULD CHANGE TO SOME-THING QUICK, QUICK...
HOW 'BOUT YOU COME SIT ON OL' SAMEDI'S LAP, EH? LET ME GET A CLOSER LOOK. MAYBE A TOUCH. A LITTLE FEEL, FEEL? A LITTLE FUCKY-FUCK?
YOU...YOU'RE DISGUSTING.
BARON SAMEDI.
GOD OF DEATH AND RESURRECTION OF EROTICISM. OF THE CLOWNISH LEER AND THE SEXUALLY RIBALD. LORD OF HEALING THE ANSWER, SOLEM OR CAPRICIOUS.

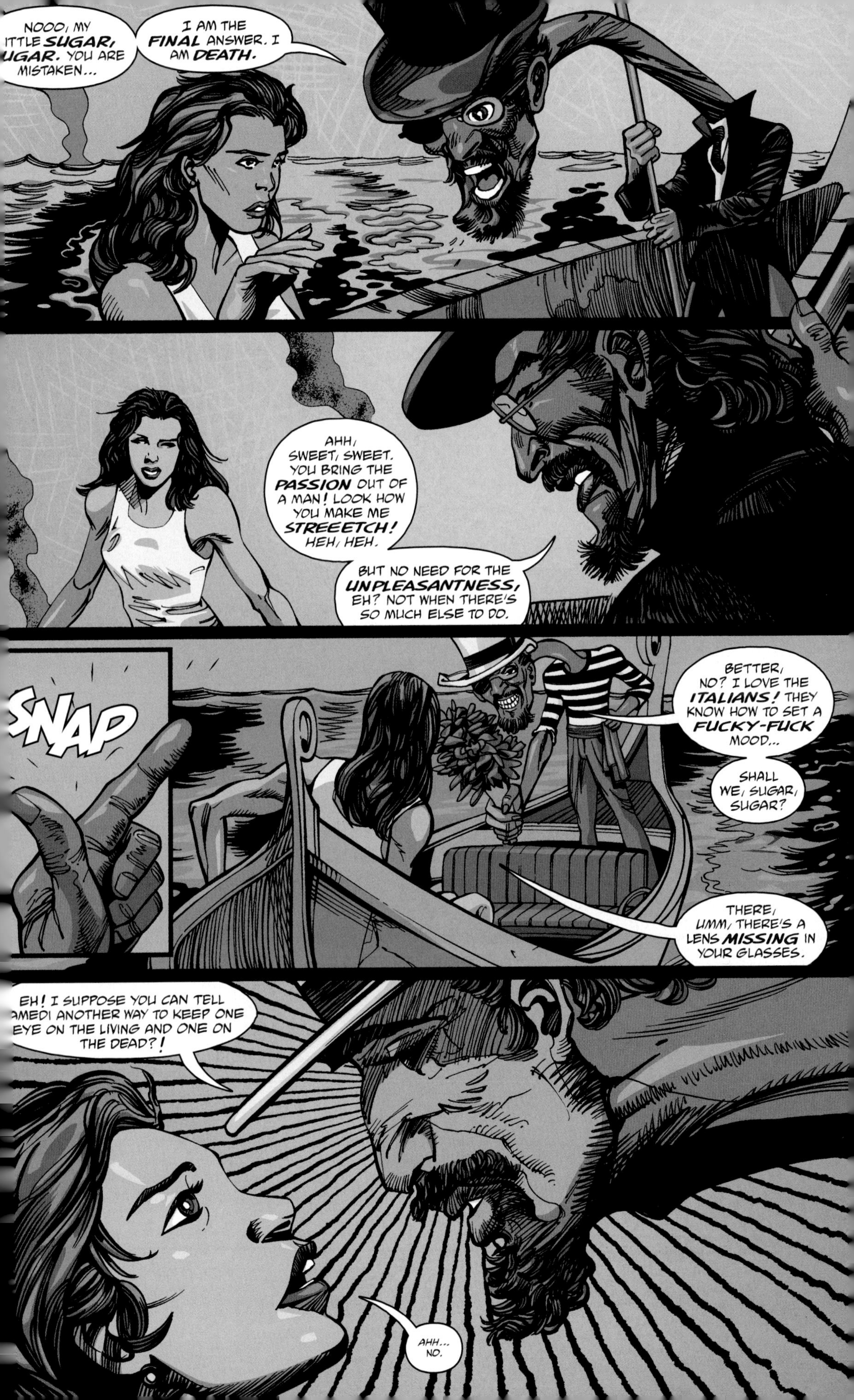

NOOO, MY LITTLE SUGAR, SUGAR. YOU ARE MISTAKEN...
I AM THE FINAL ANSWER. I AM DEATH.
AHH, SWEET, SWEET. YOU BRING THE PASSION OUT OF A MAN! LOOK HOW YOU MAKE ME STREEETCH! HEH, HEH.
BUT NO NEED FOR THE UNPLEASANTNESS, EH? NOT WHEN THERE'S SO MUCH ELSE TO DO.
SNAP
BETTER, NO? I LOVE THE ITALIANS! THEY KNOW HOW TO SET A FUCKY-FUCK MOOD...
SHALL WE, SUGAR, SUGAR?
THERE, UMM, THERE'S A LENS MISSING IN YOUR GLASSES.
EH! I SUPPOSE YOU CAN TELL SAMEDI ANOTHER WAY TO KEEP ONE EYE ON THE LIVING AND ONE ON THE DEAD?!
AHH... NO.

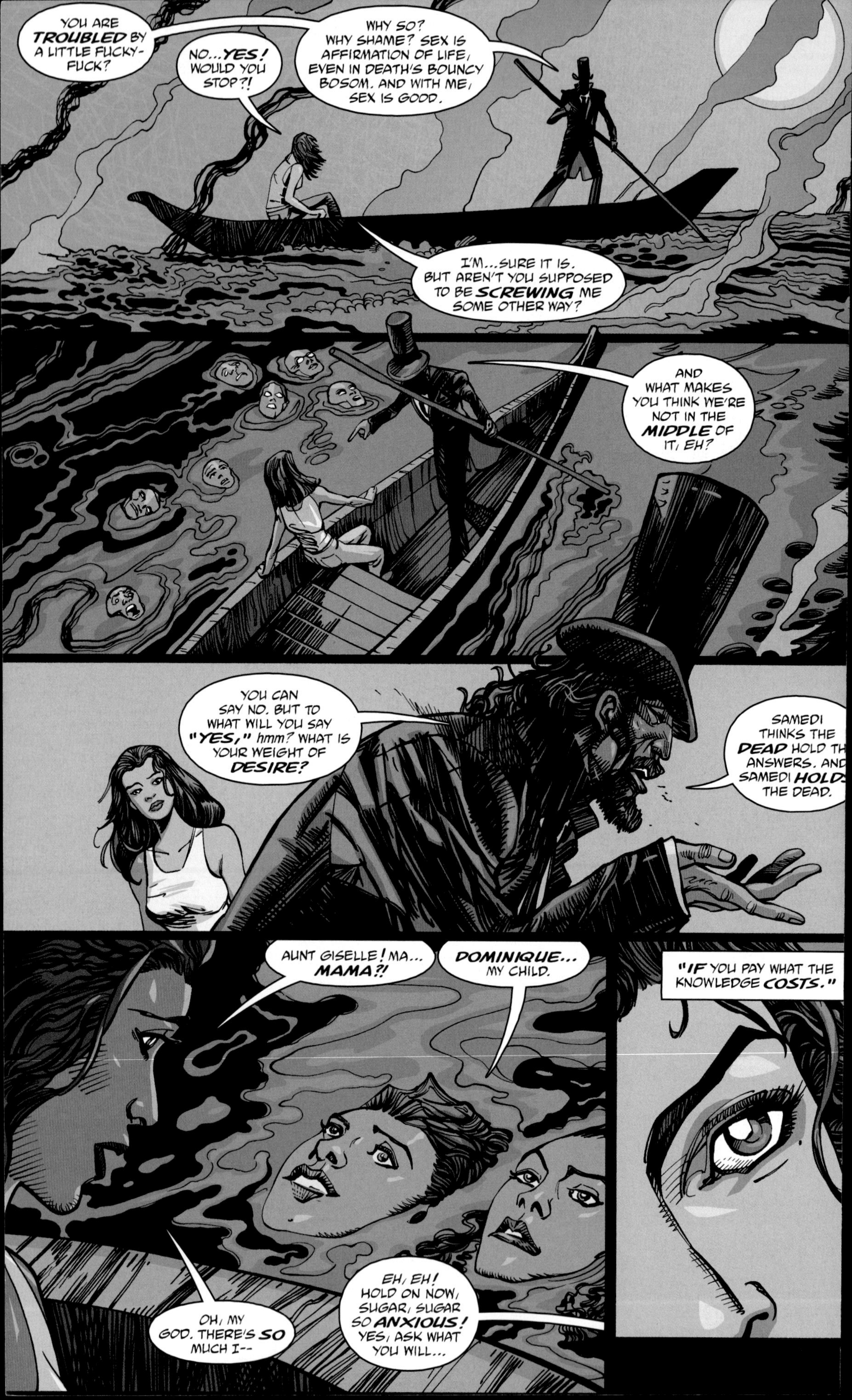
YOU ARE TROUBLED BY A LITTLE FUCKY-FUCK?
NO...YES! WOULD YOU STOP?!
WHY SO? WHY SHAME? SEX IS AFFIRMATION OF LIFE, EVEN IN DEATH'S BOUNCY BOSOM. AND WITH ME, SEX IS GOOD.
I'M...SURE IT IS. BUT AREN'T YOU SUPPOSED TO BE SCREWING ME SOME OTHER WAY?
AND WHAT MAKES YOU THINK WE'RE NOT IN THE MIDDLE OF IT, EH?
YOU CAN SAY NO. BUT TO WHAT WILL YOU SAY "YES," hmm? WHAT IS YOUR WEIGHT OF DESIRE?
SAMEDI THINKS THE DEAD HOLD TH ANSWERS. AND SAMEDI HOLDS THE DEAD.
AUNT GISELLE! MA... MAMA?!
DOMINIQUE... MY CHILD.
OH, MY GOD. THERE'S SO MUCH I--
EH, EH! HOLD ON NOW, SUGAR, SUGAR SO ANXIOUS! YES, ASK WHAT YOU WILL...
"IF YOU PAY WHAT THE KNOWLEDGE COSTS."

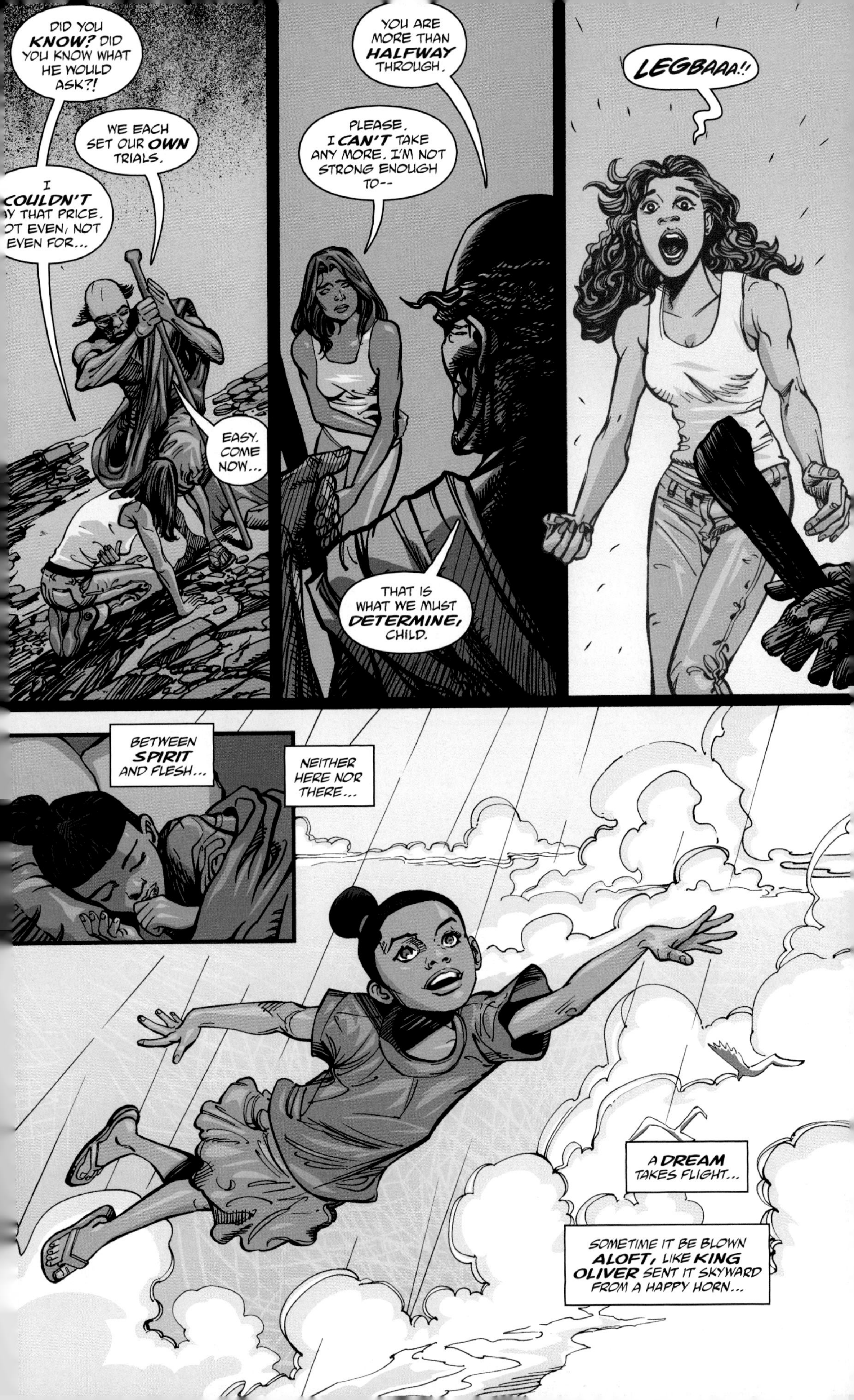
DID YOU KNOW? DID YOU KNOW WHAT HE WOULD ASK?!
WE EACH SET OUR OWN TRIALS.
I COULDN'T AY THAT PRICE. OT EVEN, NOT EVEN FOR...
EASY. COME NOW...
YOU ARE MORE THAN HALFWAY THROUGH.
PLEASE. I CAN'T TAKE ANY MORE. I'M NOT STRONG ENOUGH TO--
THAT IS WHAT WE MUST DETERMINE, CHILD.
LEGBAAA!!
BETWEEN SPIRIT AND FLESH...
NEITHER HERE NOR THERE...
A DREAM TAKES FLIGHT...
SOMETIME IT BE BLOWN ALOFT, LIKE KING OLIVER SENT IT SKYWARD FROM A HAPPY HORN...

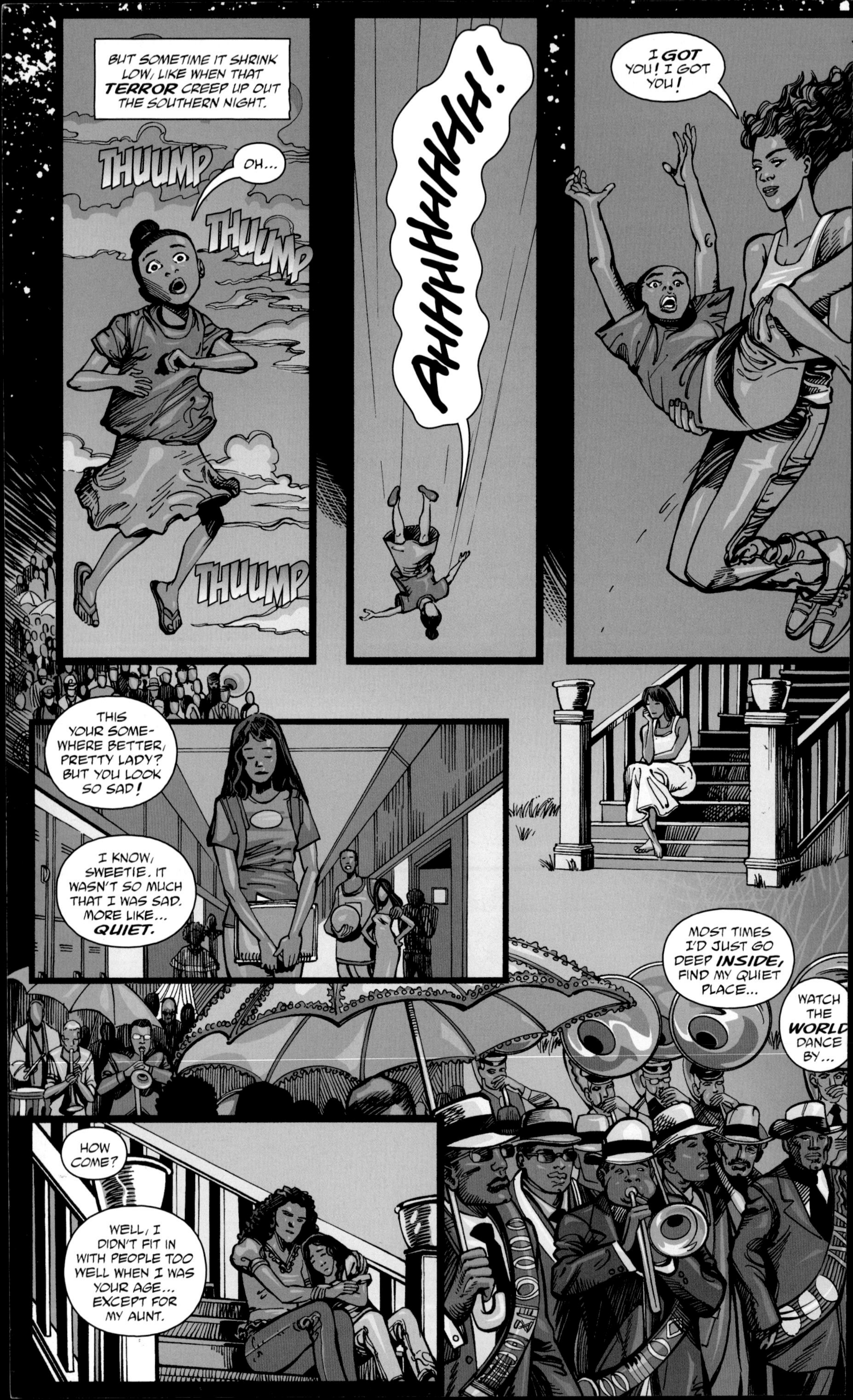
BUT SOMETIME IT SHRINK LOW, LIKE WHEN THAT TERROR CREEP UP OUT THE SOUTHERN NIGHT.
THUUMP
OH...
THUUMP
THUUMP
AHHHHHHH!
I GOT YOU! I GOT YOU!
THIS YOUR SOME-WHERE BETTER, PRETTY LADY? BUT YOU LOOK SO SAD!
I KNOW, SWEETIE. IT WASN'T SO MUCH THAT I WAS SAD. MORE LIKE... QUIET.
MOST TIMES I'D JUST GO DEEP INSIDE, FIND MY QUIET PLACE...
WATCH THE WORLD DANCE BY...
HOW COME?
WELL, I DIDN'T FIT IN WITH PEOPLE TOO WELL WHEN I WAS YOUR AGE... EXCEPT FOR MY AUNT.

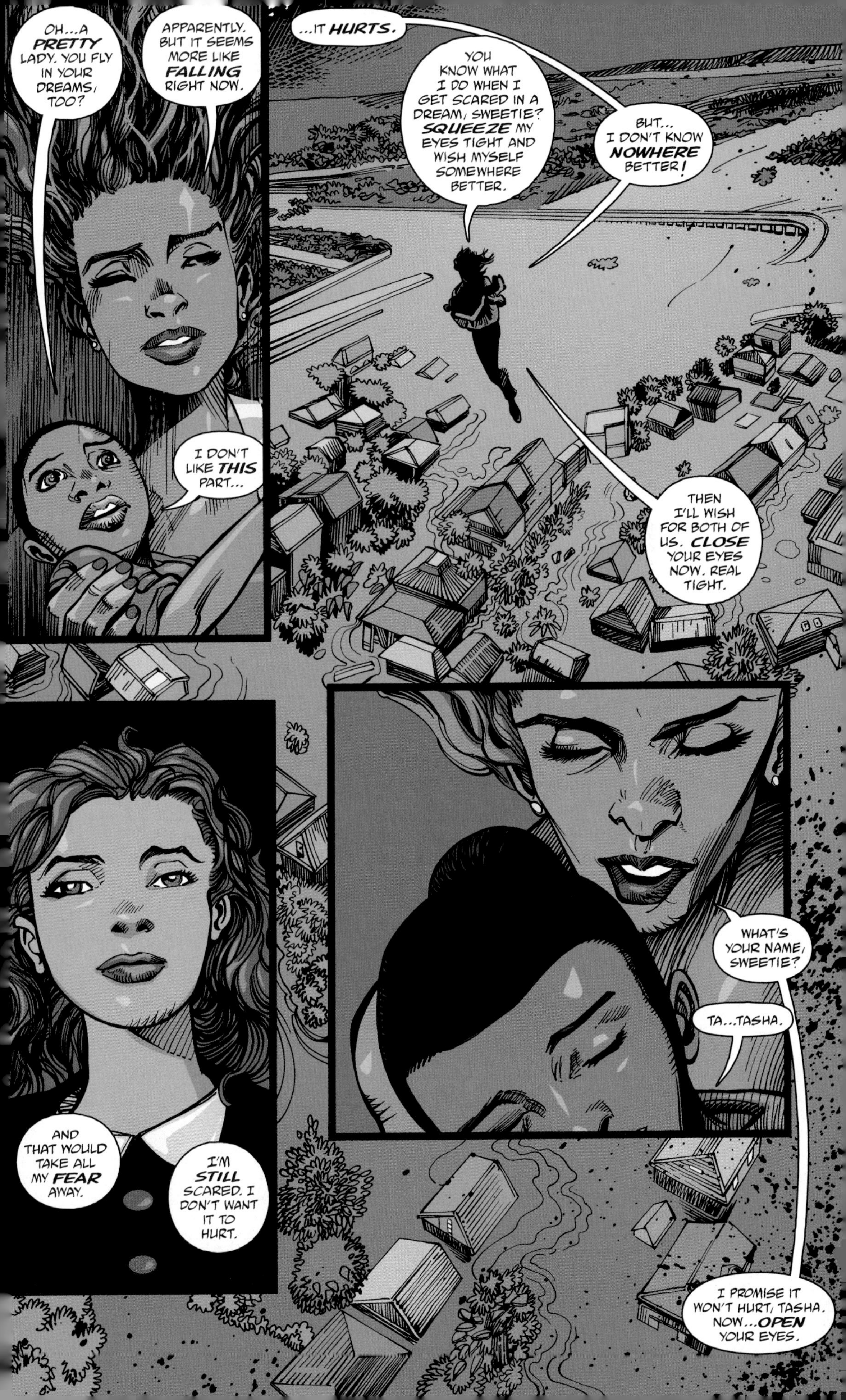
OH...A PRETTY LADY. YOU FLY IN YOUR DREAMS, TOO?
APPARENTLY. BUT IT SEEMS MORE LIKE FALLING RIGHT NOW.
I DON'T LIKE THIS PART...
...IT HURTS.
YOU KNOW WHAT I DO WHEN I GET SCARED IN A DREAM, SWEETIE? SQUEEZE MY EYES TIGHT AND WISH MYSELF SOMEWHERE BETTER.
BUT... I DON'T KNOW NOWHERE BETTER!
THEN I'LL WISH FOR BOTH OF US. CLOSE YOUR EYES NOW. REAL TIGHT.
AND THAT WOULD TAKE ALL MY FEAR AWAY.
I'M STILL SCARED. I DON'T WANT IT TO HURT.
WHAT'S YOUR NAME, SWEETIE?
TA...TASHA.
I PROMISE IT WON'T HURT, TASHA. NOW...OPEN YOUR EYES.

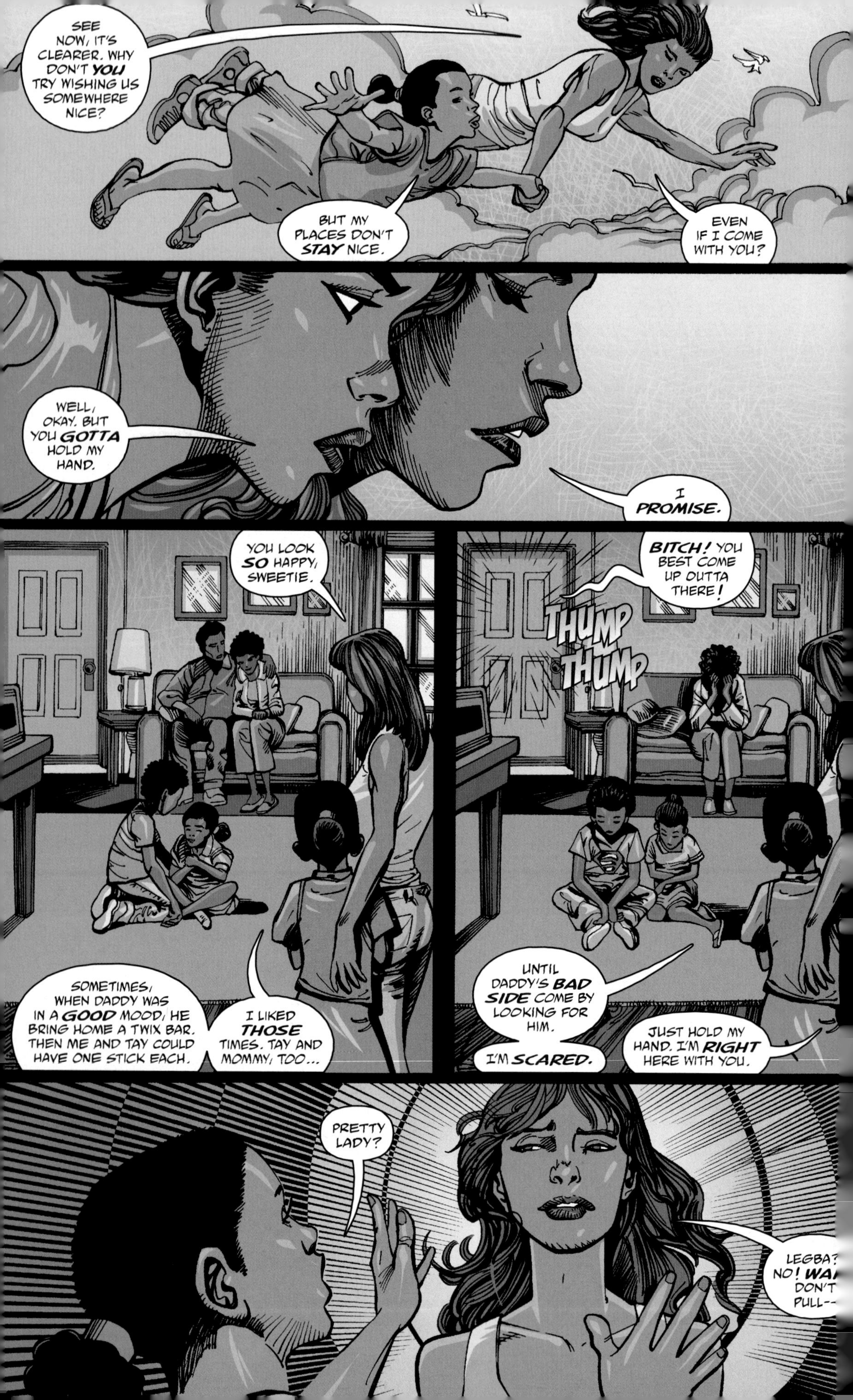
SEE NOW, IT'S CLEARER. WHY DON'T YOU TRY WISHING US SOMEWHERE NICE?
BUT MY PLACES DON'T STAY NICE.
EVEN IF I COME WITH YOU?
WELL, OKAY. BUT YOU GOTTA HOLD MY HAND.
I PROMISE.
YOU LOOK SO HAPPY, SWEETIE.
SOMETIMES, WHEN DADDY WAS IN A GOOD MOOD, HE BRING HOME A TWIX BAR. THEN ME AND TAY COULD HAVE ONE STICK EACH.
I LIKED THOSE TIMES. TAY AND MOMMY, TOO...
BITCH! YOU BEST COME UP OUTTA THERE!
THUMP THUMP
UNTIL DADDY'S BAD SIDE COME BY LOOKING FOR HIM.
I'M SCARED.
JUST HOLD MY HAND. I'M RIGHT HERE WITH YOU.
PRETTY LADY?
LEGBA? NO! WA DON'T PULL--

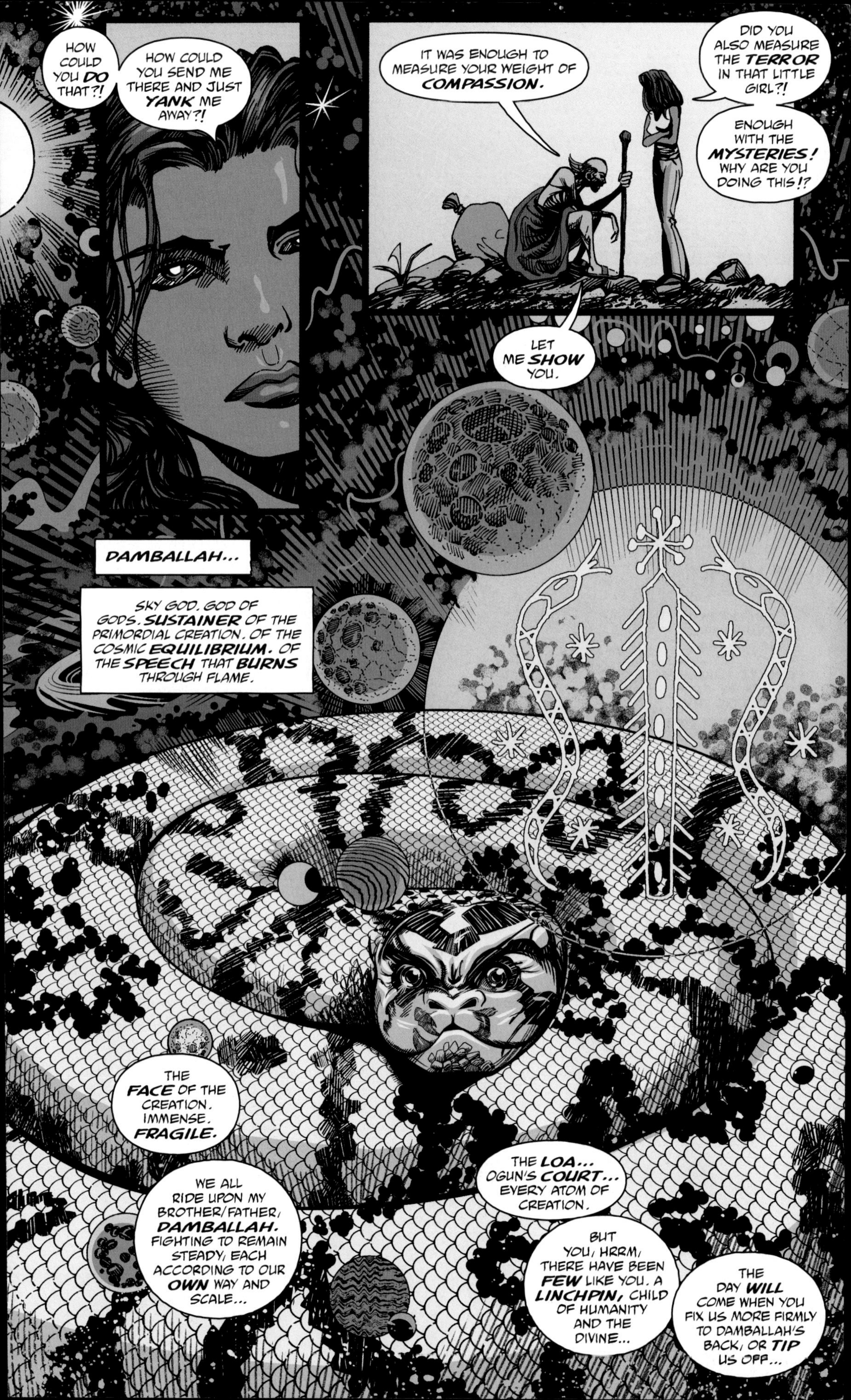
HOW COULD YOU DO THAT?!
HOW COULD YOU SEND ME THERE AND JUST YANK ME AWAY?!
IT WAS ENOUGH TO MEASURE YOUR WEIGHT OF COMPASSION.
DID YOU ALSO MEASURE THE TERROR IN THAT LITTLE GIRL?!
ENOUGH WITH THE MYSTERIES! WHY ARE YOU DOING THIS!?
LET ME SHOW YOU.
DAMBALLAH...
SKY GOD. GOD OF GODS. SUSTAINER OF THE PRIMORDIAL CREATION. OF THE COSMIC EQUILIBRIUM. OF THE SPEECH THAT BURNS THROUGH FLAME.
THE FACE OF THE CREATION. IMMENSE. FRAGILE.
WE ALL RIDE UPON MY BROTHER/FATHER, DAMBALLAH. FIGHTING TO REMAIN STEADY, EACH ACCORDING TO OUR OWN WAY AND SCALE...
THE LOA... OGUN'S COURT... EVERY ATOM OF CREATION.
BUT YOU, HRRM, THERE HAVE BEEN FEW LIKE YOU. A LINCHPIN, CHILD OF HUMANITY AND THE DIVINE...
THE DAY WILL COME WHEN YOU FIX US MORE FIRMLY TO DAMBALLAH'S BACK, OR TIP US OFF...

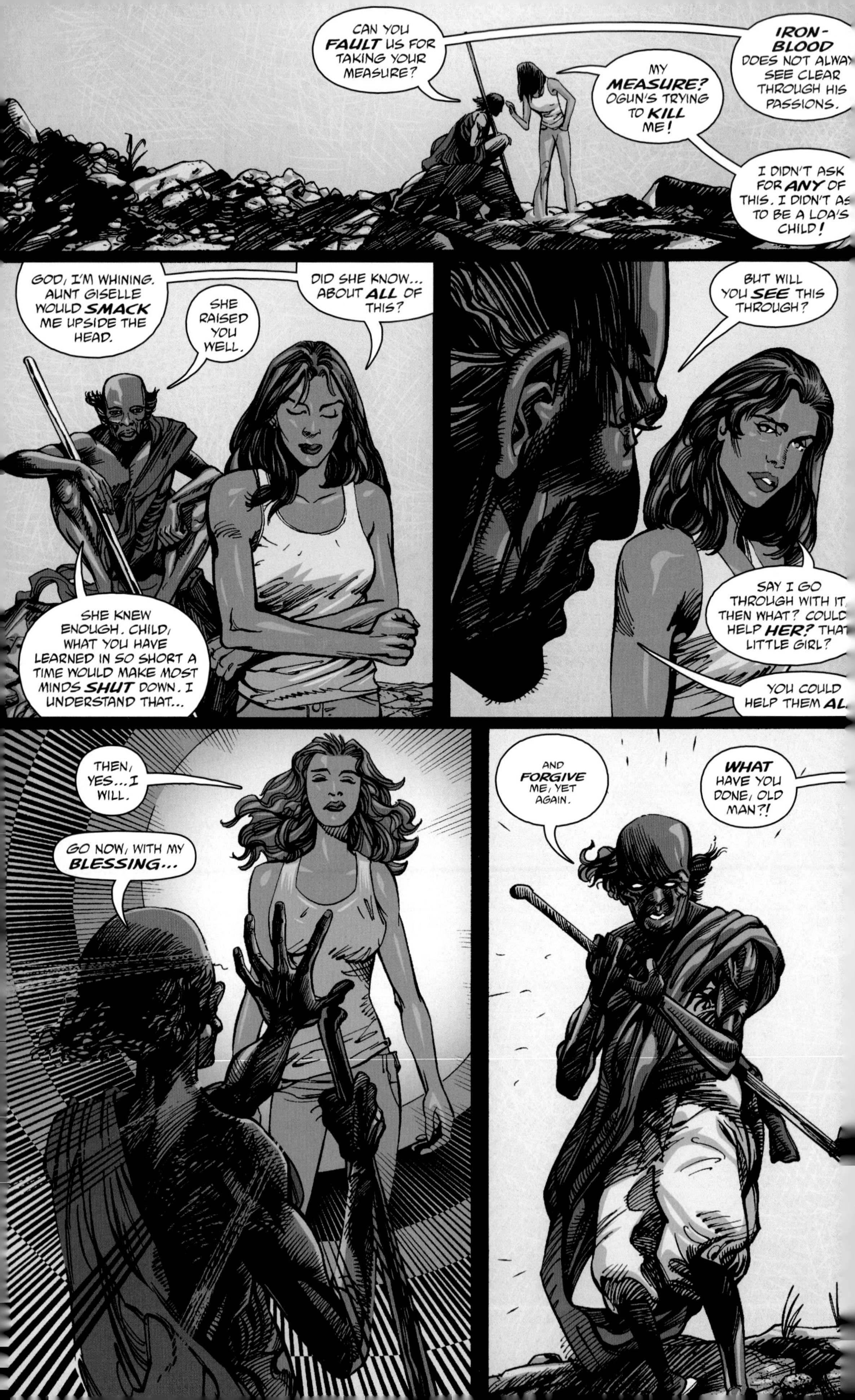
CAN YOU FAULT US FOR TAKING YOUR MEASURE?
IRON-BLOOD DOES NOT ALWAY SEE CLEAR THROUGH HIS PASSIONS.
MY MEASURE? OGUN'S TRYING TO KILL ME!
I DIDN'T ASK FOR ANY OF THIS. I DIDN'T AS TO BE A LOA'S CHILD!
GOD, I'M WHINING. AUNT GISELLE WOULD SMACK ME UPSIDE THE HEAD.
SHE RAISED YOU WELL.
DID SHE KNOW... ABOUT ALL OF THIS?
SHE KNEW ENOUGH. CHILD, WHAT YOU HAVE LEARNED IN SO SHORT A TIME WOULD MAKE MOST MINDS SHUT DOWN. I UNDERSTAND THAT...
BUT WILL YOU SEE THIS THROUGH?
SAY I GO THROUGH WITH IT, THEN WHAT? COULD HELP HER? THAT LITTLE GIRL?
YOU COULD HELP THEM AL
THEN, YES... I WILL.
GO NOW, WITH MY BLESSING...
AND FORGIVE ME, YET AGAIN.
WHAT HAVE YOU DONE, OLD MAN?!

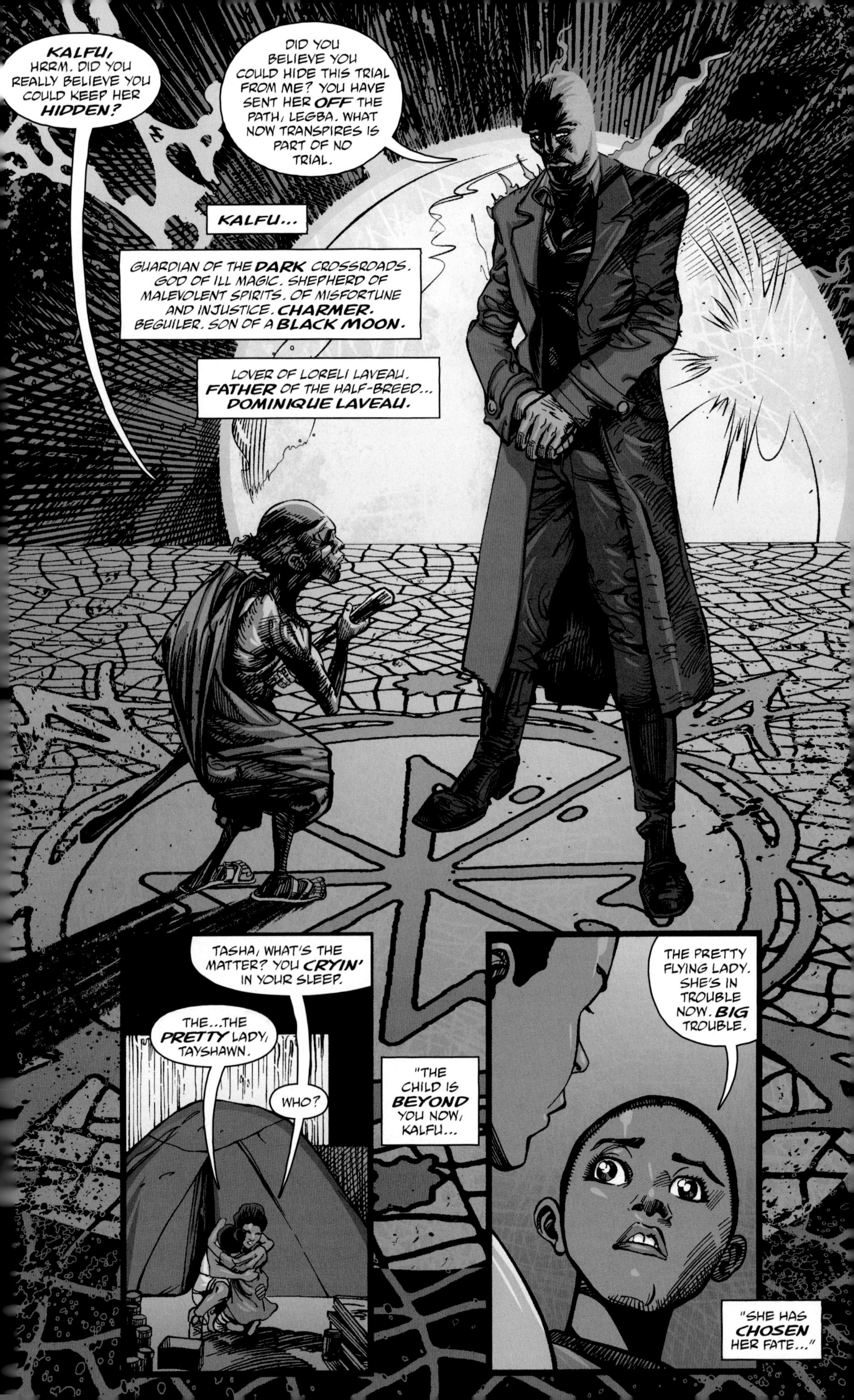
KALFU, HRRM. DID YOU REALLY BELIEVE YOU COULD KEEP HER HIDDEN?
DID YOU BELIEVE YOU COULD HIDE THIS TRIAL FROM ME? YOU HAVE SENT HER OFF THE PATH, LEGBA. WHAT NOW TRANSPIRES IS PART OF NO TRIAL.
KALFU...
GUARDIAN OF THE DARK CROSSROADS. GOD OF ILL MAGIC. SHEPHERD OF MALEVOLENT SPIRITS. OF MISFORTUNE AND INJUSTICE. CHARMER. BEGUILER. SON OF A BLACK MOON.
LOVER OF LORELI LAVEAU. FATHER OF THE HALF-BREED... DOMINIQUE LAVEAU.
TASHA, WHAT'S THE MATTER? YOU CRYIN' IN YOUR SLEEP.
THE...THE PRETTY LADY, TAYSHAWN.
WHO?
"THE CHILD IS BEYOND YOU NOW, KALFU...
THE PRETTY FLYING LADY. SHE'S IN TROUBLE NOW. BIG TROUBLE.
"SHE HAS CHOSEN HER FATE..."

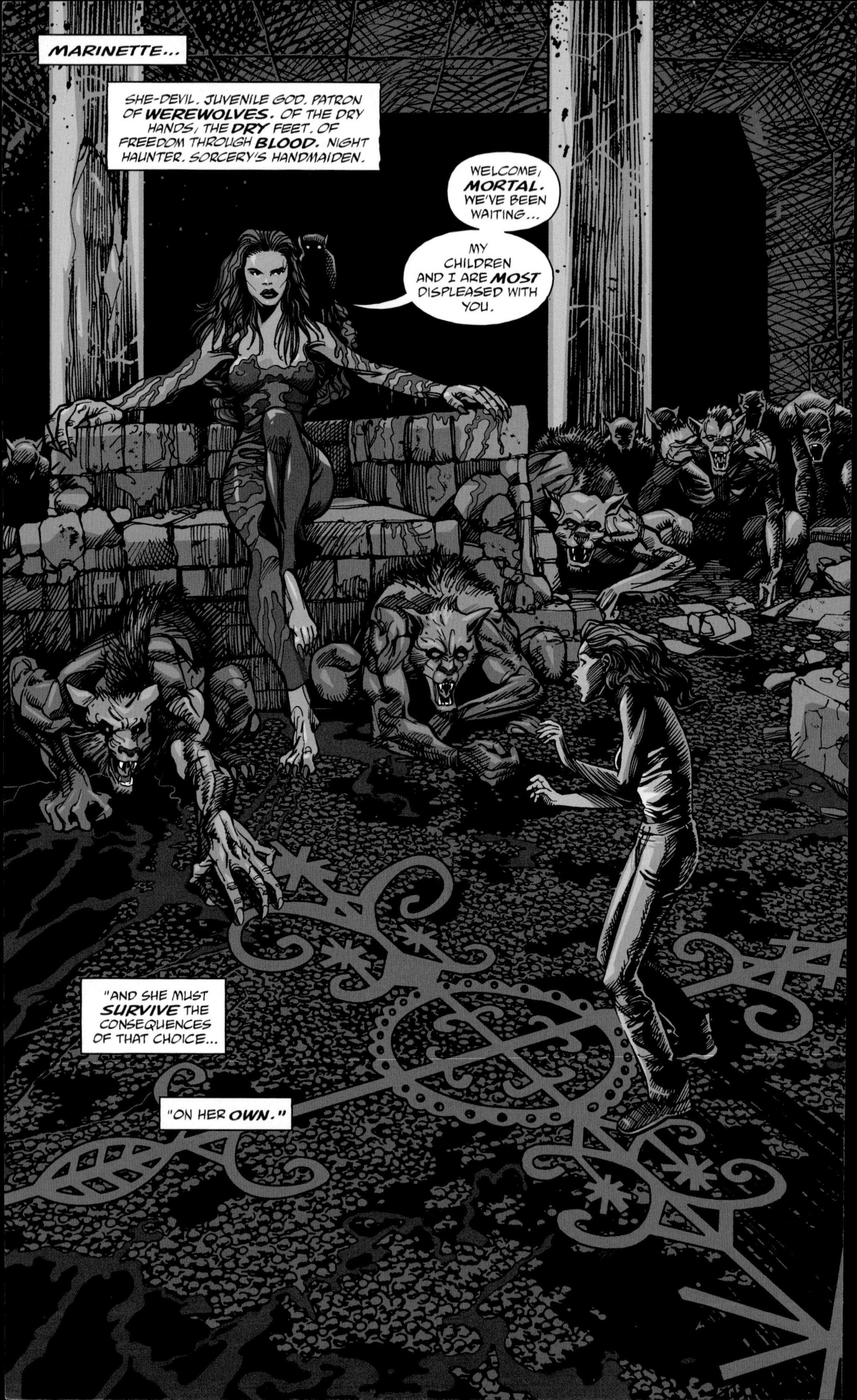
MARINETTE...
SHE-DEVIL. JUVENILE GOD. PATRON OF WEREWOLVES. OF THE DRY HANDS, THE DRY FEET. OF FREEDOM THROUGH BLOOD. NIGHT HAUNTER. SORCERY'S HANDMAIDEN.
WELCOME, MORTAL. WE'VE BEEN WAITING...
MY CHILDREN AND I ARE MOST DISPLEASED WITH YOU.
"AND SHE MUST SURVIVE THE CONSEQUENCES OF THAT CHOICE...
"ON HER OWN."

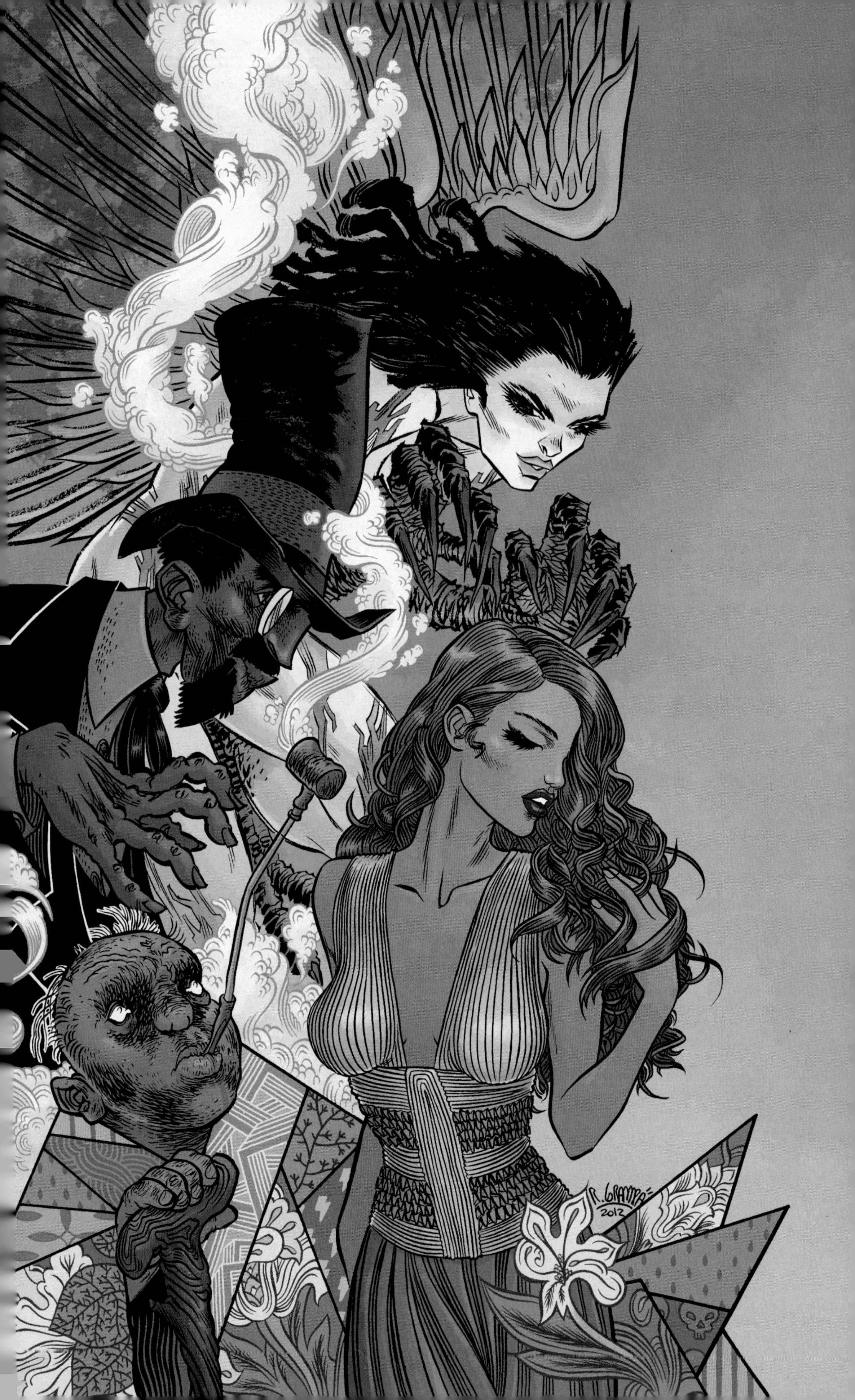
R. GRAMPA
2012

"When things appear darkest, life is the beacon that cuts through."

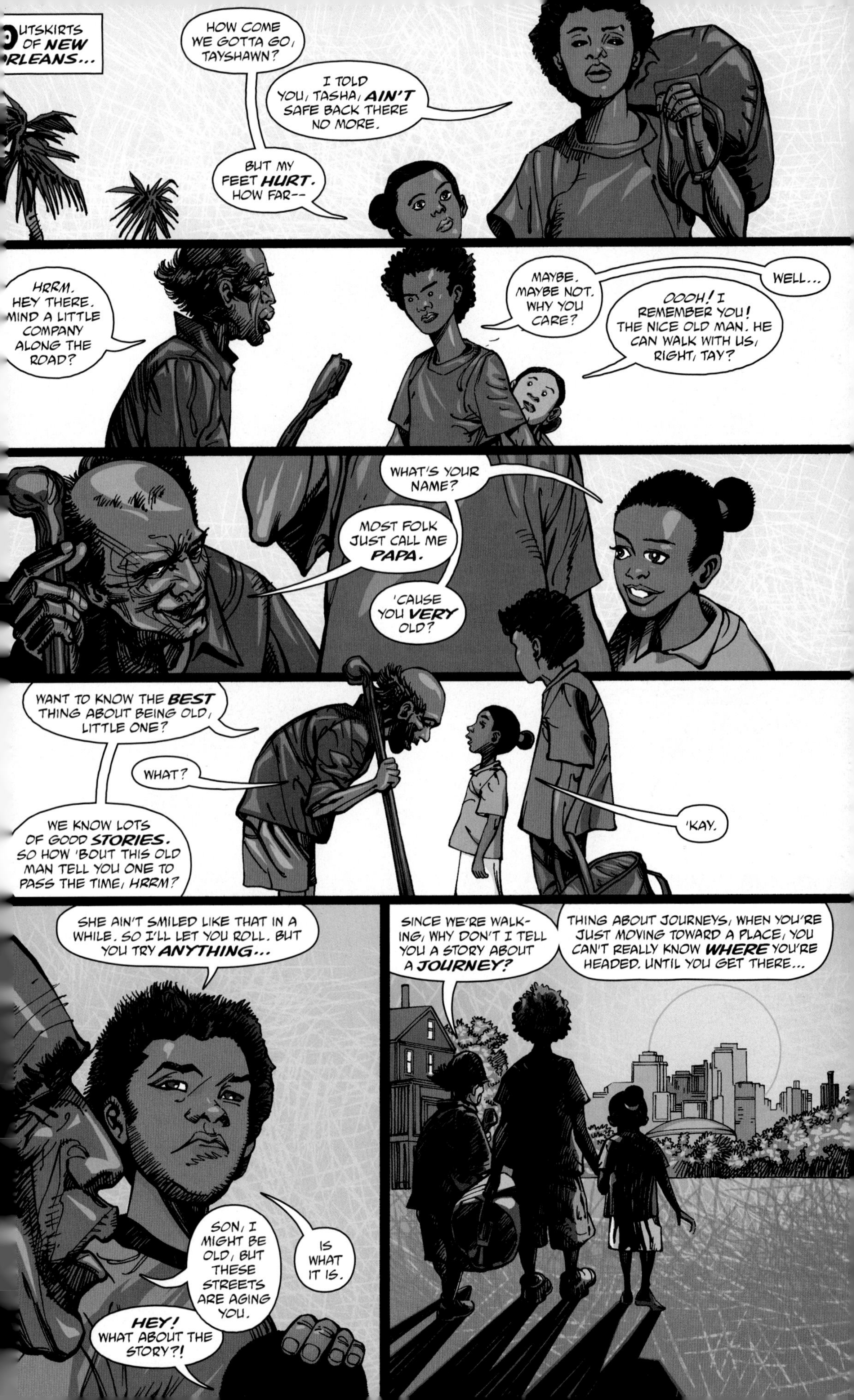
...OUTSKIRTS OF NEW ORLEANS...
HOW COME WE GOTTA GO, TAYSHAWN?
I TOLD YOU, TASHA, AIN'T SAFE BACK THERE NO MORE.
BUT MY FEET HURT. HOW FAR--
HRRM. HEY THERE. MIND A LITTLE COMPANY ALONG THE ROAD?
MAYBE. MAYBE NOT. WHY YOU CARE?
WELL...
OOOH! I REMEMBER YOU! THE NICE OLD MAN. HE CAN WALK WITH US, RIGHT, TAY?
WHAT'S YOUR NAME?
MOST FOLK JUST CALL ME PAPA.
'CAUSE YOU VERY OLD?
WANT TO KNOW THE BEST THING ABOUT BEING OLD, LITTLE ONE?
WHAT?
WE KNOW LOTS OF GOOD STORIES. SO HOW 'BOUT THIS OLD MAN TELL YOU ONE TO PASS THE TIME, HRRM?
'KAY.
SHE AIN'T SMILED LIKE THAT IN A WHILE. SO I'LL LET YOU ROLL. BUT YOU TRY ANYTHING...
SON, I MIGHT BE OLD, BUT THESE STREETS ARE AGING YOU.
IS WHAT IT IS.
HEY! WHAT ABOUT THE STORY?!
SINCE WE'RE WALKING, WHY DON'T I TELL YOU A STORY ABOUT A JOURNEY?
THING ABOUT JOURNEYS, WHEN YOU'RE JUST MOVING TOWARD A PLACE, YOU CAN'T REALLY KNOW WHERE YOU'RE HEADED. UNTIL YOU GET THERE...

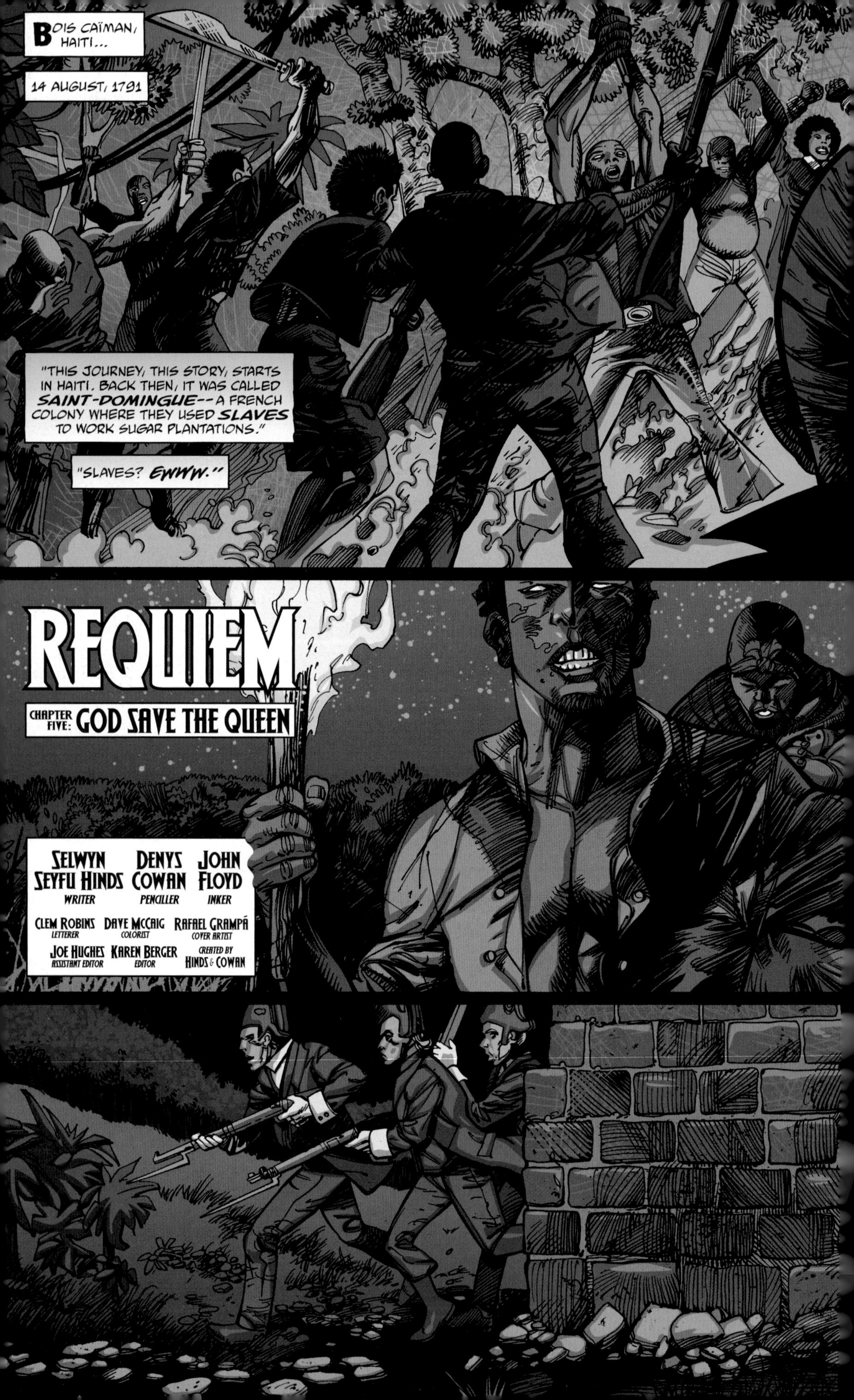

BOIS CAÏMAN, HAITI...
14 AUGUST, 1791
"THIS JOURNEY, THIS STORY, STARTS IN HAITI. BACK THEN, IT WAS CALLED SAINT-DOMINGUE--A FRENCH COLONY WHERE THEY USED SLAVES TO WORK SUGAR PLANTATIONS."
"SLAVES? EWWW."
REQUIEM
CHAPTER FIVE: GOD SAVE THE QUEEN
SELWYN SEYFU HINDS WRITER
DENYS COWAN PENCILLER
JOHN FLOYD INKER
CLEM ROBINS LETTERER
DAVE MCCAIG COLORIST
RAFAEL GRAMPÁ COVER ARTIST
JOE HUGHES ASSISTANT EDITOR
KAREN BERGER EDITOR
CREATED BY HINDS & COWAN

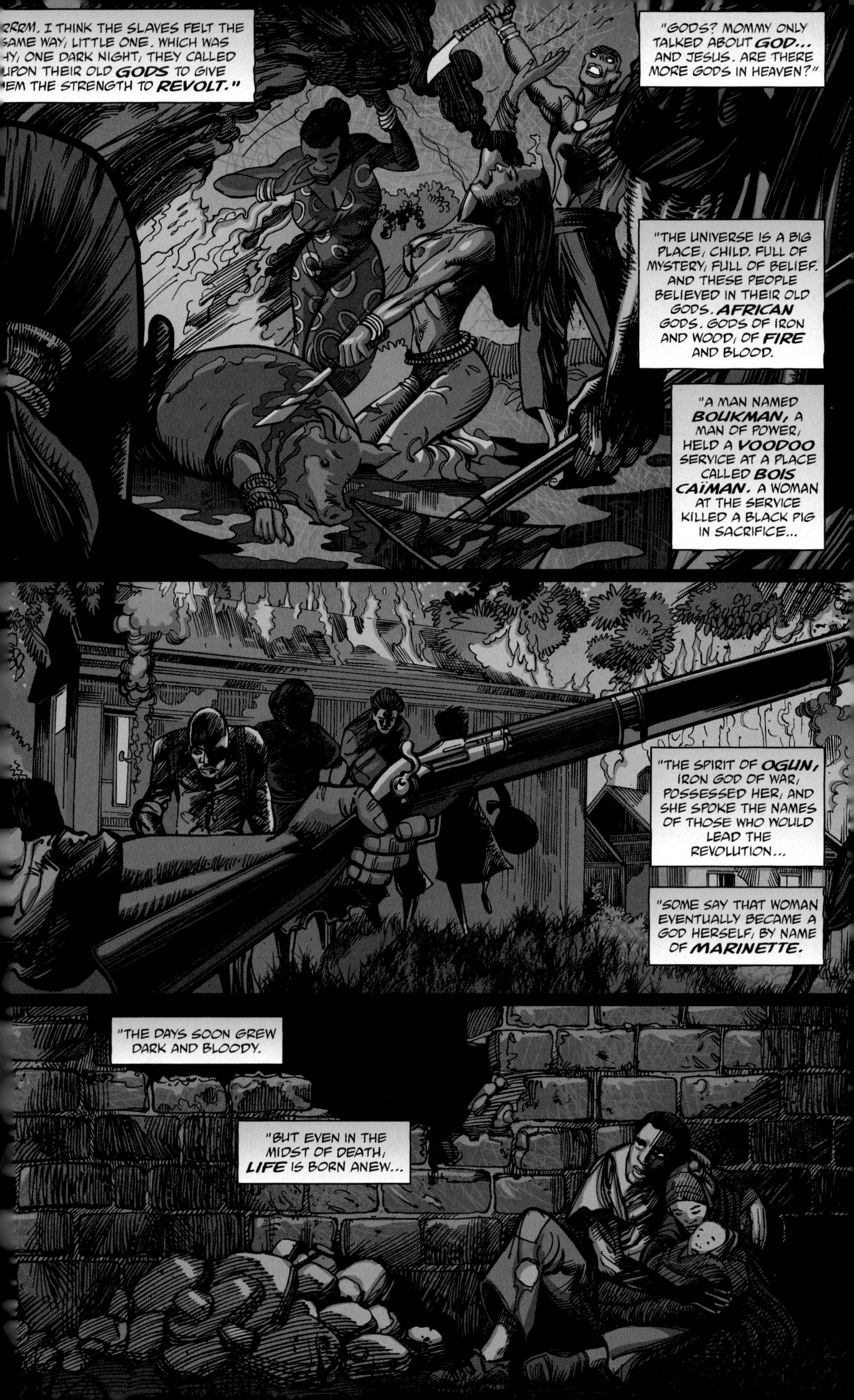

RRRM. I THINK THE SLAVES FELT THE SAME WAY, LITTLE ONE. WHICH WAS HY, ONE DARK NIGHT, THEY CALLED UPON THEIR OLD GODS TO GIVE EM THE STRENGTH TO REVOLT."
"GODS? MOMMY ONLY TALKED ABOUT GOD... AND JESUS. ARE THERE MORE GODS IN HEAVEN?"
"THE UNIVERSE IS A BIG PLACE, CHILD. FULL OF MYSTERY, FULL OF BELIEF. AND THESE PEOPLE BELIEVED IN THEIR OLD GODS. AFRICAN GODS. GODS OF IRON AND WOOD, OF FIRE AND BLOOD.
"A MAN NAMED BOUKMAN, A MAN OF POWER, HELD A VOODOO SERVICE AT A PLACE CALLED BOIS CAÏMAN. A WOMAN AT THE SERVICE KILLED A BLACK PIG IN SACRIFICE...
"THE SPIRIT OF OGUN, IRON GOD OF WAR, POSSESSED HER, AND SHE SPOKE THE NAMES OF THOSE WHO WOULD LEAD THE REVOLUTION...
"SOME SAY THAT WOMAN EVENTUALLY BECAME A GOD HERSELF, BY NAME OF MARINETTE.
"THE DAYS SOON GREW DARK AND BLOODY.
"BUT EVEN IN THE MIDST OF DEATH, LIFE IS BORN ANEW...

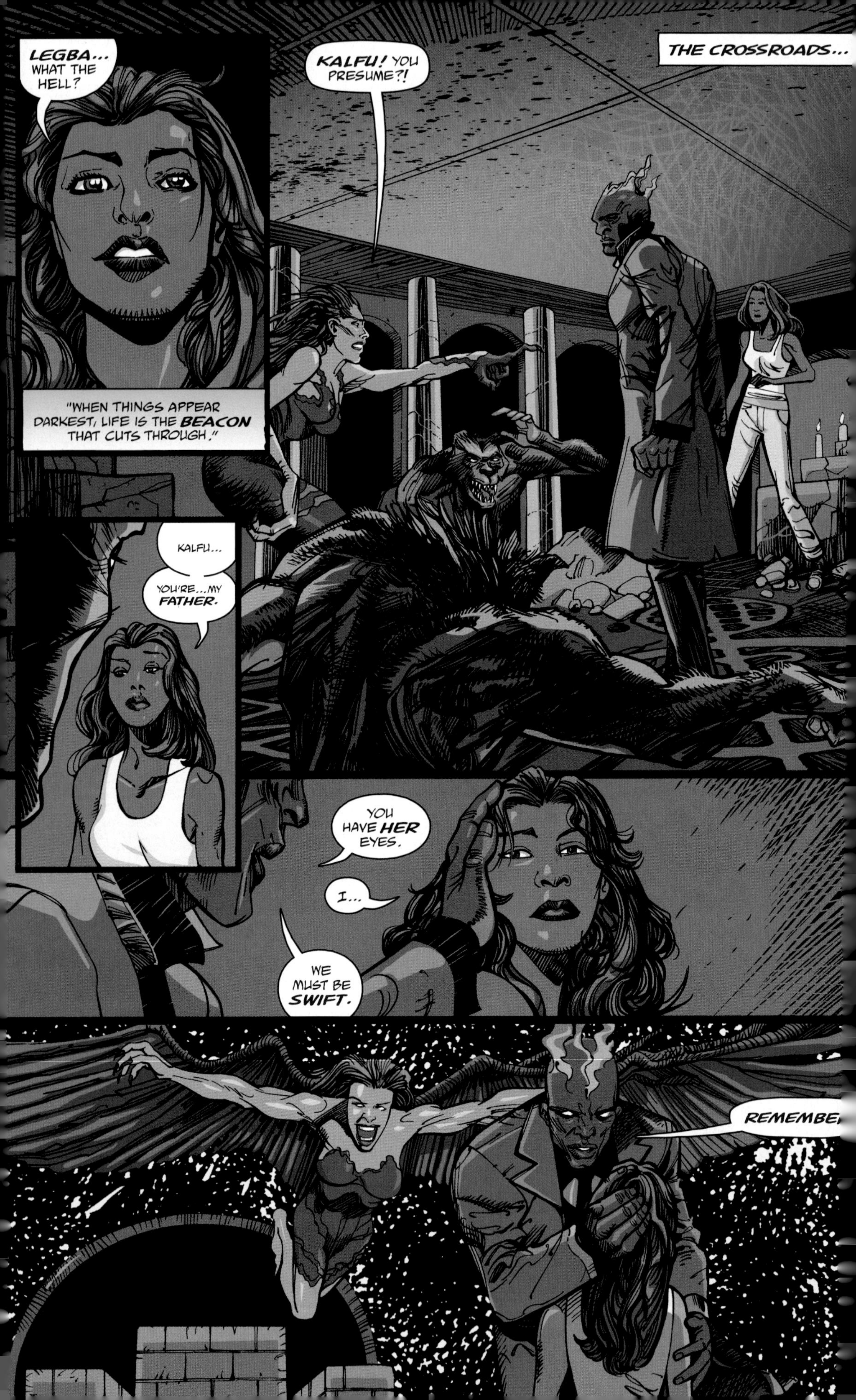
LEGBA... WHAT THE HELL?
"WHEN THINGS APPEAR DARKEST, LIFE IS THE BEACON THAT CUTS THROUGH."
THE CROSSROADS...
KALFU! YOU PRESUME?!
KALFU...
YOU'RE...MY FATHER.
YOU HAVE HER EYES.
I...
WE MUST BE SWIFT.
REMEMBE

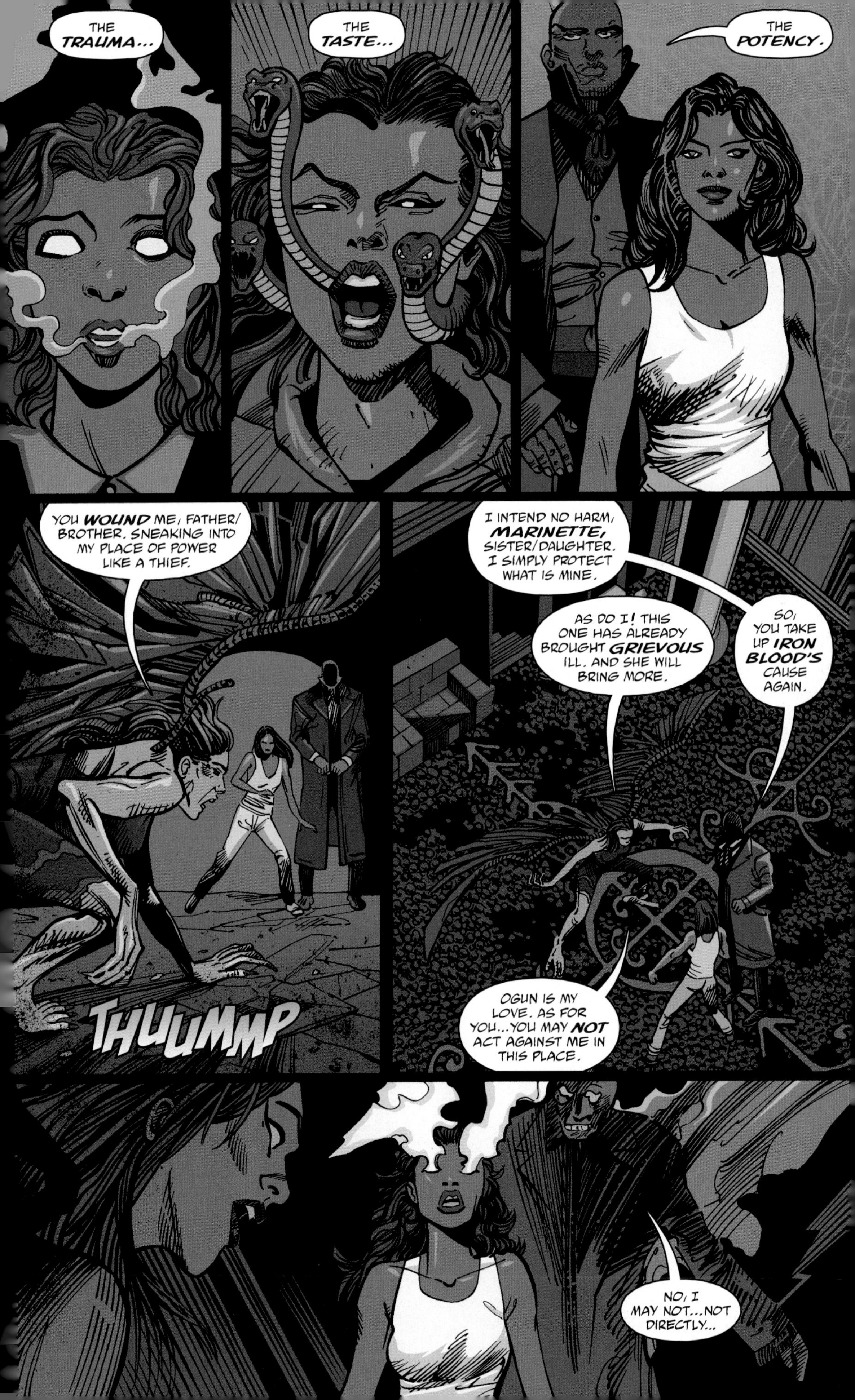
THE TRAUMA...
THE TASTE...
THE POTENCY.
YOU WOUND ME, FATHER/ BROTHER. SNEAKING INTO MY PLACE OF POWER LIKE A THIEF.
THUUMMP
I INTEND NO HARM, MARINETTE, SISTER/DAUGHTER. I SIMPLY PROTECT WHAT IS MINE.
AS DO I! THIS ONE HAS ALREADY BROUGHT GRIEVOUS ILL. AND SHE WILL BRING MORE.
SO, YOU TAKE UP IRON BLOOD'S CAUSE AGAIN.
OGUN IS MY LOVE. AS FOR YOU...YOU MAY NOT ACT AGAINST ME IN THIS PLACE.
NO, I MAY NOT...NOT DIRECTLY...

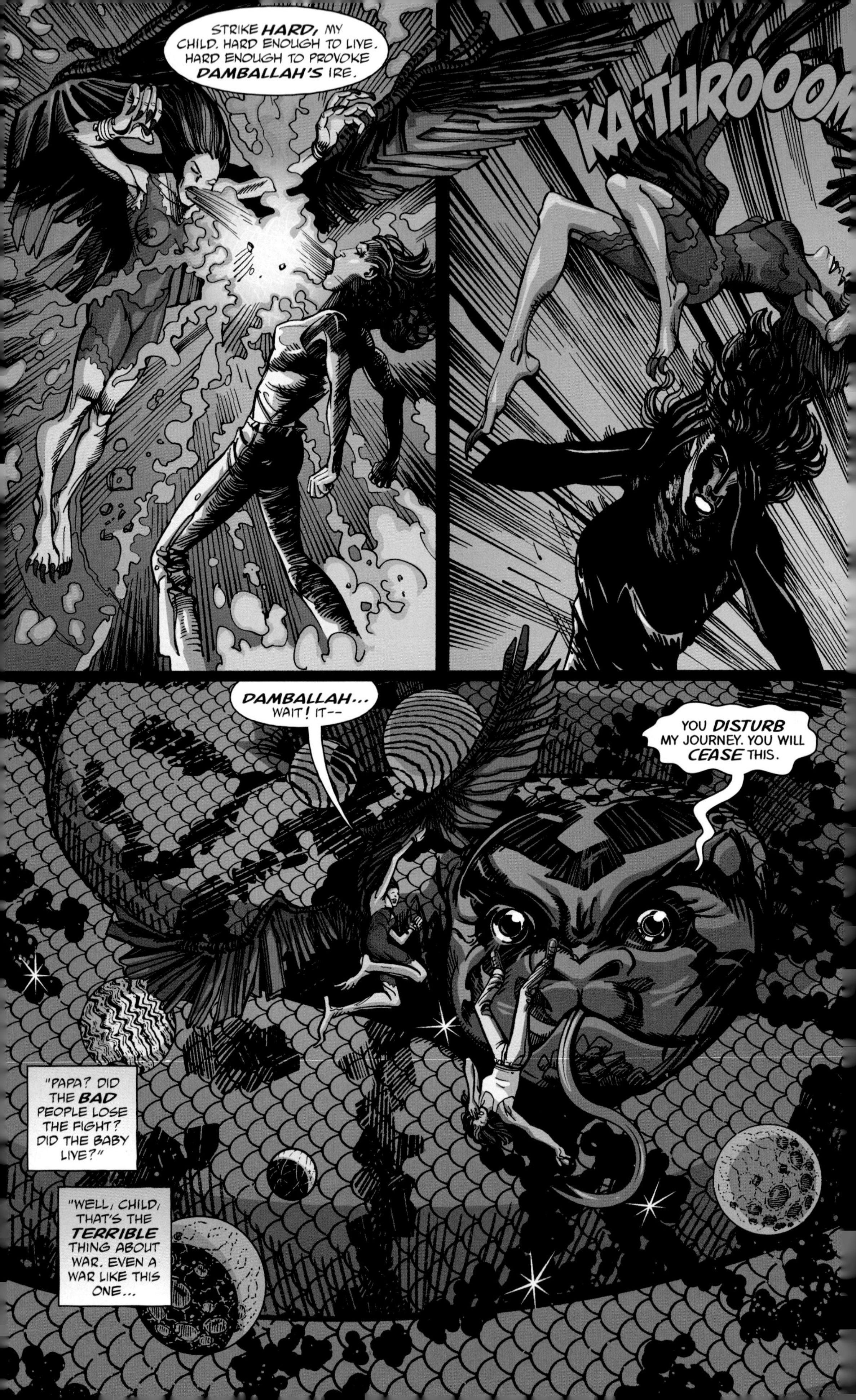
STRIKE HARD, MY CHILD. HARD ENOUGH TO LIVE. HARD ENOUGH TO PROVOKE DAMBALLAH'S IRE.
KA-THROOOM
DAMBALLAH... WAIT! IT--
YOU DISTURB MY JOURNEY. YOU WILL CEASE THIS.
"PAPA? DID THE BAD PEOPLE LOSE THE FIGHT? DID THE BABY LIVE?"
"WELL, CHILD, THAT'S THE TERRIBLE THING ABOUT WAR. EVEN A WAR LIKE THIS ONE...

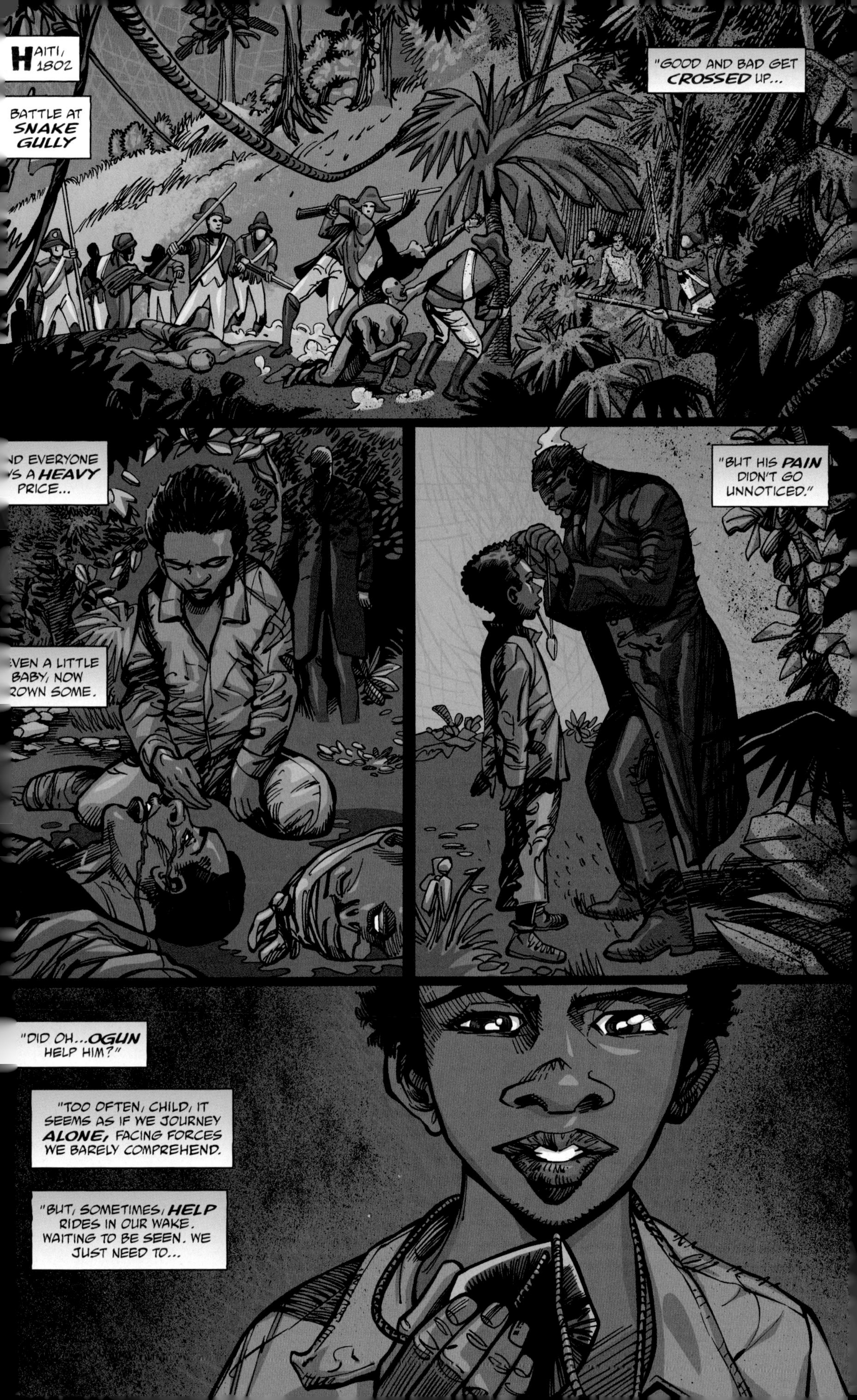
HAITI, 1802
BATTLE AT SNAKE GULLY
"GOOD AND BAD GET CROSSED UP...
ND EVERYONE 'S A HEAVY PRICE...
EVEN A LITTLE BABY, NOW ROWN SOME.
"BUT HIS PAIN DIDN'T GO UNNOTICED."
"DID OH...OGUN HELP HIM?"
"TOO OFTEN, CHILD, IT SEEMS AS IF WE JOURNEY ALONE, FACING FORCES WE BARELY COMPREHEND.
"BUT, SOMETIMES, HELP RIDES IN OUR WAKE. WAITING TO BE SEEN. WE JUST NEED TO...

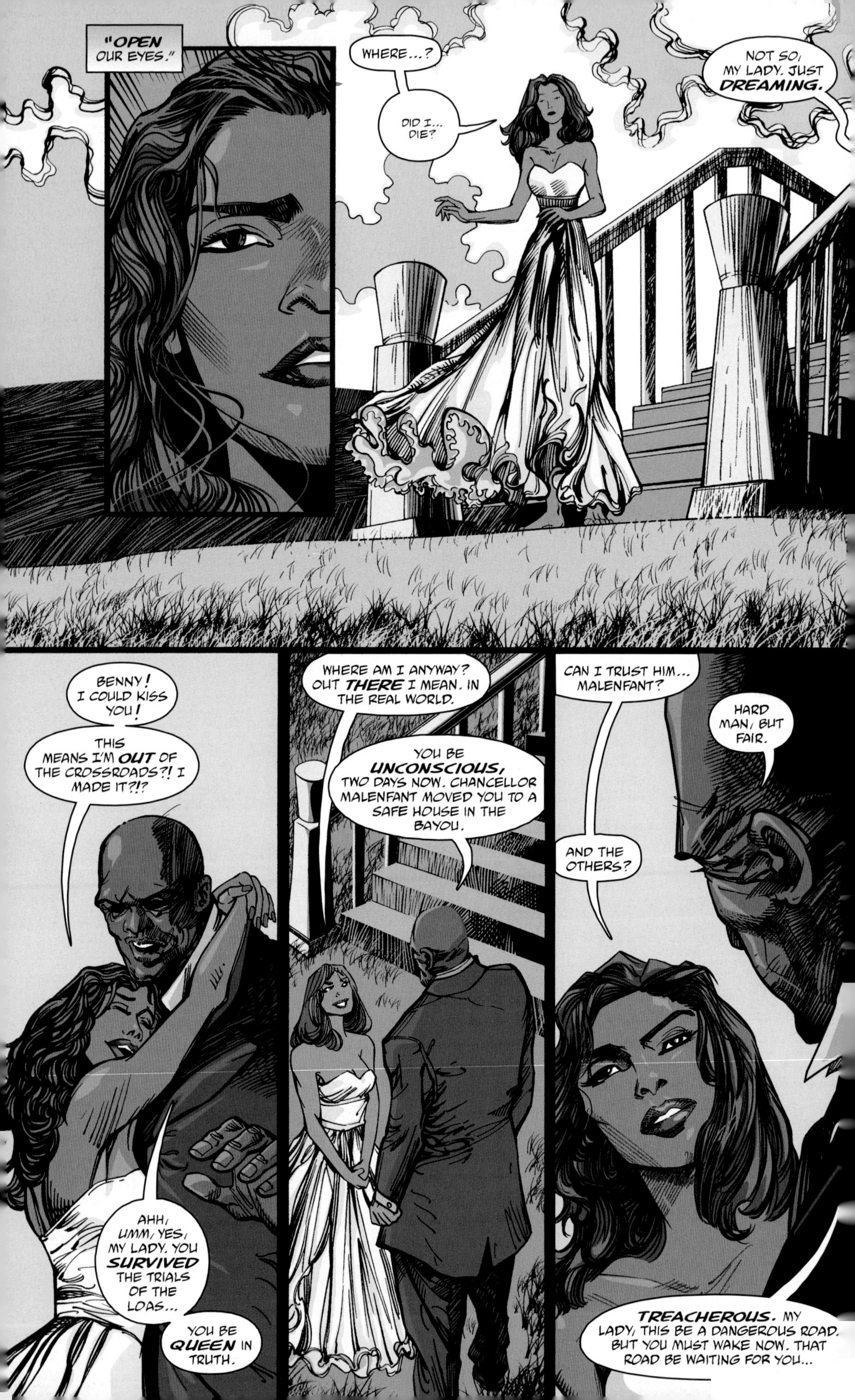
"OPEN OUR EYES."
WHERE...?
DID I... DIE?
NOT SO, MY LADY. JUST DREAMING.
BENNY! I COULD KISS YOU!
THIS MEANS I'M OUT OF THE CROSSROADS?! I MADE IT?!?
AHH, UMM, YES, MY LADY. YOU SURVIVED THE TRIALS OF THE LOAS...
YOU BE QUEEN IN TRUTH.
WHERE AM I ANYWAY? OUT THERE I MEAN. IN THE REAL WORLD.
YOU BE UNCONSCIOUS, TWO DAYS NOW. CHANCELLOR MALENFANT MOVED YOU TO A SAFE HOUSE IN THE BAYOU.
CAN I TRUST HIM... MALENFANT?
HARD MAN, BUT FAIR.
AND THE OTHERS?
TREACHEROUS. MY LADY, THIS BE A DANGEROUS ROAD. BUT YOU MUST WAKE NOW. THAT ROAD BE WAITING FOR YOU...

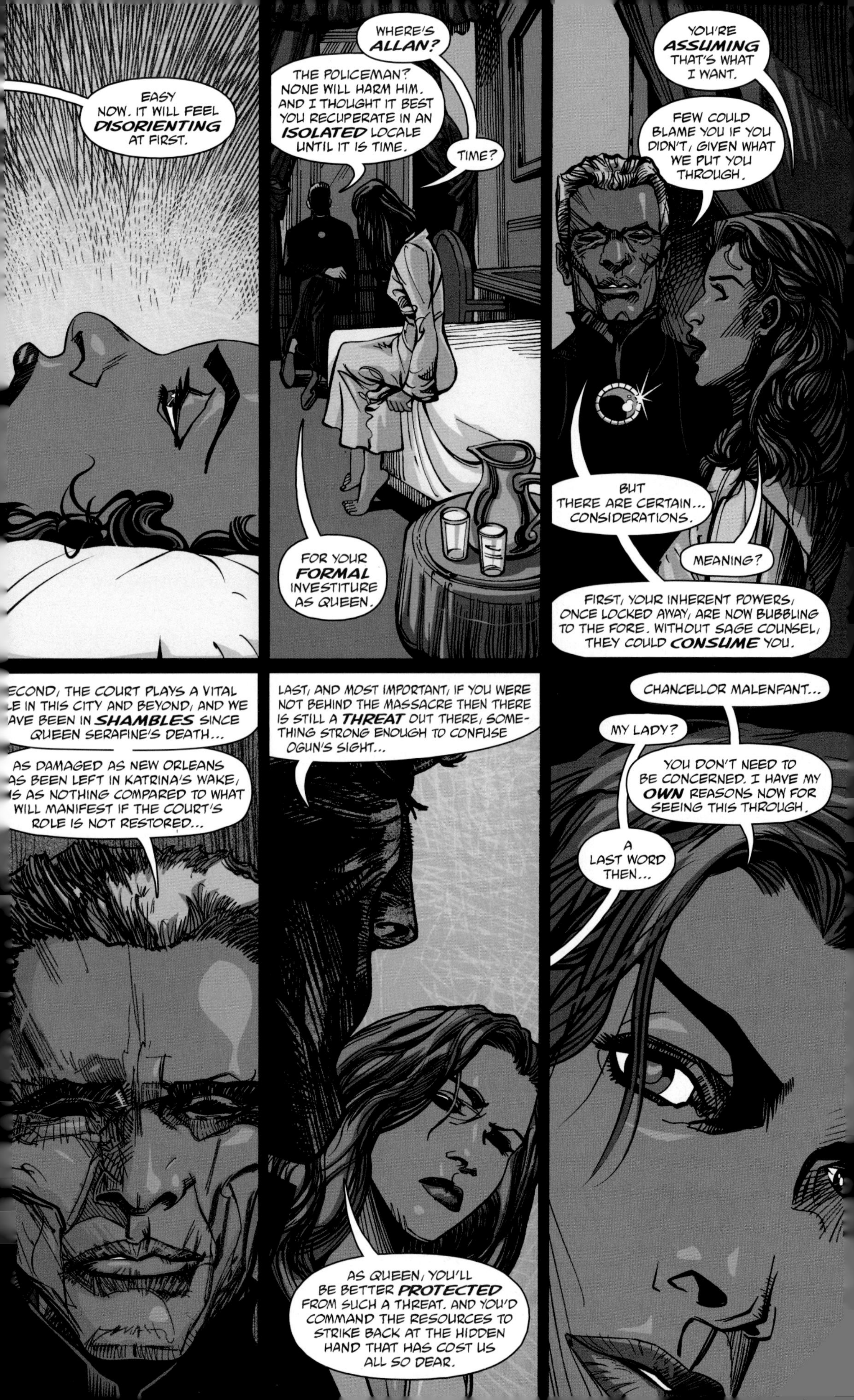
EASY NOW. IT WILL FEEL DISORIENTING AT FIRST.
WHERE'S ALLAN?
THE POLICEMAN? NONE WILL HARM HIM. AND I THOUGHT IT BEST YOU RECUPERATE IN AN ISOLATED LOCALE UNTIL IT IS TIME.
TIME?
FOR YOUR FORMAL INVESTITURE AS QUEEN.
YOU'RE ASSUMING THAT'S WHAT I WANT.
FEW COULD BLAME YOU IF YOU DIDN'T, GIVEN WHAT WE PUT YOU THROUGH.
BUT THERE ARE CERTAIN... CONSIDERATIONS.
MEANING?
FIRST, YOUR INHERENT POWERS, ONCE LOCKED AWAY, ARE NOW BUBBLING TO THE FORE. WITHOUT SAGE COUNSEL, THEY COULD CONSUME YOU.
ECOND, THE COURT PLAYS A VITAL LE IN THIS CITY AND BEYOND, AND WE AVE BEEN IN SHAMBLES SINCE QUEEN SERAFINE'S DEATH...
AS DAMAGED AS NEW ORLEANS AS BEEN LEFT IN KATRINA'S WAKE, IS AS NOTHING COMPARED TO WHAT WILL MANIFEST IF THE COURT'S ROLE IS NOT RESTORED...
LAST, AND MOST IMPORTANT, IF YOU WERE NOT BEHIND THE MASSACRE THEN THERE IS STILL A THREAT OUT THERE, SOMETHING STRONG ENOUGH TO CONFUSE OGUN'S SIGHT...
AS QUEEN, YOU'LL BE BETTER PROTECTED FROM SUCH A THREAT. AND YOU'D COMMAND THE RESOURCES TO STRIKE BACK AT THE HIDDEN HAND THAT HAS COST US ALL SO DEAR.
CHANCELLOR MALENFANT...
MY LADY?
YOU DON'T NEED TO BE CONCERNED. I HAVE MY OWN REASONS NOW FOR SEEING THIS THROUGH.
A LAST WORD THEN...

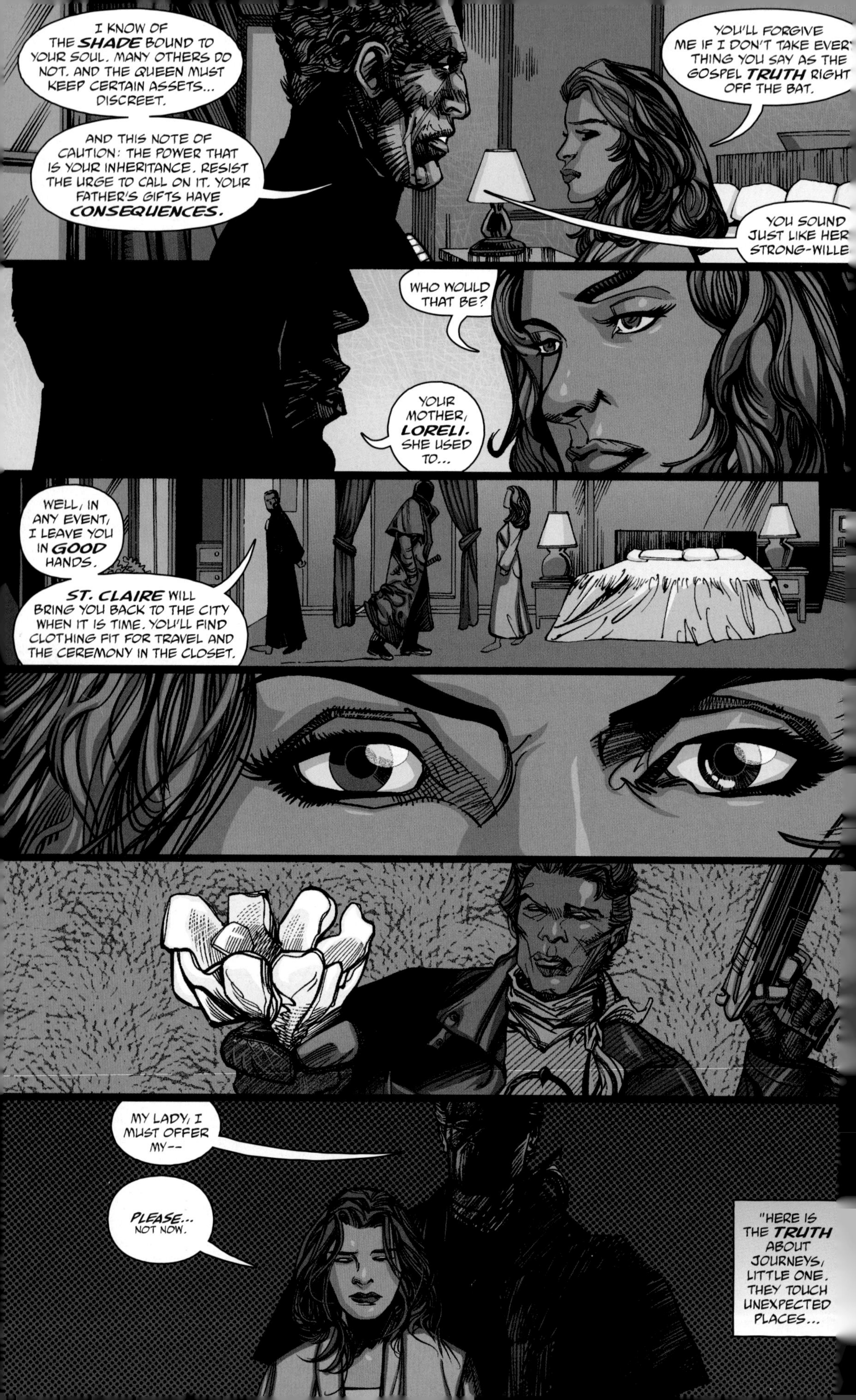
I KNOW OF THE SHADE BOUND TO YOUR SOUL. MANY OTHERS DO NOT. AND THE QUEEN MUST KEEP CERTAIN ASSETS... DISCREET.
AND THIS NOTE OF CAUTION: THE POWER THAT IS YOUR INHERITANCE. RESIST THE URGE TO CALL ON IT. YOUR FATHER'S GIFTS HAVE CONSEQUENCES.
YOU'LL FORGIVE ME IF I DON'T TAKE EVERY-THING YOU SAY AS THE GOSPEL TRUTH RIGHT OFF THE BAT.
YOU SOUND JUST LIKE HER. STRONG-WILLE
WHO WOULD THAT BE?
YOUR MOTHER, LORELI. SHE USED TO...
WELL, IN ANY EVENT, I LEAVE YOU IN GOOD HANDS.
ST. CLAIRE WILL BRING YOU BACK TO THE CITY WHEN IT IS TIME. YOU'LL FIND CLOTHING FIT FOR TRAVEL AND THE CEREMONY IN THE CLOSET.
MY LADY, I MUST OFFER MY--
PLEASE... NOT NOW.
"HERE IS THE TRUTH ABOUT JOURNEYS, LITTLE ONE. THEY TOUCH UNEXPECTED PLACES...

HAITI, 1804

"AND NOW OUR LITTLE BOY, NOT MUCH OLDER THAN YOU, FOUND HIMSELF IN THE WAR. LENDING A HAND WHERE HE COULD."

"THE FIGHTING RAGED ON..."

"BUT EVENTUALLY, AND AT GREAT COST, THE OPPRESSOR WITHDREW HIS SHACKLES."

"THE PEOPLE CELEBRATED AND GAVE THANKS TO THEIR OLD GODS."

"BUT THE PRICE PAID FOR HAITI'S VICTORY, THEN AND IN TIMES TO COME, WOULD PROVE HIGH."

"OH, NO. WHAT HAPPENED?! DID THE BOY DIE?"

"NO, MY DEAR, NOT AT ALL. IN FACT, FOR HIM..."

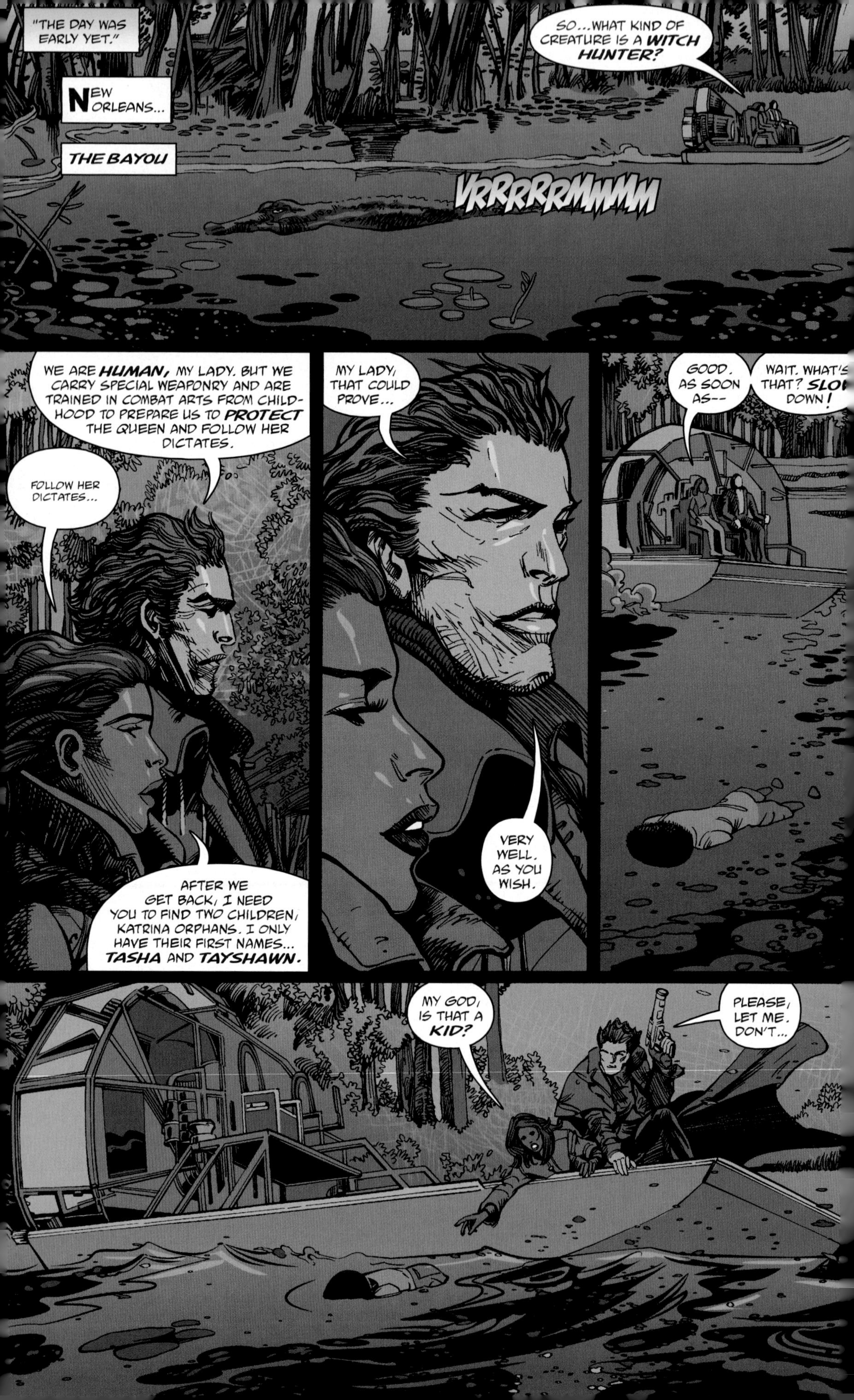

"THE DAY WAS EARLY YET."
NEW ORLEANS...
THE BAYOU
SO...WHAT KIND OF CREATURE IS A WITCH HUNTER?
VRRRRRMMMM
WE ARE HUMAN, MY LADY. BUT WE CARRY SPECIAL WEAPONRY AND ARE TRAINED IN COMBAT ARTS FROM CHILD-HOOD TO PREPARE US TO PROTECT THE QUEEN AND FOLLOW HER DICTATES.
FOLLOW HER DICTATES...
AFTER WE GET BACK, I NEED YOU TO FIND TWO CHILDREN, KATRINA ORPHANS. I ONLY HAVE THEIR FIRST NAMES... TASHA AND TAYSHAWN.
MY LADY, THAT COULD PROVE...
VERY WELL. AS YOU WISH.
GOOD. AS SOON AS--
WAIT. WHAT'S THAT? SLO DOWN!
MY GOD, IS THAT A KID?
PLEASE, LET ME. DON'T...

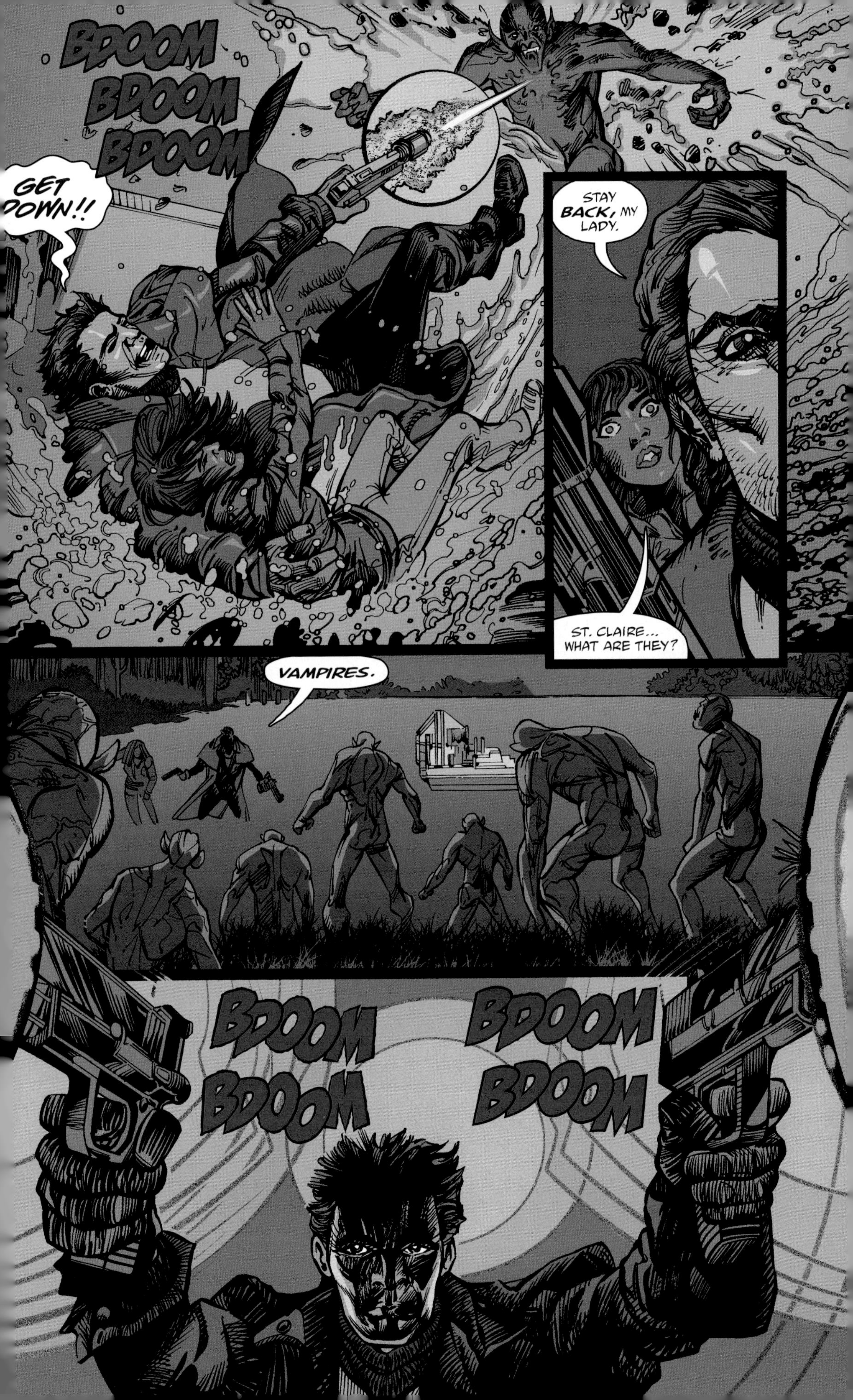
BDOOM
BDOOM
BDOOM
GET DOWN!!
STAY BACK, MY LADY.
ST. CLAIRE... WHAT ARE THEY?
VAMPIRES.
BDOOM
BDOOM
BDOOM
BDOOM

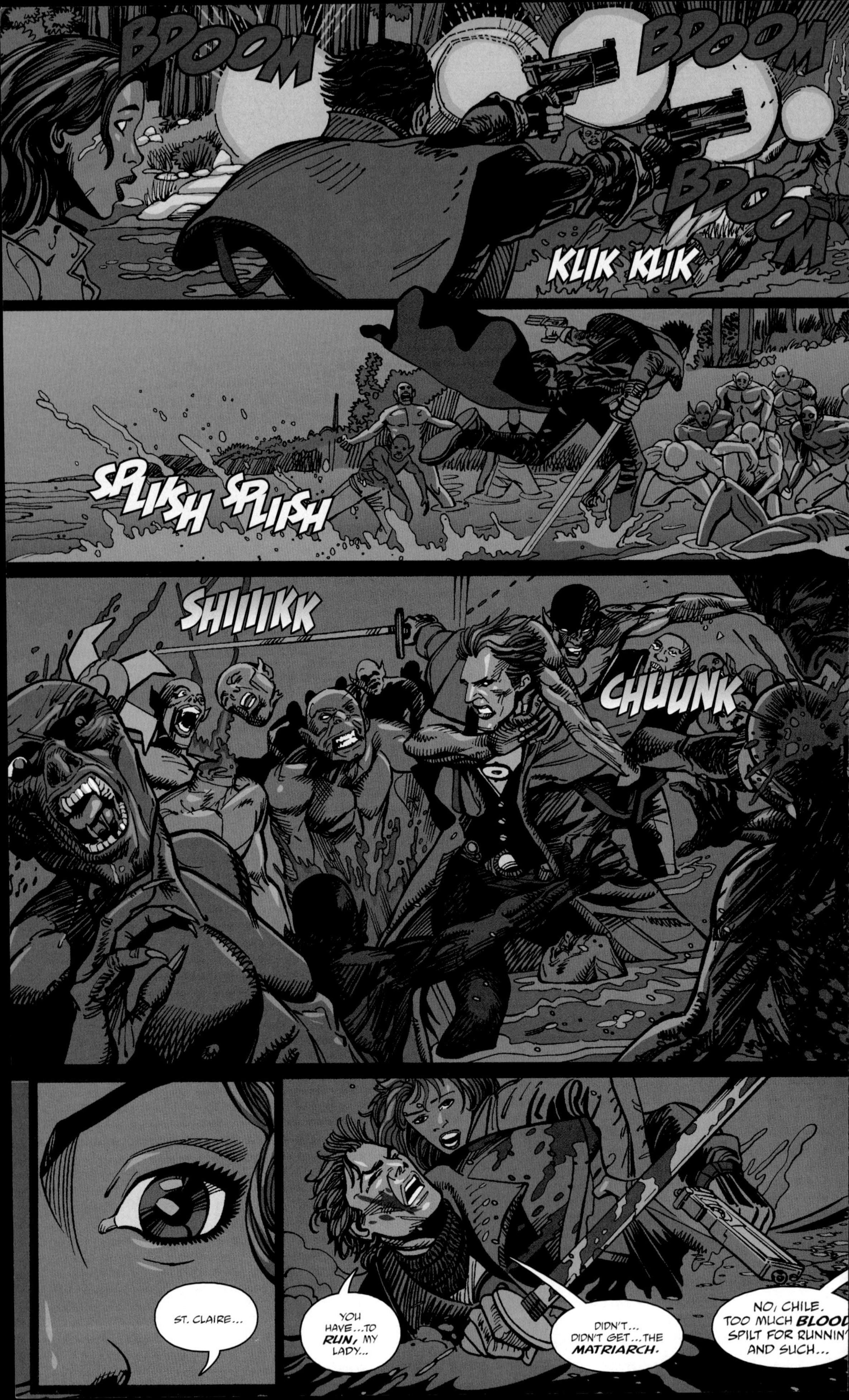
BDOOM
BDOOM
BDOOM
KLIK KLIK
SPLISH SPLISH
SHIIIIKK
CHUUNK
ST. CLAIRE...
YOU HAVE...TO RUN, MY LADY...
DIDN'T... DIDN'T GET...THE MATRIARCH.
NO, CHILE. TOO MUCH BLOOD SPILT FOR RUNNIN' AND SUCH...

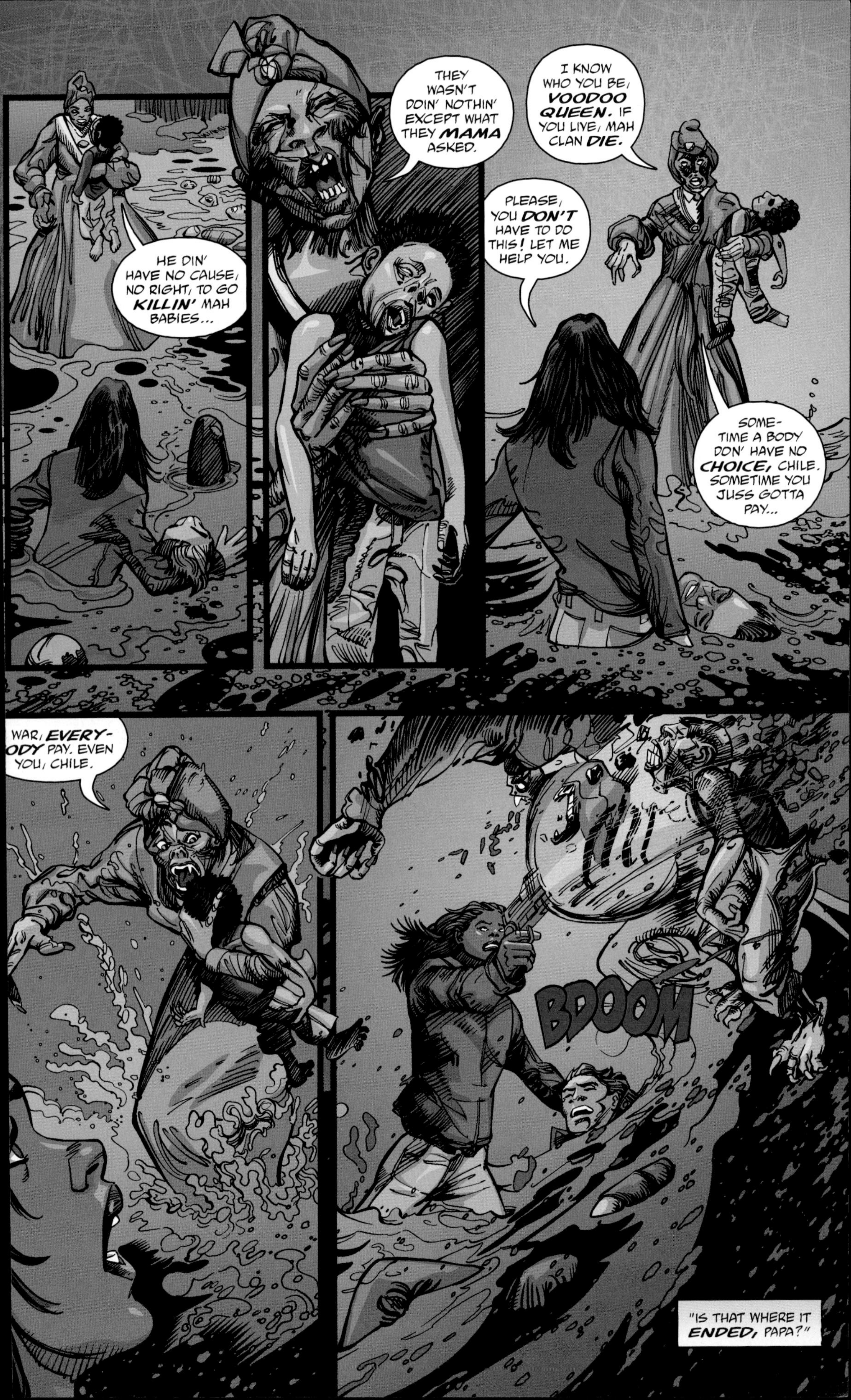
HE DIN' HAVE NO CAUSE, NO RIGHT, TO GO KILLIN' MAH BABIES...
THEY WASN'T DOIN' NOTHIN' EXCEPT WHAT THEY MAMA ASKED.
I KNOW WHO YOU BE, VOODOO QUEEN. IF YOU LIVE, MAH CLAN DIE.
PLEASE, YOU DON'T HAVE TO DO THIS! LET ME HELP YOU.
SOME-TIME A BODY DON' HAVE NO CHOICE, CHILE. SOMETIME YOU JUSS GOTTA PAY...
WAR, EVERY-ODY PAY. EVEN YOU, CHILE.
BDOOM
"IS THAT WHERE IT ENDED, PAPA?"

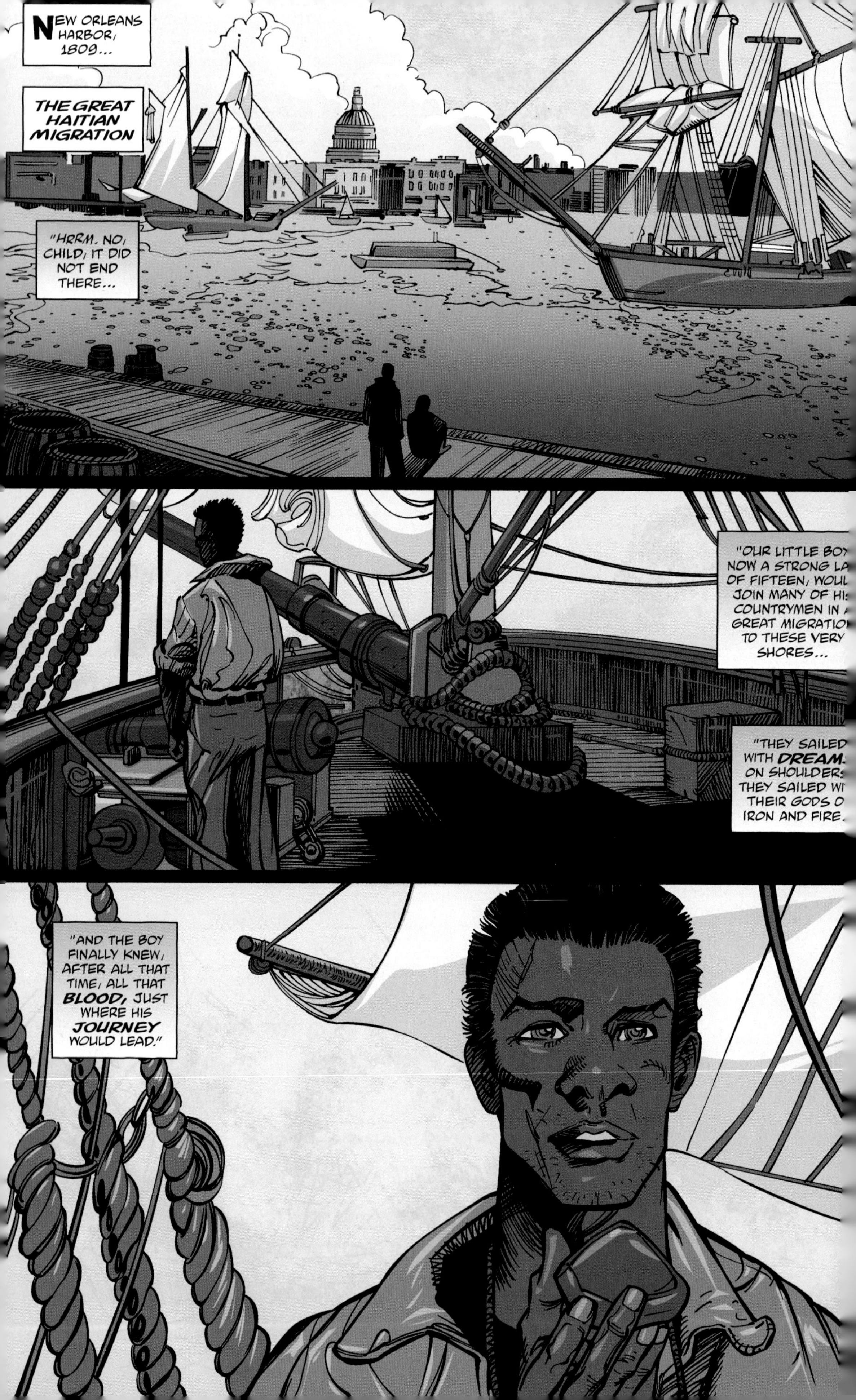
NEW ORLEANS HARBOR, 1809...
THE GREAT HAITIAN MIGRATION
"HRRM. NO, CHILD, IT DID NOT END THERE...
"OUR LITTLE BOY NOW A STRONG LA OF FIFTEEN, WOUL JOIN MANY OF HI COUNTRYMEN IN GREAT MIGRATIO TO THESE VERY SHORES...
"THEY SAILED WITH DREAM ON SHOULDERS THEY SAILED WI THEIR GODS O IRON AND FIRE.
"AND THE BOY FINALLY KNEW, AFTER ALL THAT TIME, ALL THAT BLOOD, JUST WHERE HIS JOURNEY WOULD LEAD."

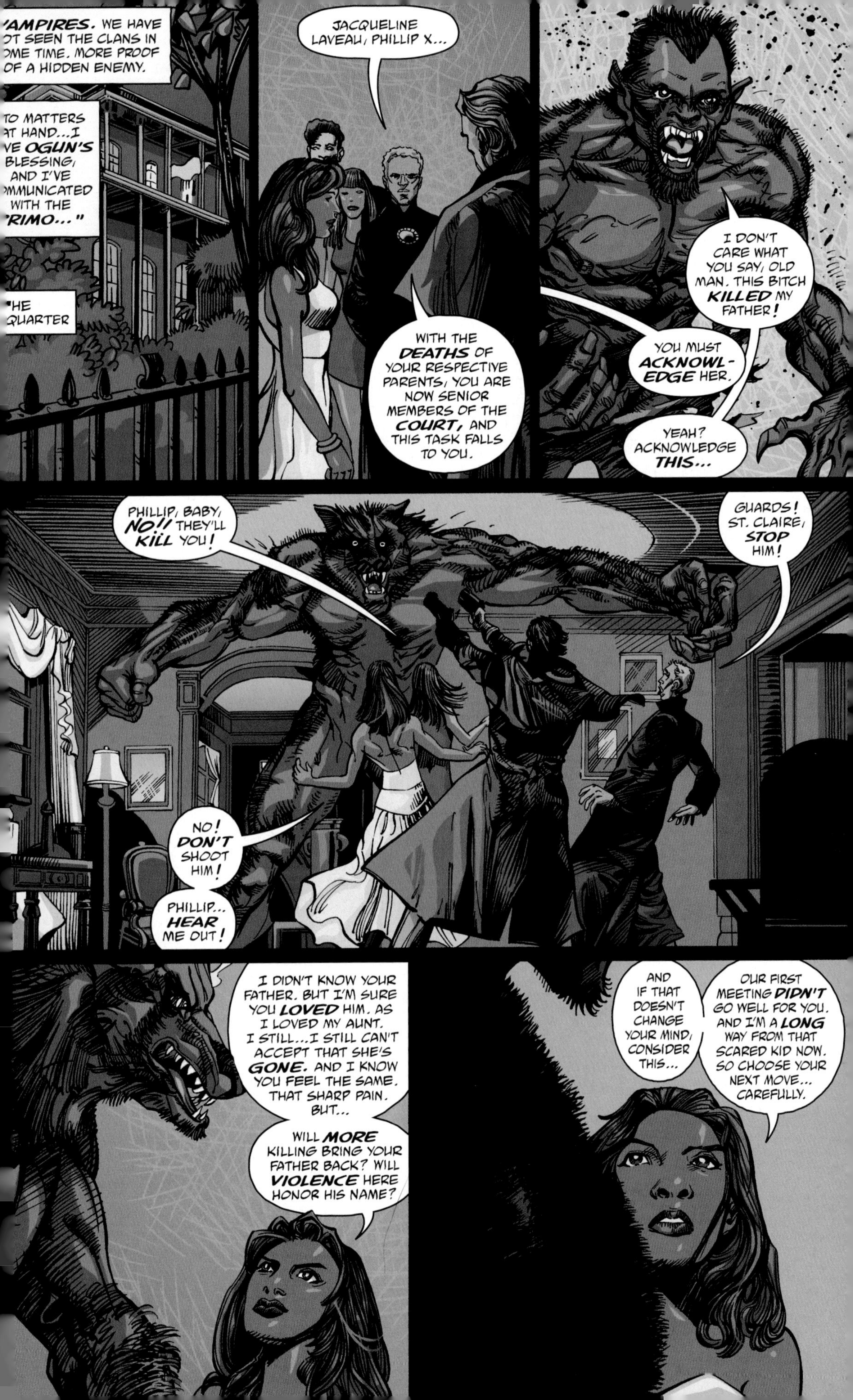
VAMPIRES. WE HAVE
OT SEEN THE CLANS IN
OME TIME. MORE PROOF
OF A HIDDEN ENEMY.
TO MATTERS
AT HAND...I
VE OGUN'S
BLESSING,
AND I'VE
OMMUNICATED
WITH THE
RIMO..."
HE
QUARTER
JACQUELINE LAVEAU, PHILLIP X...
WITH THE DEATHS OF YOUR RESPECTIVE PARENTS, YOU ARE NOW SENIOR MEMBERS OF THE COURT, AND THIS TASK FALLS TO YOU.
I DON'T CARE WHAT YOU SAY, OLD MAN. THIS BITCH KILLED MY FATHER!
YOU MUST ACKNOWL-EDGE HER.
YEAH? ACKNOWLEDGE THIS...
PHILLIP, BABY, NO!! THEY'LL KILL YOU!
GUARDS! ST. CLAIRE, STOP HIM!
NO! DON'T SHOOT HIM!
PHILLIP... HEAR ME OUT!
I DIDN'T KNOW YOUR FATHER. BUT I'M SURE YOU LOVED HIM. AS I LOVED MY AUNT. I STILL...I STILL CAN'T ACCEPT THAT SHE'S GONE. AND I KNOW YOU FEEL THE SAME. THAT SHARP PAIN. BUT...
WILL MORE KILLING BRING YOUR FATHER BACK? WILL VIOLENCE HERE HONOR HIS NAME?
OUR FIRST MEETING DIDN'T GO WELL FOR YOU. AND I'M A LONG WAY FROM THAT SCARED KID NOW. SO CHOOSE YOUR NEXT MOVE... CAREFULLY.
AND IF THAT DOESN'T CHANGE YOUR MIND, CONSIDER THIS...

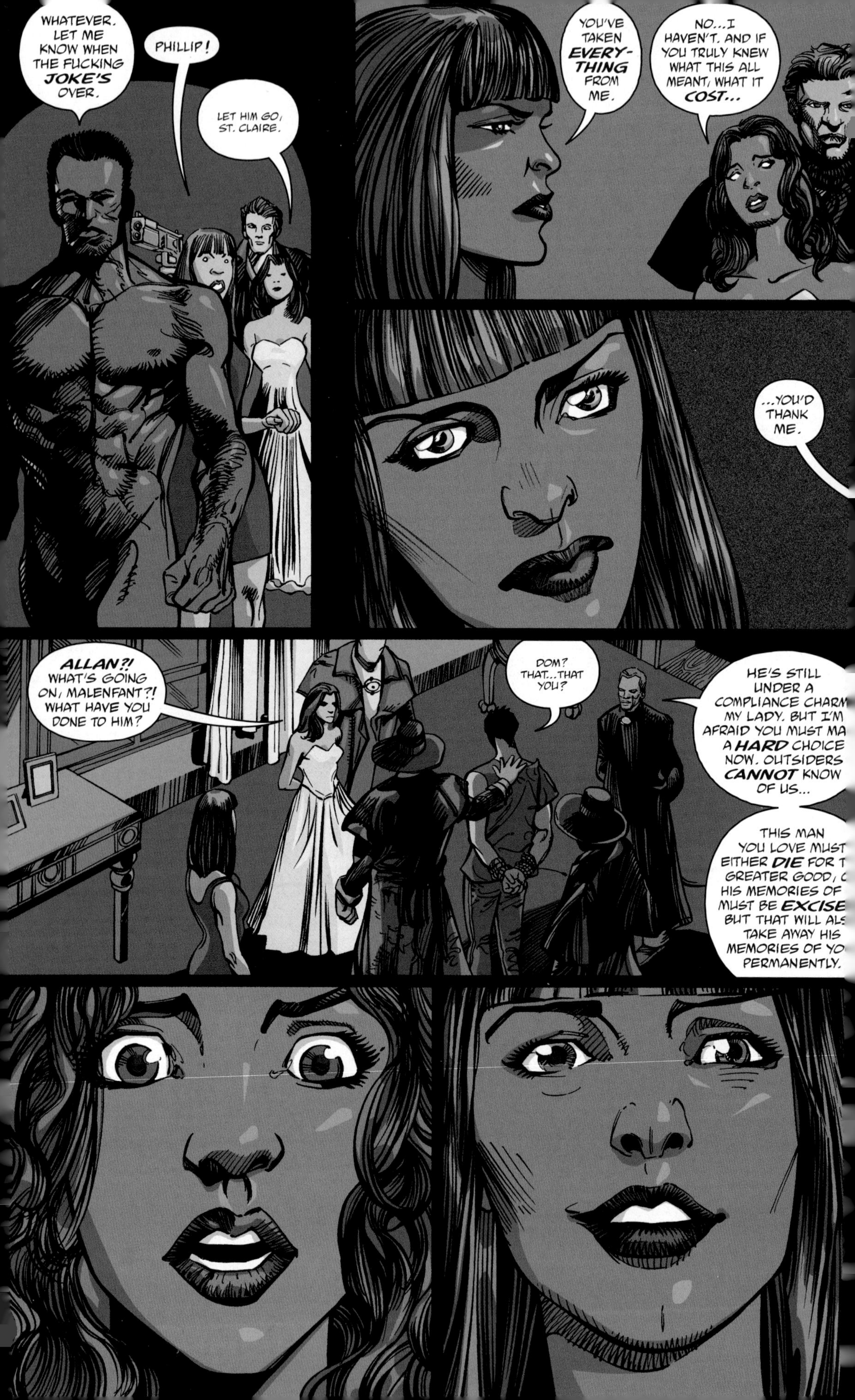
WHATEVER. LET ME KNOW WHEN THE FUCKING JOKE'S OVER.
PHILLIP!
LET HIM GO, ST. CLAIRE.
YOU'VE TAKEN EVERY-THING FROM ME.
NO...I HAVEN'T. AND IF YOU TRULY KNEW WHAT THIS ALL MEANT, WHAT IT COST...
...YOU'D THANK ME.
ALLAN?! WHAT'S GOING ON, MALENFANT?! WHAT HAVE YOU DONE TO HIM?
DOM? THAT...THAT YOU?
HE'S STILL UNDER A COMPLIANCE CHARM MY LADY. BUT I'M AFRAID YOU MUST MA A HARD CHOICE NOW. OUTSIDERS CANNOT KNOW OF US...
THIS MAN YOU LOVE MUST EITHER DIE FOR T GREATER GOOD, O HIS MEMORIES OF MUST BE EXCISE BUT THAT WILL ALS TAKE AWAY HIS MEMORIES OF YO PERMANENTLY.

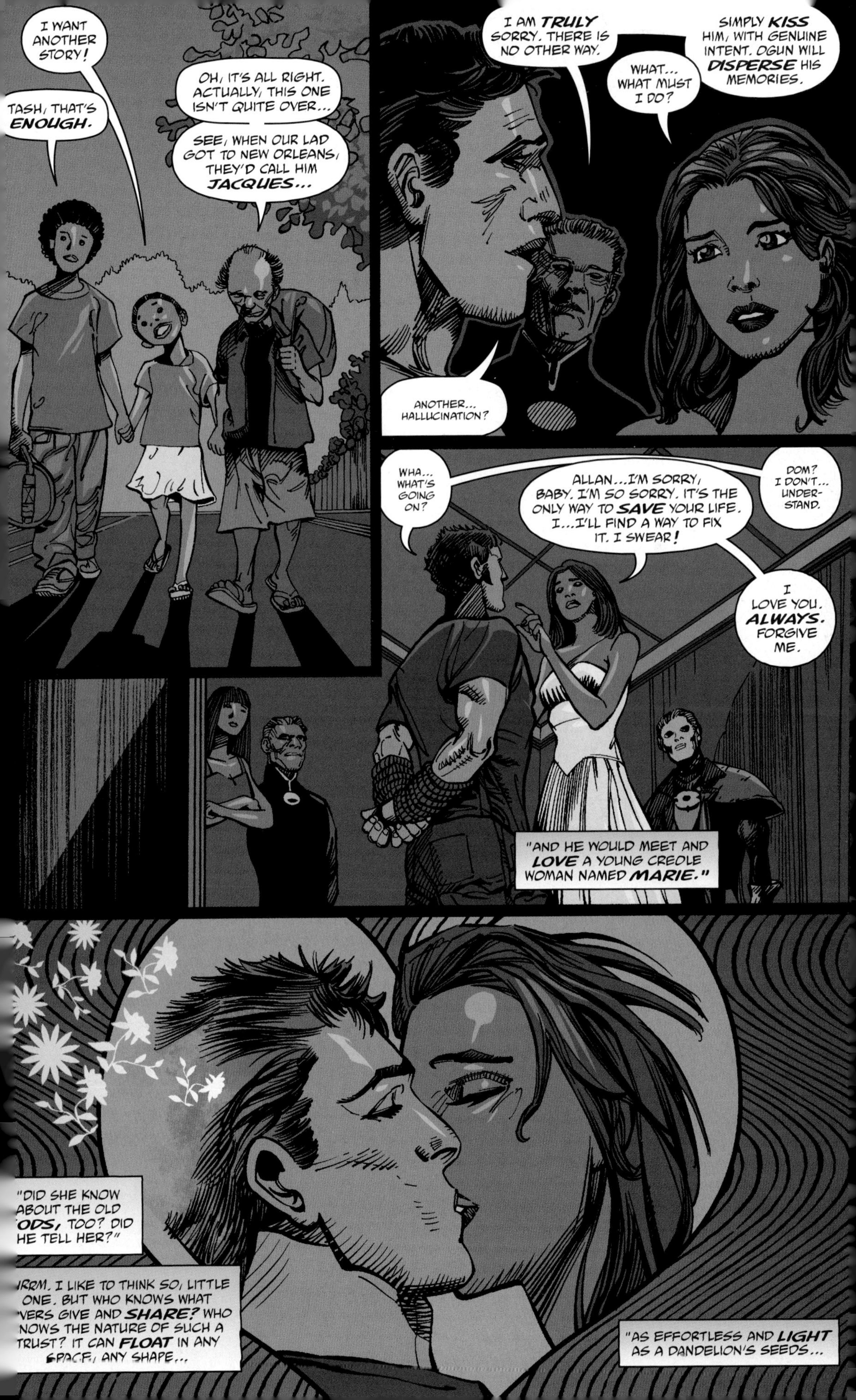
I WANT ANOTHER STORY!
TASH, THAT'S ENOUGH.
OH, IT'S ALL RIGHT. ACTUALLY, THIS ONE ISN'T QUITE OVER...
SEE, WHEN OUR LAD GOT TO NEW ORLEANS, THEY'D CALL HIM JACQUES...
I AM TRULY SORRY. THERE IS NO OTHER WAY.
WHAT... WHAT MUST I DO?
SIMPLY KISS HIM, WITH GENUINE INTENT. OGUN WILL DISPERSE HIS MEMORIES.
ANOTHER... HALLUCINATION?
WHA... WHAT'S GOING ON?
ALLAN...I'M SORRY, BABY. I'M SO SORRY. IT'S THE ONLY WAY TO SAVE YOUR LIFE. I...I'LL FIND A WAY TO FIX IT. I SWEAR!
DOM? I DON'T... UNDER-STAND.
I LOVE YOU. ALWAYS. FORGIVE ME.
"AND HE WOULD MEET AND LOVE A YOUNG CREOLE WOMAN NAMED MARIE."
"DID SHE KNOW ABOUT THE OLD ODS, TOO? DID HE TELL HER?"
RRM. I LIKE TO THINK SO, LITTLE ONE. BUT WHO KNOWS WHAT VERS GIVE AND SHARE? WHO NOWS THE NATURE OF SUCH A TRUST? IT CAN FLOAT IN ANY SPACE, ANY SHAPE...
"AS EFFORTLESS AND LIGHT AS A DANDELION'S SEEDS...

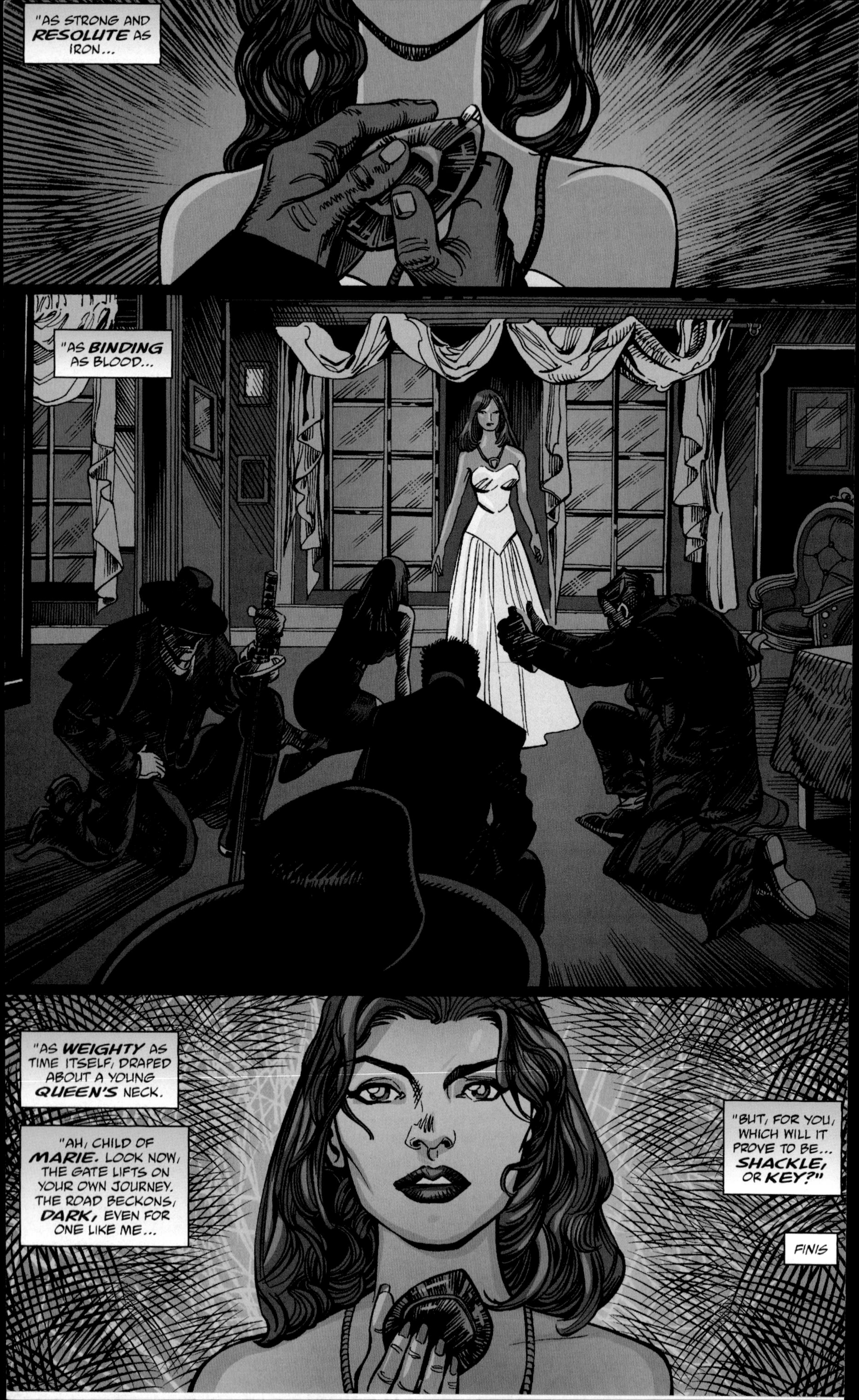

"AS STRONG AND RESOLUTE AS IRON...
"AS BINDING AS BLOOD...
"AS WEIGHTY AS TIME ITSELF, DRAPED ABOUT A YOUNG QUEEN'S NECK.
"AH, CHILD OF MARIE. LOOK NOW, THE GATE LIFTS ON YOUR OWN JOURNEY. THE ROAD BECKONS, DARK, EVEN FOR ONE LIKE ME...
"BUT, FOR YOU, WHICH WILL IT PROVE TO BE... SHACKLE, OR KEY?"
FINIS

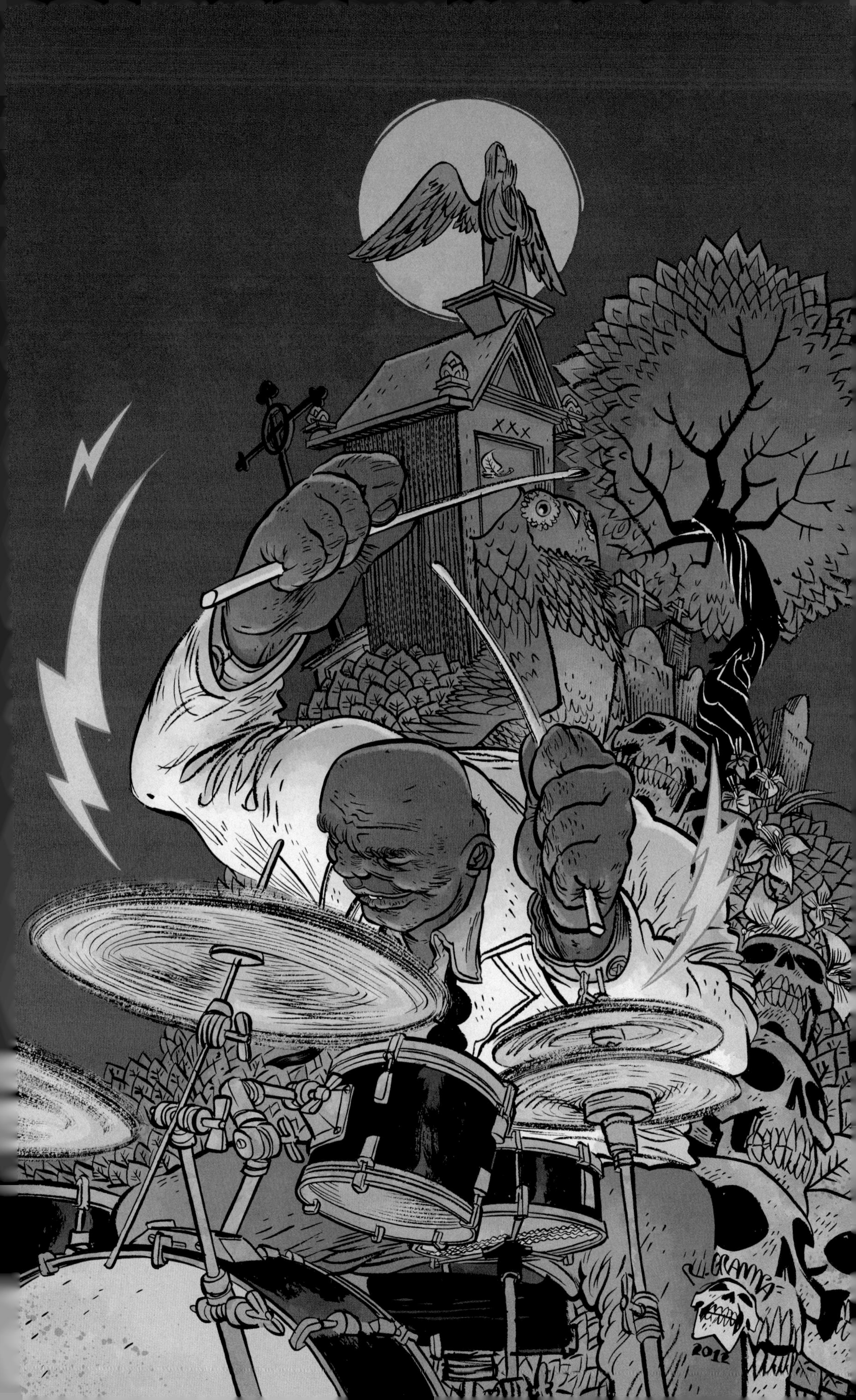
2012

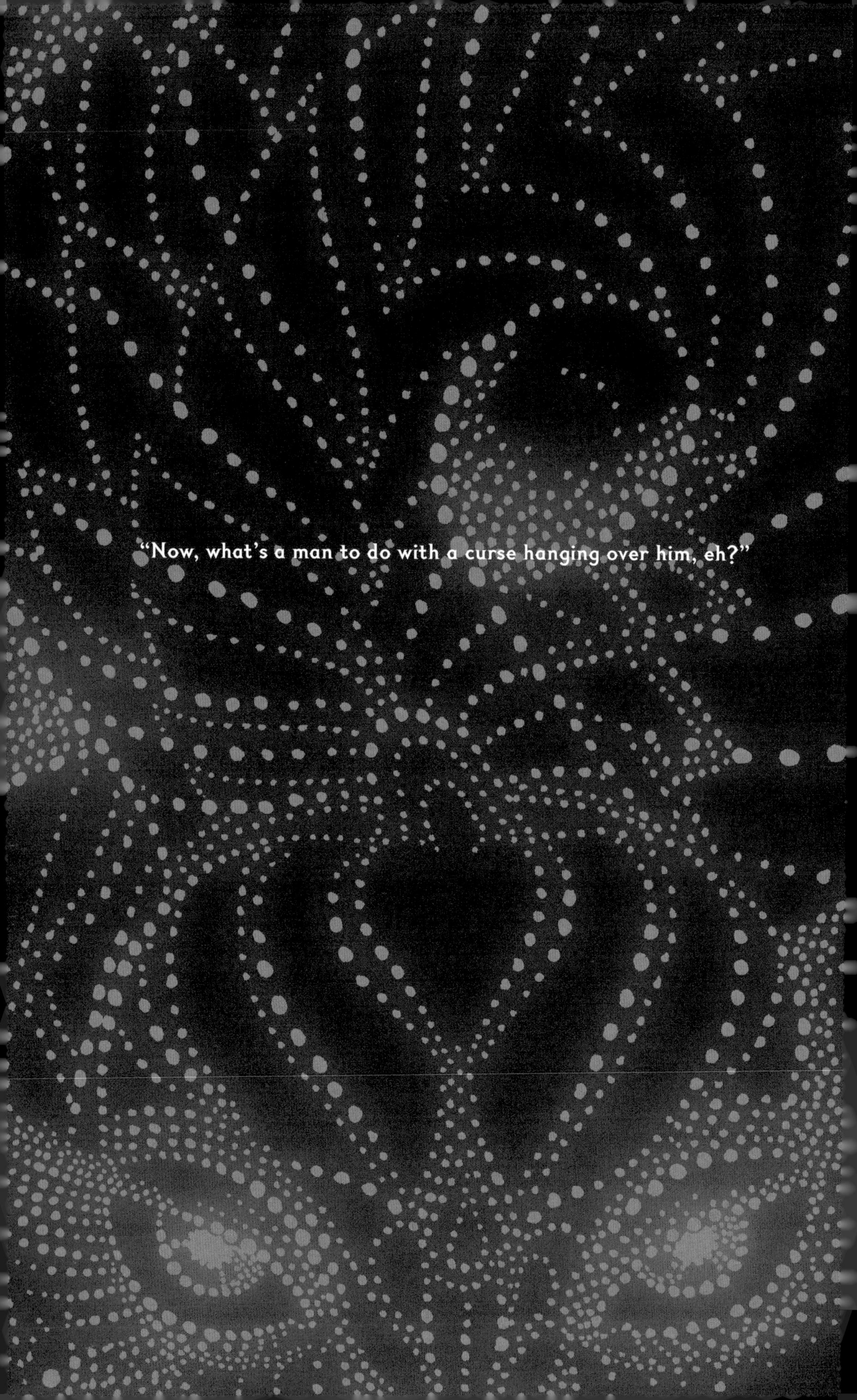
"Now, what's a man to do with a curse hanging over him, eh?"

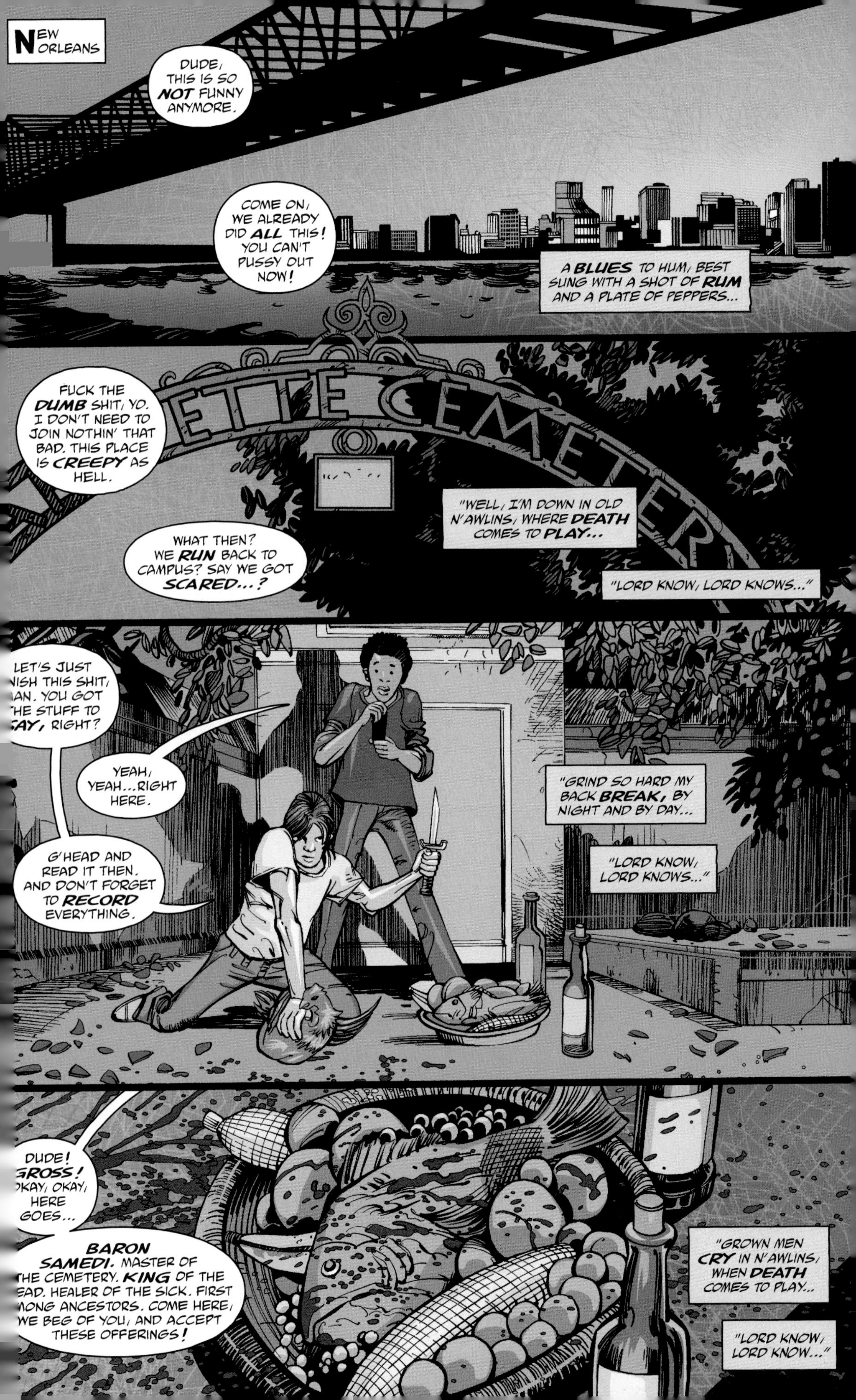
NEW ORLEANS
DUDE, THIS IS SO NOT FUNNY ANYMORE.
COME ON, WE ALREADY DID ALL THIS! YOU CAN'T PUSSY OUT NOW!
A BLUES TO HUM, BEST SUNG WITH A SHOT OF RUM AND A PLATE OF PEPPERS...
ETTE CEMETER
FUCK THE DUMB SHIT, YO. I DON'T NEED TO JOIN NOTHIN' THAT BAD. THIS PLACE IS CREEPY AS HELL.
WHAT THEN? WE RUN BACK TO CAMPUS? SAY WE GOT SCARED...?
"WELL, I'M DOWN IN OLD N'AWLINS, WHERE DEATH COMES TO PLAY...
"LORD KNOW, LORD KNOWS..."
LET'S JUST NISH THIS SHIT, AN. YOU GOT HE STUFF TO SAY, RIGHT?
YEAH, YEAH...RIGHT HERE.
G'HEAD AND READ IT THEN. AND DON'T FORGET TO RECORD EVERYTHING.
"GRIND SO HARD MY BACK BREAK, BY NIGHT AND BY DAY...
"LORD KNOW, LORD KNOWS..."
DUDE! GROSS! OKAY, OKAY, HERE GOES...
BARON SAMEDI. MASTER OF THE CEMETERY. KING OF THE EAD. HEALER OF THE SICK. FIRST MONG ANCESTORS. COME HERE, WE BEG OF YOU, AND ACCEPT THESE OFFERINGS!
"GROWN MEN CRY IN N'AWLINS, WHEN DEATH COMES TO PLAY...
"LORD KNOW, LORD KNOW..."

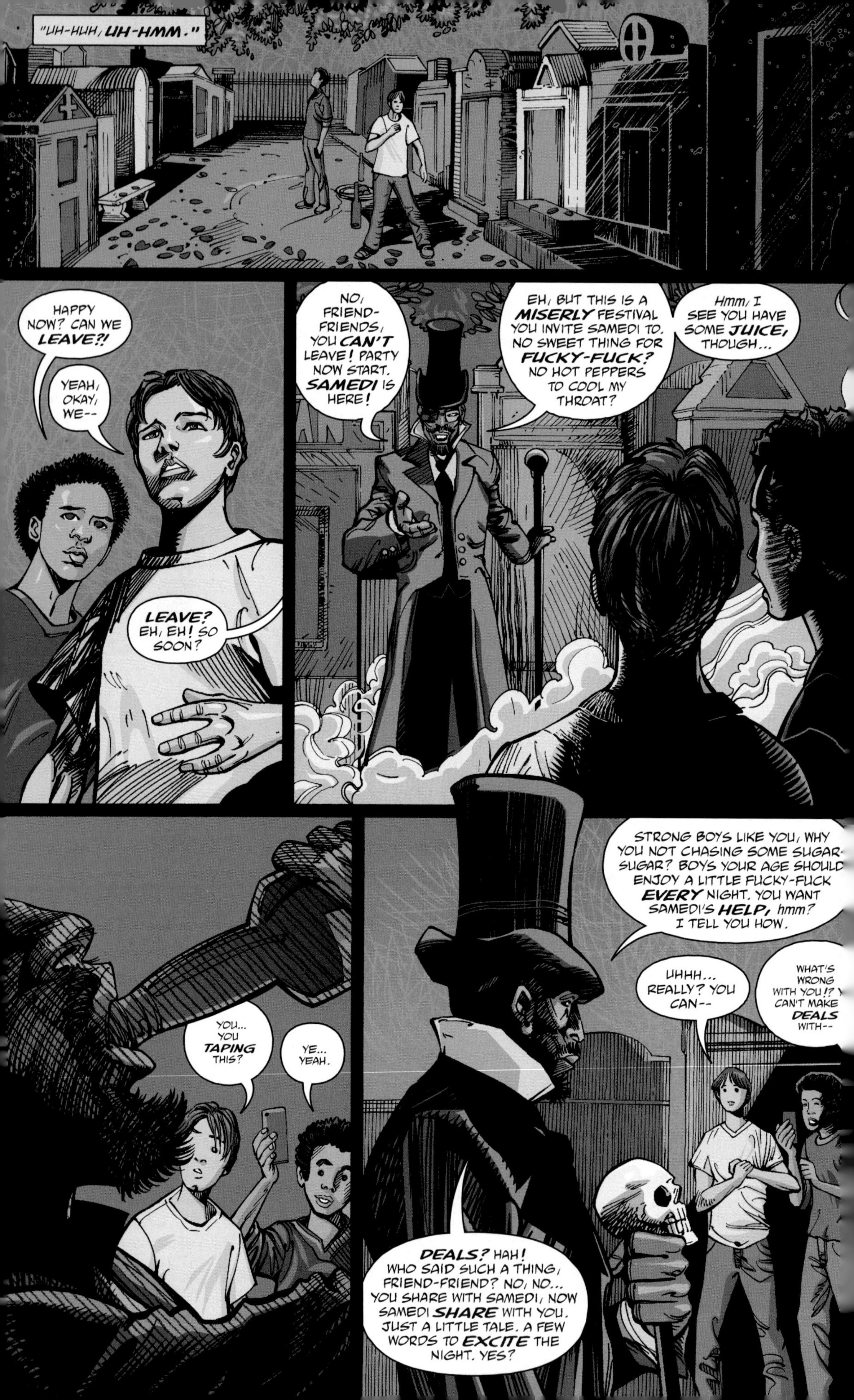
"UH-HUH, UH-HMM."
HAPPY NOW? CAN WE LEAVE?!
YEAH, OKAY, WE--
LEAVE? EH, EH! SO SOON?
NO, FRIEND-FRIENDS, YOU CAN'T LEAVE! PARTY NOW START. SAMEDI IS HERE!
EH, BUT THIS IS A MISERLY FESTIVAL YOU INVITE SAMEDI TO. NO SWEET THING FOR FUCKY-FUCK? NO HOT PEPPERS TO COOL MY THROAT?
Hmm, I SEE YOU HAVE SOME JUICE, THOUGH...
YOU... YOU TAPING THIS?
YE... YEAH.
STRONG BOYS LIKE YOU, WHY YOU NOT CHASING SOME SUGAR-SUGAR? BOYS YOUR AGE SHOULD ENJOY A LITTLE FUCKY-FUCK EVERY NIGHT. YOU WANT SAMEDI'S HELP, hmm? I TELL YOU HOW.
UHHH... REALLY? YOU CAN--
WHAT'S WRONG WITH YOU!? YOU CAN'T MAKE DEALS WITH--
DEALS? HAH! WHO SAID SUCH A THING, FRIEND-FRIEND? NO, NO... YOU SHARE WITH SAMEDI, NOW SAMEDI SHARE WITH YOU. JUST A LITTLE TALE. A FEW WORDS TO EXCITE THE NIGHT. YES?

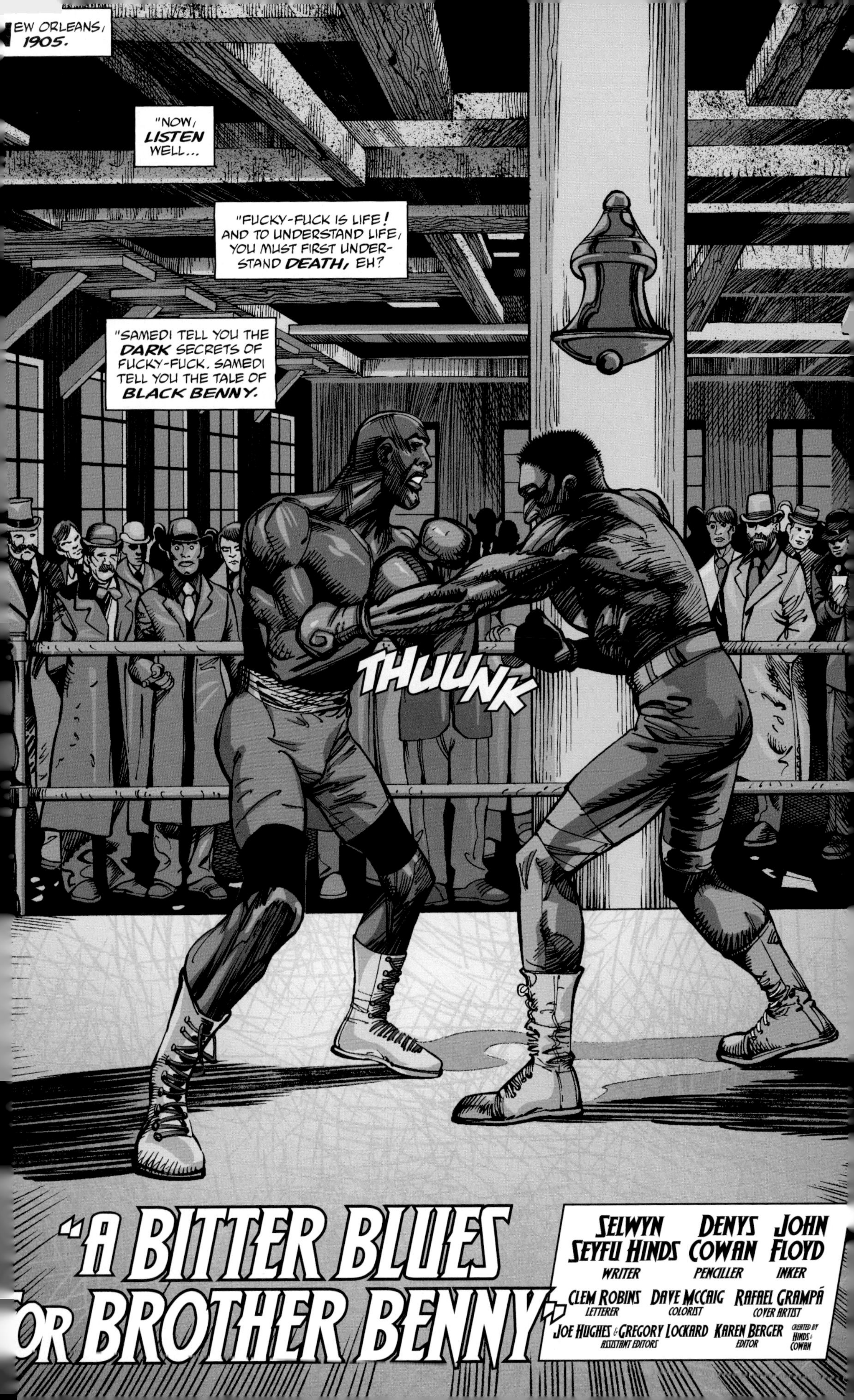

NEW ORLEANS, 1905.
"NOW, LISTEN WELL...
"FUCKY-FUCK IS LIFE! AND TO UNDERSTAND LIFE, YOU MUST FIRST UNDERSTAND DEATH, EH?
"SAMEDI TELL YOU THE DARK SECRETS OF FUCKY-FUCK. SAMEDI TELL YOU THE TALE OF BLACK BENNY.
THUUNK
"A BITTER BLUES FOR BROTHER BENNY"
SELWYN SEYFU HINDS WRITER
DENYS COWAN PENCILLER
JOHN FLOYD INKER
CLEM ROBINS LETTERER
DAVE McCAIG COLORIST
RAFAEL GRAMPÁ COVER ARTIST
JOE HUGHES & GREGORY LOCKARD ASSISTANT EDITORS
KAREN BERGER EDITOR
CREATED BY HINDS & COWAN

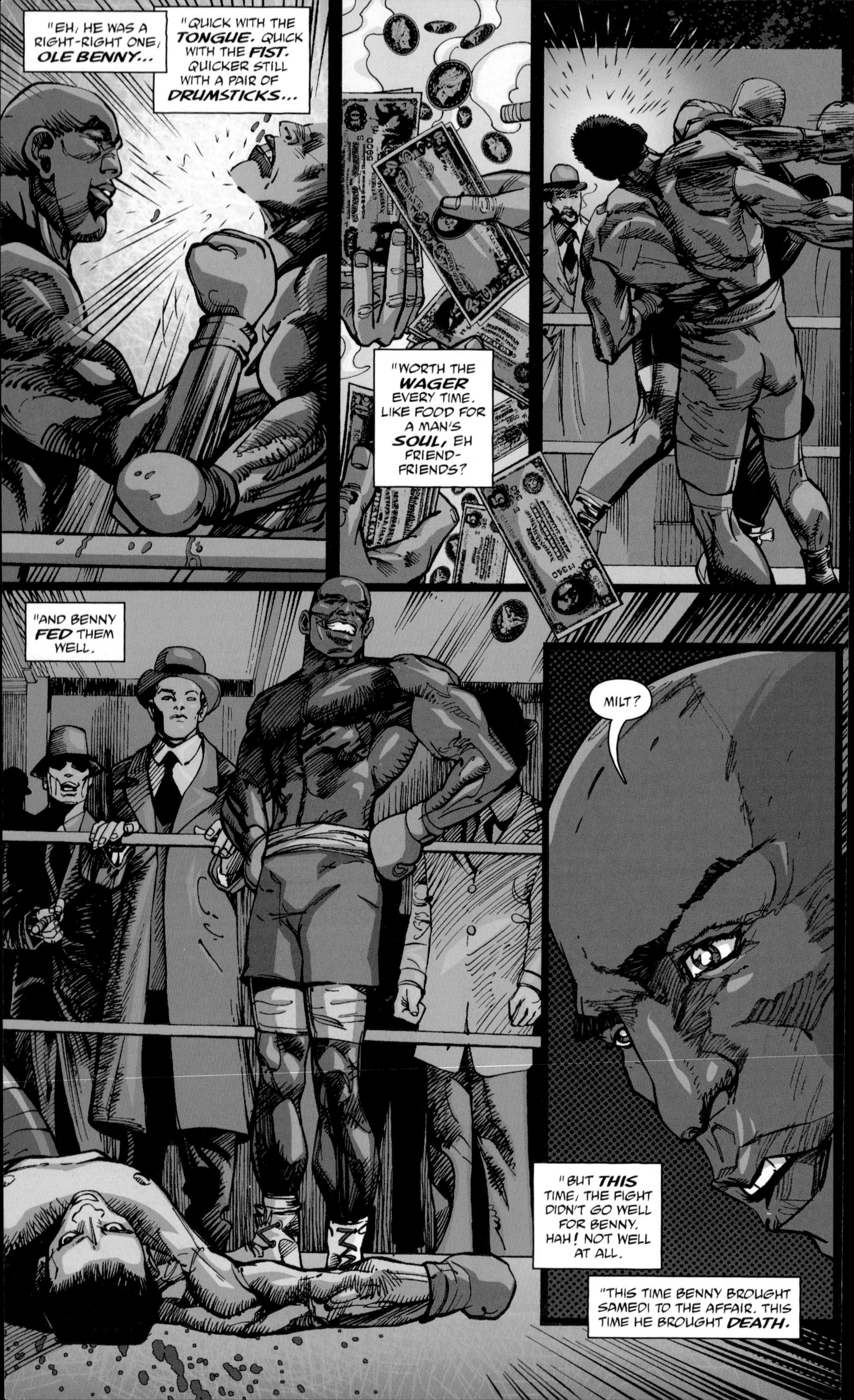
"EH, HE WAS A RIGHT-RIGHT ONE, OLE BENNY...
"QUICK WITH THE TONGUE. QUICK WITH THE FIST. QUICKER STILL WITH A PAIR OF DRUMSTICKS...
"WORTH THE WAGER EVERY TIME. LIKE FOOD FOR A MAN'S SOUL, EH FRIEND-FRIENDS?
"AND BENNY FED THEM WELL.
MILT?
"BUT THIS TIME, THE FIGHT DIDN'T GO WELL FOR BENNY. HAH! NOT WELL AT ALL.
"THIS TIME BENNY BROUGHT SAMEDI TO THE AFFAIR. THIS TIME HE BROUGHT DEATH.

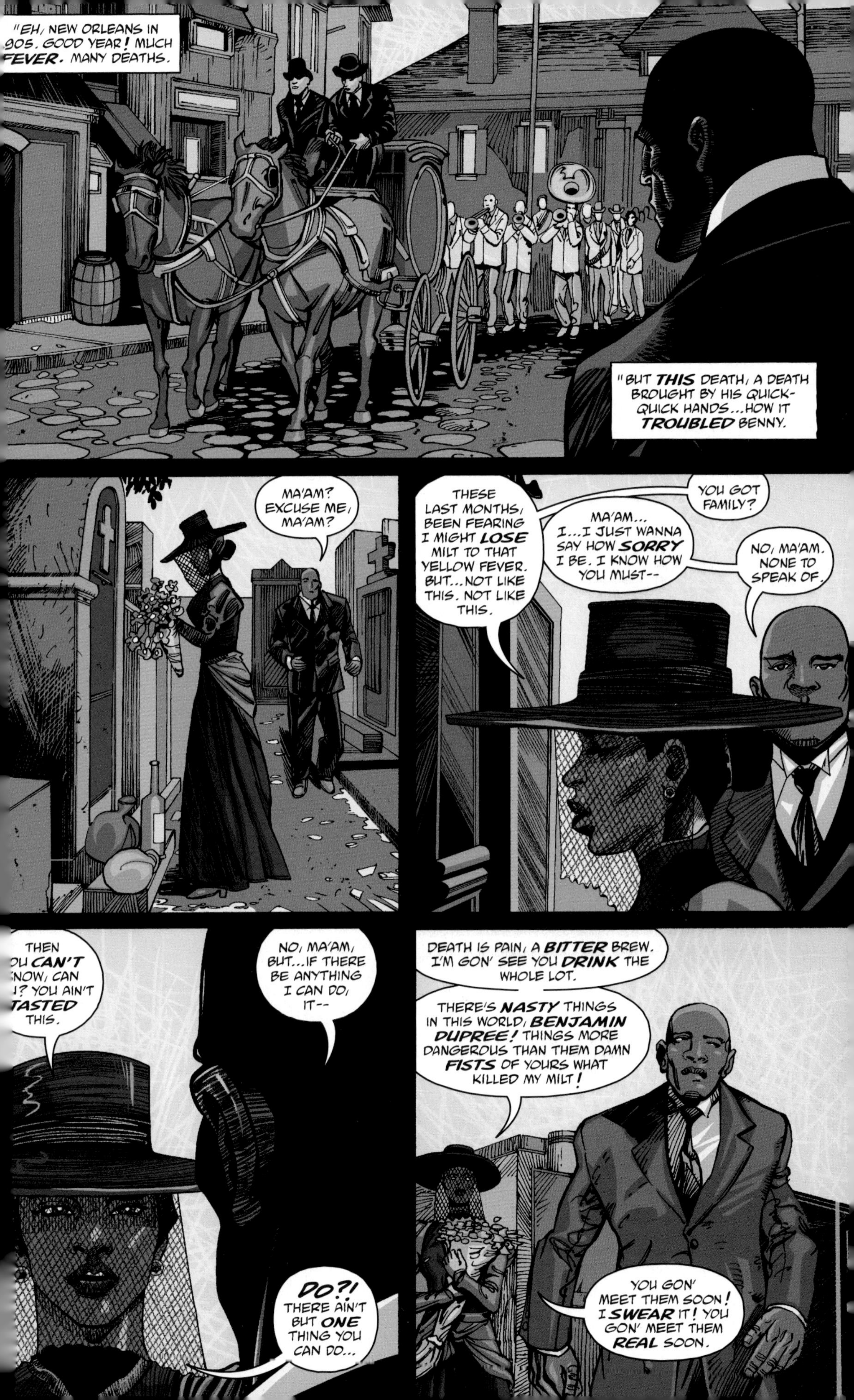
"EH, NEW ORLEANS IN 905. GOOD YEAR! MUCH FEVER. MANY DEATHS.
"BUT THIS DEATH, A DEATH BROUGHT BY HIS QUICK-QUICK HANDS...HOW IT TROUBLED BENNY.
MA'AM? EXCUSE ME, MA'AM?
YOU GOT FAMILY?
MA'AM... I...I JUST WANNA SAY HOW SORRY I BE. I KNOW HOW YOU MUST--
THESE LAST MONTHS, BEEN FEARING I MIGHT LOSE MILT TO THAT YELLOW FEVER. BUT...NOT LIKE THIS. NOT LIKE THIS.
NO, MA'AM. NONE TO SPEAK OF.
THEN YOU CAN'T KNOW, CAN YOU? YOU AIN'T TASTED THIS.
NO, MA'AM, BUT...IF THERE BE ANYTHING I CAN DO, IT--
DO?! THERE AIN'T BUT ONE THING YOU CAN DO...
DEATH IS PAIN, A BITTER BREW. I'M GON' SEE YOU DRINK THE WHOLE LOT.
THERE'S NASTY THINGS IN THIS WORLD, BENJAMIN DUPREE! THINGS MORE DANGEROUS THAN THEM DAMN FISTS OF YOURS WHAT KILLED MY MILT!
YOU GON' MEET THEM SOON! I SWEAR IT! YOU GON' MEET THEM REAL SOON.

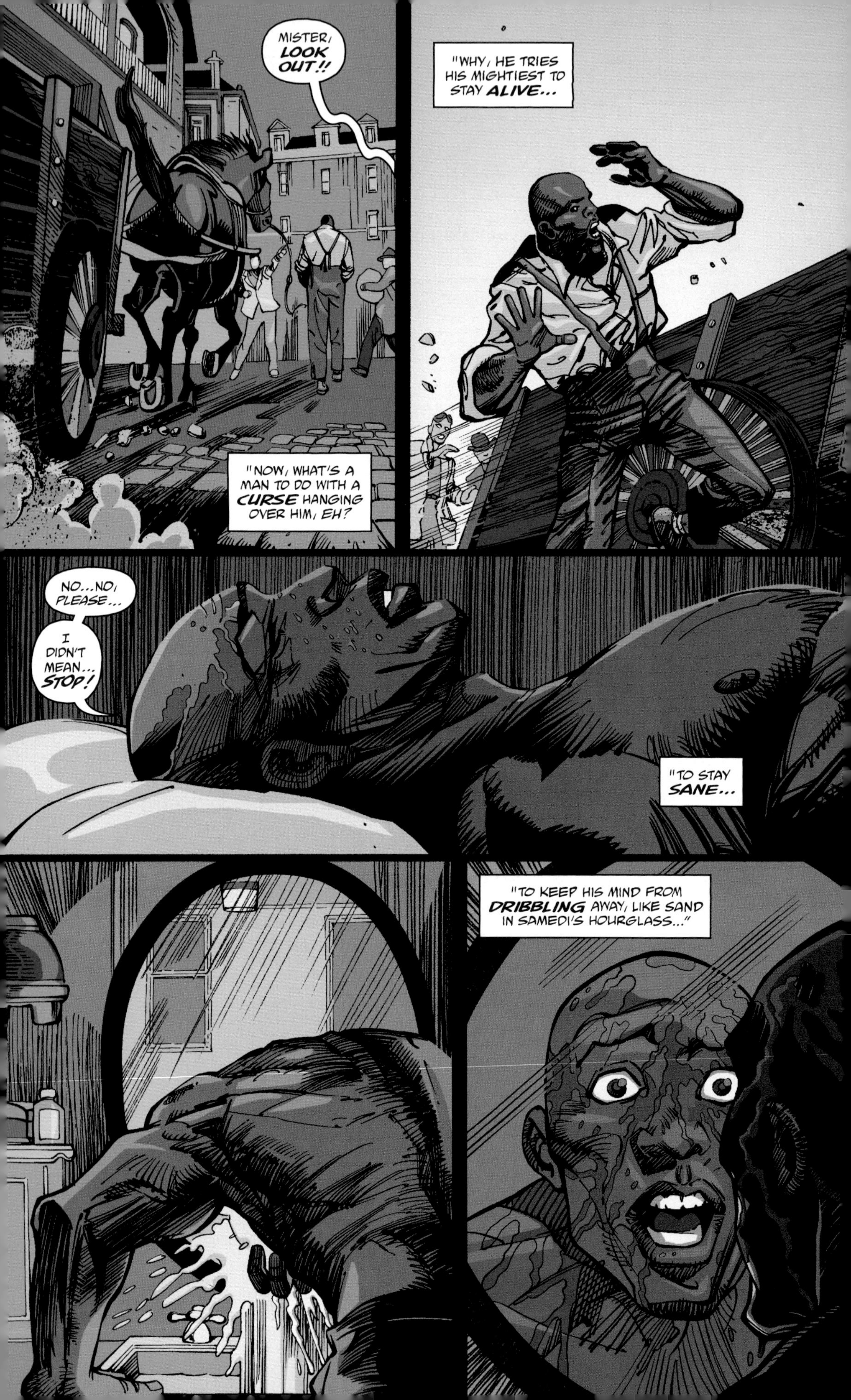
MISTER, LOOK OUT!!
"NOW, WHAT'S A MAN TO DO WITH A CURSE HANGING OVER HIM, EH?
"WHY, HE TRIES HIS MIGHTIEST TO STAY ALIVE...
NO...NO, PLEASE...
I DIDN'T MEAN... STOP!
"TO STAY SANE...
"TO KEEP HIS MIND FROM DRIBBLING AWAY, LIKE SAND IN SAMEDI'S HOURGLASS..."

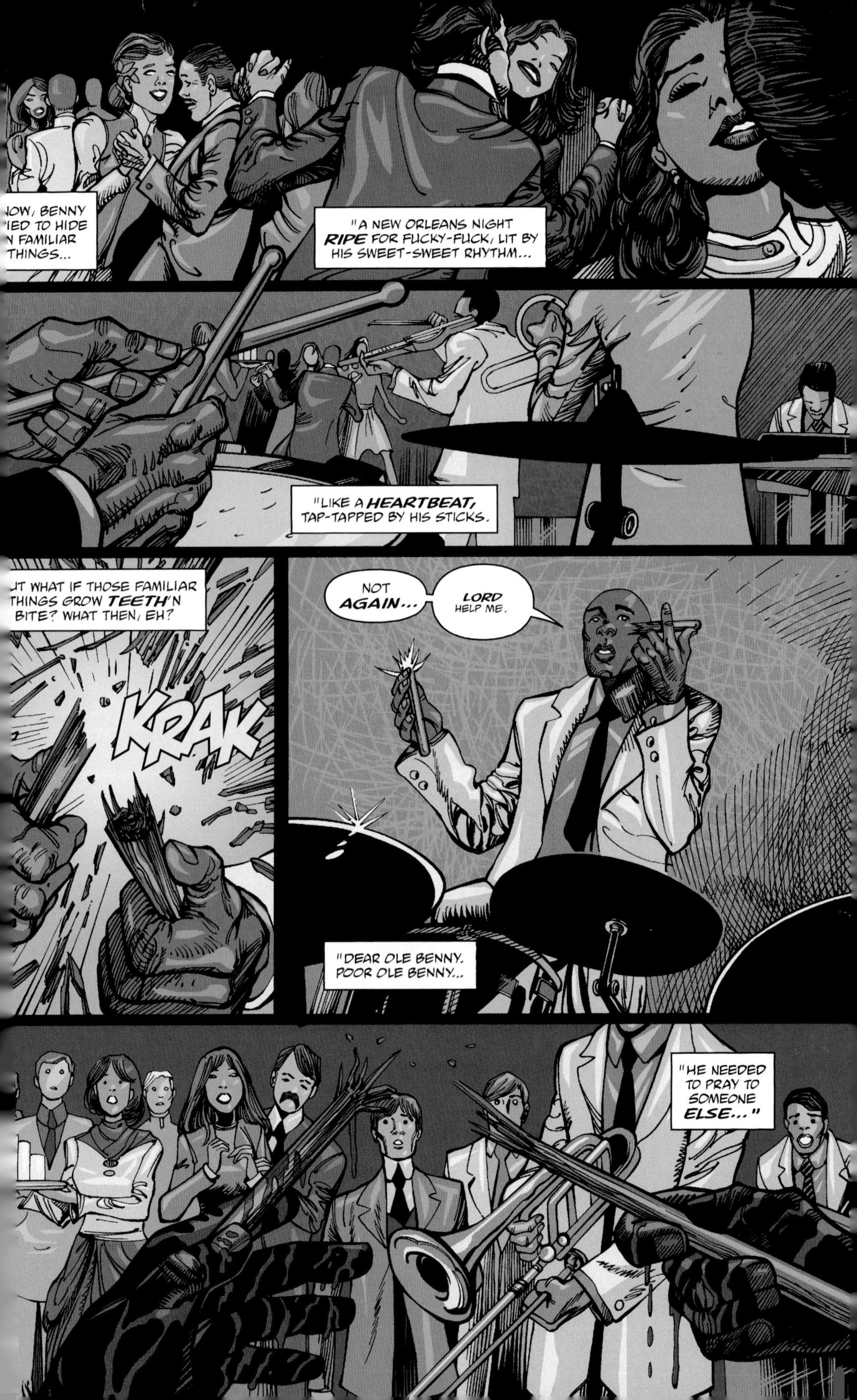

NOW, BENNY
IED TO HIDE
N FAMILIAR
THINGS...
"A NEW ORLEANS NIGHT RIPE FOR FUCKY-FUCK, LIT BY HIS SWEET-SWEET RHYTHM...
"LIKE A HEARTBEAT, TAP-TAPPED BY HIS STICKS.
UT WHAT IF THOSE FAMILIAR THINGS GROW TEETH'N BITE? WHAT THEN, EH?
KRAK
NOT AGAIN...
LORD HELP ME.
"DEAR OLE BENNY. POOR OLE BENNY...
"HE NEEDED TO PRAY TO SOMEONE ELSE..."

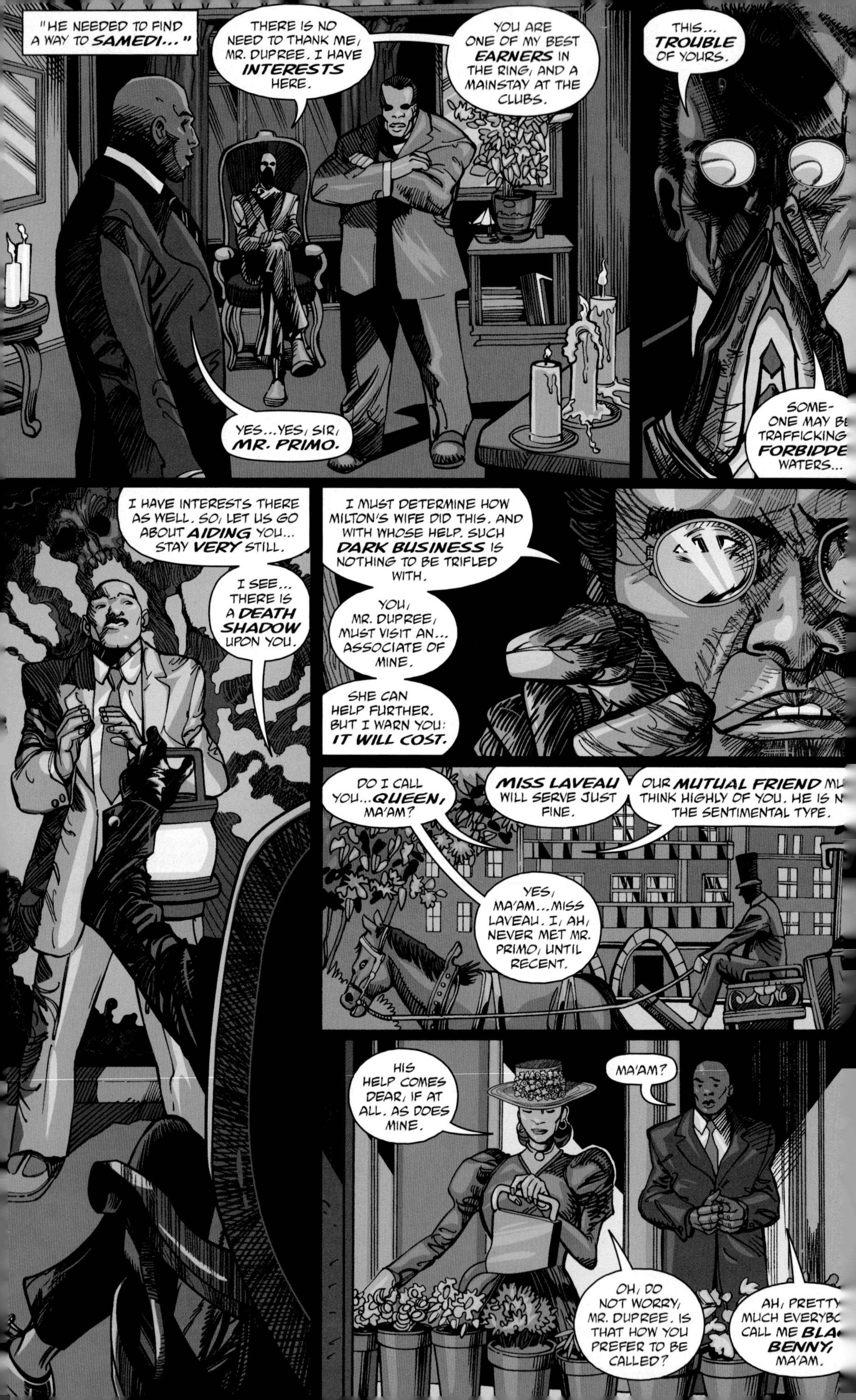
"HE NEEDED TO FIND A WAY TO SAMEDI..."
THERE IS NO NEED TO THANK ME, MR. DUPREE. I HAVE INTERESTS HERE.
YOU ARE ONE OF MY BEST EARNERS IN THE RING, AND A MAINSTAY AT THE CLUBS.
YES...YES, SIR, MR. PRIMO.
THIS... TROUBLE OF YOURS.
SOME-ONE MAY BE TRAFFICKING FORBIDDE WATERS...
I HAVE INTERESTS THERE AS WELL. SO, LET US GO ABOUT AIDING YOU... STAY VERY STILL.
I SEE... THERE IS A DEATH SHADOW UPON YOU.
I MUST DETERMINE HOW MILTON'S WIFE DID THIS. AND WITH WHOSE HELP. SUCH DARK BUSINESS IS NOTHING TO BE TRIFLED WITH.
YOU, MR. DUPREE, MUST VISIT AN... ASSOCIATE OF MINE.
SHE CAN HELP FURTHER. BUT I WARN YOU: IT WILL COST.
DO I CALL YOU...QUEEN, MA'AM?
MISS LAVEAU WILL SERVE JUST FINE.
OUR MUTUAL FRIEND MU THINK HIGHLY OF YOU. HE IS N THE SENTIMENTAL TYPE.
YES, MA'AM...MISS LAVEAU. I, AH, NEVER MET MR. PRIMO, UNTIL RECENT.
HIS HELP COMES DEAR, IF AT ALL. AS DOES MINE.
MA'AM?
OH, DO NOT WORRY, MR. DUPREE. IS THAT HOW YOU PREFER TO BE CALLED?
AH, PRETTY MUCH EVERYBO CALL ME BLA BENNY, MA'AM.

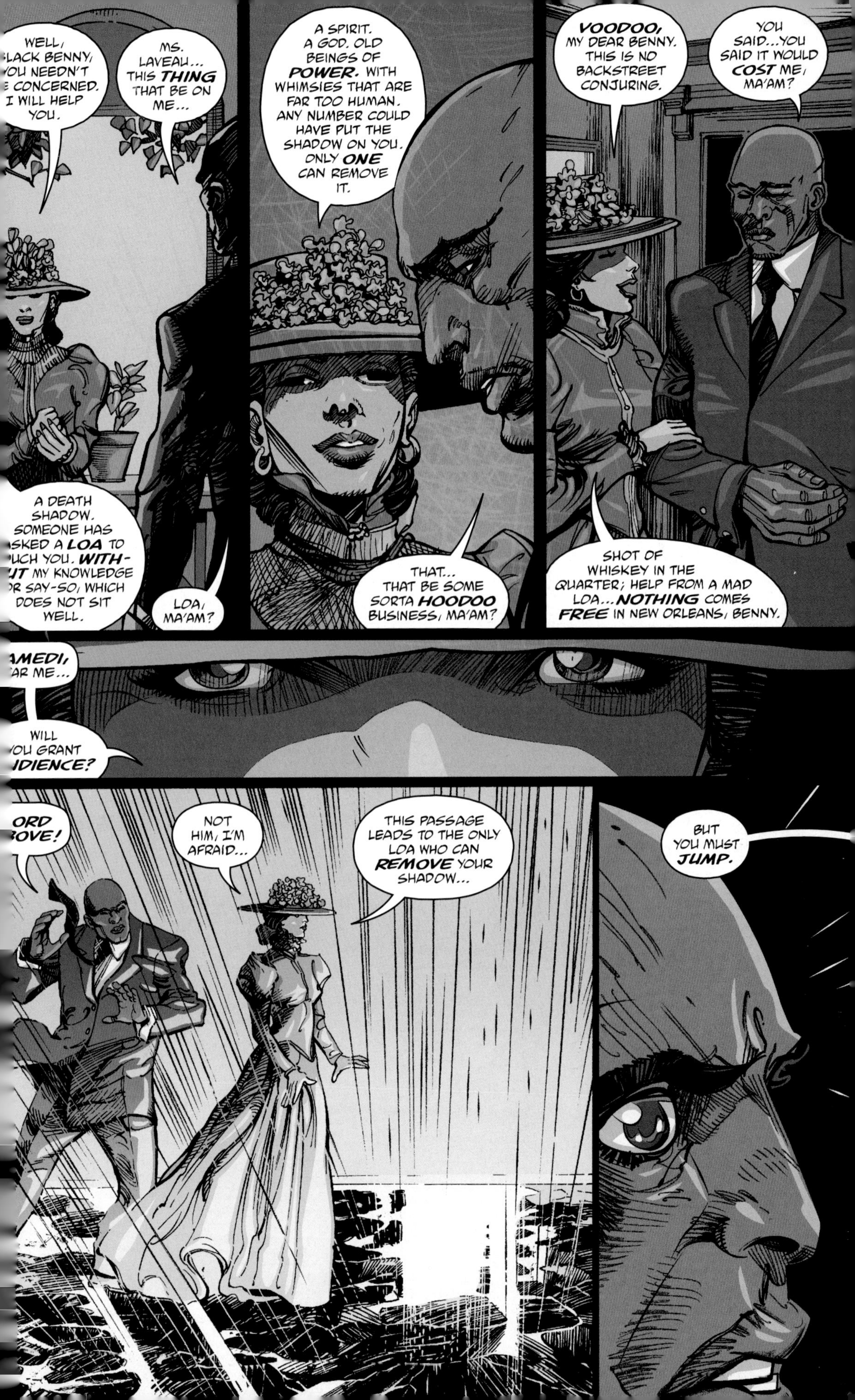
WELL, LACK BENNY, OU NEEDN'T E CONCERNED. I WILL HELP YOU.
MS. LAVEAU... THIS **THING** THAT BE ON ME...
A DEATH SHADOW. SOMEONE HAS SKED A **LOA** TO UCH YOU. **WITH-UT** MY KNOWLEDGE R SAY-SO, WHICH DOES NOT SIT WELL.
LOA, MA'AM?
A SPIRIT. A GOD. OLD BEINGS OF **POWER.** WITH WHIMSIES THAT ARE FAR TOO HUMAN. ANY NUMBER COULD HAVE PUT THE SHADOW ON YOU. ONLY **ONE** CAN REMOVE IT.
THAT... THAT BE SOME SORTA **HOODOO** BUSINESS, MA'AM?
VOODOO, MY DEAR BENNY. THIS IS NO BACKSTREET CONJURING.
YOU SAID...YOU SAID IT WOULD **COST** ME, MA'AM?
SHOT OF WHISKEY IN THE QUARTER; HELP FROM A MAD LOA...**NOTHING** COMES **FREE** IN NEW ORLEANS, BENNY.
AMEDI, AR ME...
WILL OU GRANT **IDIENCE?**
ORD BOVE!
NOT HIM, I'M AFRAID...
THIS PASSAGE LEADS TO THE ONLY LOA WHO CAN **REMOVE** YOUR SHADOW...
BUT YOU MUST **JUMP.**

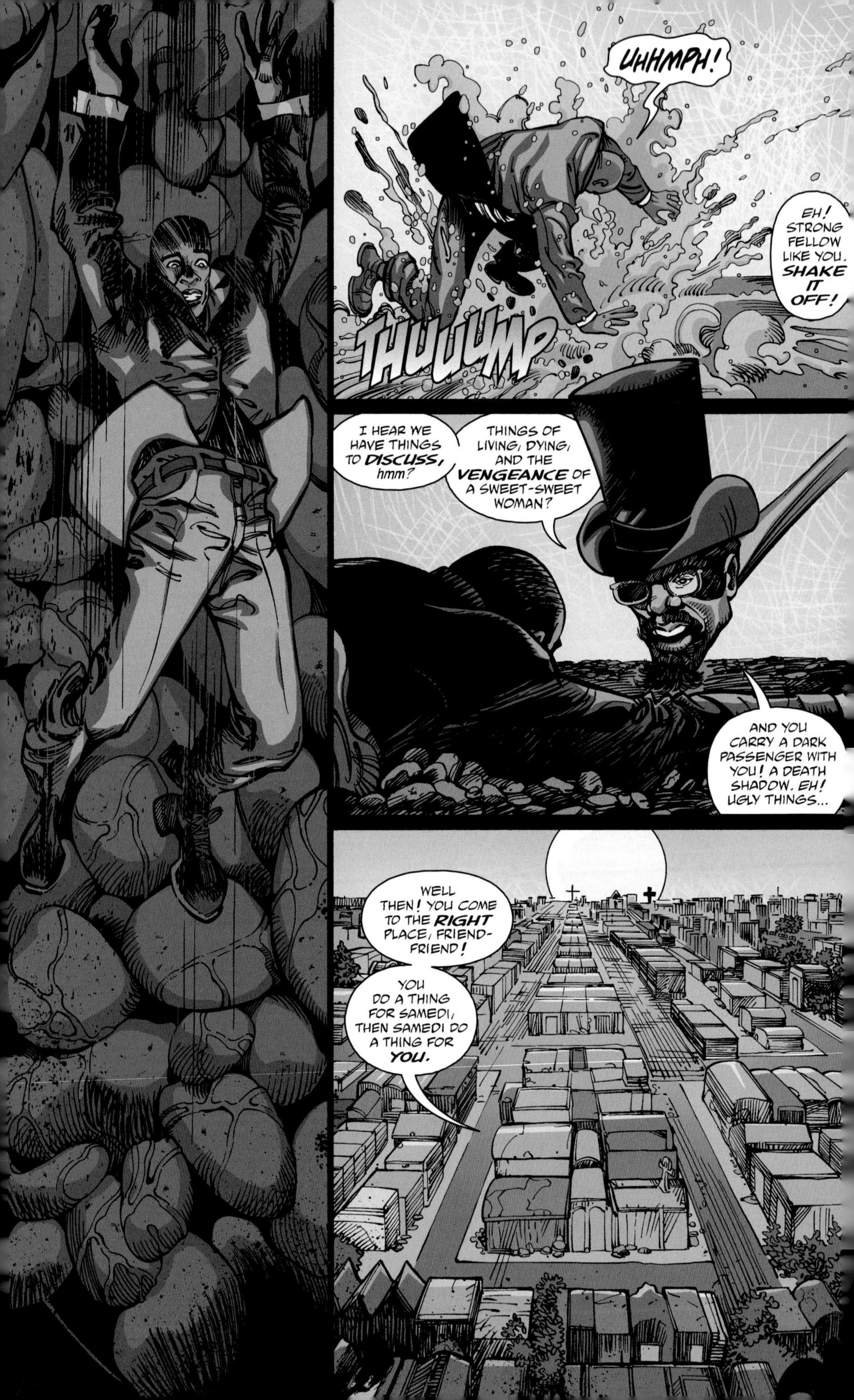
UHHMPH!
THUUUMP
EH! STRONG FELLOW LIKE YOU. SHAKE IT OFF!
I HEAR WE HAVE THINGS TO DISCUSS, hmm?
THINGS OF LIVING, DYING, AND THE VENGEANCE OF A SWEET-SWEET WOMAN?
AND YOU CARRY A DARK PASSENGER WITH YOU! A DEATH SHADOW. EH! UGLY THINGS...
WELL THEN! YOU COME TO THE RIGHT PLACE, FRIEND-FRIEND!
YOU DO A THING FOR SAMEDI, THEN SAMEDI DO A THING FOR YOU.

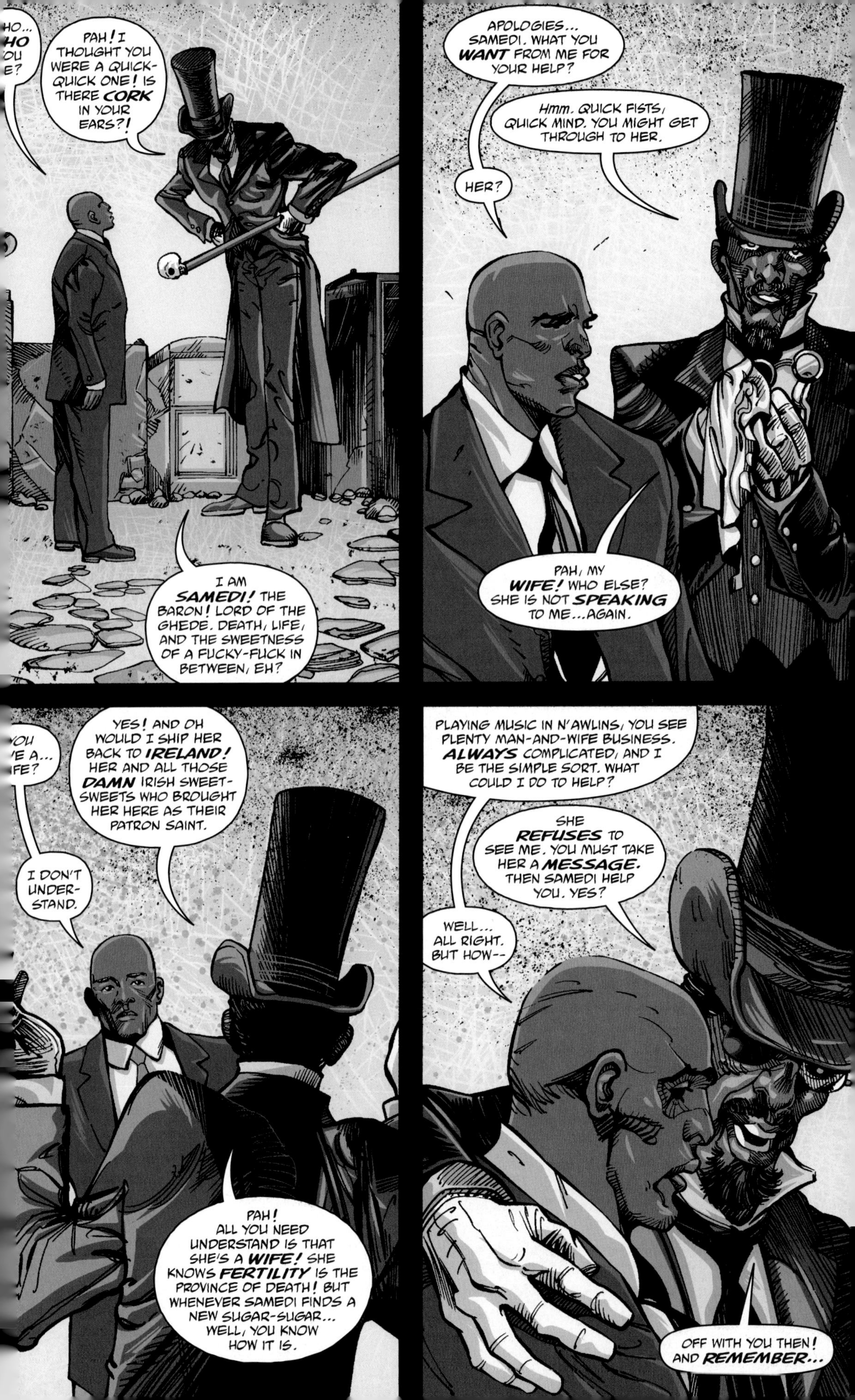
PAH! I THOUGHT YOU WERE A QUICK-QUICK ONE! IS THERE CORK IN YOUR EARS?!
I AM SAMEDI! THE BARON! LORD OF THE GHEDE. DEATH, LIFE, AND THE SWEETNESS OF A FUCKY-FUCK IN BETWEEN, EH?
APOLOGIES... SAMEDI. WHAT YOU WANT FROM ME FOR YOUR HELP?
Hmm. QUICK FISTS, QUICK MIND. YOU MIGHT GET THROUGH TO HER.
HER?
PAH, MY WIFE! WHO ELSE? SHE IS NOT SPEAKING TO ME...AGAIN.
YES! AND OH WOULD I SHIP HER BACK TO IRELAND! HER AND ALL THOSE DAMN IRISH SWEET-SWEETS WHO BROUGHT HER HERE AS THEIR PATRON SAINT.
I DON'T UNDER-STAND.
PAH! ALL YOU NEED UNDERSTAND IS THAT SHE'S A WIFE! SHE KNOWS FERTILITY IS THE PROVINCE OF DEATH! BUT WHENEVER SAMEDI FINDS A NEW SUGAR-SUGAR... WELL, YOU KNOW HOW IT IS.
PLAYING MUSIC IN N'AWLINS, YOU SEE PLENTY MAN-AND-WIFE BUSINESS. ALWAYS COMPLICATED, AND I BE THE SIMPLE SORT. WHAT COULD I DO TO HELP?
SHE REFUSES TO SEE ME. YOU MUST TAKE HER A MESSAGE. THEN SAMEDI HELP YOU. YES?
WELL... ALL RIGHT. BUT HOW--
OFF WITH YOU THEN! AND REMEMBER...

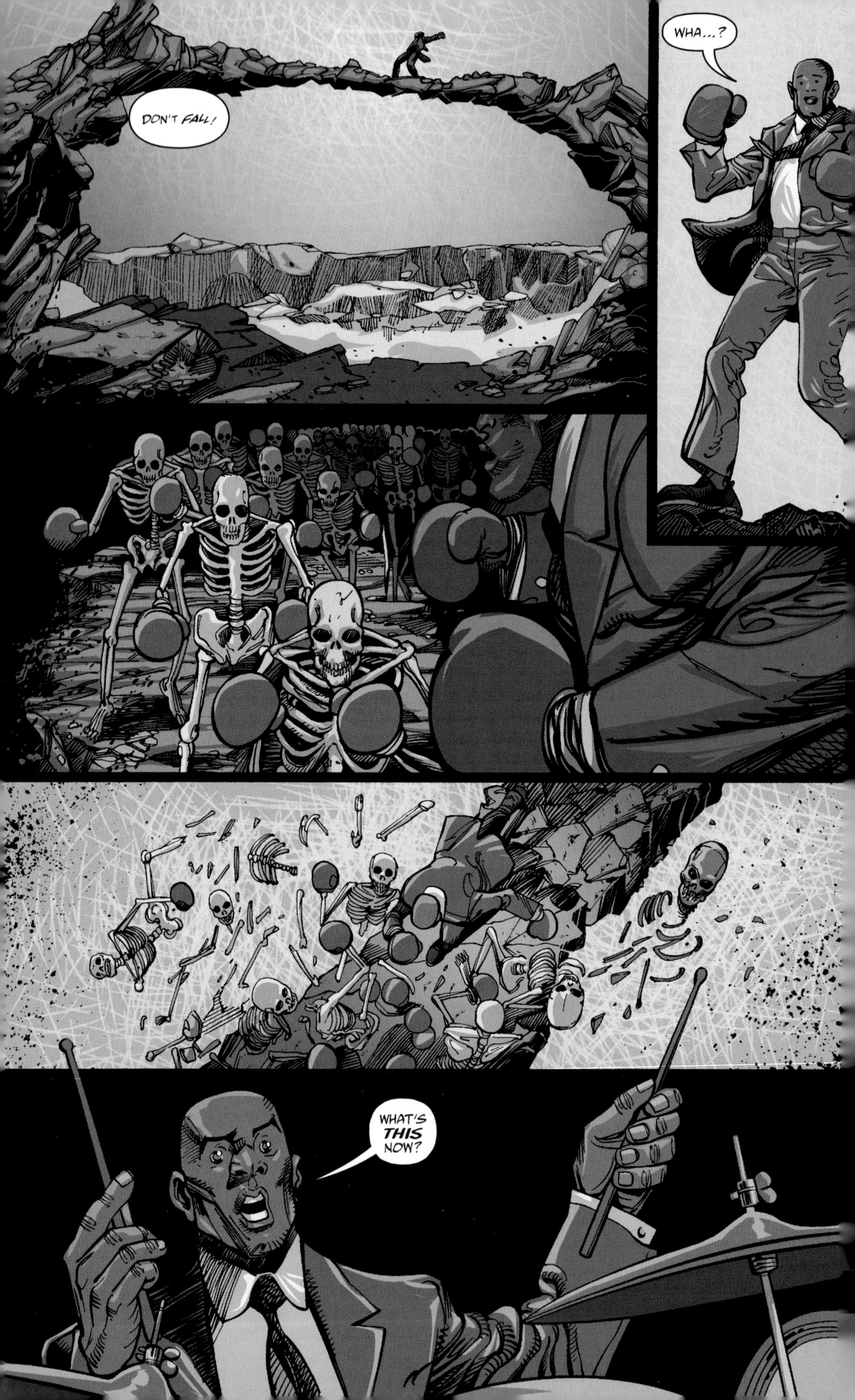
DON'T FALL!
WHA...?
WHAT'S THIS NOW?

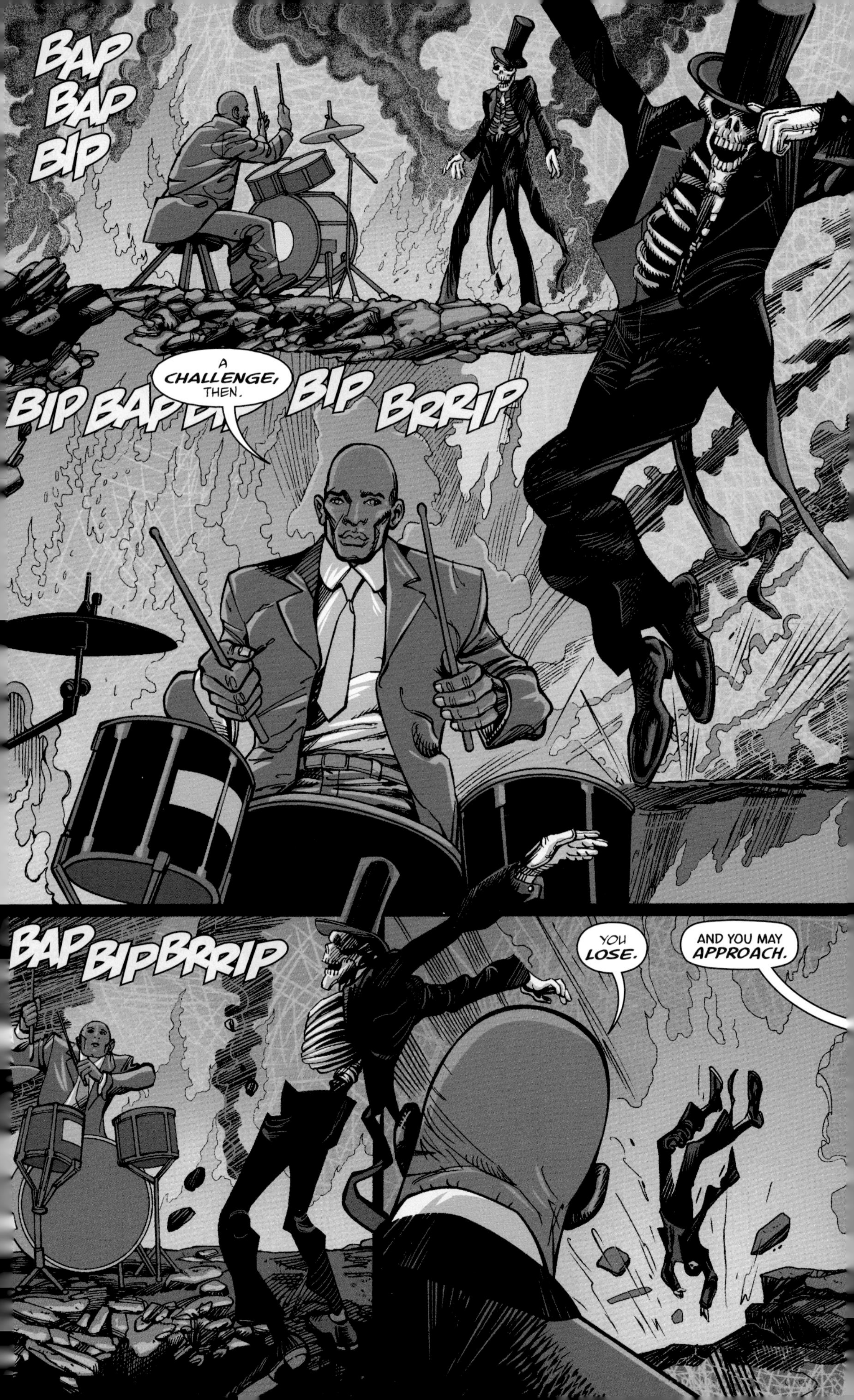
BAP BAP BIP
BIP BAP
A CHALLENGE, THEN.
BIP BRRIP
BAP BIPBRRIP
YOU LOSE.
AND YOU MAY APPROACH.

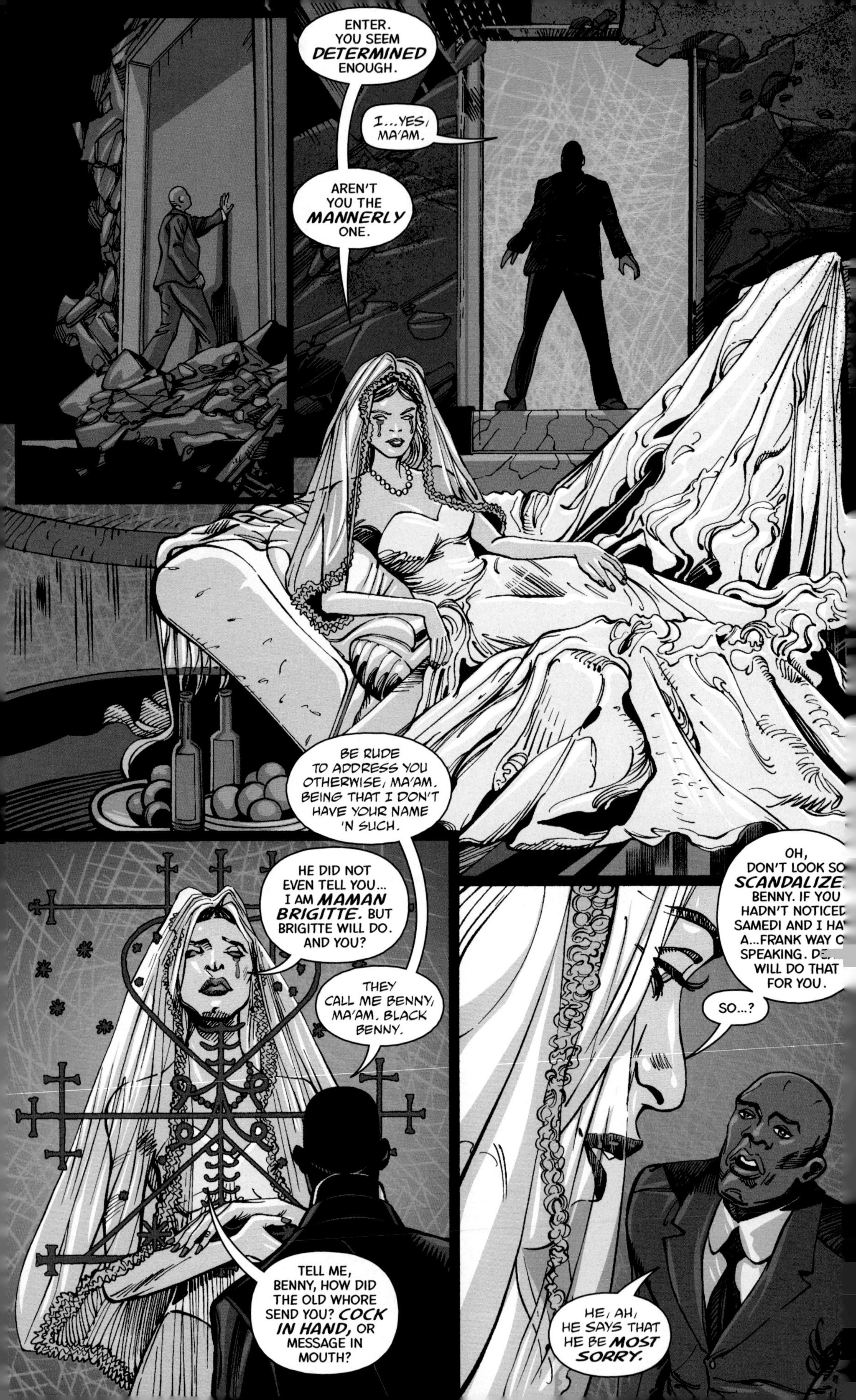
ENTER. YOU SEEM DETERMINED ENOUGH.
I...YES, MA'AM.
AREN'T YOU THE MANNERLY ONE.
BE RUDE TO ADDRESS YOU OTHERWISE, MA'AM. BEING THAT I DON'T HAVE YOUR NAME 'N SUCH.
HE DID NOT EVEN TELL YOU... I AM MAMAN BRIGITTE. BUT BRIGITTE WILL DO. AND YOU?
THEY CALL ME BENNY, MA'AM. BLACK BENNY.
TELL ME, BENNY, HOW DID THE OLD WHORE SEND YOU? COCK IN HAND, OR MESSAGE IN MOUTH?
HE, AH, HE SAYS THAT HE BE MOST SORRY.
SO...?
OH, DON'T LOOK SO SCANDALIZE BENNY. IF YOU HADN'T NOTICED SAMEDI AND I HA A...FRANK WAY O SPEAKING. DE WILL DO THAT FOR YOU.

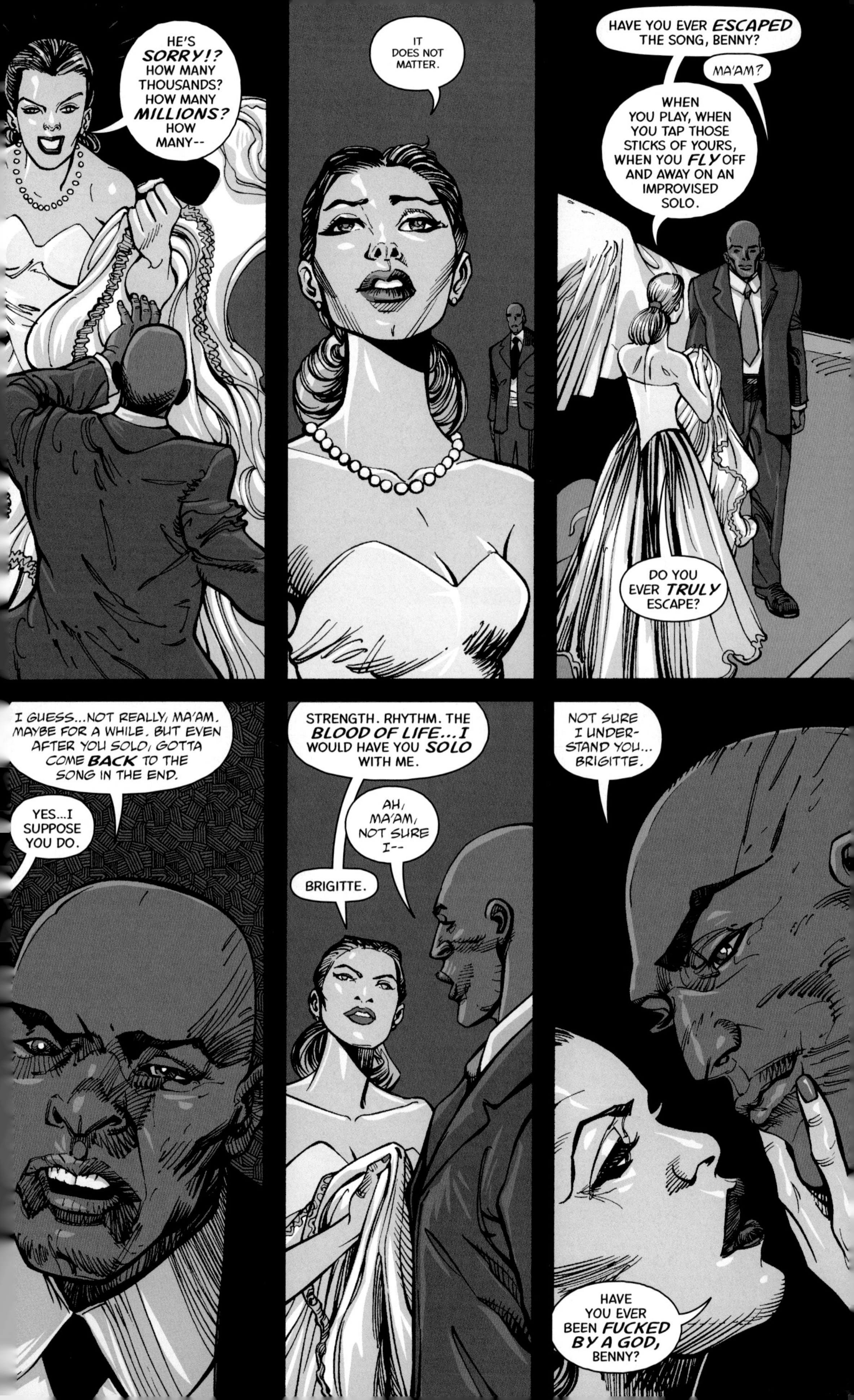
HE'S SORRY!? HOW MANY THOUSANDS? HOW MANY MILLIONS? HOW MANY--
IT DOES NOT MATTER.
HAVE YOU EVER ESCAPED THE SONG, BENNY?
MA'AM?
WHEN YOU PLAY, WHEN YOU TAP THOSE STICKS OF YOURS, WHEN YOU FLY OFF AND AWAY ON AN IMPROVISED SOLO.
DO YOU EVER TRULY ESCAPE?
I GUESS...NOT REALLY, MA'AM. MAYBE FOR A WHILE. BUT EVEN AFTER YOU SOLO, GOTTA COME BACK TO THE SONG IN THE END.
YES...I SUPPOSE YOU DO.
STRENGTH. RHYTHM. THE BLOOD OF LIFE...I WOULD HAVE YOU SOLO WITH ME.
AH, MA'AM, NOT SURE I--
BRIGITTE.
NOT SURE I UNDERSTAND YOU... BRIGITTE.
HAVE YOU EVER BEEN FUCKED BY A GOD, BENNY?

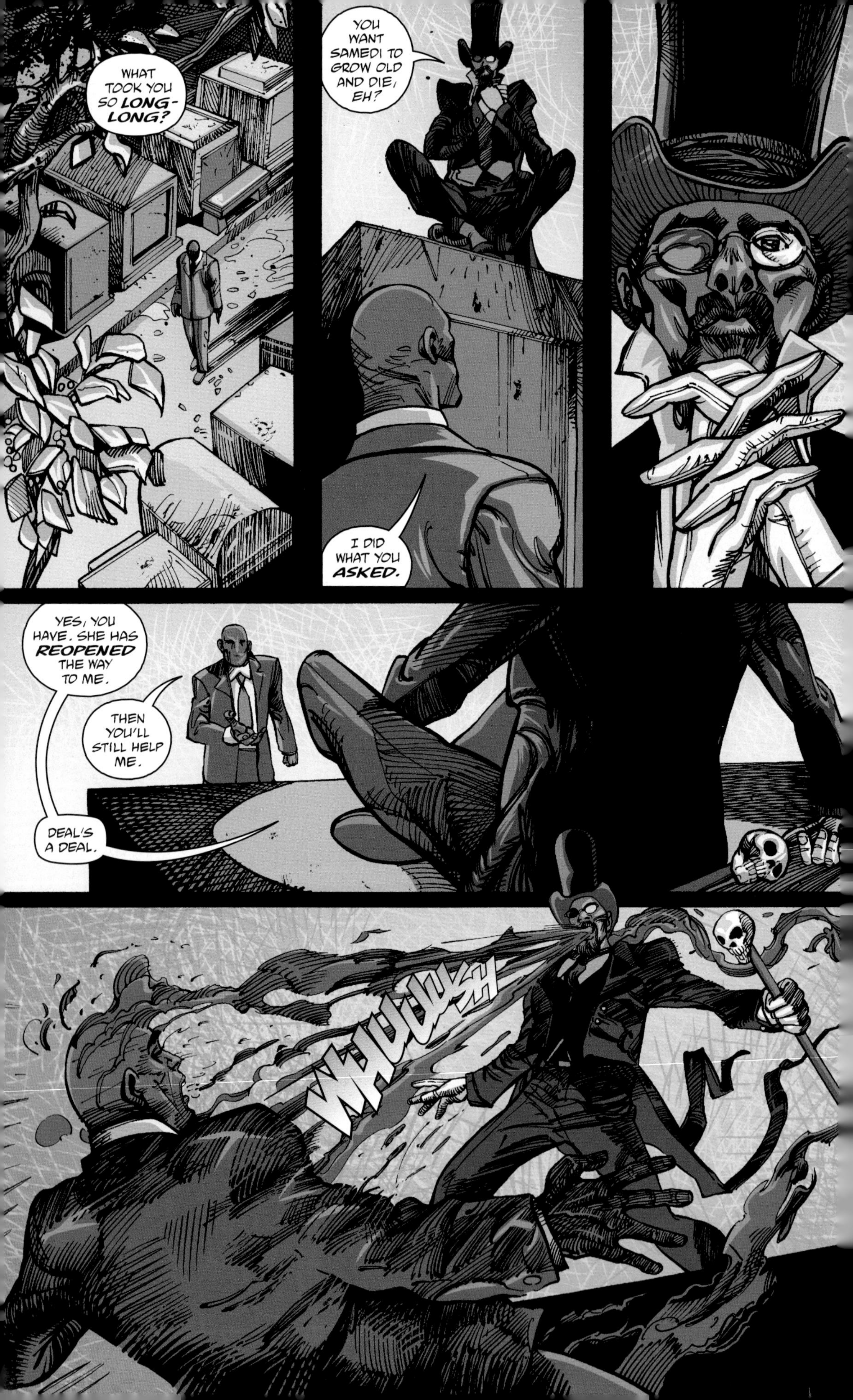
WHAT TOOK YOU SO LONG-LONG?
YOU WANT SAMEDI TO GROW OLD AND DIE, EH?
I DID WHAT YOU ASKED.
YES, YOU HAVE. SHE HAS REOPENED THE WAY TO ME.
THEN YOU'LL STILL HELP ME.
DEAL'S A DEAL.
WHUUUSH

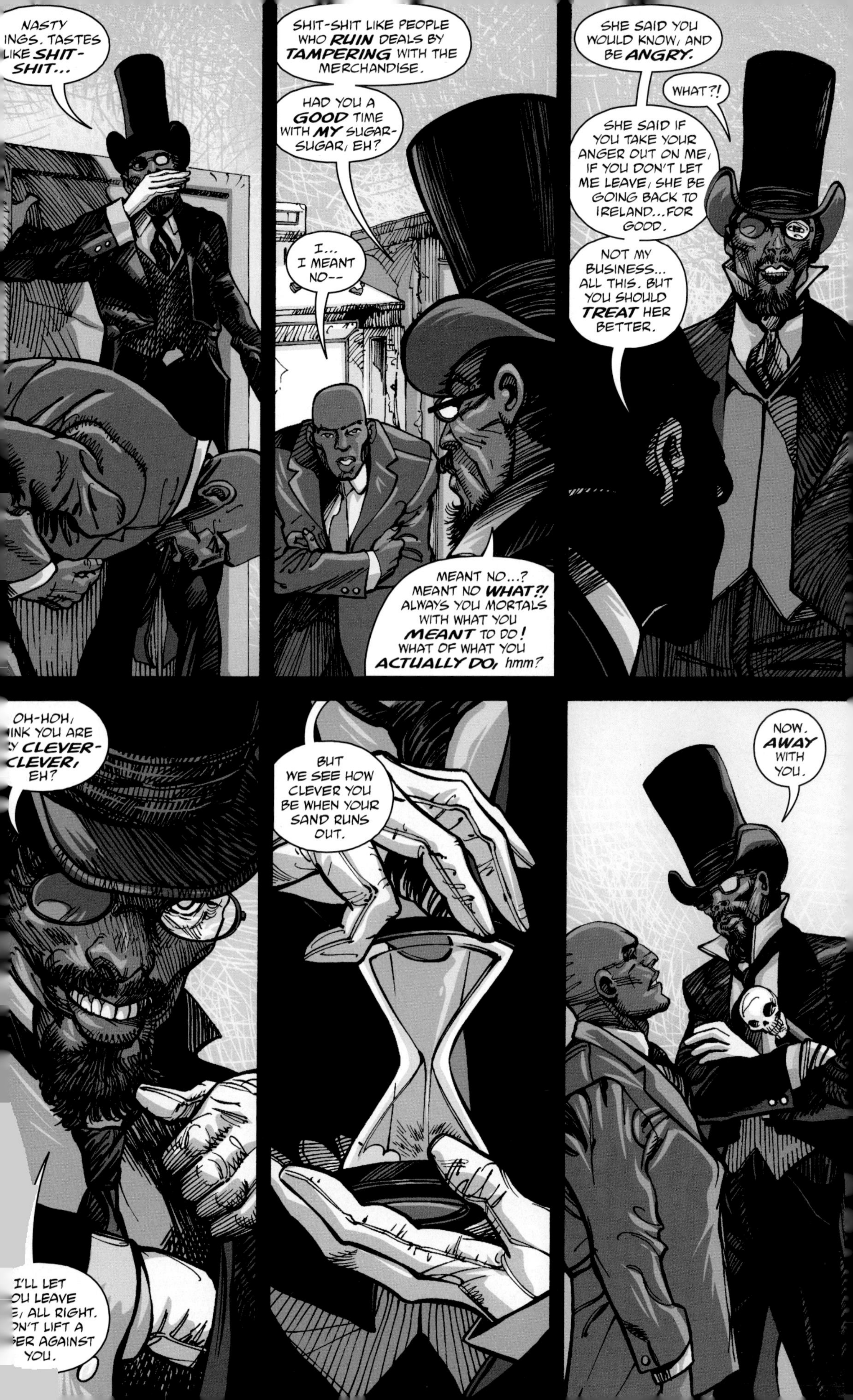
NASTY INGS. TASTES LIKE SHIT-SHIT...
SHIT-SHIT LIKE PEOPLE WHO RUIN DEALS BY TAMPERING WITH THE MERCHANDISE.
HAD YOU A GOOD TIME WITH MY SUGAR-SUGAR, EH?
I... I MEANT NO--
MEANT NO...? MEANT NO WHAT?! ALWAYS YOU MORTALS WITH WHAT YOU MEANT TO DO! WHAT OF WHAT YOU ACTUALLY DO, hmm?
SHE SAID YOU WOULD KNOW, AND BE ANGRY.
WHAT?!
SHE SAID IF YOU TAKE YOUR ANGER OUT ON ME, IF YOU DON'T LET ME LEAVE, SHE BE GOING BACK TO IRELAND...FOR GOOD.
NOT MY BUSINESS... ALL THIS. BUT YOU SHOULD TREAT HER BETTER.
OH-HOH, INK YOU ARE CLEVER-CLEVER, EH?
I'LL LET OU LEAVE E, ALL RIGHT. ON'T LIFT A GER AGAINST YOU.
BUT WE SEE HOW CLEVER YOU BE WHEN YOUR SAND RUNS OUT.
NOW. AWAY WITH YOU.

I AM SO SORRY, BENNY. SAMEDI IS *MERCURIAL,* EVEN FOR A LOA. BUT THIS *CURSE* ON YOU...

THIS BUSINESS, IT BE TOO DARK, TOO SAD.

SAMEDI WILL CLAIM YOUR SOUL WHEN YOU DIE. BUT WITH THE AID OF MY PATRON LOA, *OGUN,* THERE MAY BE A WAY TO *KEEP* IT FROM HIM...

YOU WOULD HAVE TO BE *BOUND* TO ANOTHER SOUL, ONE *BEYOND* SAMEDI'S REACH.

MA'AM, I TOOK MY FRIEND'S LIFE. AND IF THE PRICE BE MY OWN, CAN'T RIGHTLY CALL IT UNFAIR.

JUST, IF YOU CAN, LET SOMETHING *GOOD* COME OF IT. SOMETHING *LIGHT...*

WHO WOULD THAT BE, MA'AM?

ME, BENNY. YOU'D BE BOUND TO *ME.* TO THE QUEEN.

SUCH LIGHTNESS OF SPIRIT. YOU'RE A *SPECIAL* ONE, BENJAMIN DUPREE. I'M TRULY SORRY I COULDN'T DO BETTER FOR YOU.

"NOW, WHAT MAN TO DO V A *CURS* HANGING O\ HIM, EH?

"HE TRIES MIGHTIEST *STAY* ALIV

WELL, SHOOT. BETTER *YOU,* MS. LAVEAU THAN WHAT I FIGURE SAMEDI GOT IN STORE FOR ME.

"BUT NO MATTER THE *TRICK-TRICKS,* NO MATTER THE PLANS...

MISTER! LOOK OU--

"SAMEDI BE THERE WHEN THE *SANDS* RUN OUT."

"I DONE *DIE* DOWN IN N'AWLI WHERE *DEAT* COMES TO PLAY.

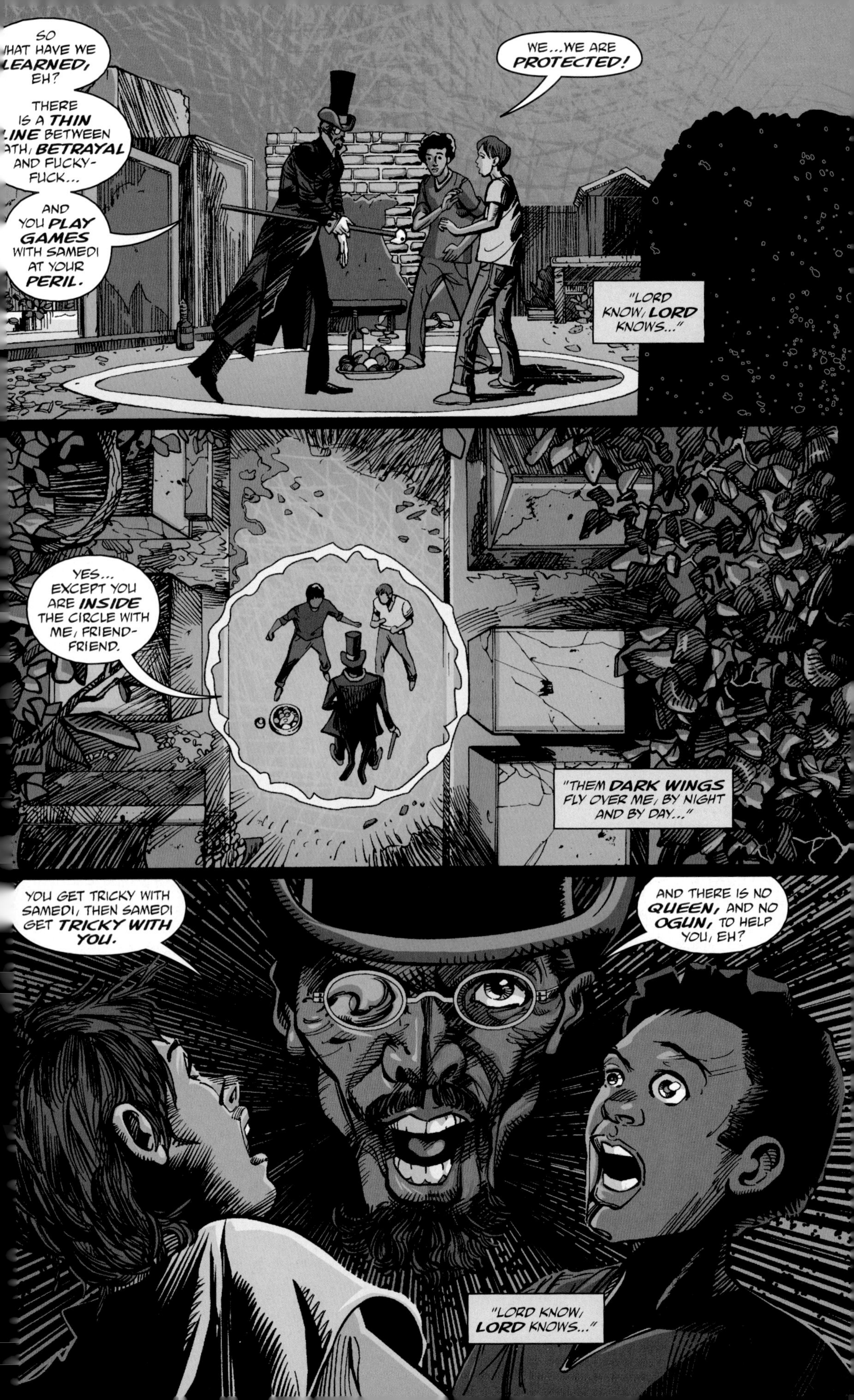
SO WHAT HAVE WE LEARNED, EH?
THERE IS A THIN LINE BETWEEN ATH, BETRAYAL AND FUCKY-FUCK...
AND YOU PLAY GAMES WITH SAMEDI AT YOUR PERIL.
WE...WE ARE PROTECTED!
"LORD KNOW, LORD KNOWS..."
YES... EXCEPT YOU ARE INSIDE THE CIRCLE WITH ME, FRIEND-FRIEND.
"THEM DARK WINGS FLY OVER ME, BY NIGHT AND BY DAY..."
YOU GET TRICKY WITH SAMEDI, THEN SAMEDI GET TRICKY WITH YOU.
AND THERE IS NO QUEEN, AND NO OGUN, TO HELP YOU, EH?
"LORD KNOW, LORD KNOWS..."

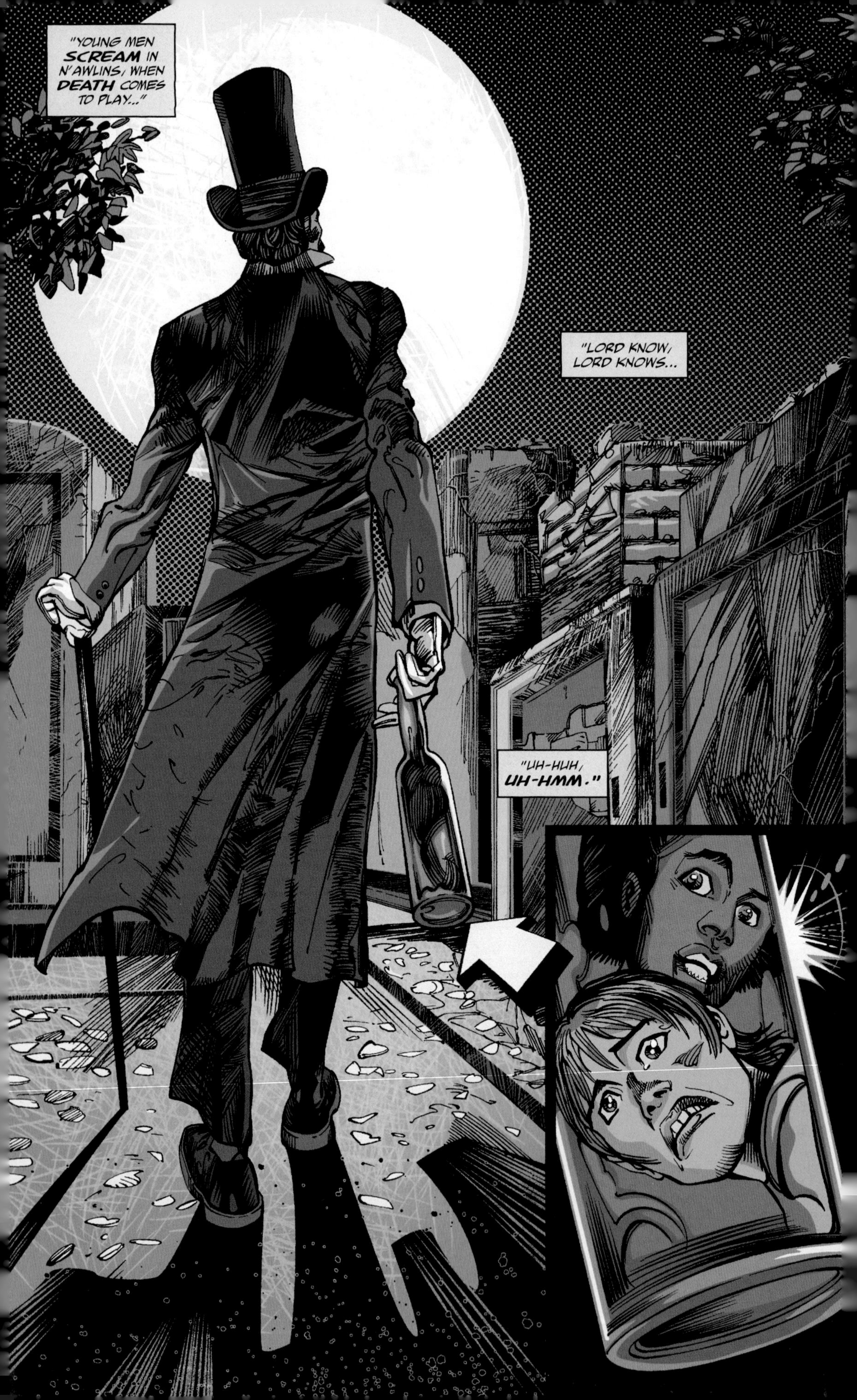
"YOUNG MEN SCREAM IN N'AWLINS, WHEN DEATH COMES TO PLAY..."
"LORD KNOW, LORD KNOWS...
"UH-HUH, UH-HMM."

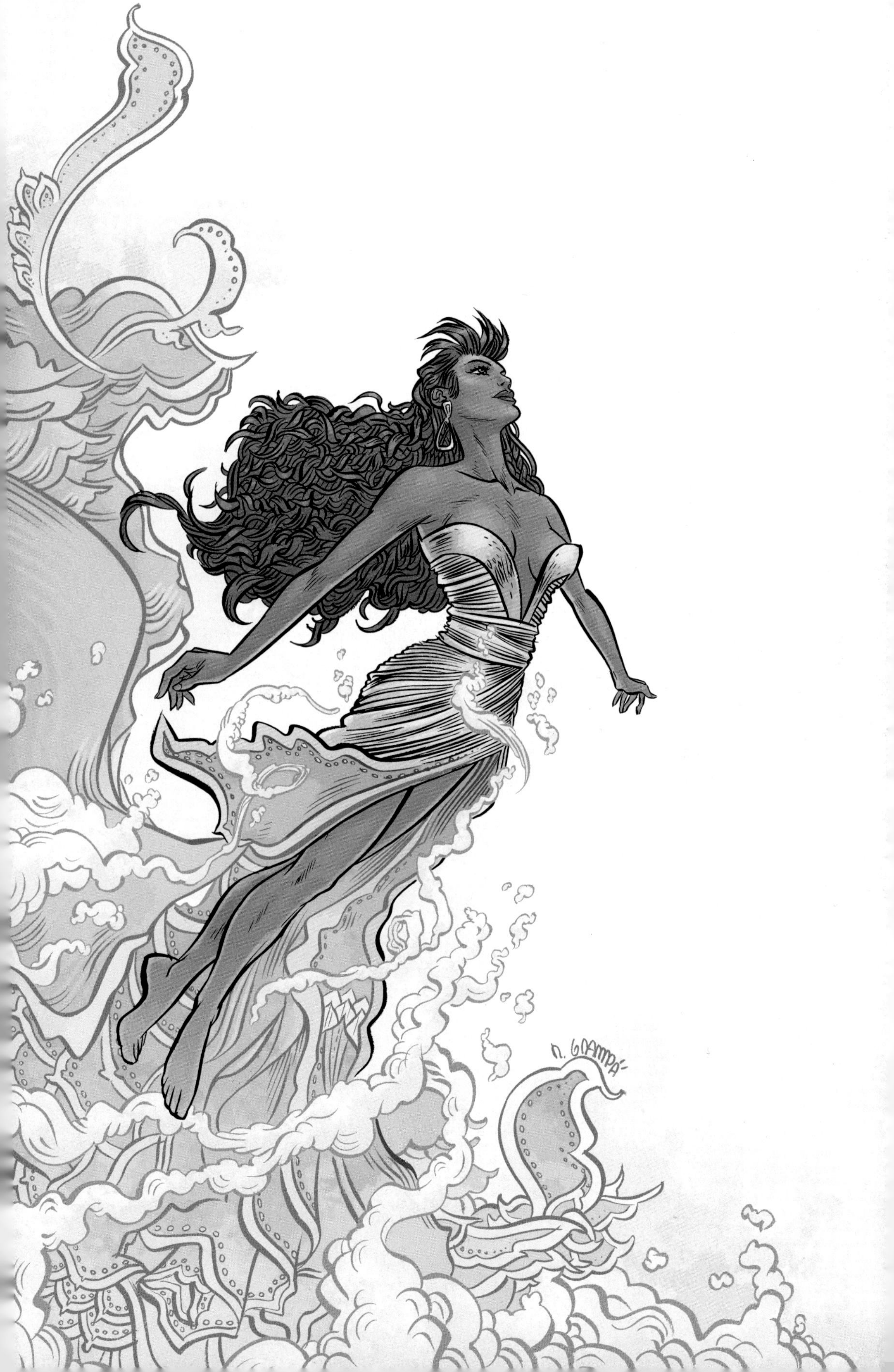

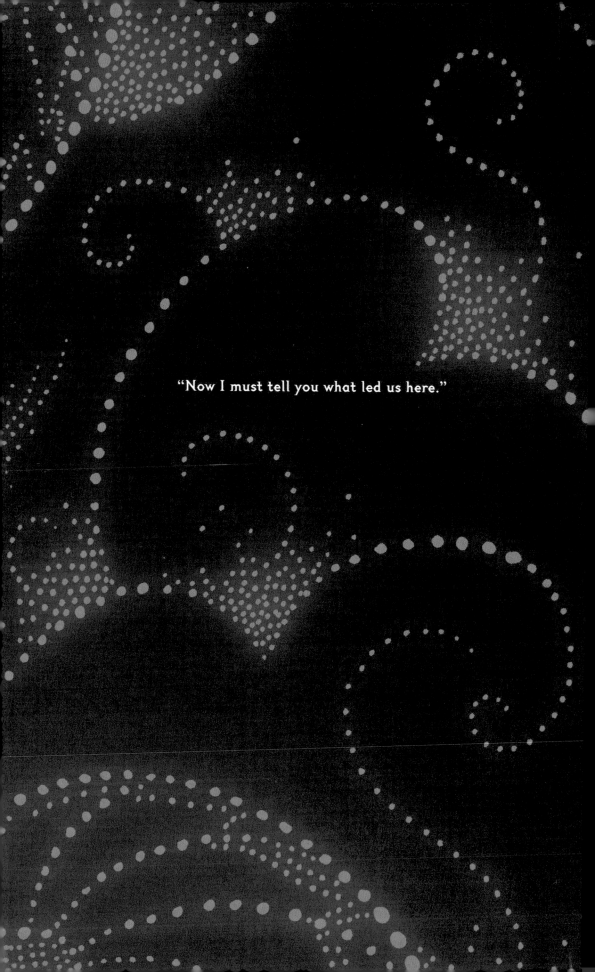

"Now I must tell you what led us here."

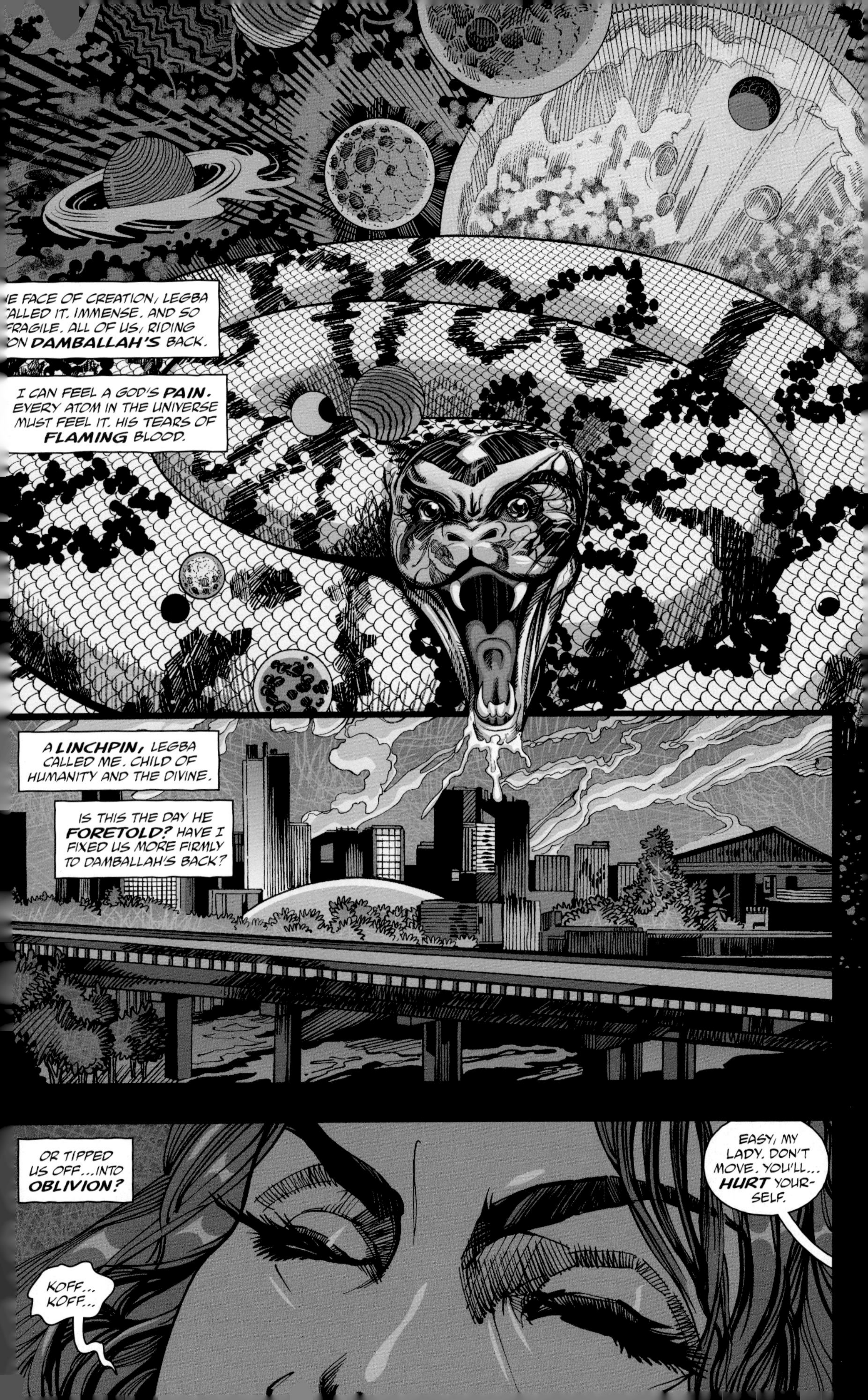
E FACE OF CREATION, LEGBA CALLED IT. IMMENSE. AND SO FRAGILE. ALL OF US, RIDING ON DAMBALLAH'S BACK.
I CAN FEEL A GOD'S PAIN. EVERY ATOM IN THE UNIVERSE MUST FEEL IT. HIS TEARS OF FLAMING BLOOD.
A LINCHPIN, LEGBA CALLED ME. CHILD OF HUMANITY AND THE DIVINE.
IS THIS THE DAY HE FORETOLD? HAVE I FIXED US MORE FIRMLY TO DAMBALLAH'S BACK?
OR TIPPED US OFF...INTO OBLIVION?
EASY, MY LADY. DON'T MOVE. YOU'LL... HURT YOURSELF.
KOFF... KOFF...

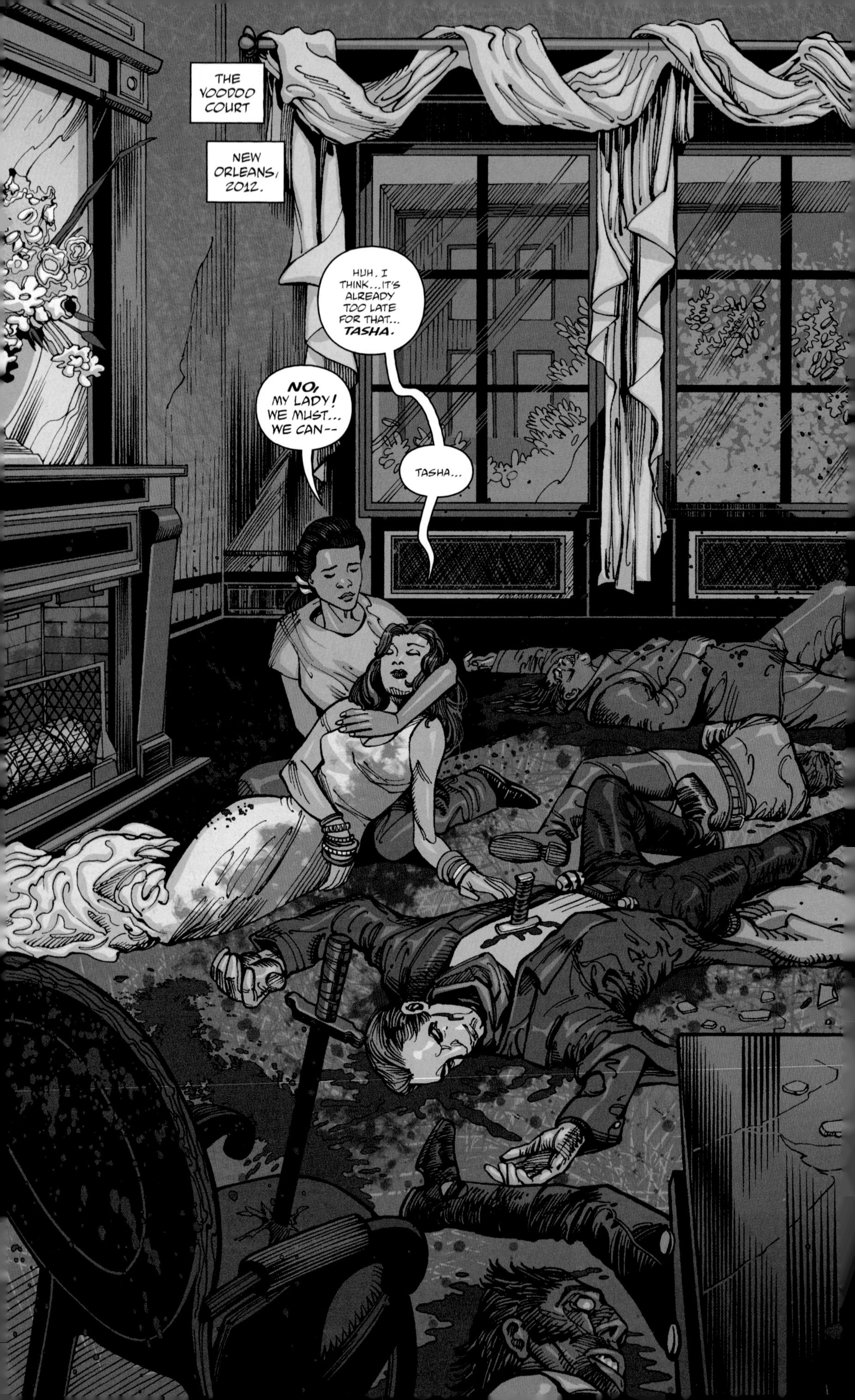
THE VOODOO COURT
NEW ORLEANS, 2012.
HUH. I THINK... IT'S ALREADY TOO LATE FOR THAT... TASHA.
NO, MY LADY! WE MUST... WE CAN--
TASHA...

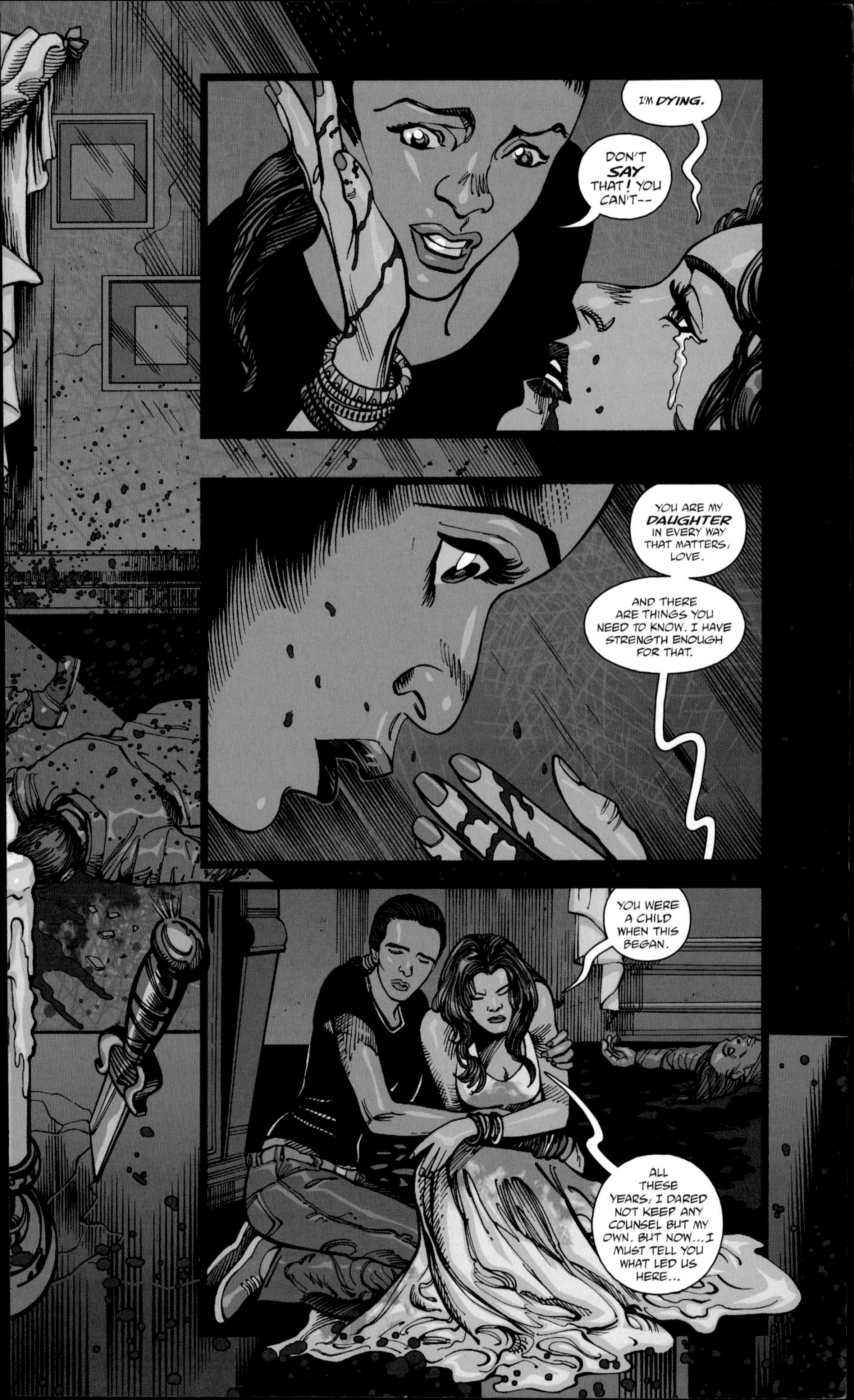
I'M DYING.
DON'T SAY THAT! YOU CAN'T--
YOU ARE MY DAUGHTER IN EVERY WAY THAT MATTERS, LOVE.
AND THERE ARE THINGS YOU NEED TO KNOW. I HAVE STRENGTH ENOUGH FOR THAT.
YOU WERE A CHILD WHEN THIS BEGAN.
ALL THESE YEARS, I DARED NOT KEEP ANY COUNSEL BUT MY OWN. BUT NOW... I MUST TELL YOU WHAT LED US HERE...

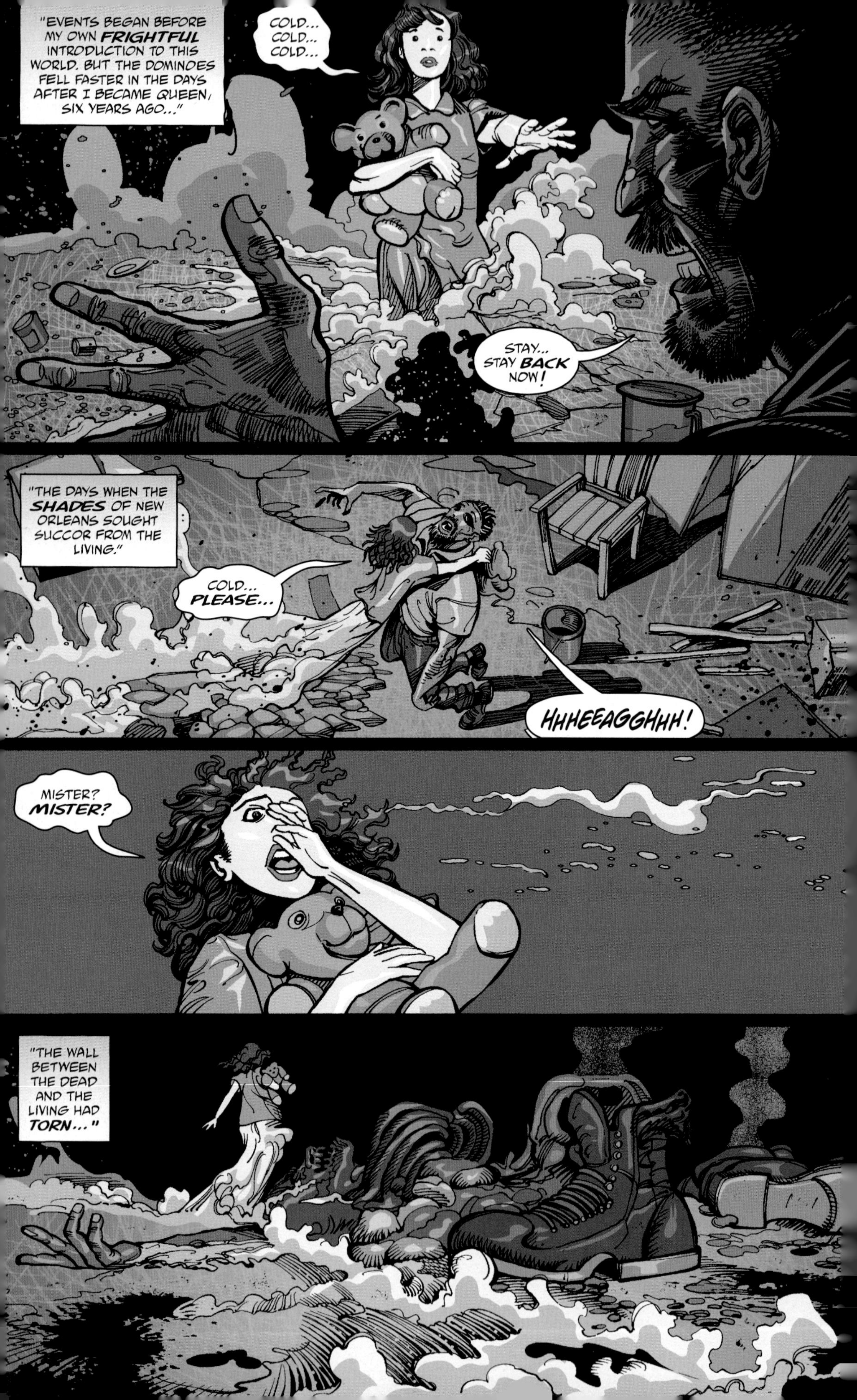
"EVENTS BEGAN BEFORE MY OWN FRIGHTFUL INTRODUCTION TO THIS WORLD. BUT THE DOMINOES FELL FASTER IN THE DAYS AFTER I BECAME QUEEN, SIX YEARS AGO..."
COLD... COLD... COLD...
STAY... STAY BACK NOW!
"THE DAYS WHEN THE SHADES OF NEW ORLEANS SOUGHT SUCCOR FROM THE LIVING."
COLD... PLEASE...
HHHEEAGGHHH!
MISTER? MISTER?
"THE WALL BETWEEN THE DEAD AND THE LIVING HAD TORN..."

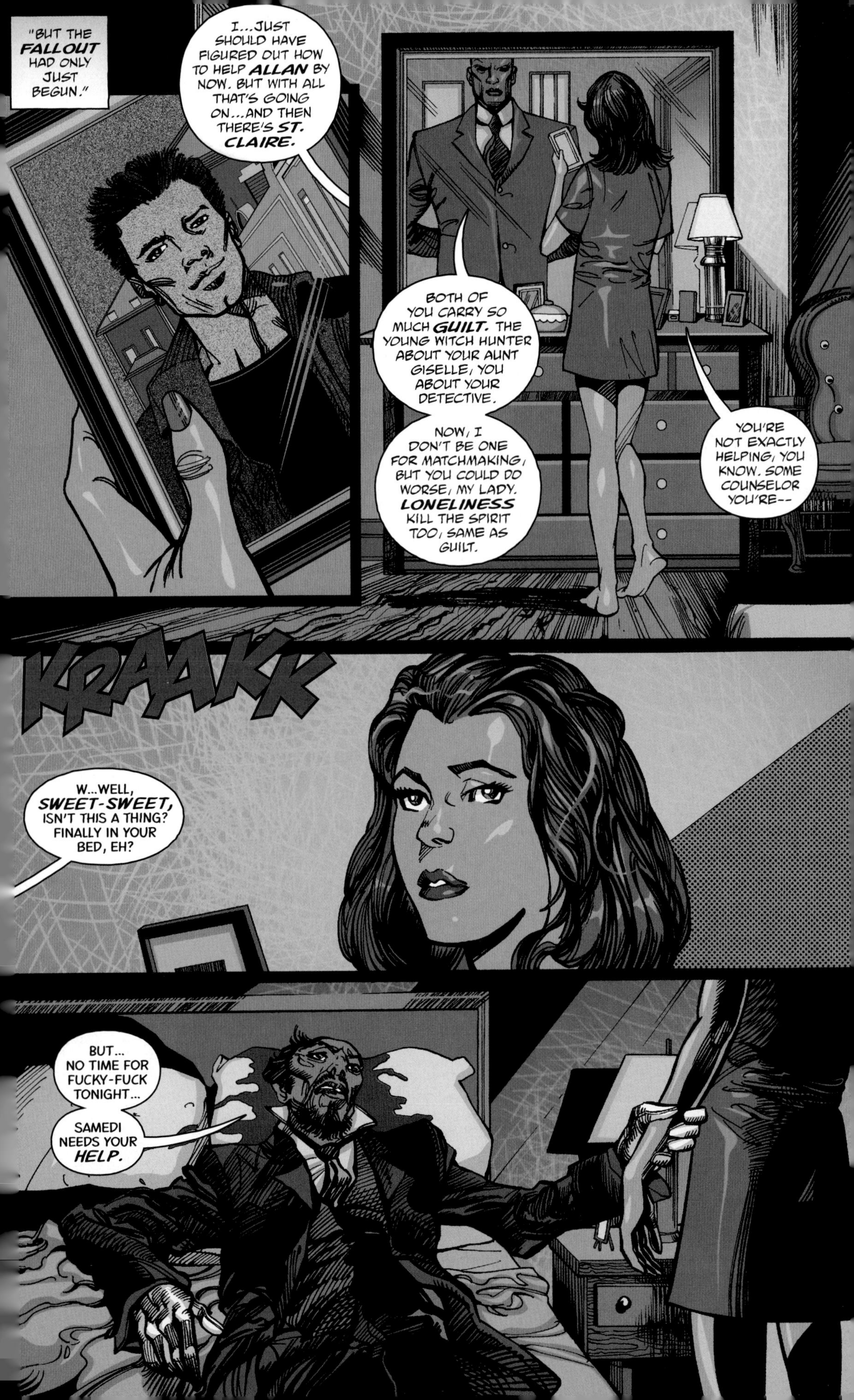
"BUT THE FALLOUT HAD ONLY JUST BEGUN."
I...JUST SHOULD HAVE FIGURED OUT HOW TO HELP ALLAN BY NOW. BUT WITH ALL THAT'S GOING ON...AND THEN THERE'S ST. CLAIRE.
BOTH OF YOU CARRY SO MUCH GUILT. THE YOUNG WITCH HUNTER ABOUT YOUR AUNT GISELLE, YOU ABOUT YOUR DETECTIVE.
NOW, I DON'T BE ONE FOR MATCHMAKING, BUT YOU COULD DO WORSE, MY LADY. LONELINESS KILL THE SPIRIT TOO, SAME AS GUILT.
YOU'RE NOT EXACTLY HELPING, YOU KNOW. SOME COUNSELOR YOU'RE--
KRAAKK
W...WELL, SWEET-SWEET, ISN'T THIS A THING? FINALLY IN YOUR BED, EH?
BUT... NO TIME FOR FUCKY-FUCK TONIGHT...
SAMEDI NEEDS YOUR HELP.

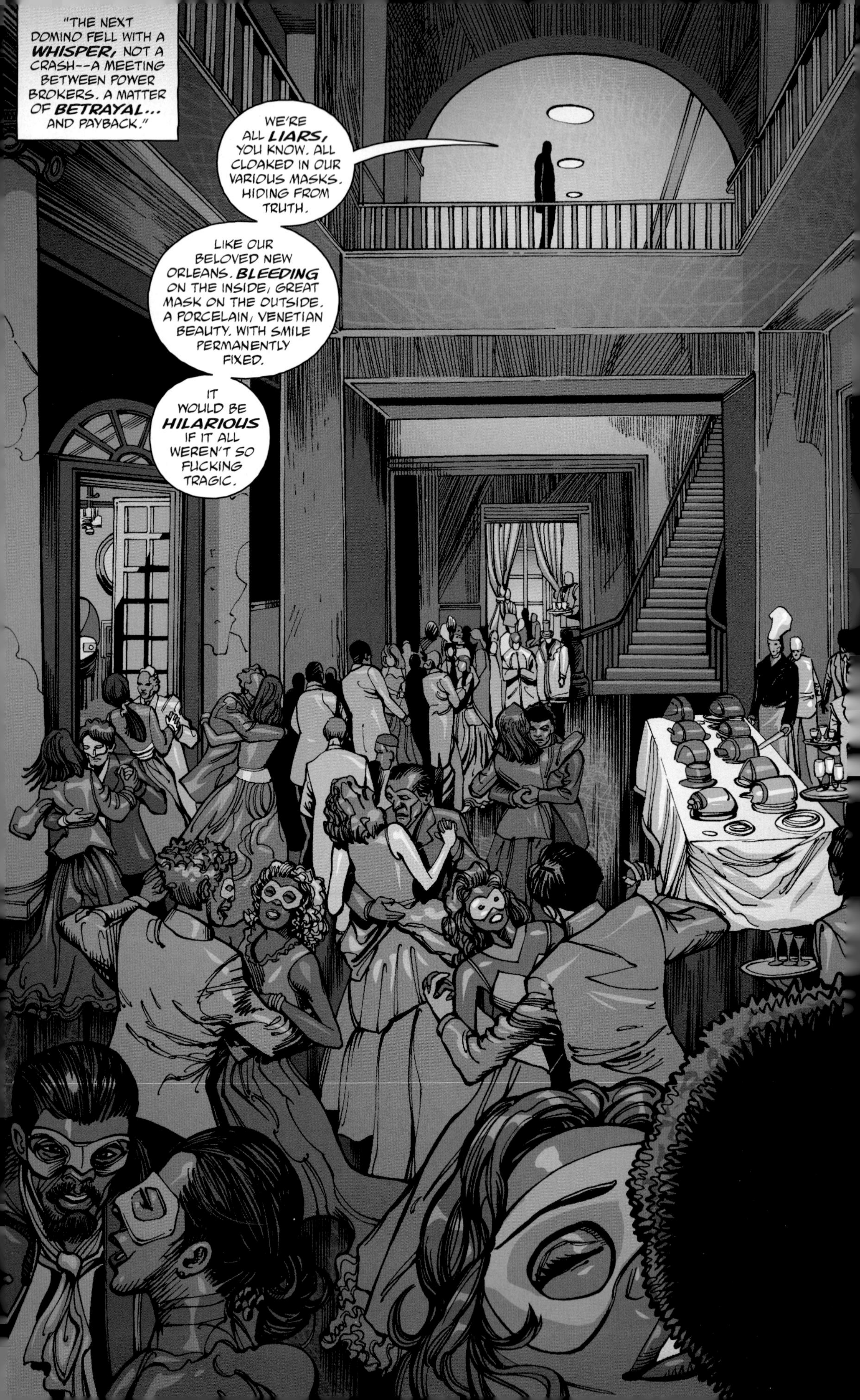
"THE NEXT DOMINO FELL WITH A WHISPER, NOT A CRASH--A MEETING BETWEEN POWER BROKERS. A MATTER OF BETRAYAL... AND PAYBACK."
WE'RE ALL LIARS, YOU KNOW. ALL CLOAKED IN OUR VARIOUS MASKS. HIDING FROM TRUTH.
LIKE OUR BELOVED NEW ORLEANS. BLEEDING ON THE INSIDE, GREAT MASK ON THE OUTSIDE. A PORCELAIN, VENETIAN BEAUTY. WITH SMILE PERMANENTLY FIXED.
IT WOULD BE HILARIOUS IF IT ALL WEREN'T SO FUCKING TRAGIC.

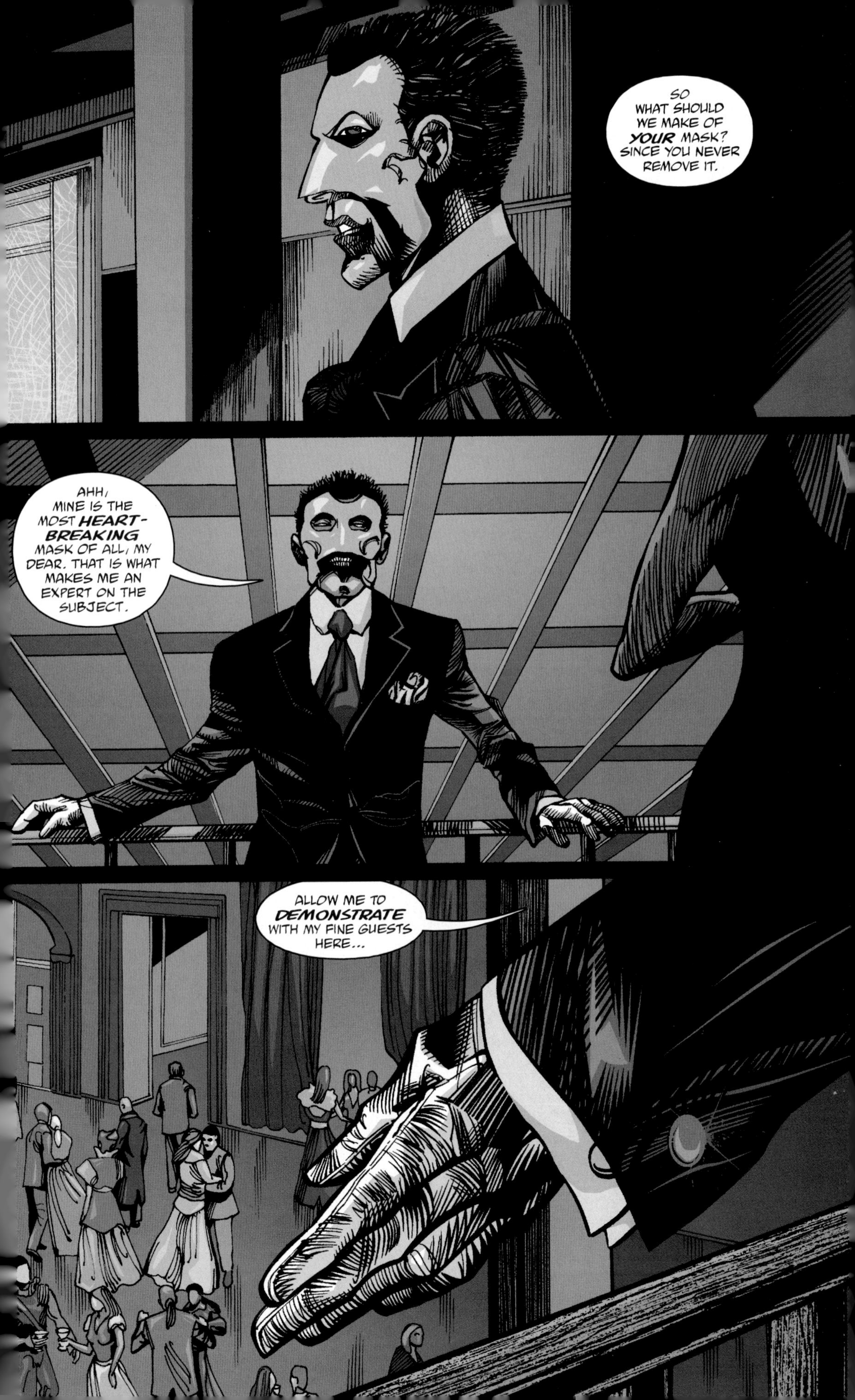
SO WHAT SHOULD WE MAKE OF YOUR MASK? SINCE YOU NEVER REMOVE IT.
AHH, MINE IS THE MOST HEART-BREAKING MASK OF ALL, MY DEAR. THAT IS WHAT MAKES ME AN EXPERT ON THE SUBJECT.
ALLOW ME TO DEMONSTRATE WITH MY FINE GUESTS HERE...

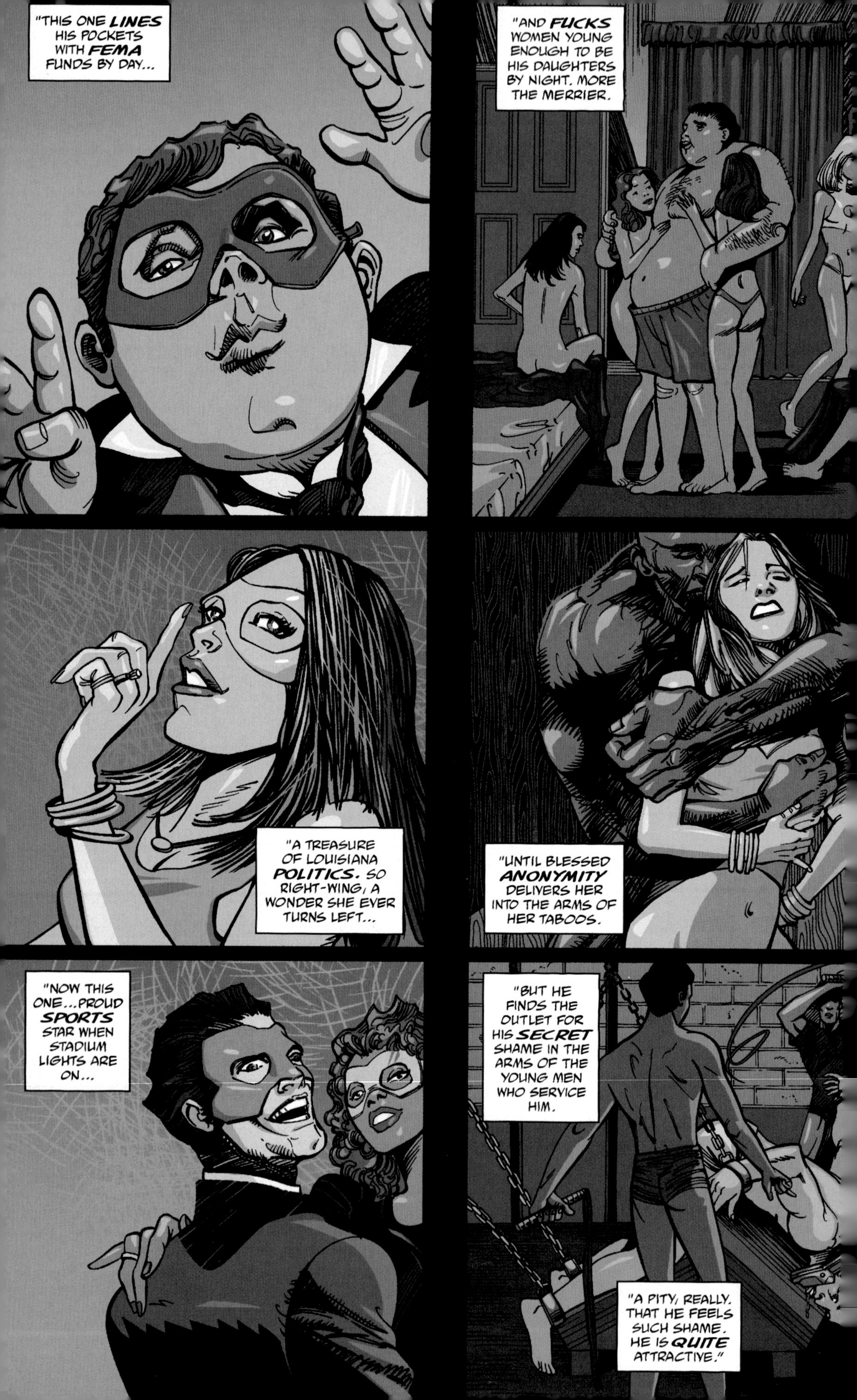
"THIS ONE **LINES** HIS POCKETS WITH **FEMA** FUNDS BY DAY...
"AND **FUCKS** WOMEN YOUNG ENOUGH TO BE HIS DAUGHTERS BY NIGHT. MORE THE MERRIER.
"A TREASURE OF LOUISIANA **POLITICS.** SO RIGHT-WING, A WONDER SHE EVER TURNS LEFT...
"UNTIL BLESSED **ANONYMITY** DELIVERS HER INTO THE ARMS OF HER TABOOS.
"NOW THIS ONE...PROUD **SPORTS** STAR WHEN STADIUM LIGHTS ARE ON...
"BUT HE FINDS THE OUTLET FOR HIS **SECRET** SHAME IN THE ARMS OF THE YOUNG MEN WHO SERVICE HIM.
"A PITY, REALLY. THAT HE FEELS SUCH SHAME. HE IS **QUITE** ATTRACTIVE."

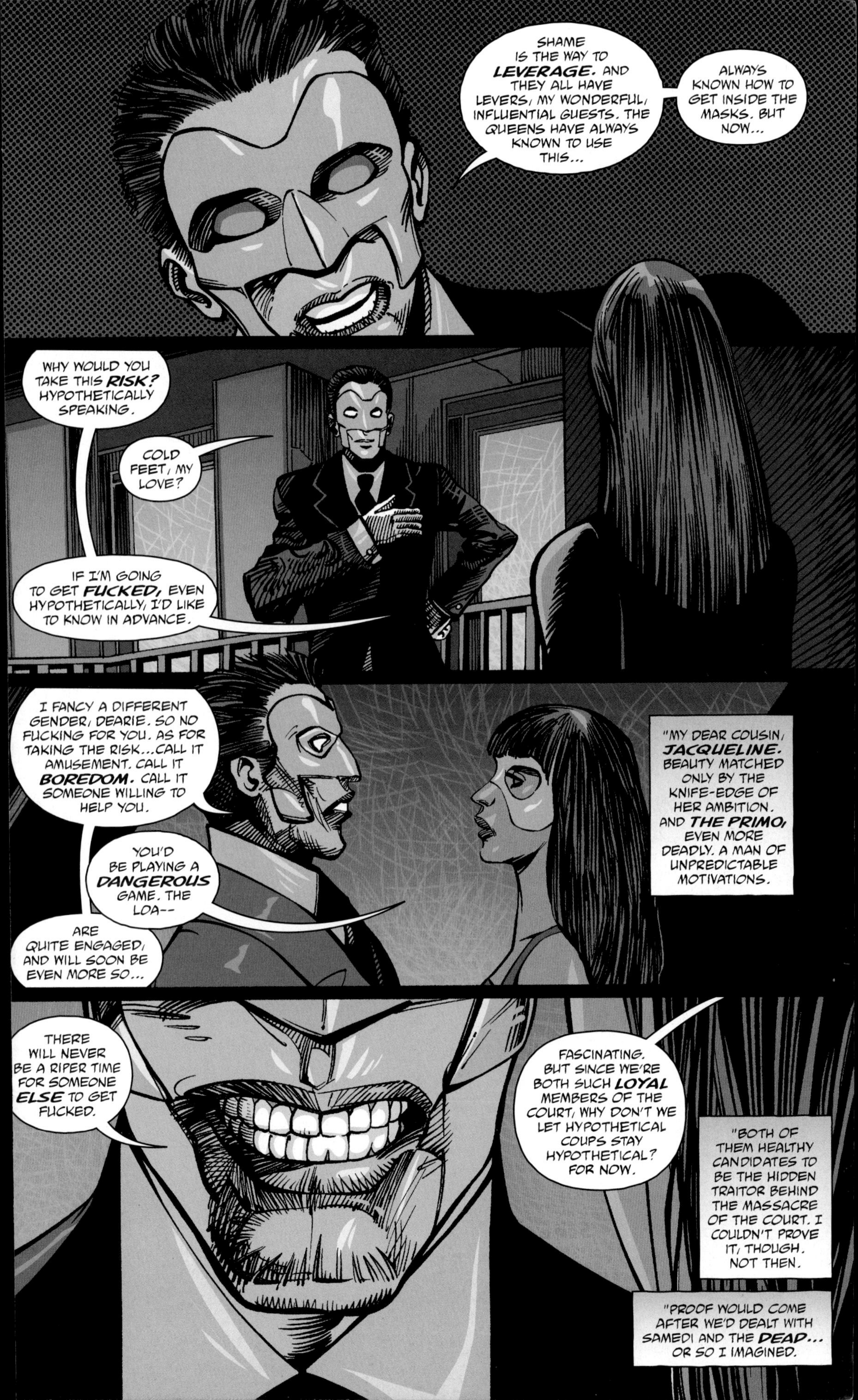
SHAME IS THE WAY TO LEVERAGE. AND THEY ALL HAVE LEVERS, MY WONDERFUL, INFLUENTIAL GUESTS. THE QUEENS HAVE ALWAYS KNOWN TO USE THIS...
ALWAYS KNOWN HOW TO GET INSIDE THE MASKS. BUT NOW...
WHY WOULD YOU TAKE THIS RISK? HYPOTHETICALLY SPEAKING.
COLD FEET, MY LOVE?
IF I'M GOING TO GET FUCKED, EVEN HYPOTHETICALLY, I'D LIKE TO KNOW IN ADVANCE.
I FANCY A DIFFERENT GENDER, DEARIE. SO NO FUCKING FOR YOU. AS FOR TAKING THE RISK...CALL IT AMUSEMENT. CALL IT BOREDOM. CALL IT SOMEONE WILLING TO HELP YOU.
"MY DEAR COUSIN, JACQUELINE. BEAUTY MATCHED ONLY BY THE KNIFE-EDGE OF HER AMBITION. AND THE PRIMO, EVEN MORE DEADLY. A MAN OF UNPREDICTABLE MOTIVATIONS.
YOU'D BE PLAYING A DANGEROUS GAME. THE LOA--
ARE QUITE ENGAGED, AND WILL SOON BE EVEN MORE SO...
THERE WILL NEVER BE A RIPER TIME FOR SOMEONE ELSE TO GET FUCKED.
FASCINATING. BUT SINCE WE'RE BOTH SUCH LOYAL MEMBERS OF THE COURT, WHY DON'T WE LET HYPOTHETICAL COUPS STAY HYPOTHETICAL? FOR NOW.
"BOTH OF THEM HEALTHY CANDIDATES TO BE THE HIDDEN TRAITOR BEHIND THE MASSACRE OF THE COURT. I COULDN'T PROVE IT, THOUGH. NOT THEN.
"PROOF WOULD COME AFTER WE'D DEALT WITH SAMEDI AND THE DEAD... OR SO I IMAGINED.

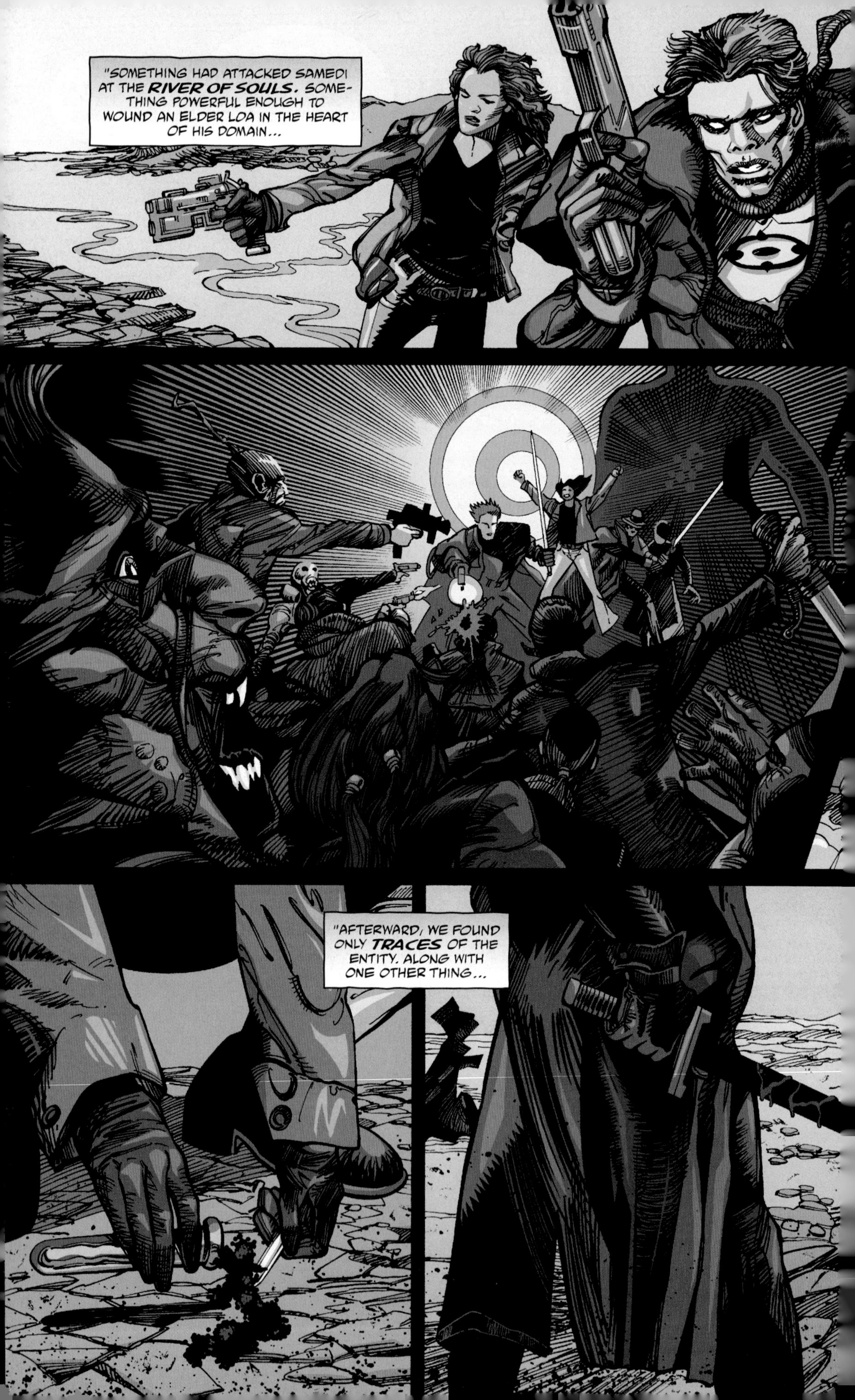
"SOMETHING HAD ATTACKED SAMEDI AT THE RIVER OF SOULS. SOMETHING POWERFUL ENOUGH TO WOUND AN ELDER LOA IN THE HEART OF HIS DOMAIN...
"AFTERWARD, WE FOUND ONLY TRACES OF THE ENTITY. ALONG WITH ONE OTHER THING...

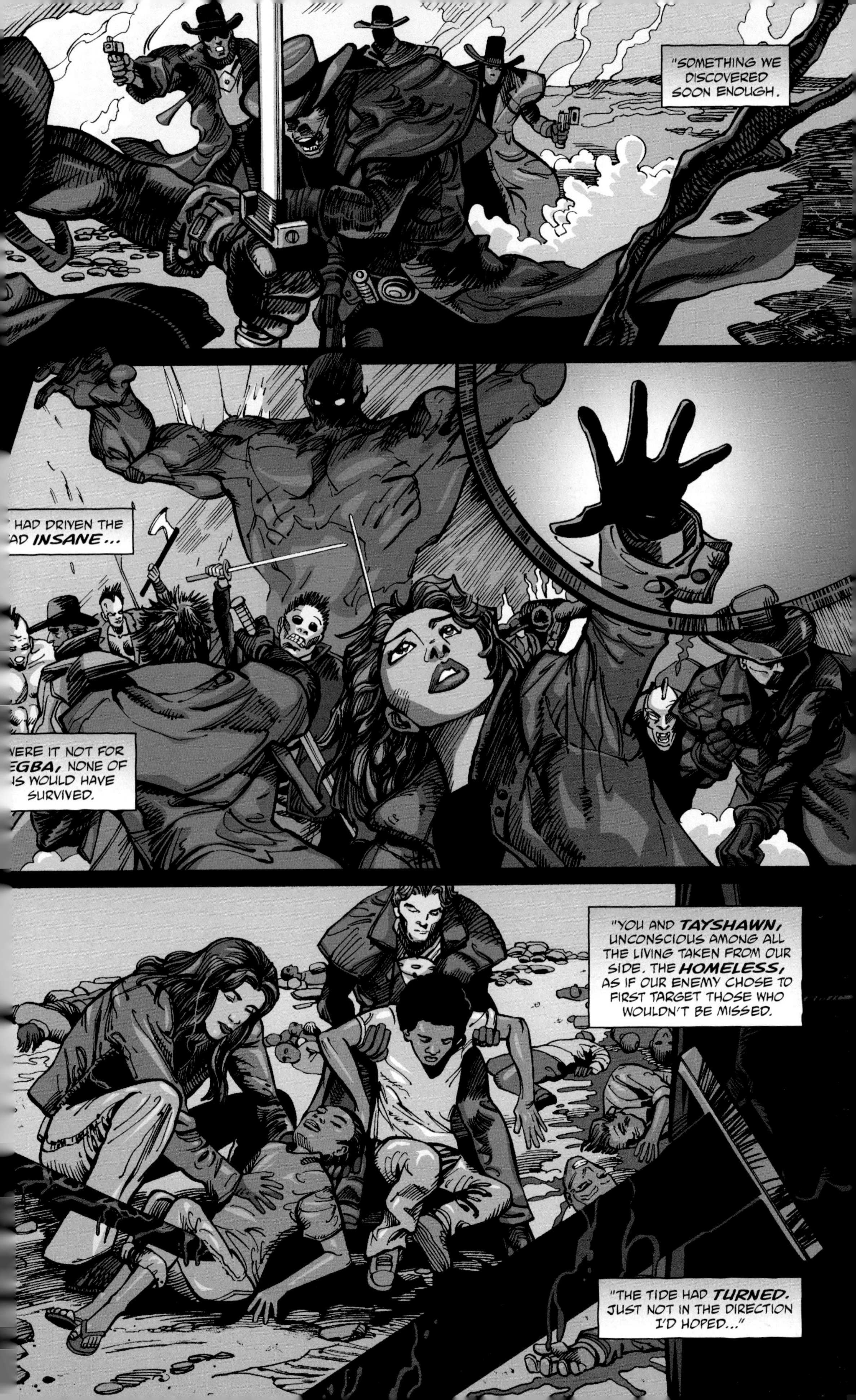
"SOMETHING WE DISCOVERED SOON ENOUGH.
HAD DRIVEN THE AD *INSANE*...
WERE IT NOT FOR EGBA, NONE OF S WOULD HAVE SURVIVED.
"YOU AND *TAYSHAWN*, UNCONSCIOUS AMONG ALL THE LIVING TAKEN FROM OUR SIDE. THE *HOMELESS*, AS IF OUR ENEMY CHOSE TO FIRST TARGET THOSE WHO WOULDN'T BE MISSED.
"THE TIDE HAD *TURNED*. JUST NOT IN THE DIRECTION I'D HOPED..."

DOMINIQUE!!

"THE **ATTACKS** KEPT COMING. EVEN FROM THOSE CLOSEST TO ME. SIX YEARS PASSES LIKE SIX WEEKS WHEN YOU'RE UNDER SIEGE. WHO COULD I TRUST?"

I **PLEDGE** MY LOYALTY TO THE QUEEN, AND SOLEMNLY VOW TO PROTECT THIS COURT.

"AT LEAST I COULD WATCH YOU AND TAYSHAW GROW UP..."

"THERE WAS LITTLE HOPE TO BE FOUND ELSEWHERE."

HRRM. WE SEEM GODLY BEINGS TO YOU, CHILD. BUT WE ARE MERELY CONSTRUCTS FOR YOUR BELIEF. AS IT **EBBS**, SO DOES OUR POWER. AND NOW THAT THIS FOE HAS COME...

WHAT **IS** IT, LEGBA?!

IT HAS NO GIVEN NAME.

BUT IT IS OUR **ANTITHESIS**, DISBELIEF. THE ABSENCE OF FAITH...

BUT THERE IS STILL **ONE** PLACE WE CAN TAKE REFUGE.

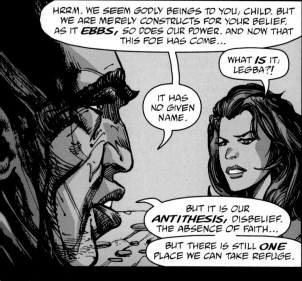

"THIS ANTITHESIS HAD FOUND AN **ANCHOR** AMONG US. WITH THE LOA IN RETREAT, I HAD TO FINALLY **FIND** THAT ANCHOR TO DRAW OUT ITS MASTER..."

"I PUSHED WHATEVER **BUTTONS** I COULD... **POWER**..

"HATE...

"AND, MOST OF ALL...**DESIRE**.

"AND THAT, FINALLY, BROUG US TO THESE LAST MOMEN' AT THE COURT."

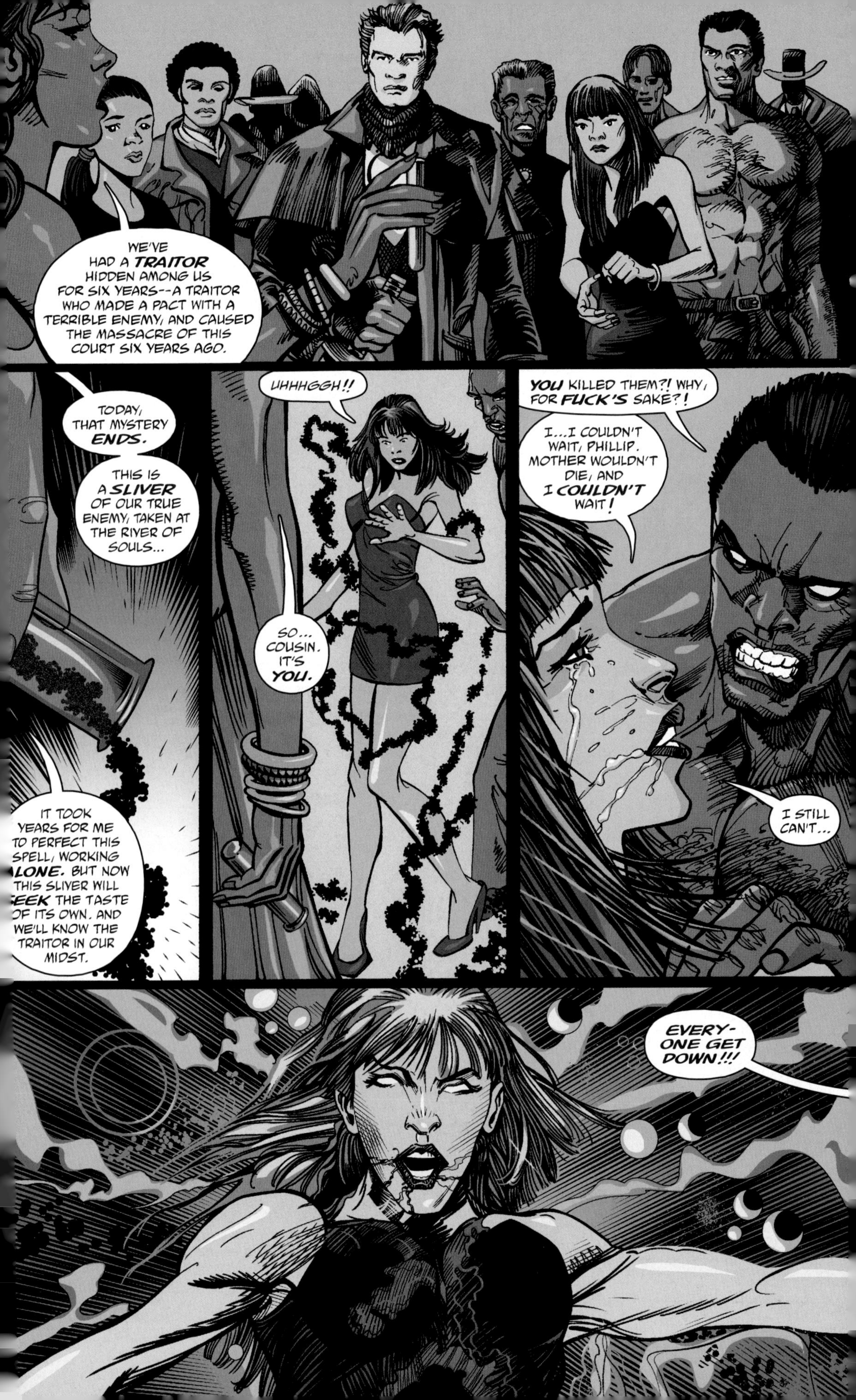
WE'VE HAD A TRAITOR HIDDEN AMONG US FOR SIX YEARS--A TRAITOR WHO MADE A PACT WITH A TERRIBLE ENEMY, AND CAUSED THE MASSACRE OF THIS COURT SIX YEARS AGO.
TODAY, THAT MYSTERY ENDS.
THIS IS A SLIVER OF OUR TRUE ENEMY, TAKEN AT THE RIVER OF SOULS...
IT TOOK YEARS FOR ME TO PERFECT THIS SPELL, WORKING ALONE. BUT NOW THIS SLIVER WILL SEEK THE TASTE OF ITS OWN. AND WE'LL KNOW THE TRAITOR IN OUR MIDST.
UHHHGGH!!
SO... COUSIN. IT'S YOU.
YOU KILLED THEM?! WHY, FOR FUCK'S SAKE?!
I...I COULDN'T WAIT, PHILLIP. MOTHER WOULDN'T DIE, AND I COULDN'T WAIT!
I STILL CAN'T...
EVERY-ONE GET DOWN!!!

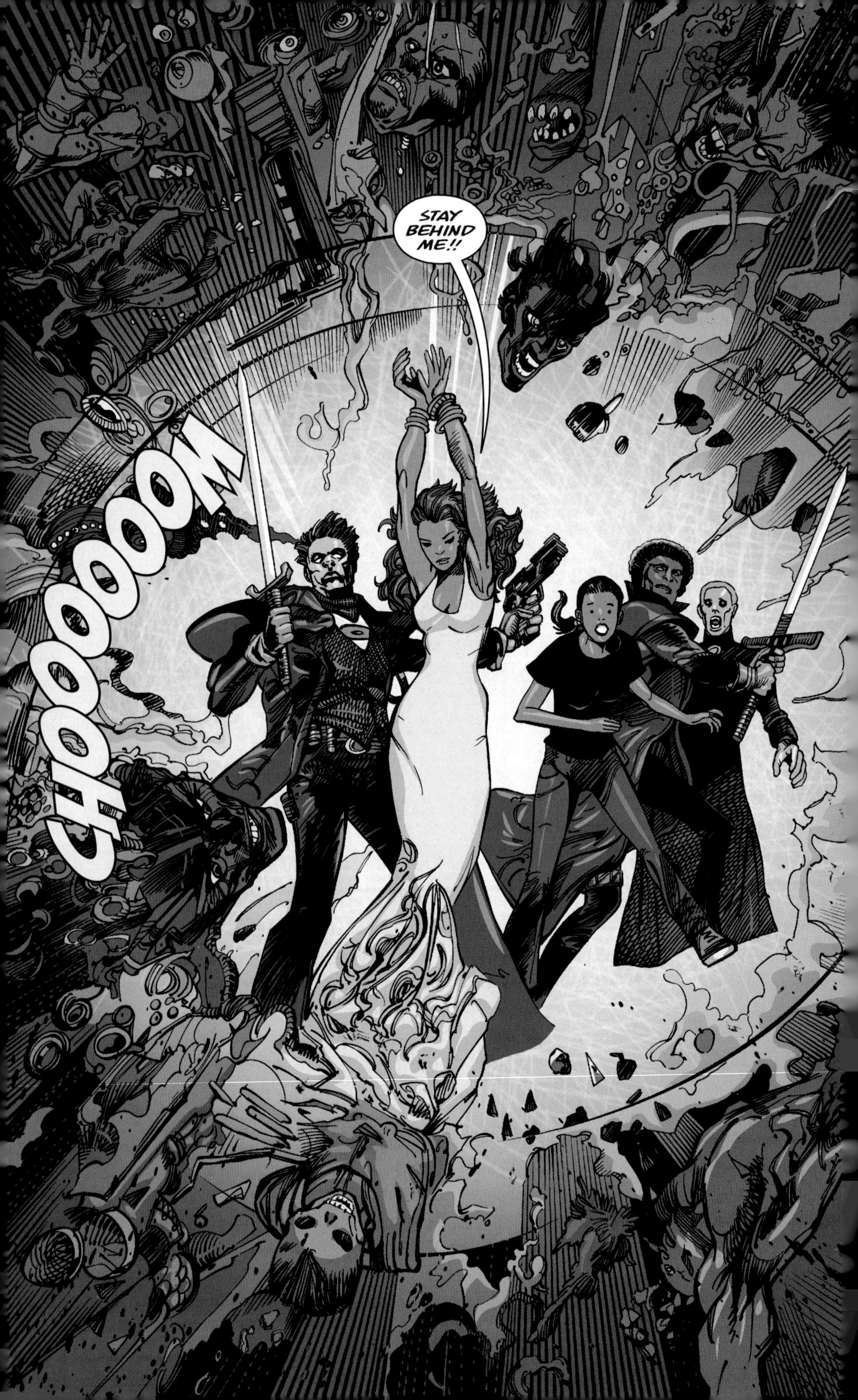
STAY BEHIND ME!!
CHOOOOOOOM

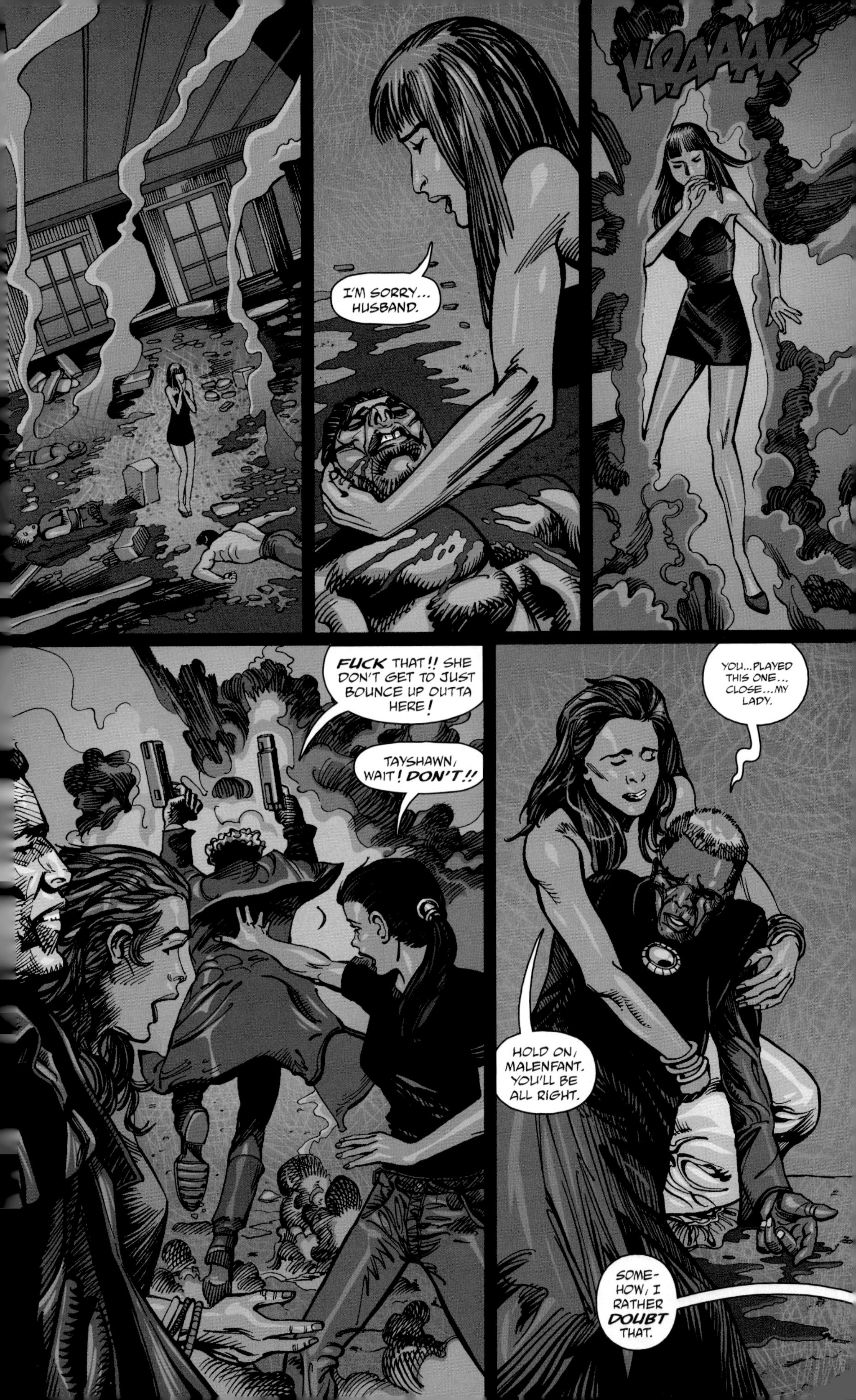
KRAAAK
I'M SORRY... HUSBAND.
FUCK THAT!! SHE DON'T GET TO JUST BOUNCE UP OUTTA HERE!
TAYSHAWN, WAIT! DON'T!!
YOU...PLAYED THIS ONE... CLOSE...MY LADY.
HOLD ON, MALENFANT. YOU'LL BE ALL RIGHT.
SOME-HOW, I RATHER DOUBT THAT.

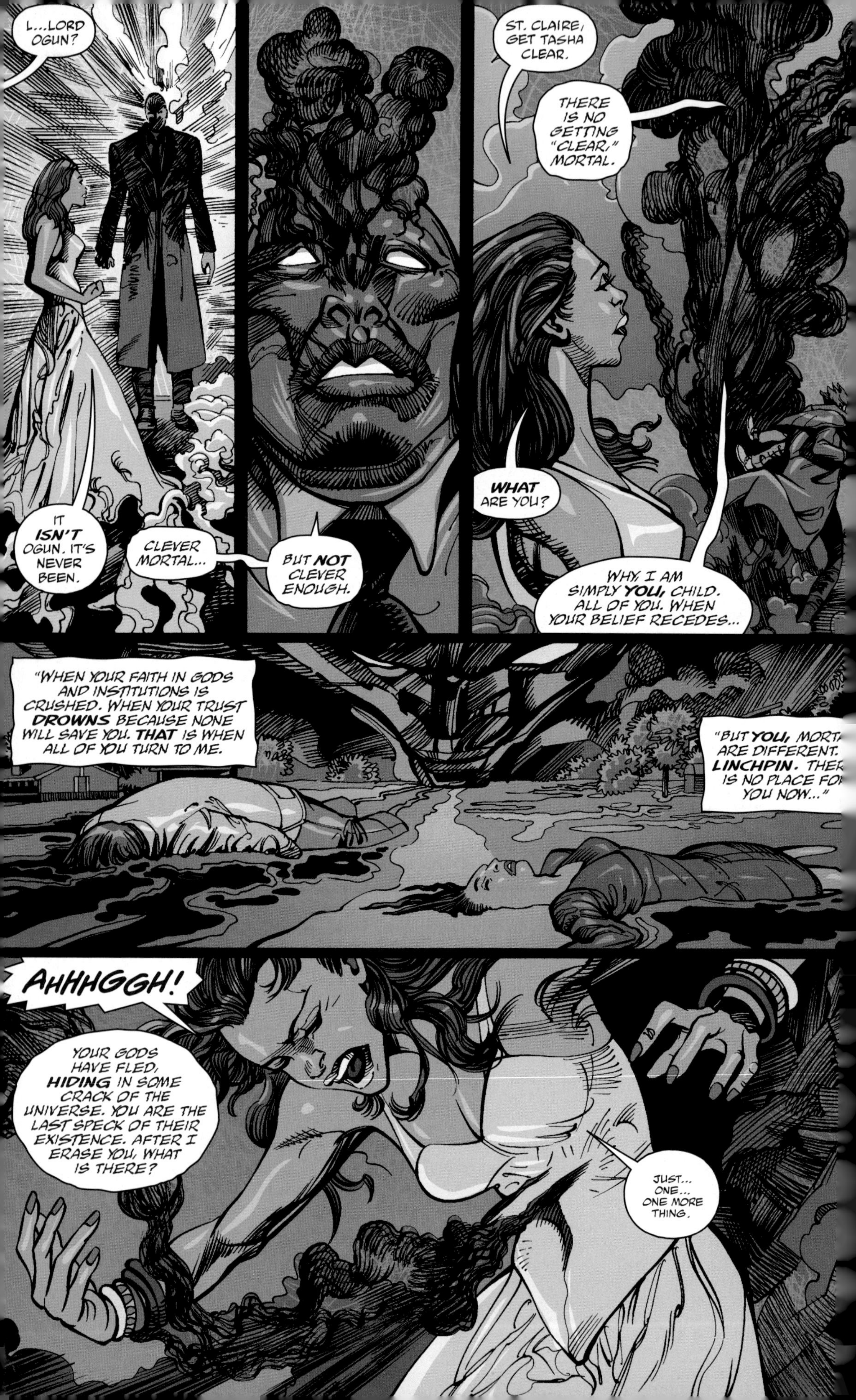

L...LORD OGUN?
IT ISN'T OGUN. IT'S NEVER BEEN.
CLEVER MORTAL...
BUT NOT CLEVER ENOUGH.
ST. CLAIRE, GET TASHA CLEAR.
THERE IS NO GETTING "CLEAR," MORTAL.
WHAT ARE YOU?
WHY, I AM SIMPLY YOU, CHILD. ALL OF YOU. WHEN YOUR BELIEF RECEDES...
"WHEN YOUR FAITH IN GODS AND INSTITUTIONS IS CRUSHED. WHEN YOUR TRUST DROWNS BECAUSE NONE WILL SAVE YOU. THAT IS WHEN ALL OF YOU TURN TO ME.
"BUT YOU, MORTA ARE DIFFERENT. LINCHPIN. THER IS NO PLACE FO YOU NOW..."
AHHHGGH!
YOUR GODS HAVE FLED, HIDING IN SOME CRACK OF THE UNIVERSE. YOU ARE THE LAST SPECK OF THEIR EXISTENCE. AFTER I ERASE YOU, WHAT IS THERE?
JUST... ONE... ONE MORE THING.

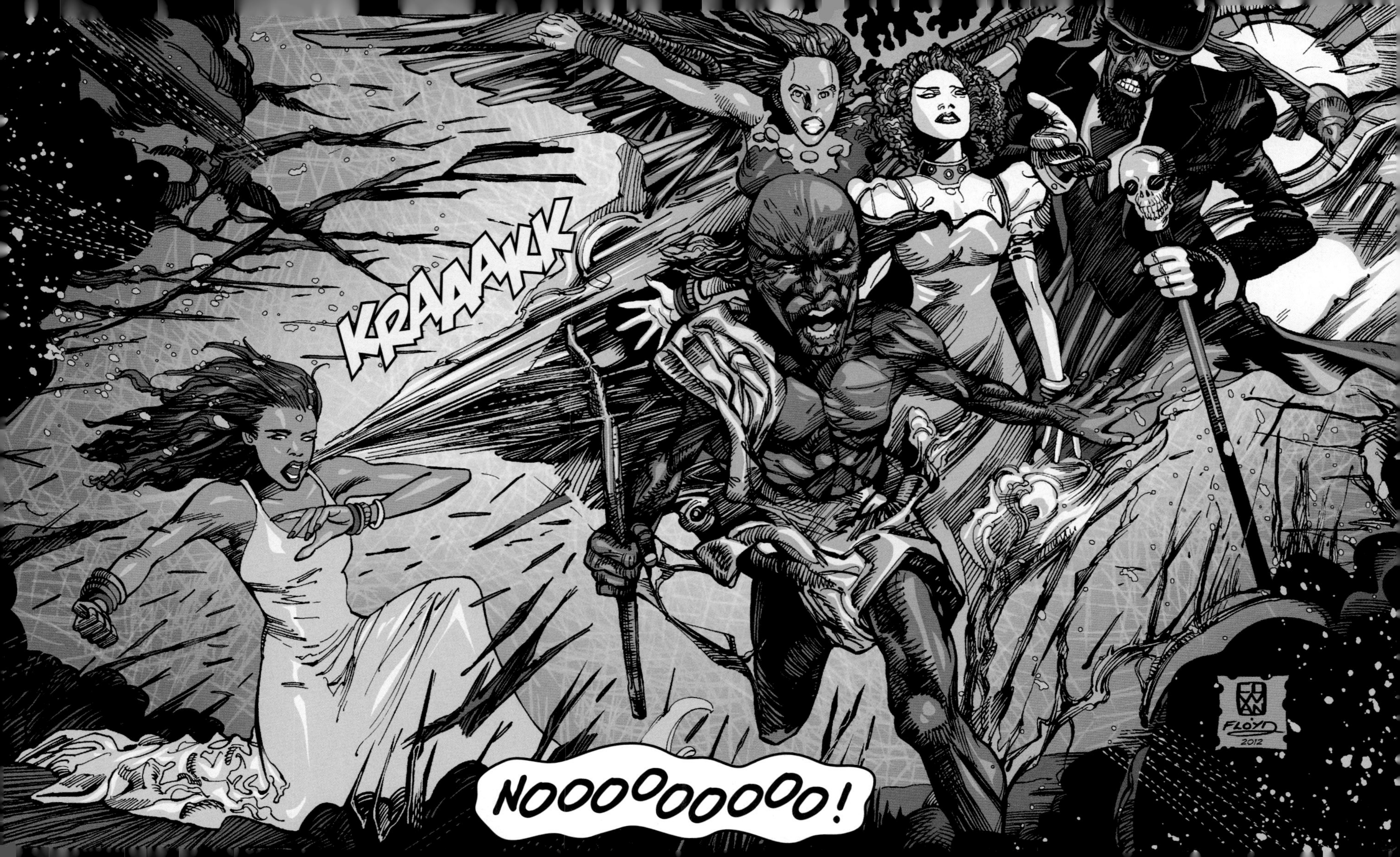
KRAAAKK
NOOOOOOOOOO!
FLOYD 2012

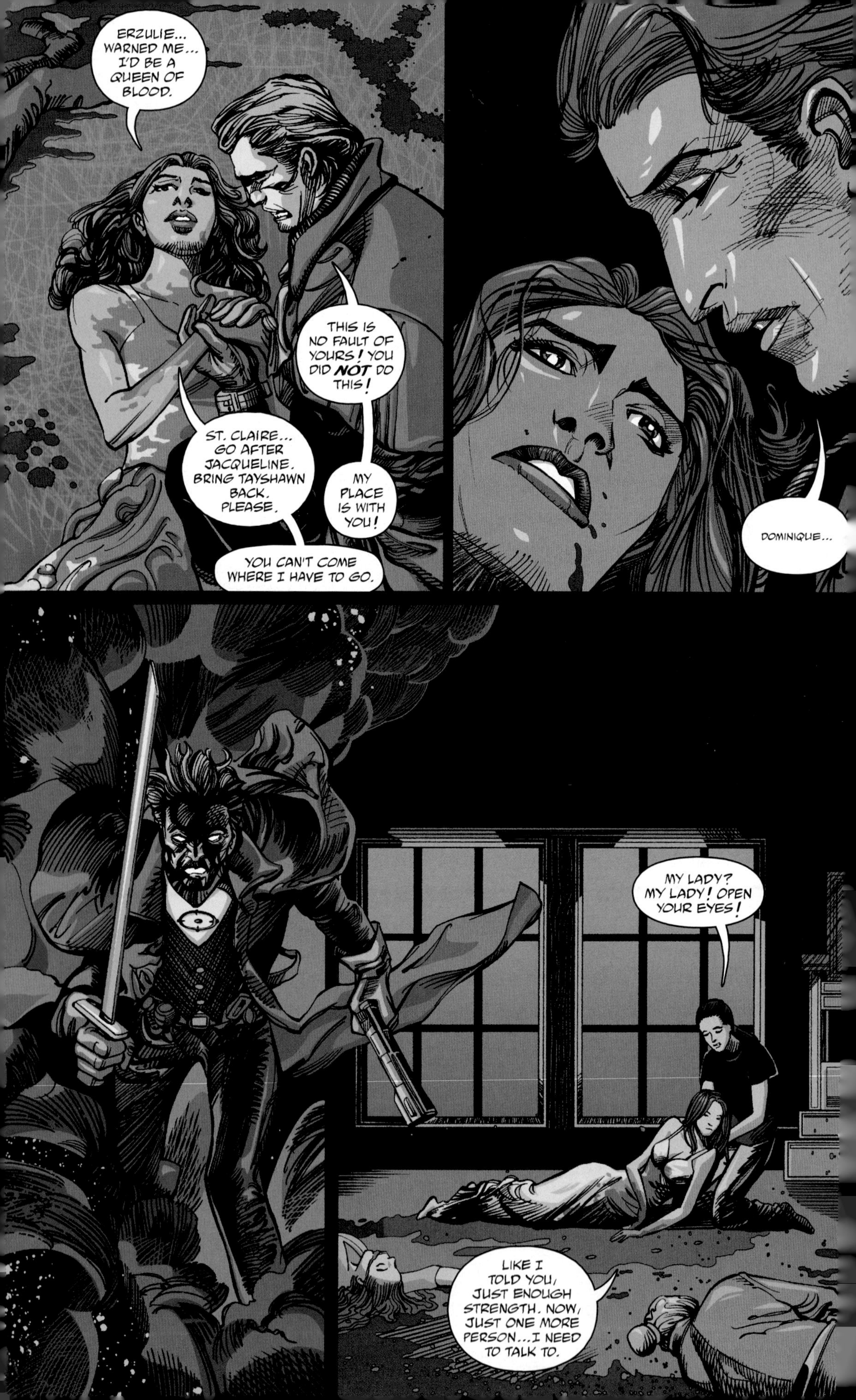
ERZULIE... WARNED ME... I'D BE A QUEEN OF BLOOD.
THIS IS NO FAULT OF YOURS! YOU DID NOT DO THIS!
ST. CLAIRE... GO AFTER JACQUELINE. BRING TAYSHAWN BACK. PLEASE.
MY PLACE IS WITH YOU!
YOU CAN'T COME WHERE I HAVE TO GO.
DOMINIQUE...
MY LADY? MY LADY! OPEN YOUR EYES!
LIKE I TOLD YOU, JUST ENOUGH STRENGTH. NOW, JUST ONE MORE PERSON...I NEED TO TALK TO.

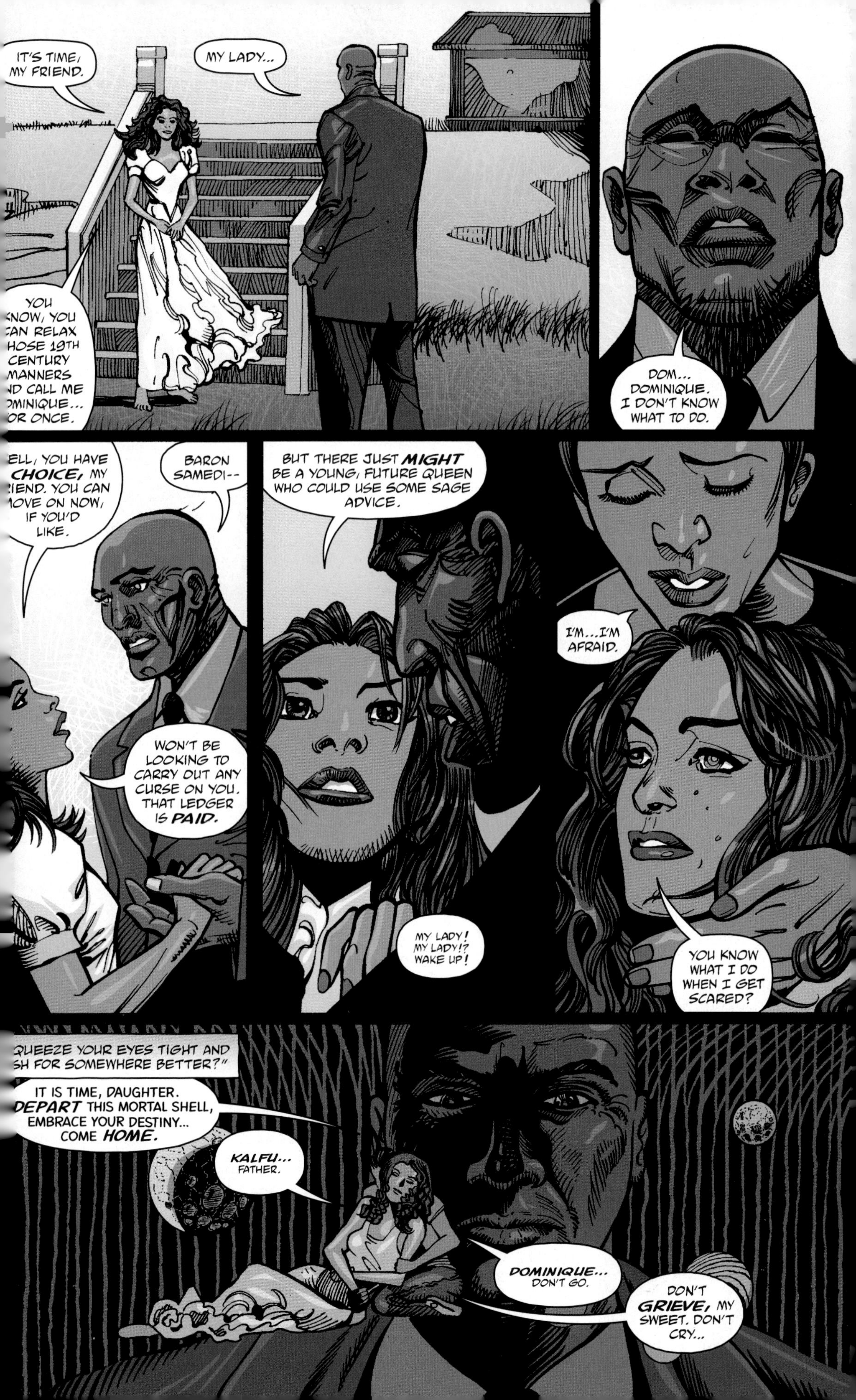

IT'S TIME, MY FRIEND.
MY LADY...
YOU KNOW, YOU CAN RELAX HOSE 19TH CENTURY MANNERS ND CALL ME OMINIQUE... OR ONCE.
DOM... DOMINIQUE. I DON'T KNOW WHAT TO DO.
ELL, YOU HAVE CHOICE, MY RIEND. YOU CAN OVE ON NOW, IF YOU'D LIKE.
BARON SAMEDI--
WON'T BE LOOKING TO CARRY OUT ANY CURSE ON YOU. THAT LEDGER IS PAID.
BUT THERE JUST MIGHT BE A YOUNG, FUTURE QUEEN WHO COULD USE SOME SAGE ADVICE.
MY LADY! MY LADY!? WAKE UP!
I'M...I'M AFRAID.
YOU KNOW WHAT I DO WHEN I GET SCARED?
QUEEZE YOUR EYES TIGHT AND SH FOR SOMEWHERE BETTER?"
IT IS TIME, DAUGHTER. DEPART THIS MORTAL SHELL, EMBRACE YOUR DESTINY... COME HOME.
KALFU... FATHER.
DOMINIQUE... DON'T GO.
DON'T GRIEVE, MY SWEET. DON'T CRY...

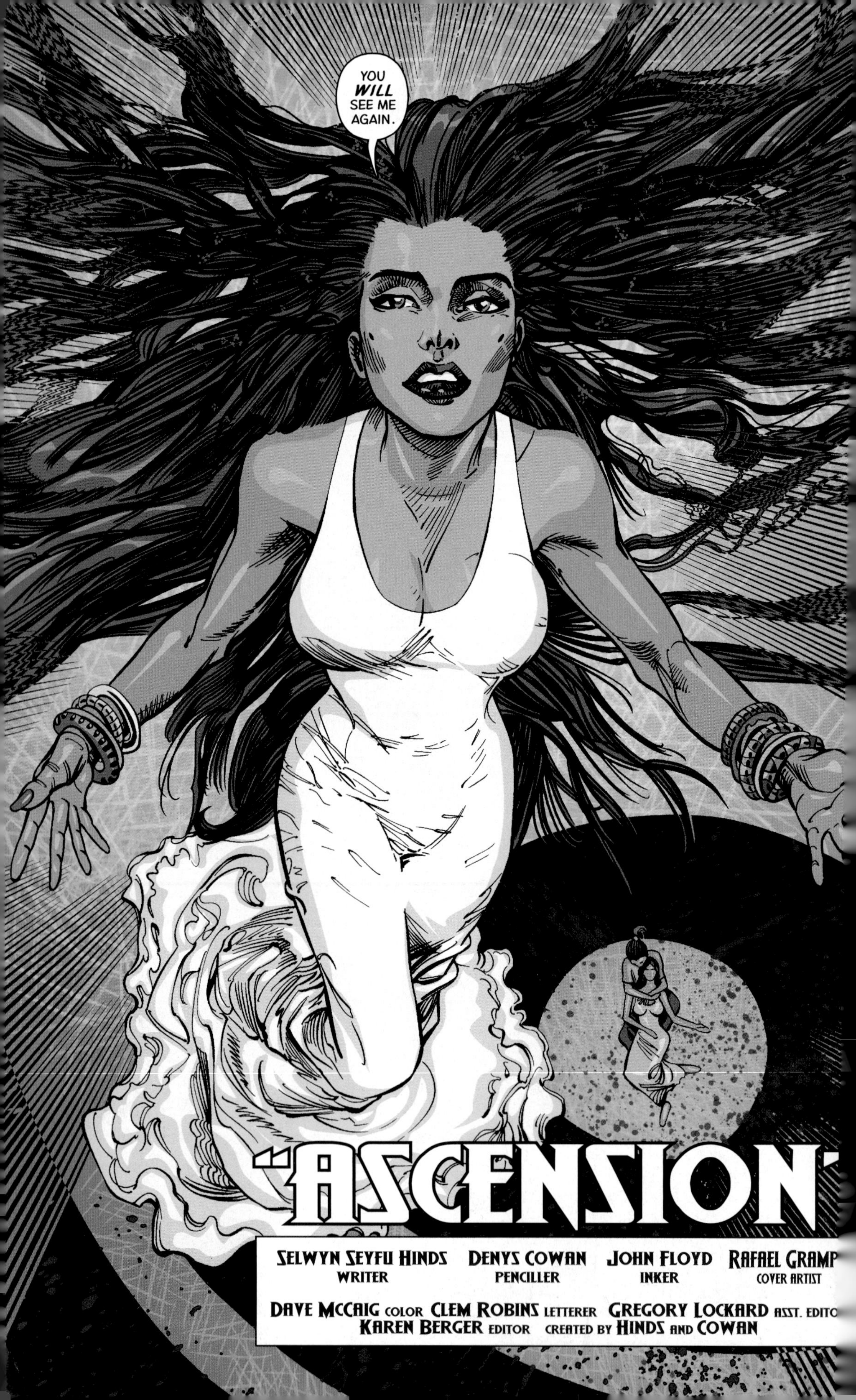
YOU WILL SEE ME AGAIN.
"ASCENSION"
SELWYN SEYFU HINDS WRITER
DENYS COWAN PENCILLER
JOHN FLOYD INKER
RAFAEL GRAMP COVER ARTIST
DAVE MCCAIG COLOR
CLEM ROBINS LETTERER
GREGORY LOCKARD ASST. EDITO
KAREN BERGER EDITOR
CREATED BY HINDS AND COWAN

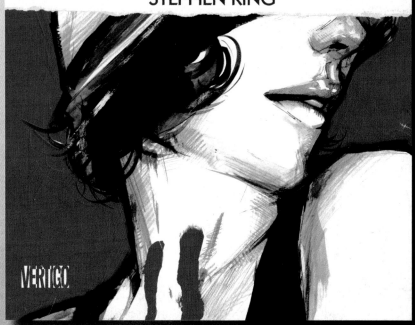